PENGUIN BOOKS

THE USER ILLUSION

Tor Nørretranders is Denmark's leading science writer and the award-winning author of more than ten books, many of them bestsellers. He has hosted numerous television programs on science and science-related topics and established a major cooperative network of scientists and artists. He lives north of Copenhagen.

Cutting

Consciousness

Down to

Size

THE USER ILLUSION

Tor Nørretranders

Translated by Jonathan Sydenham

PENGUIN BOOKS

PENGUIN BOOKS

Published by the Penguin Group

Penguin Group (USA) Inc., 375 Hudson Street, New York, New York 10014, U.S.A.

Penguin Group (Canada), 10 Alcorn Avenue, Toronto,

Ontario, Canada M4V 3B2 (a division of Pearson Penguin Canada Inc.)

Penguin Books Ltd, 80 Strand, London WC2R 0RL, England

Penguin Ireland, 25 St Stephen's Green, Dublin 2, Ireland (a division of Penguin Books Ltd)

Penguin Group (Australia), 250 Camberwell Road, Camberwell,

Victoria 3124, Australia (a division of Pearson Australia Group Pty Ltd)

Penguin Books India Pvt Ltd, 11 Community Centre,

Panchsheel Park, New Delhi – 110 017, India

Penguin Group (NZ), cnr Airborne and Rosedale Roads,

Albany, Auckland, New Zealand (a division of Pearson New Zealand Ltd)

Penguin Books (South Africa) (Pty) Ltd, 24 Sturdee Avenue,

Rosebank, Johannesburg 2196, South Africa

Penguin Books Ltd, Registered Offices: 80 Strand, London WC2R 0RL, England

First published in the United States of America by Viking Penguin,
a member of Penguin Putnam Inc. 1998
Published in Penguin Books 1999

17 19 20 18

Copyright © Tor Nørretranders, 1991
Translation copyright © Jonathan Sydenham, 1998
All rights reserved

Originally published in Danish as *Maerk verden* by Gyldendalske Boghandel.

Illustrations by Jesper Tom-Petersen.

THE LIBRARY OF CONGRESS HAS CATALOGED THE VIKING EDITION AS FOLLOWS:
Nørretranders, Tor.
The user illusion: cutting consciousness down to size / Tor
Nørretranders; translated by Jonathan Sydenham.
p. cm.
Includes bibliographical references and index.
ISBN 0-670-87579-1 (hc.)
ISBN 0 14 02.3012 2 (pbk.)
1. Consciousness. 2. Subconsciousness.
3. Human information processing. I. Title.
BF311.N675 1998 97-39580
153—dc21

Printed in the United States of America
Set in New Baskerville
Designed by Kathryn Parise

What is done
by what is called myself is, I feel,
done by something greater
than myself in me.

JAMES CLERK MAXWELL
on his deathbed, 1879

CONTENTS

PART III
CONSCIOUSNESS
211

PART IV
COMPOSURE
329

PREFACE

Consciousness is at once the most immediately present and the most inscrutably intangible entity in human existence.

We can talk to each other about consciousness, but it is fundamentally, ineradicably subjective in character, a phenomenon that can be experienced only alone, from within.

Consciousness is the experience of experiencing, the knowledge of knowing, the sense of sensing. But what is it that experiences the experience? What happens when one observes the experience of experiencing from *without* and asks, "How much does consciousness actually observe?"

In recent years, scientific investigations into the phenomenon of consciousness have demonstrated that people experience far more than their consciousness perceives; that they interact far more with the world and with each other than their consciousness thinks they do; that the control of actions that consciousness feels it exercises is an illusion.

Consciousness plays a far smaller role in human life than Western culture has tended to believe.

Historical studies indicate that the phenomenon of consciousness as we know it today is probably no more than three thousand years old. The concept of a central "experiencer" and decisionmaker, a conscious *I*, has prevailed for only a hundred generations.

Judging from the scientific experiences upon which the following account is based, the rule of the conscious ego will probably not last for many more generations.

The epoch of the *I* is drawing to a close.

≈

The User Illusion is an account of a number of astonishing scientific insights that shed light on the phenomenon of consciousness and on just how much—or how little—of human life can genuinely be described as conscious.

It is the story of what these insights signify—of their implications for our perception of ourselves and our view of free will; the possibility of understanding the world; and the degree of interpersonal contact beyond the narrow channel of language.

The starting point for this account is scientific culture, and the culture of the natural sciences in particular; but its horizon is culture as a whole. This book aims to combine science with everyday life; to shed light on everyday things we take quite for granted, against a background of breakthroughs in numerous scientific areas that apparently haven't the remotest connection with either our consciousness or our everyday lives.

This is an ambitious book, which clashes now and then with time-honored notions of such concepts as *the I* and *information* and introduces new ones such as *the Me* and *exformation,* yet its language is accessible to anyone who wants to try and read it—even though it does rather begin at the deep end.

In mathematics, physics, and computation theory, it has become increasingly clear since 1930 that the basis of objectivity is itself subjective; that no formal system will ever be able to substantiate or prove itself. This has led to a conceptual change in our view of the world, which has been realized in the natural sciences only over the last decade. The result has been a radical change in our understanding of concepts such as information, complexity, order, chance, and chaos. These conceptual shifts have made it possible to forge links with the study of phenomena such as meaning and relevance, which are vital to any description of consciousness. The first section of this account, "Computation," looks at these shifts.

In psychology and communication theory, it has become clear since 1950 that the capacity of consciousness is not particularly extensive if measured in bits, the unit of measurement for information. Consciousness contains almost no information. The senses, on the other hand, digest enormous quantities of information, most of which we never even become conscious of. So large quantities of information are in fact discarded before consciousness occurs; a state of affairs that corresponds perfectly with the understanding of the processes of computation that made their breakthrough in the 1980s. But much of the information from our surroundings that our senses detect does influence our behavior: most of what goes on in a person's mind is not conscious. The second section of this book, "Communication," is about the kind of information that is rejected but nevertheless important.

Since the 1960s, neurophysiologists have studied consciousness by comparing people's subjective reports with objective measurements of the activity in their brains. The astonishing results indicate that consciousness lags behind what we call reality. It takes half a second to become conscious of something, though that is not how we perceive it. Outside our conscious awareness, an advanced illusion rearranges events in time. These findings collide with time-honored notions of man's free will, but this book maintains that the danger is not to our free will but to the notion that it is the conscious *I* that exercises our free will. These matters are the subject of the third section of this account, "Consciousness."

The view of earth as a living system has been transformed since space travel began in the 1960s. At the same time, the advent of the computer as a scientific tool has transformed the picture of our abilities to predict the world and our actions upon it. The tendency of civilization to plan and regulate is now challenged by what we have learned in recent decades about ecological connections and the unpredictability of nature. The ability of consciousness to assimilate the world has been seriously overestimated by our scientific culture. The importance of accepting the nonconscious aspects of man is the subject of the fourth section of *The User Illusion*, "Composure": Even though consciousness is something we can experience only for ourselves, it is vital that we begin to talk about what it really is.

This book was written during a period I spent as lecturer in residence at the Royal Danish Academy of Art in 1990–91, subsidized by the Culture Fund of the Ministry of Culture. Else Marie Bukdahl, principal of the school of pictorial art, deserves heartfelt thanks for making this arrangement possible. Thanks also to Anette Krumhardt and the staff and students at the academy for an inspiring partnership.

The philosopher Ole Fogh Kirkeby has provided years of guidance and encouragement; the physicists Peder Voetmann Christiansen, Søren Brunak, and Benny Lautrup have been vital sources of inspiration.

A long list of scientists have generously found time for interviews and conversations about the matters examined in this book. Special thanks to Jan Ambjørn, P. W. Anderson, Charles Bennett, Predrag Cvitanovic, Henning Eichberg, Mitchell Feigenbaum, Walter Fontana, Lars Friberg, Richard Gregory, Thomas Højrup, Bernardo Huberman, David Ingvar, Stuart Kauffman, Christof Koch, Rolf Landauer, Chris Langton, Niels A. Lassen, Benjamin Libet, Seth Lloyd, James Lovelock, Lynn Margulis, Humberto Maturana, Erik Mosekilde, Holger Bech Nielsen, Roger Penrose, Alexander Polyakov, Per Kjærgaard Rasmussen, Steen Rasmussen, Peter Richter, John A. Wheeler, and Peter Zinkernagel.

Benjamin Libet, whose work plays a very special role in this account, displayed great openness when answers were needed to detailed questions about the scientific records of his epochmaking experiments. Thanks are also due to Jesper Hoffmeyer and Niels A. Lassen for pointing out the significance of Benjamin Libet's results.

Warm thanks to Søren Brunak, Peder Voetmann Christiansen, Niels Engelsted, Henrik Jahnsen, Ole Fogh Kirkeby, Arne Mosfeldt Laursen, Sigurd Mikkelsen, and Johs. Mørk Pedersen for their comments on the first draft of the book. Finally, a very big thank-you to Claus Clausen for editorial support during the writing process.

Copenhagen, September 1991

PART I

≈

COMPUTATION

CHAPTER 1
MAXWELL'S DEMON

"War es ein Gott, der diese Zeichen schrieb?"[1] ("Was it a god that wrote these signs?") asked the Austrian physicist Ludwig Boltzmann, drawing on Goethe to express the excitement and wonder that four brief mathematical equations could elicit in the mind of a physicist.

There were grounds for wonder. In the 1860s, a Scottish physicist named James Clerk Maxwell succeeded in summarizing all that was known about phenomena such as electricity and magnetism in four short equations possessed of as much aesthetic elegance as theoretical impact. But Maxwell did not merely succeed in summarizing in his equations everything people already knew. He also succeeded in predicting phenomena that nobody thought had anything to do with electricity and magnetism—phenomena that were not discovered until after Maxwell's death in 1879.

How could this be possible? asked Ludwig Boltzmann, a contemporary of Maxwell's and a colleague in the formulation of important theoretical landmarks. How can a summary of a rich and varied collection of phenomena occur with so few and such powerful symbols as those we find in the four famous lines that constitute Maxwell's equations?

In a sense, this is the very mystery of science: Not only can it pursue the goal of saying as much as possible in as few words or equations as possible, drawing a map of the terrain, a map that simply and clearly summarizes all the important data and thus allows us to find our way; but—and here lies the mystery—it can create a map that enables us to see details of the terrain that were unknown when the map was drawn!

≈

Physics was founded as a theoretical science through a form of cartography that unified widely disparate phenomena into a single theoretical basket. In 1687, Isaac Newton was able to undertake the first major unification of widely differing natural phenomena into a single theoretical image when he presented his theory of gravity. The theory itself was of considerable mathematical elegance, but his real achievement was in summarizing knowledge of two widely differing, already familiar, groups of phenomena. In the early 1600s, Galileo had founded the modern theory of the motion of bodies on earth—falling bodies, acceleration, oscillation, and much more besides—and during the same period, Johannes Kepler had formulated a series of laws governing the movement of the planets around the sun. Galileo and Kepler both based their theories on observations—for Galileo it was his own experiments; for Kepler, the planetary observations of the Danish astronomer Tycho Brahe.

Newton's feat was to unify these theories—Galileo's about earth and Kepler's about the heavens—into one theory that embraced heaven and earth. Only one principle mattered: gravity—something that nobody yet understands.

Newton's theory became the model for all later physics (and in effect all other science too), where Grand Unified Theories of widely different fields became the ideal.

However, it was only James Clerk Maxwell's famous equations from the last century that heralded the Second Grand Unification. Where Newton had unified heaven and earth, Maxwell unified electricity and magnetism.

The entire modern scientific view of the universe is based upon the occurrence of a handful of *forces* in nature—gravity, electricity, magnetism, and two more, which operate in the world of atoms. These forces describe how different material bodies affect each other, and the real point is that there are no more forces than the ones listed here. Everything that is known can be described with the help of these forces and their effects.

So it was tremendously significant when it was realized in the last century that there was a link between two of these forces: electricity and magnetism. In 1820, a Danish scientist, Hans Christian Ørsted, discovered that a magnetic needle is deflected by an electric current. Until then, nobody had realized there was a link between electricity and magnetism, two well-known phenomena. In 1831, Michael Faraday proved the converse of Ørsted's discovery: that a current is produced in a conductor exposed to a varying magnetic field—what we call electromagnetic induction. When Faraday was asked what practical use his discovery might have, he replied, "What use is a baby?"

James Clerk Maxwell was a few months old when Faraday discovered induction. Thirty years later, Maxwell achieved the Second Grand Unification in physics, when his equations summarized the achievements of Faraday, Ørsted, and many others.

Maxwell worked very consciously in *analogies*. He theorized about the electrical and magnetic phenomena by imagining vortices in space which represented the fields that caused the electrical and magnetic phenomena. He consciously used simple images that could be forgotten once he understood the phenomena well enough to express them in mathematical form. One had to begin with a "simplification and reduction of the results of previous investigations to a form in which the mind can grasp them," Maxwell wrote.[2]

By thinking of vortices (which later developed into a hypothetical model made up of little cogs), Maxwell arrived at the conclusion that some extra little vortices were needed if the mechanical analogy between electricity and magnetism was to work. The new vortices did not correspond to any known phenomenon but were necessary for the mental picture to make sense, for the map to be as tidy as possible.

When Maxwell calculated the velocity at which these tiny hypothetical vortices dispersed through space, he discovered that they spread at the speed of light. That was odd, because it had never occurred to anybody that light had anything to do with electricity and magnetism. But Maxwell discovered that light is electromagnetic radiation—shifting electrical and magnetic fields that travel out into the universe, alternating forever at right angles to the direction of their dispersal. An astonishing image, it explained the nature of light, an issue scientists had been discussing for centuries.

So Maxwell's equations describe not just what they were written to describe but also—as a bonus—light itself; and light turned out to have a whole range of relatives. Radio waves, X-rays, infrared radiation, microwaves, gamma rays, and TV waves (the first of them was discovered by Heinrich Herz in 1888, just nine years after Maxwell's death).

The material significance of Maxwell's equations was thus enormous.

What would the twentieth century have been like without radio, X-rays, television, and microwaves? Better, maybe; different, certainly.

As Heinrich Herz said of Maxwell's equations, "One cannot escape the feeling that these equations have an existence and an intelligence of their own, that they are wiser than we are, wiser even than their discoverers, that we get more out of them than was originally put into them."[3]

How could Maxwell hypothesize his way through his analogies to something nobody had yet discovered? That was the question Ludwig Boltzmann was really posing when he asked if Maxwell's equations had been written by a god.

In a sense, Maxwell gave his own answer, as he lay dying of cancer. Visited by Professor F. J. A. Hort, a colleague from his Cambridge days, Maxwell said, though without a thought to Boltzmann, "What is done by what is called myself is, I feel, done by something greater than myself in me."[4]

It was not the first time Maxwell had suggested that many scientific ideas arise somewhere in the mind that is beyond the control of consciousness. Shortly after his father's death, in 1856, he wrote a poem about "powers and thoughts within us, that we/know not, till they rise/Through the stream of conscious action from where the/Self in secret lies." It was not through a conscious act of will that Maxwell saw the light in his equations, "But when Will and Sense are silent, by the thoughts that come and go . . ."[5]

Such sentiments are far from unusual among the great natural scientists, who in fact speak more often than not of unconscious or even mystical experiences as the basis of their knowledge. So in that sense it was not Maxwell who wrote Maxwell's equations. It was something greater than himself *in* him.

Physicists have tried to repeat Newton's and Maxwell's feats of unifying widely differing theories about widely differing phenomena ever since. But they have not hit the unification jackpot yet.

Certainly, in this century, Albert Einstein succeeded in developing new ideas based on those of Newton and Maxwell, but his wondrously beautiful theories of relativity about motion and gravity unified no natural forces.

On the other hand, physicists studying the atomic world have discovered two fundamental forces of nature in addition to the gravitational and the electromagnetic: the strong force and the weak force, which exist at the atomic and subatomic level.

The weak force acts only in so-called radioactive decay. The strong force acts only in the atomic nuclei. In the 1960s, Abdus Salaam and Steven Weinberg succeeded in unifying the theory for the weak force and the theory for electromagnetism, enabling us to understand them as one force. In the 1970s, other physicists managed to show that the strong force, too, could be understood as a variation of this new "electro-weak force." So some new order was brought into the picture, but really all the physicists had done was to fit two newly discovered forces together with the old familiar ones. The picture may well be known as Grand Unification, but a vital piece is still missing, and without it the ultimate unification cannot take place. The missing piece is gravity.

In the 1980s, theories about entities called "superstrings" aroused great interest, because for the first time there was cause to hope that we could unify the theories of gravity (Einstein's theories of relativity) with the theories for the electromagnetic, the weak and strong forces (nuclear and particle physics). Superstrings involve incredibly tiny vibrating elements that are the building blocks of all matter in the universe. But this Third Grand Unification has turned out to be a difficult road to follow—and, in any case, it is clearly less interesting than the first two unified field theories.

Isaac Newton's great contribution was, after all, that he unified heaven and earth; Maxwell's, that he unified such everyday phenomena as magnetism, electricity, and light. Superstring theory, however, has nothing to do with everyday life; it pertains to extreme, peculiar conditions that are anything but familiar to us—and these conditions are a very long way from being available to physicists for experiments that can be performed anytime soon.

Today, despite enormous sums spent on complex apparatus—such as at the European Organization for Nuclear Research (CERN), near Geneva—nobody really believes that the Third Grand Unification—the theory that will unify all the forces of nature—can be attained in the foreseeable future. There may be much talk about such a theory being just around the corner, but as the superstring theories show, even if it did appear, it probably would not tell us much about our everyday lives that we did not already know. A pretty disappointing bit of unification at that.

During the 1980s, however, a number of astonishing, dramatic breakthroughs did take place that diverted physics from the tendency that had dominated the twentieth century.

For most of the past century, physics has been moving away from our everyday lives, away from the phenomena we can observe through our eyes. Bigger and bigger accelerators and more and more complicated apparatus have been developed to study bizarre effects physicists claim would shed light on how to unify the theories of gravity with the theories from the atomic level. So far without success.

In the 1980s, a range of new theories, such as chaos, fractals, self-organization, and complexity, once again turned the spotlight on our everyday lives. Physics may have understood lots of finicky details via experiments carried out at expensive research plants, but it is hard-pressed to explain everyday phenomena; science has a tough time answering the sort of questions children ask—questions about the shape nature takes, about the trees, clouds, mountain ranges, and flowers.

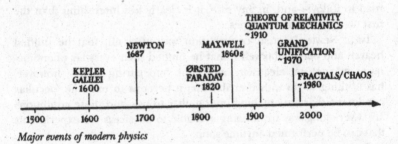

Major events of modern physics

Theories about chaos and fractals have captured great general interest, because they contain genuine new insights and have brought with them a completely new aesthetic form, especially with fractals as computer graphics.

But in fact the most interesting aspect of this new departure is that, combined, these fields contain a series of dramatic conceptual innovations that may lead to the Third Grand Unification: not a theory unifying gravity and atomic theory, but a unification of science and everyday life. A theory that will explain in the same breath the beginning of the universe and everyday consciousness; a theory that will explain why concepts of meaning, say, are related to such concepts as black holes.

This unification would easily match Newton's and Maxwell's in import. There are many indications that it must come. All because of a puzzle that was solved in the 1980s. A puzzle posed in 1867 by James Clerk Maxwell: the puzzle of Maxwell's demon.

"A specter is haunting the sciences: the specter of information."[6] With this indirect reference to the *Communist Manifesto*, the physicist Wojcieh Zurek convened a 1988 meeting in Santa Fe, New Mexico. A meeting at which forty of the world's leading physicists and a few mathematicians assembled to discuss "Complexity, Entropy, and the Physics of Information."

Zurek spoke of a number of "deep analogies" between very different extremes of physics—and between physics and everyday life. Analogies between the way steam engines work and communication theory; between measurements of atomic phenomena and the theory of knowledge; between black holes in the universe and the amount of disorder in a teacup; between calculations in a computer and the foundations of mathematics; between complexity in biological systems and the expansion of the universe.

When the same physicists assembled again two years later for the next conference, the seventy-nine-year-old American physicist John A. Wheeler convened the meeting. In 1939, Wheeler solved the theory of nuclear fission with Niels Bohr. And it was Wheeler who named the most peculiar phenomenon in Einstein's theory of gravity: the black hole. Wheeler, who liked to play the role of prophet, was the grand master of many branches of physics discussed at the meeting.

At first, the short, round man with the always amiable, always happy face peered out across the small but extremely qualified group of scientists assembled in the auditorium of the little Santa Fe Institute on 16 April 1990. Then he spoke: "This isn't just another meeting. By the end of the week, I expect us to know how the universe is put together."[7]

Wheeler then proceeded to question several sacred cows of physics. "There is no space and no time," he said, and launched an attack on the concept of reality. "There is no *out there* out there. . . .

"The idea of one universe is preposterous: The World. We are all participant observers in the universe—it's a miracle that we construct the same vision of the universe. But by the end of the week we might know how to construct all this from nothing," Wheeler told the little group of scientists.

Not everyone agreed. That week did not change our view of the universe, but the feeling spread that the time had come to start over and think everything through once again. A succession of top scientists delivered papers in which all the fundamental ideas of physics were scrutinized.

"I want to talk about what the textbooks don't say," explained Edwin T. Jaynes, another roly-poly American physicist, who, in the 1950s, formulated a new theoretical description of thermodynamics, the theory that forms the basis of entropy and information, the central issues of the 1990 conference. "Oh, maybe they say it in the sense that the formulae are there, but they don't say anything about what the formulae mean," said Jaynes. "The mathematics I am now going to use is far simpler than what we are all capable of. But the problems are not mathematical, they are conceptual."

During one intermission, Thomas Cover, a mathematician from Stanford University, asked, "Are all physics meetings like this? It's like eating candy!"

It was an exception. Such open-minded meetings were rare indeed. Here you heard the same questions that had got you in trouble with your teachers at school. "What does it mean? How can one understand it?" Here you heard the very best people exclaiming, "Why should my car be interested in what I know about the world?"

Physics seemed to have been reborn. All because of the first serious topic that was raised when Wheeler set the tone: *Maxwell's demon.*

Heat. If there is anything we humans know about, it is heat. Body heat. Summer heat. Heaters. But until the mid-nineteenth century, physics had not defined what heat was. In ancient Greece, Aristotle had regarded fire as an independent, inexplicable element on a par with air, earth, and water, and heat as one of the four irreducible qualities whose combinations define those elements.

At the beginning of the 1800s, similar ideas were prevalent, treating heat as a special substance, a thermal material, caloric, which surrounded all bodies. But coming up with a description of just what heat was had become a matter of some urgency, as James Watt's invention of an efficient new steam engine in 1769 had not only ushered in the possibility of industrialization but also put extensive discussions regarding a perpetual motion machine on the agenda. As the steam engine rolled across Europe, scientists simply had to understand thermodynamics.

The first decisive contribution was supplied in 1824 by the Frenchman Sadi Carnot, who, influenced by his father Lazare Carnot's engineering experience with heat machines, rather than with physical theories, formulated a description of steam engines that would, decades later, be expressed as the first and second laws of thermodynamics.

The first law of thermodynamics is concerned with the amount of energy in the world. That amount is constant. Energy neither appears nor disappears when we "consume" it. We can convert coal into hot steam or oil into heat, but the energy involved simply gets converted from one form to another.

This conflicts with the everyday meaning of the word "energy," which we use in terms of something we *consume*. A country has a certain level of energy consumption, we say. But that is nonsense, according to physics' definition of energy. A country converts one form of energy into another. Oil to heat, for example. But the amount of energy remains constant.

But our everyday language is not *that* silly, because it is obvious that something does get used up when we heat our houses: we cannot get our oil back.

So something or other does occur when we "consume" energy, even though the first law of thermodynamics states that the energy in the world is constant and cannot be consumed. For, as the second law of thermodynamics explains, energy can be *used*.

The second law of thermodynamics tells us that energy can appear in more or less usable forms. Some forms of energy can allow us to perform a huge amount of useful work with a machine that can access the energy. We can perform the work of heating a house, or powering a train, or vacuuming.

Energy comes in many forms—and although that energy is constant, the forms it takes most definitely are not. Some forms of energy can be used to perform lots of different kinds of useful work. Electricity is thus one of the most useful forms of energy; others cannot be used as easily. Heat is typically not much use for anything except for heating.

But heat can certainly be used for more specific things than just "heating." You can power a steam locomotive with heat. But you do not get as much out of powering a locomotive with heat as with electric current as an energy source. More energy has to be present if you use heat, which is the lowest quality of energy.

The steam engine made people realize that energy can be present without being available. Heat is a form of energy that is not available to the same extent as electricity. We have to convert more heat energy to get the trains to run. We do not consume more energy, because one cannot consume energy, when all is said and done. But more energy goes to waste when it appears in heat form than when it is available as electricity. That is, more is *converted*.

The second law of thermodynamics describes this very precisely. It says that every time we convert energy ("consume energy," as everyday language would have it), it becomes less available; we can get less work out of it. That is the way it is, says the second law; *any* conversion of energy results in the energy becoming less available than it was before. (There are very special cases where energy can be converted in a reversible way, but you mostly come across them in textbooks, and never in everyday life.)

The energy in the world is constant, but it gets less and less valuable—less and less available—the more we use it.

So the laws of thermodynamics state that energy is constant but becomes less and less available. At the end of the nineteenth century, these two laws led people to believe that the world faced a depressing future: after all, the more we converted energy, the less available it would become, until finally it would all end up as heat, the least available form of energy.

The "heat death" of the universe, people called it: everything would end as uniform, lukewarm heat, without any differences present that would allow us to use the heat to do useful work.

Experience with steam engines showed very clearly that you can use heat to do work only if there is a *difference* present: a difference between two temperatures. It is only because the steam engine's boiler is so much hotter than its surroundings that it can get the train to run. You can get useful work from heat only if you can cool the hot stuff down again. But the consequence of cooling something hot down to the temperature of its surroundings is that you cannot make it hot again without using energy. Once your coffee is cold (after having been heated by the electricity your hot plate uses), it will never heat up again (until you switch the electricity back on). The differences in heat levels are irreversibly eradicated.

So the second law of thermodynamics seems to tell us that we live in a world where everything is heading for tepidity, similarity, uniformity, and grayness: the heat death of the universe. If this was not the case, an engineer's lot would be a happy one. After all, there is enough energy in the world, and it does not disappear anywhere. We could just use the same energy over and over again. We could make perpetual motion machines without further ado. Sorry, that is a no-go. So says the second law of thermodynamics.

In 1859, a Prussian physicist, Rudolf Clausius, gave this fact a name, *entropy*. Entropy is a measure of how unavailable an amount of energy is. The greater the entropy, the less you can use the energy. The two laws of thermodynamics could thus be expressed in another way: According to the first law, energy is constant; and according to the second, entropy always increases. Every time we convert energy, the entropy in the system where the energy is converted increases.

That still does not explain what heat actually is, but it does explain quite a bit about why heat is such a special form of energy: There is lots of entropy in heat; much more than in electric current.

But soon an understanding of what heat was did develop. Some of the greatest contributions came from James Clerk Maxwell and Ludwig Boltzmann. They realized that an old idea could be formulated precisely: the idea that heat was a form of movement in matter. Their premise was the theory of atoms, the idea that matter consists of a huge number of tiny particles in constant motion.

Atomic theory was not generally accepted at the end of the last century, but today it is clear that all matter consists of atoms in constant motion. Atoms come in small groups, molecules, and every kind of matter consists of a certain type of molecule made up of a number of the ninety-two kinds of atoms that exist. But there are different forms of motion. Solids maintain their form despite the motion of their molecules; fluids are more elastic and take the shape of the bottom of the container they are in; air is completely mobile, merely filling the whole container. These are the three states or phases in which matter can be found: solid, fluid, and gaseous. (There is actually a fourth state, plasma, where the atoms have been smashed to bits; in everyday life, this state is familiar as fire.)

The difference between the three states is not as great as one might think. From one common or garden material, H_2O (which consists of oxygen atoms—O—and hydrogen atoms—H, with two of the latter per molecule), we are familiar with the three states: ice, water, and vapor. At low temperatures, the molecules move very slowly. The structure can be maintained. If the temperature goes up a bit, the molecules move a little faster and are able to change places with each other; but they still stick together. At temperatures over 100 degrees centigrade, all the molecules separate and move freely around in the shape of steam—as gas. The transitions between these states or phases are known as "phase transitions." In all these heat motions, the molecules move around chaotically, hither and thither. There is no direction to their heat-induced motion.

But heat is not the only form of motion in matter; an electric current is also a manifestation of motion. But with electricity, not all the molecules move around haphazardly. In an electric current, it is one constituent of the atoms in the molecules—the negatively charged electrons—that flows in a particular direction. There is more order in an electric current than during chaotic heat motion. Similarly, an atmospheric wind is something other than heat: An enormous number of molecules flow in a particular direction instead of just tumbling around among each other. That is why windmills are a clever way of generating current, while oil-fired and nuclear power stations are less elegant, because they use fuel to heat water so it can drive a turbine. The detour via hot water is a high price to pay for the engineers' favorite toys.

Anyway, we can understand many things about matter by understanding it as consisting of tiny identical components in some state of motion. Motion implies a certain amount of energy, whether it be ordered, as with wind, or disordered or confused, as with heat. Wind is more useful than heat for generating current, precisely because it has a direction of motion. But there is still plenty of energy in heat; it is just difficult to harness, because it is caught up in such disorderly motion.

Temperature is an expression of the characteristic speed at which the molecules are moving. What we mean by heat and measure in temperature is disordered movement.

Does that mean, then, that all molecules in a gas share precisely the same speed? How do they keep in step with each other when we turn on the heater?

This was exactly the dilemma Maxwell solved. He introduced statistical concepts to physics for the first time. The molecules do not all move at the same speed. Some have enormous speed, others far less. But their speeds have a characteristic distribution, the Maxwell-Boltzmann distribution, which states that the molecules have a certain average speed but display a variation off this average. If the average is high, the temperature is high; if the average is low, the temperature is low.

But in matter at a given temperature, molecules evince many different speeds. Most have speeds close to the average. We find more high-speed molecules in hot matter than in cold matter. But we also find speedy molecules in cold matter and lethargic ones in hot.

This allows us to understand evaporation. The higher the temperature, the more high-speed molecules. If we imagine evaporation as tiny molecular rockets shooting spaceward, we can see that the hotter a liquid is, the more molecules get away.

But the statistical distribution of speeds has an interesting consequence: We cannot tell from the individual molecule to which temperature it belongs. In other words, the individual molecule can have no idea which temperature it is part of.

Temperature is a concept that means anything only if we have a lot of molecules at once. It is nonsensical to ask each molecule how much temperature it has. Because the molecule does not know. It knows only one speed: its own.

Or does it? After a while, a molecule in a gas will have bumped into other molecules and therefore acquired a certain "knowledge" of the speeds of the other molecules. That is precisely why matter assumes an even temperature: the molecules keep bumping into each other and exchanging speed; a state of balance is achieved. When we heat matter, we might as well do it from underneath. The ensuing great speed spreads rapidly among all the molecules.

Maxwell's contribution was to found the study of the laws governing this behavior. The motion and collisions of the tiny molecules can be described beautifully according to Newton's old laws of motion and collisions involving billiard balls. It turns out that if you have sufficient balls (and there are an awful lot of molecules in air—roughly 1,000,000,000,000,000,000,000,000,000 [10^{27}] molecules in an ordinary room), Newton's laws of motion result in the statistical rules for matter with which we are familiar: rules for temperature, pressure, and volume; rules for the declining availability of the energy in heat.

But there is something strange about this picture. Newton's laws for billiard balls and other mechanical phenomena are beautifully simple laws. They describe phenomena that are reversible: They can be reversed in time. In Newton's universe, time could go backward and we wouldn't be able to tell the difference. But in the world of thermodynamics, the behavior of the balls leads to oddities like the second law of thermodynamics. If you mix something hot and something cold, you can't unmix it. Something irreversible has occurred once your coffee has cooled.

A crowd of high-speed molecules is mixed with a lower-speed crowd; the balls collide and assume a new average speed. That settles the difference once and for all; you cannot separate the molecules that were high-speed before from the molecules that were low-speed, because the individual molecule hasn't the faintest idea which temperature it was part of at a given moment.

Once the molecular deck has been shuffled, you cannot unshuffle it.

It was Ludwig Boltzmann, in the years around Maxwell's death, in 1879, who formulated these matters precisely: It is not particularly probable that Newton's laws will lead to all the molecules suddenly reverting to their original premix speeds. Actually, it is highly improbable. As time passes, mixtures will become more and more mixed. Cold and heat will equalize into lukewarmth.

That is why entropy grows. Entropy is the expression of the unavailability of a given energy. If this energy comes in heat form—measured as temperature—it can be exploited only by mixing something hot with something cold (steam and cool air from the surroundings mixed via a steam engine, for example). But once you have mixed these goodies, you can't separate them and expect the process to work all over again.

The reason for this is the equalization that occurs—an equalization that is irreversible and is the reason why the entropy of the universe is increasing. Irreversibly.

Boltzmann attained an understanding of heat and an understanding of what soon came to be regarded as the most fundamental law of nature: the second law of thermodynamics. In one sense, too, even an understanding of what the passing of time actually means: The molecules exchange speed, their motion equalizes; they assume an average speed, a balance. There is a difference between then and now; we are moving from difference to uniformity.

But many physicists of his day criticized Boltzmann's view. One cannot, they said, deduce such irreversible, irrevocable laws as those of thermodynamics from Newton's laws of motion and kinetics, the physics of the pool table. Because reversibility imparts Newton's picture with such majesty: All equations can go backward in time, all processes are the same, forward and backward.

Based upon practically any experience from everyday life we choose to mention, we can state that things in this world quite simply are irreversible: When something breakable falls on the floor, it does not repair itself; heat goes up the chimney; an untidy desk gets only more untidy. Time passes and everything perishes. Things fall apart. Have you ever seen a smashed plate rise from the pieces?

But this did not interest Boltzmann's critics, for Newton's theories constituted the very ideal of physical theories, and there was something hideously wrong with a picture that would deduce something irrevocable from the revocable, irreversible from the reversible. The physicists of his time said that Boltzmann had misunderstood time.

The theory that matter consists of atoms was not generally accepted around the turn of the nineteenth century. The theoretical basis of all Maxwell's and Boltzmann's ideas about heat as a statistical phenomenon in huge conglomerations of molecules came under heavy fire. It was not until the first decades of the twentieth century that physicists such as Einstein, J. J. Thomson, and Bohr established once and for all that atoms do indeed exist.

In 1898, in the foreword to a book about the theory of molecular motion in air, Boltzmann wrote that he was "convinced that these attacks are merely based on a misunderstanding" and he was "conscious of being only an individual struggling weakly against the stream of time."[8]

When Boltzmann had turned sixty-two, in 1906, he was no feted hero, despite his enormous contributions to the development of physics. He was tormented by depression and by fear of lecturing. He had to turn down a professorship in Leipzig and confront his scientific isolation.

The previous year, he had written in a popular book, "I might say that I am the only one left of those who embraced the old theories with all their hearts; at least the only one to fight for them with all my strength."[9]

But his strength ran out. While on summer holiday near Trieste, on 6 September 1906, Ludwig Boltzmann took his own life.[10]

The unification of the reversibility in Newton's sublime equations and the irreversibility of everyday life was not to be Boltzmann's lot, despite the fact that this was precisely the problem Maxwell had encountered in 1867 when he conceived the mischievous demon who would, through more than a century of discussion, illuminate and explain the difficulty that had proved irreversible for Ludwig Boltzmann.

"Maxwell's demon lives on. After more than 120 years of uncertain life and at least two pronouncements of death, this fanciful character seems more vibrant than ever," wrote two American physicists, Harvey Leff and Andrew Rex, in 1990 when they published a book of historical sources elucidating the story of Maxwell's demon—a story the two physicists consider an overlooked chapter in the history of modern science. "Maxwell's demon is no more than a simple idea," they wrote. "Yet it has challenged some of the best scientific minds, and its extensive literature spans thermodynamics, statistical physics, information theory, cybernetics, the limits of computing, biological sciences and the history and philosophy of science."[11]

≈

In 1867, the physicist Peter Guthrie Tait wrote to his close friend and university chum James Clerk Maxwell to ask if Maxwell would take a critical look at a manuscript on the history of thermodynamics before it was published. Maxwell replied that he would be happy to do so, although he was unfamiliar with the details of the history of thermodynamics; but he could perhaps point out a hole or two in the presentation. Whereupon Maxwell continued his letter by pointing out an enormous hole in the presentation he had not yet even seen: a hole in the second law of thermodynamics.

Maxwell's idea was simple: A gas is confined in a container with two chambers, A and B. A hole in the diaphragm separating the two chambers can be opened and closed without any effort of work being done—in other words, through some kind of superslide.

LEFT *Maxwell's demon in a twin-chambered container. The molecules in both chambers have the same velocity.*
RIGHT *Maxwell's demon after sorting through the molecules: high-speed molecules on the right, slow-speed molecules on the left.*

"Now conceive a finite being who knows the paths and velocities of all the molecules by simple inspection but who can do no work except to open and close a hole in the diaphragm by means of [this] slide without mass," Maxwell wrote to Tait.[12] He went on to describe how the little creature opens the slide every time a fast molecule in the chamber on the left is heading for the little slide. When a slow molecule in the same chamber approaches the slide, it remains closed.

So only the fast molecules pass from the left-hand chamber to the right-hand one. Conversely, only slow molecules from the right-hand chamber are let into the left-hand one.

The result is a buildup of fast molecules on the right and slow ones on the left. The number of molecules is constant in both chambers, but their average speed changes in each chamber. The temperature rises in the chamber on the right, while it falls in the chamber on the left. A difference is created. "And yet no work has been done," Maxwell wrote. "Only the intelligence of a very observant and neat-fingered being has been employed."[13]

Maxwell had apparently discovered a hole in the second law of thermodynamics: a clever little fellow can create heat out of luke-warmth without doing any work. "In short," wrote Maxwell, "if heat is the motion of finite portions of matter and if we can apply tools to such portions of matter so as to deal with them separately, then we can take advantage of the different motion of different proportions to restore a uniformly hot system to unequal temperatures or to motions of large masses. Only we can't, not being clever enough."[14]

We are too big and clumsy to be able to get around the second law of thermodynamics. But if we were a bit more neat-fingered and obser-vant, we would be able to separate the molecules in the air in our kitchens into a refrigerator and an oven, without it ever appearing on our electricity bills.

Three years later, Maxwell wrote to Lord Rayleigh, another physicist: "Moral. The 2nd law of thermodynamics has the same degree of truth as the statement that if you throw a tumblerful of water into the sea, you cannot get the same tumblerful of water out again."[15]

Maxwell wanted to show that the second law of thermodynamics was valid only statistically: It is a law that applies at *our level* and not to small creatures of great intelligence. When we describe the world as we know it, in the form of very large congregations of molecules, the law of increasing entropy and decreasing availability of energy *does* apply. But if only we were just a little more clever, we would be able to obtain heat from cold simply by opening the window when fast molecules were on their way from the night frost (rare though they may be) or when slow molecules wished to leave the room.

A perpetual motion machine based on intelligent observance.

Maxwell published the idea of the little fellow in a book, *Theory of Heat*, in 1871, and three years later, another physicist, William Thomson, nicknamed the creature a demon—not a creature of malice but "an intelligent being endowed with free will and fine enough tactile and perceptive organization to give him the faculty of observing and influencing individual molecules of matter."[16]

Maxwell's demon tells us a teasing tale: The reason we have to work in order to obtain warmth in winter is because of our own inadequacies, not the universe's. Everything is descending into disorder and confusion for no other reason than that we are too big and clumsy to manipulate the individual components of matter.

Maxwell thereby pointed out the difference between the description of the haphazard rushing to and fro of individual molecules—as proved by Newton's sublime equations—and the description of finite portions of matter—as proved by the heat death of thermodynamics—which would, a few decades later, be the death of Boltzmann.

Thermodynamics is a statistical theory that tells us about a world that we can know but never attain, because we are not clever enough. In reality, there is no difference between various forms of energy: They are all equally available—to anyone who knows how to use them.

The fact that energy becomes more and more unavailable is thus linked to our description and the possibilities for intervention in the world our description gives us.

In the ninth edition of the *Encyclopaedia Britannica*, 1878, Maxwell wrote about the increasing unavailability of energy, its dissipation, the way it slips through the fingers, the growth of entropy.

He pointed out a peculiarity: If you take a jar with two gases, you can make a gain by allowing them to mix. The disappearance of the difference during the mixing process gives access to some work. If, however, the gases are of the same kind, you will not get anything out of mixing them—which intuitively seems quite right and proper. But this leads to an odd thing. Maxwell wrote, "Now, when we say that two gases are the same, we mean that we cannot distinguish the one from the other by any known reaction. It is not probable, but it is possible, that two gases derived from different sources, but hitherto supposed to be the same, may hereafter be found to be different, and that a method may be discovered of separating them by a reversible process." So it is possible that in time we will grow more clever and be able to detect differences we could not before. Consequently there would suddenly be available energy present where it had not been before. Dissipation of energy is apparently not defined without knowledge of our ability to discriminate. That ability is not constant! Maxwell continues with the following remarkable observations:

"It follows from this that the idea of dissipation of energy depends on the extent of our knowledge. Available energy is energy which we can direct into any desired channel. Dissipated energy is energy which we cannot lay hold of and direct at pleasure, such as the energy of the confused agitation of molecules which we call heat. Now, confusion, like the correlative term order, is not a property of material things in themselves, but only in relation to the mind which perceives them."

Maxwell goes on: "A memorandum-book does not, provided it is neatly written, appear confused to an illiterate person, or to the owner who understands it thoroughly, but to any other person able to read it appears to be inextricably confused. Similarly the notion of dissipated energy could not occur to a being who could not turn any of the energies of nature to his own account, or to one who could trace the motion of every molecule and seize it at the right moment. It is only to a being in the intermediate stage, who can lay hold of some forms of energy while others elude his grasp, that energy appears to be passing inevitably from the available to the dissipated state."[17]

Maxwell's demon is laughing in our faces: The second law of thermodynamics can be circumvented, if we are clever enough. Only we aren't that clever.

The exorcism of the demon became a major theme of the twentieth-century scientific picture of the universe. Because unless there is something wrong with Maxwell's concept of a demon, all that stands between us and perpetual motion is our own stupidity. Purely because mortals are not clever enough, we are condemned to earning our living by the sweat of our brow.

But might there be a price to pay for being as clever as Maxwell's demon?

CHAPTER 2

THROWING AWAY
INFORMATION

A demon had to be exorcised. The first decades of the twentieth century had been one long succession of victories for the notion that matter was made up of atoms and molecules. Maxwell's and Boltzmann's ideas on the statistical behavior of large aggregations of such atoms and molecules had been validated, despite the considerable resistance that proved so fatal to Boltzmann.

At the end of the nineteenth century, the argument over the existence of atoms was still raging so strongly that the problem of Maxwell's demon could be left to rest. But the further we moved into the twentieth century, the clearer it became that there was a serious problem with this demon. After all, it showed that there was a problem with the second law of thermodynamics—i.e., if only we know enough about the world, we can have things any way we want them. But as we all know, we cannot.

The Hungarian physicist Leo Szilard posed a very good question in 1929: Can you know all about the world without changing it? The answer was simple: No, you cannot.

In a paper formidably entitled "On the Decrease of Entropy in a Thermodynamic System by the Intervention of Intelligent Beings," Szilard asked the cost of attaining knowledge and whether paying such a price could "save" the second law from Maxwell's demon.

Leo Szilard provided the answer to his own question. He worked out that the cost of knowing is just high enough to save the second law. If you want to be as clever as Maxwell's demon, you have to convert a whole lot of energy, thereby creating a load of entropy and counterbalancing the entire knowledge gain. The demon does gain by having its eye on every single molecule and being ready with a closed trapdoor at the right instant, but any gains are outweighed by the cost: in order to be able to open and close the trapdoor between the two chambers at the right moments, you have to know the motion of every single molecule. So you have to measure all the particles. And that costs. Szilard explained:

"One may reasonably assume that a measurement procedure is fundamentally associated with a certain definite average entropy production, and that this restores concordance with the Second Law."[1]

An ingenious idea that has decisively affected science this century, from information theory via computer science to molecular biology.

The physicists were delighted: The demon was exorcised. It works only because it knows something about the world—and this knowledge costs. Since then, science historians have laid out the battleground: "Why did not Maxwell think of that?" Edward E. Daub asked in 1970 in a journal on the history and philosophy of science. He replied, "Because his demon was a creature of his theology."[2]

Maxwell's theology, Daub posited, came from Isaac Newton, the founder of modern physics. Newton talked of the God who sees, hears, and understands everything "in a manner not at all human, in a manner not at all corporeal, in a manner utterly unknown to us. As a blind man has no idea of color, so we have no idea of the manner by which the all-wise God perceives and understands all things," Newton wrote.[3]

It was this divinity that Szilard dismissed. "Maxwell's demon was not mortal," wrote Daub, "because he was made in the image of God. And like God, he could see without seeing and hear without hearing. In short, he could acquire information without any expenditure of energy. . . . In essence, Szilard made Maxwell's doorkeeper mortal."[4]

Leo Szilard's analysis of Maxwell's demon started the study of knowledge as part of the physical world—insight as a participation that carries a cost; measurement as a material act; sensation as metabolism; knowing as work: the thermodynamics of thought; the insight of the mind into its own physicality.

A very significant event in the history of human knowledge. A milestone in man's perception of the surrounding world and of himself.

All the more remarkable, then, that Szilard's analysis happens to be incorrect. You cannot exorcise the demon using Szilard's arguments. They do not hold water, even though people believed them for half a century, right up until 1982.

"It's one of the great puzzles in the sociology of science why this obviously inadequate argument met with wide and uncritical acceptance," the physicist Rolf Landauer wrote in 1989, adding with barely concealed impatience: "Only in recent years have clearer discussions emerged, and these are not yet widely appreciated."[5]

Landauer, who works at the IBM research laboratories in Yorktown Heights, New York, was himself one of the leading figures behind the insights that led to the final exorcism of the demon. It was performed by Landauer's close associate at IBM, Charles Bennett, in 1982.

The measuring, the obtaining of information, is not what costs at all. What costs is getting rid of that information again. Knowledge is not what costs. Wisdom does.

As is so often the case in the history of science, a flawed conclusion proved to be extraordinarily fertile. Leo Szilard's analysis does not hold water, but it is no less interesting because of it. For Szilard had grasped much of the point.

In fact, Szilard does not write that he has exorcised Maxwell's demon at all. He writes, as quoted above, that "one may reasonably assume" that a measuring process costs a certain amount of produced entropy; a certain amount of inaccessibility of the existing energy. He goes on to show that the amount of entropy produced is at least equal to the energy gained through the activity the demon can perform by dint of its knowledge.

So in reality Szilard merely assumes that measuring costs something, in the form of more entropy. He does not prove it.

But not many people notice that, which is what puzzled Landauer. For how could Szilard's argument lead to half a century of fruitful acceptance when it was actually incorrect? One major reason is, of course, that it seemed a touch embarrassing that this demon could disprove the most fundamental law of physics: The second law was so fundamental to physics that it was as clear as daylight that Maxwell's demon could not work. Because if it did, we could build all kinds of perpetual motion machines and tap hot air from the frosty night. So nobody could dispute that something was wrong, and Szilard was a skillful physicist who had supplied an elegant argument showing that something was wrong.

It was not that there were no protests to Szilard's analysis. But they came mostly from philosophers. Physicists have never had much respect for philosophers who argue with the results of physics research because these results happen to conflict with philosophical views. The protests came from philosophers like Karl Popper, Paul Feyerabend, and Rudolf Carnap,[6] three of the twentieth century's most influential philosophers of science. They protested not least because it did not accord too well with their philosophy if mental phenomena were to be understood as physical quantities. So their objections did not make that much of an impression.

Moreover, in many ways Szilard's 1929 notion resembled what quantum physicists in the 1920s had experienced regarding the significance of the measuring process on the study of the bits and pieces that make up matter. Niels Bohr and his student Werner Heisenberg had pointed out that measurements disturb the systems you are measuring. It had nothing to do with the case, certainly, but that is what people thought, especially when a number of physicists crystallized Szilard's reasoning most beautifully.

"Maxwell's demon cannot operate,"[7] asserted Leon Brillouin, a physicist at the IBM laboratories in New York, in an article that tried to expand on Szilard's arguments. Brillouin had already discussed the demon in "Life, Thermodynamics and Cybernetics," published in 1949, and he became well known for his book *Science and Information Theory* (1956).[8] The subjects Brillouin throws into the ring in his discussions of Maxwell's demon are pretty interesting ones: life, information, and control mechanisms (cybernetics).

The argument is seemingly crystal clear: Maxwell's demon is located in a gas-filled container at a given temperature. It keeps an eye on the various molecules and sorts them by speed so all the speedier molecules are collected in one of the container's two chambers.

However, everything is equally hot at first. This means that the radiation and matter inside the container are in balance, and you cannot see anything: because if everything is equally hot, you cannot see differences. "The demon cannot see the molecules, hence, he cannot operate the trap door and is unable to violate the second principle," Brillouin wrote.[9]

Maxwell's demon does not work because it cannot see anything. This may seem a peculiar assertion, but it concerns a thought experiment: a hypothetical world that does not resemble everyday life but is meant to illustrate physical laws in all their simplicity.

In everyday life, everything we look at is equally hot or roughly so, about room temperature (apart from the sun and the stars, whose surfaces are very hot). But since there is plenty of light in our ordinary world, we can see things. The light that enables us to see originates from a body far hotter than what we are looking at (the sun's surface or the filament in an electric lightbulb). We can see things in our everyday lives because the light comes from something hotter than the objects in our everyday world. We live in a composite world, so we can see, while the demon lives in a world in balance and therefore cannot.

However, Brillouin comes to the aid of the demon. "We may equip him with an electric torch and enable him to see the molecules."[10] But a flashlight would cost. Brillouin calculates the presence of a charged battery and a bulb that emits light. The light disperses through the container after it strikes the molecules and turns to heat. The flashlight converts the accessible energy from the battery into heat from the dispersed light. The entropy grows. At the same time, the entropy decreases, because the molecules rushing around get sorted into the two chambers, according to their speed. But the amount of energy to which we can gain access in this manner is less than the amount of energy to which we lose access as the battery goes dead.

Brillouin expanded his analysis into a more general theory as to how physicists can perform experiments that involve measuring nature. His conclusion was clear. "The physicist in his laboratory is no better off than the demon. . . . He needs batteries, power supply, compressed gases, etc. . . . The physicist also needs light in his laboratory in order to be able to read ammeters or other instruments."[11]

Knowledge costs.

Leon Brillouin had clarified a wide-ranging point in Szilard's work: Maxwell's demon does not work because information is a material quantity. Brillouin was delighted. "We have discovered a very important physical law," he wrote. "Every physical measurement requires a corresponding entropy increase. . . ."[12] This is what could be learned from the demon's difficulties in seeing in the dark.

But Brillouin failed to ask whether Maxwell's demon could *feel* its way around. So he concluded—like other physicists since, such as Denis Gabor, inventor of holography—that it was the demon's use of flashlights that rescued the second law. But the demon is a clever fellow, so who says it needs light to make it more knowledgeable?

In 1982, Charles Bennett, the physicist from IBM, demonstrated that the demon could get along just fine in an unlit container. Bennett set up an ingenious apparatus that would allow the demon to determine the location of each molecule at no cost. The idea was not to obtain this knowledge without converting any energy—that would be impossible, even for a demon. The idea was to feel your way around in such a way that all the energy you convert is also accessible to you after the measurements are completed.

When you use a flashlight, the light is dissipated and ends up as heat. The energy is made inaccessible. But when you feel your way around, you can find out where a molecule is without rendering the energy you have used inaccessible.

The apparatus Bennett designed was pretty refined. Actually, it works only on a special edition of Maxwell's demon, whose container contains a gas that consists of a single molecule! This may sound like a pretty weird version of the demon hypothesis, but it is precisely the one Szilard conceived of back in 1929 when he wanted to show that the cost of learning the location of that one molecule was just enough to rescue the second law. Simply by analyzing the cost of the very simple measurement—is the molecule to the left or to the right?—Szilard arrived at the foundations for all subsequent information theories: the answer to a yes/no question.

By posing the problem so simply, Szilard was able to ask how much such a simple piece of knowledge would cost. This has since become known as the bit, the smallest unit of information: a concept that was to become one of the most common technical terms in everyday use by the end of the twentieth century. In his article on Maxwell's demon, Szilard founded the whole of modern information theory.

Szilard considered that measuring one's way to such a bit would always cost something. But Bennett proved that this cost could be made arbitrarily small in the case Szilard had analyzed.

If you think about it, it is not so strange: The obtaining of information as to the location of the molecule means copying information that already exists. You "read" a state, and copying information like that does not necessarily cost much in the form of energy made inaccessible. After all, you can make lots of copies, rendering each of them relatively very cheap to produce. This is actually something highly characteristic for information, unlike most other consumer goods: An arbitrary number of copies can be made without wearing it out. You can use information without using it up. So why should it cost the demon anything to obtain knowledge?

Rolf Landauer and Charles Bennett could prove that it did not need to cost anything at all. But that does not mean that Maxwell's demon can break the second law of thermodynamics. It merely means that it's not the measuring that necessarily costs. It's not the obtaining of information that costs the demon anything. It's forgetting it again.

In 1961, Landauer proved that forgetting *always* costs. When you get rid of information by erasing it, you have to pay by way of increased entropy. You have to get rid of information because the measurement has to be repeated: you have to clear the memory in order to reset the measuring apparatus to zero.

For Maxwell's demon, this means that it can find out where the molecules are in the dark without this costing more than the advantage of knowing. But the demon rapidly runs into the problem of keeping track of its knowledge about a whole bunch of molecules from which it has already obtained the work. The demon drowns in its knowledge of prior observations.

Bennett summarized his point in 1987: "We have, then, found the reason why the demon cannot violate the second law: in order to observe a molecule, it must first forget the results of previous observations. Forgetting results, or discarding information, is thermodynamically costly."[13]

One might object that the demon could just remember everything. Then it wouldn't need to forget and thereby create entropy. The rest of us would soon be exhausted by such traffic, but then we are not demons. What that exhaustion shows is that there *is* a cost: Memory costs; entropy builds up as the memory gradually fills with molecules that went by ages ago. The bother of keeping track of this huge memory exceeds the gain of having it.

A look at relative sizes in the real world shows that this is actually a major problem in practice. There is a vast number of molecules in the air. Even if the demon needed only a single bit of information about each molecule (through the trapdoor or not), it would soon run out of memory. Even a demon equipped with the memory of all the computers in the world put together (ten million billion bits) would run out of memory in which to store its measurements before it had reduced the entropy in one gram of air by as little as a tenth of a millionth of a percent![14] There are inconceivably many molecules in the air—they just happen to be very, very small. We live in a world where the equivalent of all the information the human brain can handle in a lifetime is not enough to recall just one bit about each molecule in a single liter of air.[15]

So the fact of the matter is that the demon cannot function because it has to forget everything again, which costs more than the value of all its efforts. This may seem like a weird idea, but it indicates a very important fact: The interesting thing about information is getting rid of it again. In itself, information is very tedious. What is interesting is getting rid of it—and the means of discarding it.

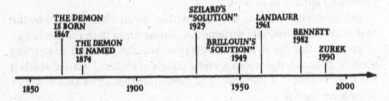

Major events in the life of Maxwell's demon

For example, you are standing at the checkout at a supermarket. Your purchases are being totaled. Each item in your basket has a price. The cashier enters each price, adds them, and arrives at a sum—a total price of, say, $27.80. This amount is the result of a calculation involving the addition of a lot of numbers.

What contains the most information, the sum or the calculation itself? The sum is one number ($27.80), while the calculation was a collection of several numbers—twenty-three different prices, say. We might feel that on the face of it there must be more information in the result, because when we did sums at school our teacher instructed us to come up with the right answer.

But in fact there is far less information in the result than in the problem: After all, there are lots of different combinations of goods that can lead to the same total price. But that does not mean you can guess what is in each basket if you know only the price.

The cashier and the register discard information as they calculate the total. In this situation, the cashier does not care which goods you take out of the store with you and how much they each cost. As long as you pay up.

The total price is what matters, even though it contains very little information—or more accurately, the fact that it contains very little information is what matters. It contains precisely the information that is relevant in the context.

Calculation is a method of getting rid of information in which you are not interested. You throw away what is not relevant.

This contradicts our everyday perception of information as being something highly positive, a good. We are accustomed to viewing information as a positive thing, but this may well be completely unreasonable—a prejudice that affects man on the threshold of the information society.

As Charles Bennett states, "We pay to have newspapers delivered, not taken away. Intuitively, the demon's record of past actions seems to be a valuable (or at worst a useless) commodity. But for the demon 'yesterday's newspaper' (the result of a previous measurement) takes up valuable space, and the cost of clearing that space neutralizes the benefit the demon derived from the newspaper when it was fresh. Perhaps the increasing awareness of environmental pollution and the information explosion brought on by computers have made the idea that information can have a negative value seem more natural now than it would have seemed earlier in this century."[16]

At the IBM labs, they know that information is closely related to entropy, which is a measure of disorder. Once upon a time, we could simply pile up our old newspapers in the basement. But information has to be recycled, too, if things are not to drown in so much information that they end in chaos.

But we all feel information is a boon, an expression of order, meticulousness, and correct results. That is what we learned when we did arithmetic at school: to discard all our rough calculations on scrap paper in order to present a neatly written sum on a nice clean sheet. We learned to discard information, not to obtain it. Yet we live in a world which believes that information is what's valuable in an information society.

So there is something wrong with our everyday perception of information (or with the natural scientists' perception of information; at any rate, they do not match up). Maxwell's demon has already indicated part of the problem. But it has more up its sleeve. Which brings us back to Ludwig Boltzmann.

A few years before James Clerk Maxwell died, Boltzmann published a series of papers in which he expounded a wonderful theory for the link between the notion of entropy, which arose from the study of the limitations to the efficiency of steam engines, and the theory of heat as a statistical whirl of the smallest components of matter. Maxwell never learned of these works, and in the words of the historian Martin Klein, he thus "missed the pleasure of seeing the relationship between entropy and probability."[17]

Boltzmann's idea was simple. He distinguished between what are known as *macrostates* and *microstates:* between the properties of large conglomerations of matter and the properties of the individual components of that matter. Macrostates are such things as temperature, pressure, volume. Microstates consist of accurate descriptions of the behavior of each individual component.

The temperature of a cloud of gas is a macrostate that does not tell us much about the microstates. The temperature tells us that the molecules are rushing about among each other in a highly disorganized way at an average speed that is expressed by the temperature and a distribution of speeds that is statistical and known as the Maxwell-Boltzmann distribution. It tells us that most molecules move at a speed close to average, while a few molecules have speeds that are much higher or much lower than average. In fact, this is not of much interest to us: We might know the macrostate, a specific temperature, but it does not tell us very much at all about the condition of the individual molecules.

As we've got one hundred seventeen thousand million billion molecules flitting about at one temperature (and normally we would have far more than that), it really does not matter much which molecules have which speeds, as long as all together they distribute themselves the way the Maxwell-Boltzmann distribution says they should—and they do, because they keep bumping into each other.

There is an enormous number of different ways of distributing speed among the umpteen billion molecules that would match the given temperature. There are many microscopic states that correspond to the macrostate the temperature expresses—and it really does not matter which of them is actually present in the room.

The higher the temperature, the more speeds there are from which to choose. So the number of microstates that correspond to the given macrostate grows with the temperature.

Ludwig Boltzmann's idea, so to speak, was that macrostates which can be realized by many different microstates are more disorganized than those corresponding to just a few microstates. According to Boltzmann, the more microstates that go with a macrostate, the greater the entropy of the latter.

There happen to be extremely many microstates that correspond to the macrostate "the temperature in this room is 21 degrees centigrade," so counting them all is pretty difficult. Boltzmann therefore used a mathematical trick that had been known since the Renaissance when the numbers got too big to handle: He took the logarithm for the number of microstates and made this logarithm equal to the entropy. This merely means that you ask not if there are a million billion (10^{15}) microstates or a billion billion (10^{18}) but whether the logarithm of the number is 15 or 18. Rather easier to keep track of. Moreover, using logarithms means other major advantages when you are counting microstates.

But most important of all is the basic idea, no matter how it is expressed mathematically: Entropy is a measure of how many microstates we cannot be bothered to keep track of and why we choose to talk about one macrostate instead. Entropy is a measure of how much we cannot be bothered to keep tidy but decide to sweep under the carpet by using a general term that tells us what we need to know—e.g., a temperature.

As humans, we like heat. Temperature interests us. We could not care less about the motion of the molecules (in the same way as political figures are often interested in their constituents only when there are enough of them for a macrostate such as one that might swing an election). The macrostate is an expression of an interest, a relevancy. It encapsulates what interests us. What we are interested in knowing.

Poker is a good example.[18] You have a deck of cards. When you buy it, it is in a very specific macrostate. The individual cards are in order of suit and rank. This macrostate corresponds to one microstate alone, the one where all the cards are in the order in which they came from the factory.

But before the game begins, the cards must be shuffled. When you have a deck of shuffled cards, you still have only one macrostate—shuffled cards—but there is an almost infinite number of microstates that correspond to this macrostate. There are differences between all the ways the cards can be shuffled, but we do not have enough energy to express them. So we just say they have been shuffled.

To start the game, five cards, a "hand," are dealt to each player. This hand is now the macrostate that the players are interested in. It can take various forms. Some macrostates consist of very similar cards—for example, five cards of the same suit, though not in sequence: a "flush." Other macrostates consist of five cards in sequence, though not of the same suit: a "straight." There are lots of ways of forming a straight, but not vastly many. There are far more ways of making a nonstraight.

Among the many microstates described by the macroscopic "straight," there is a small group of good straights known as "straight flushes." Here the cards are not only in sequence; they are in the same suit. Best of all is the "royal flush," the sequence ten to ace in one suit. There are only four microstates that correspond to the royal flush macrostate, but an astronomical figure corresponding to the macrostate known as a "pair."

The order of value in poker is an expression of how many microstates correspond to the macrostate. Your hand is "strong" if it is one that does not assume many variants (and therefore seldom occurs).

There is a clear link between probability and entropy. The greater the number of different cards that can be put together for a particular hand, the greater the probability that you will be dealt such a hand. So you are most likely to get a "weak hand" (with lots of entropy) rather than a "strong hand," where the macrostate can have only a very small number of corresponding microstates.

The purpose of the game is to see who has the macrostate with the lowest entropy.

The vast majority of microstates are actually so boring that they do not even have names in poker—there is no pattern to your cards and the only bid you can make is "high cards," a macrostate corresponding to any microstate. As people play poker for enjoyment, the game includes the opportunity to affect your macrostate by changing the microstate—i.e., the individual cards: You draw. This may enable you to improve your macrostate to one that does not correspond to so many microstates. You play Maxwell's demon—if you are lucky and draw good cards to replace those you discard.

The game involves pretending that the macrostate you actually possess corresponds to only very few microstates, even though this may not be true. This is known as bluffing and presupposes more advanced theories than those Boltzmann can help us with. They come later, in Chapter Five.

The link between entropy and probability may give an idea of why entropy is growing: The probability of receiving a low-entropy macrostate is smaller than the probability of a high one. So everything is proceeding in the direction of higher entropy.

When changed, a macrostate will inexorably lead to another macrostate, with higher entropy—and thus more microstates corresponding to it than the first. Keeping track of the world becomes ever more difficult and tedious.

There is nothing mysterious about that. It is self-evident, once the macrostate has been defined. But how can the world know what we find so boring that we cannot be bothered to keep track of it?

Boltzmann explained that entropy is an expression of the number of microstates that correspond to a given macrostate. It sounds like a highly subjective concept, because entropy seems to express what we do not know when we know the macrostate. A high temperature corresponds to high entropy because the higher the speed of the molecules, the more ways there are in which we can compose their patterns of movement. Our lack of knowledge about the actual microstate grows the hotter it is in our living room. Entropy is a measure of ignorance, but it is convenient ignorance: There is in fact no reason for us to know where every single molecule in the room is heading, or at what speed.

Entropy is a measure of the coarse graining that applies to the level at which we describe things. Heat is a very coarse concept; there are stacks of knowledge we happily ignore. Heat is a concept that involves lots and lots of entropy because it is very coarse and discards a great deal of knowledge of microstates that we cannot be bothered to possess. Wind and current are slightly less coarse concepts, because we know quite a bit more about where the molecules are heading when we say that there is a warm breeze than when we just say "It's warm out."

Entropy is a measure of information that is of no immediate interest—microstates that make us tired simply thinking about them. Entropy is a concept that assumes meaning only when we have explained what it is we cannot be bothered to keep track of. The concept of entropy presupposes that we have explained which macrostates interest us. But no matter which ones we choose, their entropy grows.

The second law tells us that the world is constantly getting harder to describe: The mess is growing, disorder is on the up-and-up, everything will end up as friction and heat. Mess is a kind of order that is so rich in detail that it is a mess.

How can the world know what we think is a mess? Why do our physics textbooks never tell us that a concept like entropy is meaningless unless one explains which macrostate one has in mind? Why teach schoolchildren and university students thermodynamics without telling them that Maxwell and Boltzmann always referred to the way in which we describe the world? Because subconsciously, physicists know that what interests human beings is heat.

This is the unspoken premise for the whole of modern thermodynamics: that people like heat. It is why thermodynamics is about heat and similar macrostates—or what interests people. In turn, the microstates are the arrangement of atoms and molecules—or what interests physicists.

But entropy is defined only when we know who has defined it. Entropy is not defined until we know the coarseness of the observer. This seems so obvious to physics teachers that they see no reason to tell their students.

This was exactly what physicist Edwin Jaynes hinted at when he spoke at Santa Fe in 1990 on the importance of asking what things mean—the things printed in our physics textbooks. Jaynes has reworded the modern version of thermodynamics and illuminated Boltzmann's old points very clearly. In 1979, he wrote, "The entropy of a thermodynamic system is a measure of the degree of ignorance of a person *whose sole knowledge about its microstate consists of the values of the macroscopic quantities X, which define its thermodynamic state.* This is a completely 'objective' quantity, in the sense that it is a function only of the X, and does not depend on anybody's personality. There is then no reason why it cannot be measured in the laboratory."[19]

So entropy is clearly defined once you know the level of description.

It is not a subjective concept in the sense that every observer has his own entropy. Anyone interested in the same macrostates and microstates will find the same measure of entropy. But it is subjective in the sense that it is meaningless until you ask the person who asks about the entropy just what he is interested in.

This does not prevent entropy from being a measure of ignorance. Because it is exactly a measure of the ignorance that accompanies a given coarseness.

"But why should my car be interested in what I know about the world?" one physicist asked at Santa Fe with concern when Jaynes explained these matters. The answer is really quite simple: because it was built by people like you. Because the car engine has exactly the coarseness people have when we describe the world: We sense heat, but we do not sense molecules. Our description of the world is obtained through a refinement and elaboration of this sensing. So it reappears in the machines we build on the basis of this knowledge.

As philosopher Paul Feyerabend said of Boltzmann, "With his realization of the hypothetical character of all our knowledge, Boltzmann was far ahead of his time and perhaps even of our own."[20]

In 1948, Claude Shannon, an engineer, posed a very good question: How much does it cost to transmit messages from one place to another? Szilard had asked how much it cost to measure. Shannon asked how much it cost to communicate. The point of departure was the concept of the bit—distinguishing between two identical conditions: a yes/no answer to a question.

Shannon's analysis was revolutionary. Based on Szilard, he founded modern information theory.

When we talk about information in our everyday lives, we think of meaning. But meaning was not what interested Claude Shannon. He was interested in the length of telephone calls.

Shannon was an engineer at Bell Laboratories, AT&T's famous research unit. He was studying the difficulty of transmitting messages in signal form. His interest was in defining what is required in order to transmit a specific message via a specific connection—for example, a telephone or telex line.

How can one measure the difficulty of transmitting a message?

Shannon proposed that the surprise value was what expressed the difficulty of communicating. How can one measure the surprise value of a line of letters from the alphabet?

We know that the next symbol to appear will be a letter. We also know that the alphabet consists of twenty-six letters. So our surprise is expressed via the fact that each symbol consists of one of twenty-six possible letters. When we see the letter, we are surprised to the extent that it is precisely that letter—and not one of the other twenty-five possibilities.

Shannon's theory can be expressed by saying that each symbol is a macrostate that can correspond to twenty-six different microstates—the individual letters. Each symbol contains an ability to surprise that is expressed by the possibility of its being one of twenty-six letters. The reception of a specific letter thus contains a surprise value that derives from the fact that it precludes the arrival of the other twenty-five letters.

This makes it possible to express with precision the difficulty of communicating: A character is a macrostate whose surprise value is determined by how many microstates correspond to this macrostate.

Shannon was very much in doubt as to what to call this quantity. He considered using the word "uncertainty" and the word "information." The mathematician John von Neumann, known as the father of the logical structure of today's computers, tried to persuade Shannon to call this surprise value "entropy," because the similarity to the concepts of thermodynamics was so striking and, he reportedly argued to Shannon, "it will give you a great edge in debates because nobody really knows what entropy is anyway."[21]

In the end, Shannon chose "information entropy," but as nobody knew what entropy was, his theory passed into history as a theory of information.

In reality, the "information society" is thus an "entropy society"—a society of ignorance and disorder.

This concept of information is defined most simply if we limit ourselves to communicating via a very special alphabet—that of binary numbers. When we use binary numbers, as people do everywhere nowadays in the communications and computer industries, we have just two fundamental means by which to express ourselves: 0 or 1.

As a macrostate, a binary digit corresponds to just two equally probable microstates. When we receive a binary symbol, our surprise is limited: either/or. But exactly this degree of surprise, where we distinguish between two equally probable possibilities, had been discovered by Szilard and has since been dubbed "one bit": the information contained by a yes/no answer to a question, or distinguishing between two possibilities. When we receive a bit, we receive a piece of information that corresponds to distinguishing between two microstates. So you have to receive quite a few bits before the surprise seems significant.

There is slightly more information in a symbol known to be part of an alphabet. Here the arrival of a specific letter excludes not just one other possibility but twenty-five. So you receive a handful of bits when you receive a single letter—more precisely, you receive between four and five bits.

In practice, of course, things are a bit more complicated. Language is full of redundancy, or superfluous symbols. We do not need to know all the letters to guess a word on *Wheel of Fortune*. So in practice the letters have a lower average information value than five bits. In Danish, the information content per letter is about two bits, while for a more systematic language like German, the value comes down to about 1.3 bits per letter.[22]

What is more, the letters are not used equally, so there is not quite so much information in receiving an *e* as in receiving a *z*. On average, each microstate (letter) has a probability proportional to the number of different microstates. But the probability of each letter is proportional to its frequency, which is also linked to the number of different microstates there are overall. As *Wheel of Fortune* contestants know, the information value of a letter is inversely proportional to its frequency. The rarer the letter, the more information its presence contains.

Furnished with this exact definition of information that can be measured as a number of bits, Shannon was able to derive a shoal of very useful equations governing the maintenance of telephone lines and the cable dimensions required. His main conclusion was that you can always transmit a message error-free if you have sufficient bandwidth.

Bandwidth expresses the ability of a communications channel to transmit information in terms of bits per second. A telephone can transmit four thousand bits per second, for example, while television transmits four million—a thousand times as much. A good radio receiver is somewhere in between, at about sixteen thousand bits per second.[23]

Shannon knew that as long as the bandwidth was greater than the information content per unit of time of the message, you could get your message across without losing anything on the way.

That is nice to know when you make your living by selling telephone lines to people.

But it does not necessarily have much to do with information in the everyday sense. As we are all aware, it's possible to hold protracted telephone conversations without transmitting very much meaning at all—or to write reams of words without their seeming particularly meaningful.

The term "information" was not what mattered most to Shannon. In fact, he did not like the word much and emphasized that what he had come up with was a theory for communication, a theory for the transmission of information, not its meaning. A given volume of information may contain profound insights or a load of baloney. It does not matter. The phone bill will be the same.

But that does not make Shannon's analysis a load of baloney. For what Shannon called "information" is just as genuine and real as what Clausius called "entropy." Making a phone call costs. Signals have to be transmitted in order for your mother-in-law to prattle. But they do not necessarily have anything to do with meaning.

Information is a measure of everything she could have said. Not of what she *did* say.

The information content of a communication is an expression of the volume of communications that *could* have been transmitted. Not of the one that was.

Just as entropy at a given temperature is an expression of how many different ways the molecules could have been arranged without making any difference, information is an expression of how many ways the letters could have been arranged without requiring another cable.

Thermodynamics is about macrostates that interest people: heat. Information theory is about macrostates that interest telephone utilities: symbols.

But there is something bizarre about Shannon's definition of information. It precludes any notion of meaning and concerns itself only with meaning that *could* have been present but is not necessarily so. Compared to our everyday ideas about information, it is a very meager definition. On the other hand, it is incredibly precise, and we might accept a certain hollow ring to it for the sake of precision.

However, information is not always a particularly precise term. It is an enormously subjective concept: It's about how surprised we can be at a message. It tells us that an *a* contains a certain information value because we know that any one of twenty-five other letters could have arrived but did not: the *a* did.

But what if we did not know that we were dealing with a letter from an alphabet of twenty-six letters? How much information would there be in an *a* then? Shannon's definition of information tells us nothing about that.

Information is defined only once you have defined who is talking to whom and in what context. You cannot define Shannon information until you know which common assumptions the transmitter and the receiver are making by mutual agreement. So Shannon's maneuver is a peculiar one: First he throws out any talk of meaning, and then he defines information as something that depends on a connection so fundamental that we do not even talk about it.

Unless we know how many microstates correspond to each macrostate, we cannot talk about information at all. Only when we define what macro- and microstates are can we know the amount of information. Just as in the case of entropy.

Information is very closely related to entropy: The entropy of a given macrostate is measured by the number of corresponding microstates. The more there are, the greater the entropy. Information is something we possess when we know which of the microstates is involved.

A letter in a piece of writing has an entropy defined by the fact that it may be one of twenty-six characters. Information consists of knowing which of those characters it is. The information value of knowing which microstate is involved depends on how many microstates could be involved. The character has specific entropy, and knowledge of its actual microstate—which letter?—yields a specific amount of information, which corresponds to the entropy possessed by that character.

So we cannot define entropy or information unless we know the context.

This has given rise to many misunderstandings, primarily because "information" is a value-laden "plus" word, an expression we spontaneously associate with something "good." For decades, information was identified with order and entropy with disorder.

That is an idea originating from the mathematician Norbert Wiener, who founded cybernetics, the theory of control systems. In his book *Cybernetics* (1948), he says that the information theory occurred to him at about the same time it did to Shannon (who published it in 1948).[24] A few lines later, Wiener declares that "Just as the amount of information in a system is a measure of its degree of organization, so the entropy of a system is a measure of its degree of disorganization."[25]

This view is a far cry from Shannon's. More accurately, Wiener's notion is *the opposite* of Shannon's. But it was very influential, especially regarding the study of Maxwell's demon. Leon Brillouin developed Wiener's idea enthusiastically, summarizing it in the concept of negentropy,[26] dis-disorder—i.e., order.

It sounds intriguing. But it cannot be correct. Indeed, to make it correct, Brillouin had to change the sign of Shannon's concept of information. Decades of misunderstandings arose from this change of sign. Shannon information is entropy: the number of choices, the number of microstates, indeterminacy. Brillouin simply changed the symbol: Information is order—i.e., negative entropy.

The perception of information as order lies closer to our everyday understanding of "information" than does Shannon's notion of the same name. So Wiener and Brillouin's notion of negentropy is enticing. The problem is simply that you cannot fiddle with the symbols in an equation without losing the whole point.

As the Danish physicist Peder Voetmann Christiansen put it, "People thought they could get hold of the meaning by changing the sign of meaninglessness."[27] Wiener and Brillouin were too impatient.

Entropy is a measure of an amount of information we have no interest in knowing. Information is something to be found in bulk in a state where the entropy is great. That does not mean we possess this information; it means only that it is there, that we could obtain it if we could be bothered.

Information is something that is to be found in disorder. There is more information in disorder than in order. The more disorder, the more information. The more microstates, the more information. The more microstates epitomized by the macrostate, the more information we have discarded when we restrict our thoughts to the macrostate. The macrostate "heat" refers to an inconceivably large number of microstates that we do not know when we merely refer to the temperature.

A mess is hard to describe. Especially in detail.

The late American physicist Richard Feynman put it this way: "We measure disorder by the number of ways that the insides can be arranged, so that from the outside it looks the same."[28]

Entropy is a measure of the amount of information we have discarded when we view a system from the outside: the movements of a gas as a temperature, a series of letters as a number of symbols. If we are inside a system, we can obtain this information if we can be bothered. If we are outside the system, we have "thrown it away"—or have never possessed it.

Information is an expression of the difference between being inside and outside: temperature/molecules; number of characters/message. Information and entropy tell us something about the difference between describing or controlling a system from the inside or from the outside.

If we look at a gas from the outside, from our level of description, where heat is most interesting, we can summarize things in a succinct, overall description: the macrostate *heat* measured as temperature. If we look at the gas from "its own" level of description, where everything consists of molecules in motion, we have to enumerate enormous numbers of bits that describe enormous numbers of single states: the microstates of molecular motion measured as speeds.

If we view the gas from the outside, we can extract a certain amount of energy from the heat as long as we obey the second law of thermodynamics, which is about gases described from without. If we look at it from the inside, we can obtain much more energy from the molecular motion of the gas—that is, if we can get rid of all the information now in our possession.

As long as we are outside, we can be utterly indifferent to the information inside the gas. But meanwhile we must abide by the second law of thermodynamics and call this information "entropy."

If we want to make the energy in the chaotic heat motion accessible, we must get to know all the microstates of molecular motion we previously ignored by simply saying that heat involves a certain entropy. We must obtain information about every single one of all these microstates.

But then we're in trouble: We'll either have to exert ourselves keeping control of all the information or forget it all again. In the long run, either will prove too costly.

Maxwell's demon wants to describe the gas from within and without at once. It wants to know where the molecules are and at the same time enjoy the heat. But you cannot do that, even if you are a demon.

In 1988, Wojcieh Zurek posed an important question: What if the demon is so cunning that it starts by measuring all the molecules and then summarizes its knowledge in a very simple description, such as "All the molecules are in the chamber on the left"? This information does not contain many bits; just one, actually. It does not cost much to get rid of this bit again, yet it contains a piece of knowledge that can be used to hit the jackpot.

Now, what is interesting about our knowledge of the world is that once in a while it can be summarized with such strange beauty that enormous insight may be packed into just a few lines. The demon must be able to do the same—and at the same time enjoy the gains within.

Is the demon, then, not mortal after all?

CHAPTER 3

INFINITE ALGORITHMS

If science can attain its goal, then Maxwell's demon can also attain its goal: to knock holes in the most fundamental law of nature discovered by science.

In reality, this is the consequence of the question Wojcieh Zurek posed in 1988: If the only reason Maxwell's demon does not work is that the demon expends masses of energy on forgetting everything it has learned, the demon could simply summarize its knowledge in a few formulae it would not cost much to forget again. Then it would be able to cash in on almost the entire benefit of knowing the world at the molecular level—it would be able to extract heat from the night frost—at no cost. The second law of thermodynamics would be violated, the perpetual motion machine possible—and the natural science view of the world would be in deep trouble.

So it must be impossible for the demon to "compress" its knowledge into a few simple formulae and data that tell the whole history of the molecules in the container in which the demon operates.

But if it is impossible for the demon to do so, surely it must be impossible for human beings? The goal of science has always been to draw up the most concise description of the world possible. But there must be limits as to how concisely the world can be described. Or there will be problems with Maxwell's demon.

That is the consequence of Wojcieh Zurek's question: If we can prove that we can describe the whole world in an arbitrarily concise form, the most fundamental assertion in our perception of the world breaks down: the second law will be breached.

Maxwell's demon is *not* just a problem for the study of heat and thermodynamics. Maxwell's demon is a problem for our entire cosmography—unless the notion that the entire world can be described in all its details by just a few brief equations of almost divine beauty is incorrect.

It is. This was proved in 1930 in a study of the most basic problems in the foundation of mathematics. It was a realization that totally transformed the situation of the mathematicians and logisticians; a realization that forced scientists to admit that they would never be able to prove everything in this world, that human understanding of the world will forever contain intuitive insights that cannot be proved; that human beings know more about the world than they can explain via a formal system.

This realization, understandably called the most profound proof ever carried out, concerns the limits of the certainty of human knowledge, the limits of what we can prove. It is proof that we cannot prove everything, even when we know it is true.

That this should be remotely connected to thermodynamics and the impossibility of building perpetual motion machines can hardly have occurred to mathematician Kurt Gödel when he published his proof of a theorem in January 1931. It took another half century, and it came almost as a relief, to realize that it was precisely Gödel's theorem that led to the explanation of why Maxwell's demon did not work.

For in Gödel's theorem we simply come to grips with the very limits of all formal knowledge—and thereby, in one sense, the only certain knowledge we will ever possess: An infinity of truth can never be embraced by a single theory.

Only the world is big enough to understand the whole world. No map of the whole world can ever be made that includes everything, unless the map is the terrain itself; in which case, of course, it is not a map.

Modern mathematics' account of its own foundations was annihilated at a stroke. The dream of certitude withered.

"Wir müssen wissen. Wir werden wissen." This was the great mathematician David Hilbert's conclusion to his great summarizing lecture when

his native town, Königsberg, made him an honorary citizen on 9 September 1930. "We *must* know. We *shall* know."[1]

For decades, David Hilbert had been the great spokesman for the possibility of a clear, definitive account of the logical foundations of mathematics. In 1900, he had listed the problems yet to be solved before the foundations of mathematics were under complete control. It had to be shown that mathematical science comprised a coherent, uncontradictory, exhaustive logical system.

Again and again during the early decades of the twentieth century, Hilbert emphasized that such an absolute clarification of the foundations of mathematics was in sight, that there was sense in the belief that any mathematical problem could be solved. "We are all convinced of that," he said, and went on to describe the mathematician's dream: "After all, one of the things that attract us most when we apply ourselves to a mathematical problem is precisely that within us we always hear the call: Here is the problem, search for the solution; you can find it by pure thought, for in mathematics there is no *ignorabimus* [we shall not know]."[2]

In 1930, when Hilbert was sixty-eight and retired from his professorship in Göttingen, capital of German mathematics, one of the many honors bestowed on him was especially gratifying: honorary citizenship of his native town. The ceremony was to take place in the autumn, when the Gesellschaft deutscher Naturforscher und Arzte (German Society of German Scientists and Physicians) was to have its ninety-first convention in Königsberg, which has played a very special role in the intellectual history of Germany because the philosopher Immanuel Kant lived and worked all his life there.

David Hilbert decided to give a grand lecture on the occasion of his investiture: a lecture in which he would be able to forge the link back to Kant, regarded as one of the greatest philosophers of modern times, if not the greatest. Under the title *Naturerkennen und Logik*, he directed sharp but politely formulated criticism at Königsberg's great son.

At the end of the 1700s, Kant had realized that human knowledge was based on a number of preconditions that precede experience. We can know the world only because our knowledge is based on a series of concepts or categories, such as time and space, that themselves cannot be known. We see through very specific spectacles, which we cannot question, for they themselves constitute the precondition for our being able to see at all. Kant talked about the *a priori* of knowledge, concepts and categories that are preconceived prerequisites to any understanding.

Hilbert did not agree. "Kant has greatly overestimated the role and the extent of the *a priori*," he said in his address. "We see now: Kant's *a priori* theory contains anthropomorphic dross from which it must be freed. After we remove that, only that *a priori* will remain which also is the foundation of pure mathematical knowledge."[3]

In other words, his project was to anchor mathematics in a handful of logical, mathematical principles from which anything could be proved in a final, conclusive fashion. This meant that logic would be able to explain most of human intuition, so there would be no need for Kant's *a priori*—things in our understanding that we cannot account for rationally, so that in the final analysis the explanation of understanding rests in the fact that we are what we are and we perceive the world the way we do. Hilbert wanted to do away with this illogical *a priori*. He wanted a thoroughly transparent explanation of our knowledge.

In the 1800s, the French philosopher Auguste Comte founded positivism, the philosophical school which says we must stick to knowledge that can be positively underpinned—i.e., through experience or logical and mathematical proofs. Anything else is unscientific. Comte's was an attitude highly critical of Kant.

But positivism did not go far enough for Hilbert. In his address, he referred to Comte and his discussion of the problem of unsolvable problems (which is a problem for any philosophy that will accept only knowledge the correctness of which can be proved).

Hilbert stated, "In an effort to give an example of an unsolvable problem, the philosopher Comte once said that science would never succeed in ascertaining the secret of the chemical composition of the bodies of the universe. A few years later, this problem was solved. . . . The true reason, according to my thinking, why Comte could not find an unsolvable problem lies in the fact that there is no such thing as an unsolvable problem."[4]

There are no limits to thought, everything can be understood, one day everything will be understood. *Wir müssen wissen. Wir werden wissen.*

A local radio station received a visit from Hilbert that day. Two mathematicians from Königsberg had arranged for him to repeat the conclusion of his address in the studio, so his words would go out on the air and be recorded for posterity.

Constance Reid, who has written a nicely balanced biography of Hilbert, relates: "His last words into the microphone were firm and strong: 'Wir müssen wissen. Wir werden wissen.' As he raised his eyes from his paper and the technician snapped off the recording machine, he laughed. The record which he made of this last part of his speech at Königsberg is still in existence. At the end, if one listens very carefully, he can hear Hilbert laugh."[5]

What Hilbert did not know was that in the audience for his address was an unknown twenty-four-year-old mathematician from Vienna, who had two days earlier, on 7 September 1930, for the first time, apparently quite nonchalantly, in that very same town of Königsberg, told his fellow mathematicians of a discovery he had made[6]—a discovery founded upon Hilbert's program for settling the foundations of mathematics, but one that devastated this program.

The young man was Kurt Gödel. Not many of his fellow mathematicians took much notice of his announcement. He made it at a seminar on the epistemology of the sciences, attended by many of the greatest mathematicians of the day, yet it was not until his theorem had been published that its significance began to dawn on them.

On 17 November, Gödel submitted an article containing his proof to *Monatshefte für Mathematik und Physik*. It was published in January 1931, but on Christmas Eve, 1930, Hilbert's assistant, Paul Bernays, wrote to Gödel asking for a copy of the printer's proofs.[7] When Bernays told Hilbert about Gödel's work, Hilbert was "somewhat angry."[8] But Hilbert demonstrated his stature as a man and as a scientist in 1939, by expanding, together with Bernays, Gödel's work with a number of important technical details.

The words remain on the headstone of Hilbert's grave in Göttingen:[9] *Wir müssen wissen. Wir werden wissen.* But he lived long enough to know that we never will.

In 1910–13, the British philosopher and mathematician Bertrand Russell and the mathematician A. N. Whitehead had published *Principia mathematica*, a work that was meant to deduce all mathematical theory from the laws of logic. While preparing the work, Russell had come upon what is known as Russell's paradox, which had to all intents and purposes spoiled their project. It turned out that there were contradictions inherent in mathematics; paradoxes emerged from the otherwise so logical system. It was particularly when mathematical quantities began to refer to themselves that things went wrong. But Russell thought these problems could be dealt with. A neat technical solution was apparently found.

Kurt Gödel's January 1931 article bore the title "On formally undecidable propositions in *Principia mathematica* and similar systems." In other words, it was with direct reference to the work of Russell and Whitehead that Gödel delivered his realization.

Bertrand Russell was an all-embracing intellect and became one of the dominant philosophers of the twentieth century, busying himself with almost all the disciplines of philosophy (and adopting widely differing philosophical stances in the course of his life). He abandoned mathematical logic once he, as he thought, had solved its fundamental problems in *Principia mathematica.*

"It is fifty years since I worked seriously at mathematical logic," he wrote in 1963, "and almost the only work that I have read since that date is Gödel's. I realized, of course, that Gödel's work is of fundamental importance, but I was puzzled by it. It made me glad that I was no longer working at mathematical logic."[10]

Yet it was through Gödel's work that the theme of the century began to unfurl for real.

"I am lying." This statement, the paradox of the liar, has plagued European thought for thousands of years. If it is true, it is false, and vice versa. A liar who says he is lying must be speaking the truth; if he is lying, he is not lying when he says he is.

There are lots and lots of more technical versions of this paradox, but in essence they are the same: Self-reference causes difficulties. This applies to claims that one is lying and also to claims that one has said things as concisely as possible. Such paradoxes are quite loathsome. One of them is known as "Richard's antinomy" and is about the uncountability of numbers.

Gödel demolished the hope for mathematical logic by studying propositions reminiscent of these paradoxes—or antinomies, as the philosophers prefer to call them. One of the very few nonmathematical sentences in his 1931 paper reads: "The analogy of this argument with the Richard antinomy leaps to the eye. It is closely related to the 'Liar' too."[11]

Gödel's ingenious idea was to take the assertion "I cannot be proved." If this is true, we cannot prove it. If it is false, then we can prove it—i.e., we have proved something that is false. The assertion is true if and only if it cannot be proved.

This was not too good for mathematical logic, but not because it was a paradox, a contradiction. The problem rather is that the assertion "I am unprovable" is *true*. It means that truths exist which we cannot prove. There are truths we cannot arrive at through mathematical and logical proofs.

This is an informal version of Gödel's proof[12]—even though, of course, it was originally expressed in a far more stringent version, in far more formal terms. Gödel showed that statements could be coded as numbers. He thereby translated problems with statements that refer to themselves into numbers that "refer to themselves."

A simple yet very profound idea, it leads to the realization that a logical system can never prove its own consistency. The truth or correctness of a logical structure or language can never be proved from within. You have to stand outside the system and say, "It is consistent. It hangs together." Consistency and freedom from contradiction can never be proved from within a system.

The mathematician Andrew Hodges has since put it thus: "Gödel's special assertion was that since it was not provable, it was, in a sense, true. But to say that it was 'true' required an observer who could, as it were, look at the system from outside. It could not be shown by working within the axiomatic system."[13]

Logic can never do without man.

"People often think of Gödel's theorem as something negative," the British mathematician Roger Penrose wrote in 1988.[14] Gödel's realization is usually perceived as a signal of everything man cannot do. Or, as Danish philosophical literature puts it, as an *axiom of impotence*.[15] Indeed, Gödel's proof is also proof of impotence. Not, however, of the impotence of man—but of the impotence of logic.

We will never escape the need for our own powers of judgment. Gödel proved that people know more than they can know whence they know it. Insight reaches further than any logical recipe can lead the mind. Gödel's theorem is an unparalleled tribute to the creativity of the human mind.

But historical circumstances meant that Gödel's revelation was reminiscent of the conclusion of a previous epoch more than it signified the start of a new one.

Hilbert's program was merely the mathematical expression of an overconfidence that infected the philosophy of science at the turn of the century. Comte's positivism condemned any knowledge that could not be positively founded in experience or logical deduction. In the Vienna of the 1920s, this philosophy was refined and honed in a direction known as logical positivism. A circle of philosophers and mathematicians honed the positivist requirement into a requirement that one must be able to verify knowledge before it could be taken seriously. One must be able to prove that it was correct.

The consequence of this refinement was the death of positivism. It turned out that it was irreconcilable with the use natural science made of induction, where one derives a general law from a series of observations. After all, one never knows whether the next phenomenon one observes will violate the law one has just drawn up.

That positivism could collapse this way could have been no surprise to Gödel, who attended the meetings of the Vienna circle; his entire mathematical philosophy was inspired by Kant, who stressed that we cannot prove all that we know but must accept that it is based on premises that cannot be proved—the *a priori* categories.

But Gödel was not merely an opponent of positivism. He was a Platonist. His views on the quantities mathematics involved derived from the Greek philosopher who drew up a philosophy of ideas in about 400 B.C. Plato's idea was that behind the reality we perceive through our senses there was an even more real reality, composed of fundamental principles, ideas, of which the reality we perceive is merely an impression. But it exists, whether we realize it or not.

This view was in powerful contrast to most of the views in mathematics in the early twentieth century (but is far more widespread today). David Hilbert thought that mathematics was a kind of game that showed its correctness through its formal consistency. Bertrand Russell considered mathematics simply a type of applied logic. Others, such as the Dutchman Luitzen Brouwer, considered that mathematical quantities were refinements of human practice—i.e., our intuition.

But Gödel thought that the reality of these quantities had nothing to do with whether we could prove that they were consistent or could be proved logically or applied in practice. Integers and other mathematical quantities exist "out there" long before we realize their existence.

Gödel held these views from the mid-1920s through the 1930s, when he achieved one profound result in mathematical logic after another. He considered that these views were vital to his scientific achievements. But he did not discuss them. He did not publish his philosophical views, even though philosophy was his major interest all his life. Only in 1944 did his views find public expression, in a Festschrift for Bertrand Russell. The mathematician and philosopher Solomon Feferman says of this article: "Hilbert died in 1943, the year before Gödel (1944) appeared."[16]

"In the course of preparing an introductory chapter on Gödel for a forthcoming comprehensive edition of his works, I was struck by the great contrast," wrote Feferman, principal editor of Gödel's *Collected Works*,[17] "between the deep platonist convictions Gödel held concerning the objective basis of mathematics and the special caution he exercised in revealing these convictions."[18]

One may ask what this silence cost him. Gödel did not share the source of his insights with many people. He did not reveal directly what he believed about the world. He told others only what he could prove.

Gödel lived a very isolated life, trusted few people, and was admitted on several occasions to sanatoriums, for treatment of depression and overwork. He was reserved and suspicious—not least where doctors were concerned, despite being preoccupied by his own health. His depression increased, and in the 1970s it developed into paranoia and the classic syndrome of fear of poisoning. The situation became critical in 1977 when his wife was hospitalized and could no longer cook for him. He would not open the door to nurses, and on 14 January 1978 he died, in the fetal position. "Malnutrition and inanition" resulting from "a personality disturbance" was given as the cause of death.[19]

He had presented the most beautiful tribute to the reach of the human mind beyond the domain of the formally provable that has ever emerged from the realm of logical thought. But it was regarded as an assertion of impotence, a technicality, from the historical point of view, a localized rebellion against excessive faith in science.

Kurt Gödel himself accepted the following formulation, which comes to us from the mathematical logician Hao Wang: "In philosophy Gödel has never arrived at what he looked for: to arrive at a new view of the world, its basic constituents and the rules of their composition. Several philosophers, in particular Plato and Descartes, claim to have had at certain moments in their lives an intuitive view of this kind totally different from the everyday view of the world."[20]

Gödel certainly had such revelations. But he did not dare discuss them. He dared only to reveal to us what he could unambiguously recount from them. He dared only to share his revelations as they appeared from the outside. From the viewpoint of the rest of the community.

The miracle of mathematics is that it sufficed to enable others to see the light.

In spring 1935, twenty-two-year-old Alan Turing, who had just completed his doctorate, attended lectures given by the mathematician M. H. A. Newman in Cambridge, England. The subject was the fundamental problems of mathematics. The point of departure: Hilbert's program. The lectures reported that Gödel had clearly and plainly shown that the central elements in Hilbert's program did not hold water. But one question remained, which Gödel had not settled: Hilbert's so-called *Entscheidungsproblem*—the problem of decidability.

This *Entscheidungsproblem* faces the other way: If we have a mathematical system that talks about a particular proposition, can we decide whether it is possible to deduce this proposition from that system? Gödel had shown that in any closed system, questions will arise that cannot be answered—true statements that cannot be deduced. That was decisive, for it showed that the dream of a mathematics settled once and for all was impossible.

The problem of deciding or not whether one specific proposition or another can be deduced seems to be far more suited to engineers, a problem that concerns specific, concrete questions. Of course it interests mathematicians, but to the rest of us it must appear considerably less important than the fundamental problem itself: that we cannot prove everything.

But no. Even though the question may sound dull, the answer certainly was not.

In his lectures, Newman asked whether we could conceive of some kind of "mechanical process" we could apply to a mathematical problem in order to see if there was a solution. Fundamentally, this was what Hilbert had been asking: Was there a recipe that could tell us if we could deduce a specific consequence from a theory? Preferably a recipe that did not require too much imagination but was indeed highly mechanical—an algorithm, as mathematicians call it.

"A *mechanical* process." Alan Turing considered Newman's expression. He thought about machines; machines that could calculate. There were such things in 1935, but they were not especially interesting. So Turing considered the principles for machines: What is required for a machine to be able to solve a mathematical problem and figure out if a proposition can be derived from a theoretical system?

Not much was required. Turing invented a simple logic machine, which could not do very much. It could follow a few instructions: write, read, and do corrections in its memory. Not much more than a typewriter.

But Turing equipped his logic machine with an infinitely large memory. He envisaged the machine recording its activities on a roll of

A Turing machine—the logical precursor of the computer. A simple logic machine with an infinite memory

paper infinitely long, paper that could be moved back and forth so that the machine—just like a typewriter—operated on only one spot at a time. This infinite roll of paper—a ribbon, a tape—possessed an infinity that meant it really did not matter how clumsy the machine was at performing its instructions. Because it had enough memory, and enough time.

Turing realized that such a simple machine—known today as a Turing machine—could actually solve many of Hilbert's problems of deduction, precisely because Gödel had invented elegant logical maneuvers by which to treat all manner of mathematical constructions disguised as numbers. It was a universal machine capable of solving any kind of arithmetical problem. Any calculation known to be performable could be performed by a Turing machine, which thus embodied the principle of a calculating machine in pure and general form.

But Turing soon realized something else: Algorithms could be described that the machine could not chew its way through in comprehensible fashion. There were quantities it could not arrive at. Not because the figures were too big, but because the algorithm was too inscrutable: One could not say whether the machine would arrive at the number until it had done so, and that might take infinitely long. So within a finite period of time, one could not know whether it would ever arrive at the result.

This meant that Hilbert's *Entscheidungsproblem* was unsolvable. We cannot provide an algorithm that tells us whether anything can be deduced from a mathematical system.

An important conclusion in its own right, and one that was arrived at simultaneously and independently by another scientist, the American logician Alonzo Church.

But the interesting thing about Turing's findings was that he had made two discoveries at once, one summer day when he was lying in a meadow. In his biography of Alan Turing, the mathematician Andrew Hodges puts it this way:

"Alan had proved that there was no 'miraculous machine' that could solve all mathematical problems, but in the process he had discovered something almost equally miraculous, the idea of a universal machine that could take over the work of any machine."[21]

Turing had created the theory for machines that could calculate. A few years later, the Second World War brought the resources necessary for the urgent development of electronic computers, particularly in Britain and the United States. Under Turing, the British used them to crack Germany's secret communication codes. The Americans used them for building the atom bomb, among other things.

Since World War II, computers have become common property. For decades now, man has been dominated by the idea of the endless possibilities computers allow us for controlling the world and monitoring absolutely everything.

But the fact is that the concept and theory of computing were invented at the very instant Alan Turing realized that we cannot compute everything. The human mind was able to formulate the idea of a universal calculating machine at the very moment it became obvious that we cannot calculate everything mechanically; that there are questions that we know as answerable only once they have been answered, and not before.

The depth of this relationship may seem alien to us. The Church-Turing thesis simply states that you can compute anything that has already been computed. You can do whatever you know you can do. And you know whether you can do more only once you've done it!

Today, when computers are omnipresent, this finding is more familiar as the Turing halting problem: In general, can we figure out when a computer will have finished a specific calculation? The answer is no; we cannot know in advance when a computer will finish a calculation (unless, of course, we have tried it before).

Similarly, we cannot know whether a computer will ever finish a calculation until it has finished. Until it has finished, we don't know whether it will finish or whether it will just go on forever.

This is not the case for the simple sums of everyday life, of course, for we have plenty of experience with them. But it is only because we have experience of them that we know this. There are no principal universal logical rules that tell us anything we did not already know.

The Church-Turing thesis and Turing's halting problem tell us that we can learn nothing unless it is through experience. There is no possibility of telling in advance what will happen.

In this respect, computers are similar to seekers of the truth and little children. All we can do is wait until the cry comes: "I've *finished!*"

"Many mathematicians would perhaps prefer to limit the disclosure of the present status of mathematics to members' of the family," Morris Kline wrote in 1980 in his preface to a book about mathematics' loss of certainty. "To air these troubles in public may appear to be in bad taste, as bad as airing one's marital difficulties."[22]

Indeed, many years did go by in which the crisis made few waves. As

Rudy Rucker summarizes the sequence of events in a book published in 1987: "Gödel's theorem shows that human thought is more complex and less mechanical than anyone had ever believed, but after the initial flurry of excitement in the 1930s, the result ossified into a piece of technical mathematics. Gödel's theorem became the private property of the mathematical logic establishment, and many of these academics were contemptuous of any suggestion that the theorem could have something to do with the real world."[23]

The philosophers were not doing much better either, although in the early 1930s the Polish philosopher Alfred Tarski did present a Gödel-like argument demonstrating that one could never deduce the truth of a system from within the system itself.[24]

But Gödel's theorem did become widely known, not least because in 1979, the American computer scientist Douglas Hofstadter published a very beautiful, very difficult, and very famous book, *Gödel, Escher, Bach*,[25] in which he points out the spiritual kinship of Johann Sebastian Bach (1685–1750), whose contemporaries found his music too mathematical; the graphic artist Maurits Escher (1898–1972), still not properly acknowledged by his fellow artists; and Kurt Gödel (1906–1978), news of whom is only now reaching wider circles.

There was another reason why the world began to take notice of Gödel: It became clear that the phenomenon he had pointed out was not limited to the quaint paradoxes of the ancient Greeks. Unprovability and undecidability are fundamental features of our world.

The further development of Gödel's theorem in the 1960s was given several names—the theory of Algorithmic information, algorithmic complexity, algorithmic randomness—whichever name we choose, it had three fathers: Ray Solomonoff, Andrei Kolgomorov, and Gregory Chaitin.

Complicated? Not so bad as it sounds. Actually, this theory makes it far simpler to express just what it was that Gödel and his successors had discovered. For it gives us a sensible definition of what *randomness* really is; and that is important because it thereby gives us a hint as to what *order* is.

Its point of departure is numbers. What is a random number? As the three gentlemen are mathematicians, they have a penchant for binary numbers—i.e., numbers consisting of 0's and 1's. 010110100110 . . .

A number like that is a real eye-strainer, but we can just put a period up front and make it look like a good old-fashioned decimal: 0.10110100110. Is this a random number? Well, we just jotted down a series of random binary digits. But were they just chance?

We could also have tossed a coin twelve times and noted heads as 1 and tails as 0. Surely then the number would have been random? We can try it: 100010000111—no, there was no cheating: a coin was tossed twelve times. But if we try again, the number will definitely be different: 110011010000.

Of course, we could have done something quite different. For example, we could have arranged a test of our knowledge of binary numbers. By writing, for example, 0.010101010101.

That does not look so random at all. It is a sequence of 01's. So it could be expressed much more simply: "0 period 6 times 01." But as a matter of fact, this was a particularly devious example,[26] for it can be expressed even more concisely: It is the binary representation of $1/3$.

The point is that there are some numbers that can be expressed much more concisely. 111111111111111111 can be written "18 times 1."

If we use the decimal system, 0.42857142857 can be written as $3/7$, and 1234567891011121314151617181920 can be written as "the sequence of numbers from 1 to 20."

But can the coin-tossing sequences be described more concisely? No, they cannot. After all, they are a kind of report of twelve successive events, completely independent of one another. There is no system to decide whether a 0 or a 1 will appear in the next position. Oh, we would expect a long string of 0's and 1's to contain roughly the same number of 0's and 1's, because we expect roughly the same number of heads and tails. But the order is random. There is no system in it.

Of course, we could toss the coin twelve times and come up with the sequence 010101010101, which can be expressed very concisely, but it would not happen very often. In fact, we would have to reckon on tossing the coin many thousands of times before we came up with precisely that sequence (or any other specific sequence). We can't be bothered.

So random numbers cannot be described more concisely. But other kinds of numbers can be, such as 0.42857142857, which can be written as $3/7$.

So we can differentiate between random numbers and ordered numbers: Random ones are the ones that cannot be described more concisely, while ordered ones are the ones that can. That is what we mean by order.

The three gentlemen's theory says that we thereby have a very nice theory for order and randomness. Randomness is that which cannot be expressed more concisely by an algorithm. A random number is a number that cannot be expressed more concisely than itself.

The opposite is the case with ordered numbers. "$3/7$" is a rule of arithmetic, an algorithm that tells us how to obtain the sequence 0.42857142857 (when we tacitly agree that we will make do with the first twelve digits). So this sequence is less random than the sequence 0.32857142877—where two digits have been altered, thereby *presumably* creating a number that cannot be reduced to a simple fraction.

But can we be sure? Who says that 0.32857142877 is not some simple fraction or other that we merely failed to grasp in the rush?

Perhaps there is a reader out there who will find an algorithm for the sequence 0.32857142877 that is shorter than the sequence itself. If so, that will prove that this sequence is not random. But until then, we can assume that it is.

However, one never knows what a cunning reader might come up with; and in a sense, that is what Gödel proved.

We cannot propose a general rule that tells us how to figure out whether a number is random or not—whether it can be expressed more concisely or not. This is a direct consequence of Gödel's realization. It *is* Gödel's theorem; it is what he proved.

We know whether a number can be expressed more concisely only when we realize that it can be. Until then, we cannot decide.

There are far more random numbers than ordered ones. Most numbers cannot be expressed more concisely than they are already. We can understand this intuitively from the way in which we created our (hopefully) random number: We simply took an "ordered" number ($3/7$), wrote it as a decimal, and changed two digits. The result was a (presumably) random number. But we could have changed two other digits, or changed the two we did change into something quite different. The result would (presumably) have been just as random. (It is important that the algorithm describing the way we create our "messy" number cannot be expressed more concisely than the number itself, or things will go wrong: 0.32857142877 can be expressed as $3/7 - 0.1 + 2 \times 10^{-10}$, which is almost shorter than the number itself, which would then not be random at all.)

It is possible to prove that a number is not random because it can be described more concisely—namely, by giving an algorithm for it. But it is not possible to say that it cannot be described more concisely.

That is Gödel's realization: We can know that it is order when we see it. But we cannot know that it is not order just because we cannot see it—and no mathematics, logic, or computers can help us.

Order is order. The rest is undecided.

Of course, the three gentlemen have expanded on these ideas. The shortest way of describing a series of numbers can also be expressed as the shortest instruction we can give a machine to make it print out the number. A random number requires that we tell the machine the whole sequence, while a number such as 0.42857142857 can be entered more concisely as $3/7$.

The idea is, then, to define the algorithmic information content of a sequence of numbers as the shortest algorithm that will make a Turing machine print the sequence out. This concept is also known as algorithmic complexity or algorithmic randomness.

But—we could object—that means that random numbers contain more information than ordered ones. Indeed they do. The information content expresses how difficult it is to transmit a message. A longer telephone conversation is required to describe the twelve tosses of the coin than $3/7$, for the random is what cannot be said more concisely.

Information is associated with entropy, a measure of thermodynamic disorder. The macrostate "12 tosses" corresponds to more microstates (binary digits) than the macrostate "$3/7$." There is more information in the twelve tosses of the coin.

Information is a measure of randomness because randomness is a measure of disorder: something that is difficult to describe.

Information is a measure of how surprised we are; and there are more surprises in disorder than in order. In fact, that is precisely what we mean by order: something that cannot surprise us because it is ordered.

The peculiarity of Shannon's notion of information thereby becomes comprehensible: Information is defined only when we know the context; when we say which macrostates and microstates we are talking about. Information is defined only when we explain what we mean by order.

Gödel's theorem tells us that we can never know whether there is order in something random. An order we have not yet caught sight of. To know how much information there is in a piece of disorder, we must know how much order has already been discovered in this disorder. We cannot define information until we know what order the receiver of the information has discovered. Information cannot be defined without knowing the context. Not because there is anything wrong with our notion of information, but because the notions of order and randomness necessarily include an element of subjectivity.

Each of the three gentlemen came up with the theory of algorithmic information independently of one another. Andrei Kolgomorov, one of the greatest mathematicians of the century, was working in Moscow; Raymond Solomonoff in Cambridge, Massachusetts; and Gregory Chaitin in New York. Gregory Chaitin in particular pursued the theory even further. In the 1960s, when the theory was born, Chaitin was studying at City University of New York. Today he works at the IBM laboratories in Yorktown Heights near New York (where Rolf Landauer and Charles Bennett work).

Chaitin has proved that Gödel's findings are natural and easy to understand: Gödel showed that any formal system consisting of a finite series of postulates or axioms will always contain incomplete propositions. You cannot completely explore such a system from within. You can never get to know it completely if you restrict yourself to formal methods of proof.

"Gödel's theorem may be demonstrated using arguments having an information-theoretic flavor," Chaitin writes. "In such an approach it is possible to argue that if a theorem contains more information than a given set of axioms, then it is impossible for the theorem to be derived from the axioms. In contrast with the traditional proof based on the paradox of the liar, this new viewpoint suggests that the incompleteness phenomenon discovered by Gödel is natural and widespread rather than pathological and unusual."[27]

But Chaitin also derived his theorem as an extension of Gödel's. Chaitin started with Turing's halting problem—can we know when a computer will halt as it solves a problem? The answer is that we can know only once it halts.

Chaitin asked what the probability was of a Turing machine, given a perfectly random program, halting because it had found a solution. He proved that this probability is unknowable. We cannot calculate it. It is a number by the name of Omega. It is somewhere between 0 and 1. But we can *never* know it.

Chaitin proved that this meant that the very theory for whole numbers must be riddled by randomness. Number theory cannot be described without random elements entering the picture.

In 1988, the British mathematician Ian Stewart, who must surely be the clearest commentator on mathematical science today, wrote in *Nature*: "For the foundations of mathematics, and even the philosophy of its application to science, this century has been one of shattered illusions. Cosy assumption after cosy assumption has exploded in mathematicians' faces. The assumption that the formal structure of arithmetic is precise and regular turns out to have been a time-bomb, and Chaitin has just pushed the detonator."[28]

Later the same year, Chaitin wrote in *Scientific American*: "How have the incompleteness theorem of Gödel, the halting problem of Turing and my own work affected mathematics? The fact is that most mathematicians have shrugged off the results. Of course, they agree in principle that any finite set of axioms is incomplete, but in practice they dismiss the fact as not applying directly to their work. Unfortunately, however, it may sometimes apply. Although Gödel's original theorem seemed only to apply to unusual mathematical propositions that were not likely to be of interest in practice, algorithmic information theory has shown that incompleteness and randomness are natural and pervasive."[29]

Mathematics is apparently too important to be left to mathematicians.

Chaitin would agree. "The fact that many mathematical problems have remained unsolved for hundreds and even thousands of years tends to support my contention. Mathematicians steadfastly assume that failure to solve these problems lies strictly within themselves, but could the fault not lie in the incompleteness of their axioms?" He adds: "This may seem like a ridiculous suggestion to most mathematicians, but to a physicist or a biologist it may not seem so absurd."[30]

"It's the Watergate question: what does Maxwell's demon know—and when does he know it?" said Wojcieh Zurek enthusiastically during his introductory address at the seminar on complexity, entropy, and information physics at the Santa Fe Institute in 1990.

Zurek had a pretty good idea, as he had explained at the first meeting of the group, two years earlier. His address then was entitled "Algorithmic Information Content, the Church-Turing Thesis, Physical Entropy, and Maxwell's Demon."[31] His idea linked these hitherto disparate areas of physics and mathematics together.

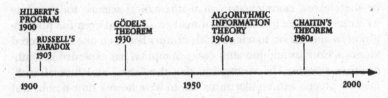

Major events in mathematical logic this century

Landauer and Bennett were in the audience. Zurek quoted their solution to the problem of Maxwell's demon—a solution which indicated that the problem for the demon was forgetting everything again: Once it had measured where all the molecules in the container were and the way they were moving, so that it could let the swifter ones into one chamber, it had scored a gain, certainly, but also taken on an awful lot to remember. The problem was not, as Szilard and later Brillouin thought, measuring where the molecules were. The problem was all the knowledge the demon had acquired. Landauer had proved that getting rid of this information was costly; Bennett had proved that the cost of doing so redeemed the second law of thermodynamics. The demon could not power a perpetual motion engine.

But then an idea had occurred to Zurek: What if the demon was so clever that it could compress its knowledge? What if it could describe the molecular motion in very concise form so it wouldn't cost so much to clear its memory again? If it could remember, for example, that all the swifter molecules were in a particular location (the bottom of the container) that it would not cost so many bits to describe—and then forget? Would this intelligent demon then be capable of making perpetual motion machines and a mess of our view of the world?

With great pleasure, Zurek described how he had solved this problem: for there are limits to how clever the demon can be. Physical limits. It cannot describe the molecular pattern in a way that is less complicated than it already is—and the laws of physics tell us the least degree of complexity things may assume.

Certainly, it does not cost many bits to describe a situation where all the molecules are gathered in the left-hand portion of the container. But physically such a situation is highly improbable—it is precisely the one the demon wants to bring about through its clever attempt to make a gain.

The demon must therefore respect the fact that there is always disorder in a concourse of molecules in equilibrium; and the description cannot be made more concise than the reality of this disorder. Deviations from equilibrium occur, but they are rare, so they do not mean anything in the long run.

So Zurek had translated physical disorder into notions of description. The key to this operation had proved to be algorithmic information theory, for an enormous assemblage of molecules can be described as a very long string of numbers. They are produced by all the molecules being measured and weighed from tip to toe—resulting in a series of numbers.

The complexity of these numbers must reflect the complexity of the state of the molecules. Precisely because we are dealing with a random movement of heat, the numbers that describe the molecular motion must also contain a whole bunch of randomness. A major feature of such randomness is that it cannot be described with arbitrary conciseness.

So Zurek had used algorithmic information theory to translate physical randomness into the length of the shortest description. This gave him a measure for how much information the demon had to discard in order to "keep its head cold."

This measure could be compared to the work the demon could achieve by having the description. If the second law was to hold water, the randomness in the molecules should be reflected in the randomness in the description, which would make it just long enough to render the gain less than the cost.

Zurek had discovered that a particular theorem in information theory, the *Kraft inequality*, saved the second law. "The success of an intelligent Maxwell's demon is ruled out as a consequence of a theorem which was proposed a century after the second law in a very different context of the theory of communication!"[32] Zurek explained eagerly.

While the audience buzzed and applauded this splendid example of the link between widely differing fields of research and shared in the pleasure of this discovery, Zurek began to describe a lecture he had given a few months earlier in which he had shared his triumph with an audience at an American university.

"Then somebody asked one of those questions one does not know how to answer. A highly intelligent question," said Zurek, and glanced good-humoredly at the physicist who had been asking all morning why his car was interested in entropy when it was merely a subjective notion.

The audience quickly gathered that none other than William Unruh from Vancouver had asked the question. Bill Unruh belongs to the beautiful line of physics best described as clear-sighted sassiness—*Herr Warum*, Mr. Why, as Gödel had been called in his childhood. At this meeting too, Mr. Unruh played that role.

"He asked what would happen if the demon was so intelligent that it only measured the molecules it could pay to measure," said Zurek, "and just forgot about the others."

Bill Unruh had asked, but Zurek had not answered at the time. Because the answer did not spring to mind.

But he did have the answer ready for Santa Fe. A detailed analysis of a logical sequence revealed that it was very simple. The demon would of course have to forget all the molecules it could not pay to remember.

And forgetting is what really costs, Zurek explained. "That's right!" agreed the audience, led in its laughter by Unruh, who has asked so many questions over the years, many of them very good ones, that he has no problem living with the fact that most of them turn out stupid in the end.[33]

Bill Unruh's question proves that the argument can be reversed: Once in a very rare while, the demon will find itself in a container where all the molecules are congregated on the left. This situation is just as physically improbable as it is easy to describe: 1 bit. Hard to find, easy to forget: There are no "bad" molecules to remember. But when a demon encounters this situation (without having created it itself), it will be able to obtain work from it. Otherwise there would be something wrong with the information-theoretic analysis. As the physicist Carlton Caves puts it, "The demon wins occasionally, but not in the long run."[34]

≈

Zurek's paper was a triumph not just for Zurek but for the whole gathering. People had come for a project aimed at describing physics in terms of information. No new idea, certainly—since Shannon's information theory in 1948, people had been trying to explain practically anything in terms of information.

What was new was that now they looked as if they were getting somewhere; as if the algorithmic information theory suddenly made it possible to link physical entropy to the information of the description; as if disorder and randomness could be captured by a physics that was mostly about order and rules.

Maxwell's demon had proved to be the key. Studying this tricky little mischiefmaker had been most useful for understanding these new ideas.

Scientists had succeeded in creating a "computational counterpart of the second law of thermodynamics," as Zurek immodestly phrased it in *Nature*. Physical entropy can be understood as a disorder one can account for via algorithmic information theory. Plus, of course, the ignorance we ourselves supply. The irrevocability of discarding information had itself solved the problem: "I have demonstrated that the second law is safe even from 'intelligent beings,' as long as their abilities to process information are subject to the same laws as those of universal Turing machines. . . . Turing's halting theorem implies that the information required to attain maximum efficiency can be secured only through an indefinitely long computation. Gödel's undecidability can be regarded as an additional source of dissipation."[35]

Maxwell's demon has not been exorcised. It may no longer be a threat to the second law, but instead of being a mischievous devil, it has turned into a true friend, evidence of profound affinities in our world, of molecular details we do not wish to know and therefore never will. We would rather feel the warmth.

If the world could be exhaustively described in an arbitrarily brief number of algorithms, there would be a problem with Maxwell's demon. But it cannot. The scientists' ancient dream of a total all-embracing theory, the world formula that predicts everything, is passé.

As the German biologist Bernd-Olaf Küppers puts it, ". . . in the framework of algorithmic information theory, there is a strict mathematical proof for the assertion that we can never know whether we are in possession of the minimum formula by means of which all the phenomena of the real world can be predicted. The completeness of a scientific theory can in principle never be proved."[36]

We can take pleasure in such concise, elegant expressions as Maxwell's formulae for electromagnetism. But we can never know whether we could express them even more concisely. Not until the day we do so.

Life will forever be open to us. We will never know that it cannot be expressed more beautifully.

The beauty in the world is growing.

CHAPTER 4

THE DEPTH OF COMPLEXITY

"What apple?" Seth Lloyd was quick. Very quick. Actually, he defused a rather good practical joke.

The physicist from the California Institute of Technology was standing with his back to the audience. He was writing formulae on the board as he explained how he would derive the existence of things from notions of information.

It was Friday afternoon, 20 April 1990, and at the beginning of the week John Wheeler had prophesied that by this stage the assembly would have arrived at an explanation of how the universe was put together. Of course, this had not been fulfilled yet at the Santa Fe Institute, but many of the physicists felt that the conference on complexity, entropy, and information physics was really onto a very good thing. "It from bit," as the graying visionary John Wheeler had put it—deriving the theory of things from the theory of information.

Seth Lloyd had kicked off his lecture on "Logical Friction" by talking about an apple and its itness. "I want to try and do what Wheeler suggested, and derive *it* from *bit*," said Lloyd, and took a bite of the apple.

But he soon switched from his tangible apple to more theoretical matters, dressed up in a very long series of equations that Lloyd scribbled on the board as a couple of dozen physicists struggled to keep their eyes open at the end of the last day of the week.

During one of Lloyd's longer calculations, the physicist John Denker from AT&T's famous Bell Laboratories swiped the apple from Lloyd's lectern. It vanished. Another colleague from Bell Labs, Yan LeCun, caught on to the idea and interrupted Seth Lloyd's flow of words as he calculated. "How does that particular notion relate to the itness of the apple?" His question was not especially shrewd, but everyone waited for Lloyd's reaction with bated breath.

Seth Lloyd turned to face the audience to make his reply, but he spotted the trap quick as a flash. "What apple?" he asked, and he turned back to the blackboard and went on calculating.

The next time he was interrupted, this time by a more serious question, he turned to the audience and remarked, "I refuse to answer any more questions until I've gotten my apple back!" But by now the apple was on the lectern again, and the audience tried to pretend they did not know what he was talking about.

When the lectern was over, tumult arose. Doyne Farmer, who headed up the nonlinear-studies group at the Los Alamos lab near Santa Fe, tried to capture Lloyd's apple. "I want that apple so bad," he shouted, but Lloyd was not going to give it up just like that. The apple of discord ended up on the floor of the lecture room at the Santa Fe Institute, smashed to bits.

That week, *it* did not get derived from *bit*. But the prospects for its being so are so good that scientists are already racing to see who will solve the riddle of complexity.

"Complexity covers a vast territory that lies between order and chaos,"[1] the physicist Heinz Pagels wrote in his visionary book *The Dreams of Reason* (1988). For the fact is, the spectrum of possibilities that the notions of order and disorder offer our cosmology is a very poor one.

Total disorder is uninteresting. A mess. Not worth talking about, because we cannot describe it in any explanatory way. There is no more to be said about disorder than it says itself.

Similarly, total order is not particularly interesting either. A lattice of atoms in a crystal, a meticulously arranged pattern of reiterations. What there is to say about such order is quickly said and soon becomes trivial.

So there must be a third possibility, which is neither total disorder nor total order, something that is definitely not trivial but is complicated without being chaotic: complexity.

This territory between order and chaos encompasses practically everything worth talking about, everything we talk about and experience in our everyday lives: living beings, changes in the weather, wonderful landscapes, friendly conversation, delicious salads, and fun and games.

Take a piece of writing. If it is totally ordered and predictable, it is of little interest. There is an enormous amount of order in a text composed of regular series of letters such as AAAAAAAAAA. The algorithmic information theory explains why it is boring. It is not difficult to prepare a concise description that permits the reproduction of such a text: 10 times A.

Conversely, a total mess of a text isn't that interesting either: LIUQWEGAEIUJO. According to algorithmic information theory, the shortest program that can reproduce this string of random letters is the string itself. Because it is a random string of letters.

Widespread acceptance of information theory has always been plagued by the fact that there is far more information in a text written by a monkey than in a text written by a famous author. But this is only natural, because there is no system in what the monkey writes (as far as we can see, at any rate), so it cannot be expressed more concisely, whereas the author's text always includes an amount of redundancy—a meaningful text can always be expressed a bit more concisely because language contains a degree of superfluous characters. You u_ders_and w_at is _rint_d her_ even _houg_ ever_ fift_ lett_r has _een r_move_, righ_?

A totally ordered text contains very little information and is therefore very easy for the telephone engineer to compress and transmit, whereas a totally disordered text requires very accurate reproduction, and even that cannot make it especially interesting.

So meaning and information cannot have much to do with each other as regards pieces of text. Similarly, complexity and information cannot have much to do with each other as regards the physical world. Of course, there has to be a certain amount of information before we can talk of meaning or complexity. But the amount is not what matters most.

Information is an interesting concept but not a particularly good measure of complexity.

The scientific view of the world is characterized by the same problem: It includes order and disorder but not this third possibility, which is the really interesting one.

Newton's classical physics is characterized by a majestic order expressed in equations that can be reversed in time: All the processes described are so neat and regular that they might just as easily happen backward. The planets orbit around the sun with such regularity that we would have the same picture if we reversed their motion so that they orbited in the opposite direction. Mechanics and other classical disciplines of physics consist of reversible laws in which the direction of time is irrelevant. These laws correspond more to the situation in space than on earth, for they work only if there is no friction—air resistance and adhesion such as always exist on earth in practice. However, these are only corrections, and we can allow for them, or so we are taught at school.

But we can ask the same question as American physicist Richard Feynman: "Are all the laws of physics reversible? Evidently not! Just try to unscramble an egg! Run a moving picture backward, and it takes only a few minutes for everybody to start laughing. The most natural characteristic of all phenomena is their obvious irreversibility."[2]

On the other hand, the field of physics that actually does explain friction and other irrevocably irreversible matters ends in utter chaos. Thermodynamics explains that entropy grows as time passes, so films of eggs smashing on the floor look strange if viewed in reverse; thermodynamics is closer to everyday life than Newton's equations. But then thermodynamics ends in the heat death of the universe: Everything is heading for gray on gray and a huge mass of entropy. Fundamentally the world is wearing out. Time is passing and everything is constantly deteriorating.

Thermodynamics also does not correspond to the world about us: Every spring, the trees burst out in an orgy of color, spiders swarm from the cracks, and new generations of bird beaks begin to sing. The winter cold creates wondrous patterns of ice on our windowpanes, the autumn storms bring with them ever-changing cloud formations, and the summer waves sculpt the sand on our coasts into unpredictable patterns. In the heavens we see stars shining in a darkness of nothing.

The world is not made of sameness. It may end up like that, but most of our lives revolve around the fact that there are other things to think about than dust bunnies and doing the dishes. Life evolves and—as far as we can tell from the fossils—gets more and more complicated.

So there is something missing, something radically different, which is neither Newton's order nor the disorder of thermodynamics but lies in between and has to do with complexity. Or meaning.

Life has always been a complicated affair, and the world forever characterized by complexity. So why, one might ask, is science suddenly beginning to show an interest in the fact that the world is considerably more difficult than the simple circles scientists are used to studying?

The answer is the advent of the computer during and after the Second World War. The computer meant the end of the arrogance scientists displayed toward everyday phenomena.

Classical science as founded by Newton described a simple, comprehensible world composed of simple systems that could be understood by simple equations. Certainly it did not have much to do with the world to be found outside the physicists' windows, but that did not bother them; they could not have understood it anyway.

Scientists have always been indifferent to the kinds of questions children ask: Why do trees look like they do, why do clouds look like lambs or ducks, why does the world not look like our geometry books? Or more accurately, scientists were not so much indifferent as they were aware that they could not answer such questions. They knew the equations for the world, but they just did not have the energy to do the calculations all the way through; if only they had, they would of course have understood why clouds looked like animals and the evening mist gave shape to elves and trolls. . . .

Everyday things are so complicated that calculating them cannot be worthwhile, or so the scientists told one another—and left it to teachers and parents to shut the traps of their curious offspring.

Then the computer changed everything. Suddenly the calculations could be performed full-scale, and it now became clear that even the simplest equations gave rise to very complicated solutions. Though the world is described in simple formulae that look just as comprehensible as the examples in our textbooks, these formulae turned out—now that we had finally done the calculations—to contain an enormous complexity. Buzzwords like "chaos" and "fractals" are not the only tellers of this tale. Anywhere computers are used in science, it turns out that we can generate highly complex worlds from even the simplest formulae.

Oh, scientists could not tell from the formulae what kinds of patterns they would lead to, for most systems turned out to be computationally irreducible: We do not know the pattern until we have computed the formula. This phenomenon is a variation of Gödel's theorem—and very deep. We can regard physical processes as calculations that transform simple laws and a few basic conditions into a final result. This means that many of the difficulties that have arisen in computation theory must also appear in the description of the physical world. Physical systems are computationally irreducible too: We do not know where they end or even if they end until we have computed them on the premises of the physical systems themselves. It is not much good to make rough calculations in which we ignore friction, for example; we will not know where the system is heading.

In 1985, the twenty-four-year-old American physicist Stephen Wolfram wrote: "Computational irreducibility is common among the systems investigated in mathematics and computation theory. This paper suggests that it is also common in theoretical physics."[3]

For hundreds of years, scientists had been going around believing they had a grip on their formulae—that simple equations would lead to simple behavior. But such formulae proved to be computationally irreducible. Nobody could know their content until they had been computed, and nobody could be bothered to compute them in the days when all the calculations had to be performed by hand.

So scientists stuck to their formulae and closed their eyes to the world beyond the windowpane.

One day, though, something curious happened. Complexity appeared from amidst all the well-ordered simplicity computers were given to calculate. Simple calculations were repeated again and again in a loop known as an "iteration." The simple calculations led to a vast complexity when they were reiterated a sufficient number of times, and when complexity appeared on computer monitors around the world, the scientists looked out the window and saw a familiar sight.

They realized that the world was not divided into well-ordered formulae and a disorderly everyday world. It hangs together! Disorder can emerge from order—the process just happens to be complex.

A new field had been created, and scientists crowded into it. Complexity became a respectable subject even to scientists. The computer became their tool. "A new paradigm has been born," wrote Stephen Wolfram.[4]

Wolfram set the agenda for science for decades to come. "It is common in nature to find systems whose overall behavior is extremely complex, yet whose fundamental component parts are each very simple. The complexity is generated by the cooperative effect of many simple identical components. Much has been discovered about the nature of the components in physical and biological systems; little is known about the mechanisms by which these components act together to give the overall complexity observed. What is now needed is a general mathematical theory to describe the nature and generation of complexity."[5]

There is a terrain between order and chaos: a vast undiscovered continent—the continent of complexity. The precondition for discovering it is that we learn to steer between the two poles of our worldview—order and randomness, supervision and surprise, map and terrain, science and our everyday lives.

We have to navigate between more than just the order and the disorder in the structure of things. Complexity appears midway between the predictable and the unpredictable, the stable and the unstable, the periodic and the random, the hierarchical and the flat, the closed and the open. Between what we can count on and what we cannot.

Complexity is that which is not trivial. That which is not dull. That which we all intuitively sense but which is hard to express.

All this may seem obvious; but the curious thing is that it is not many years since an internationally influential and uncommonly well-informed German physicist, Peter Grassberger, from the University of Wuppertal, had to admit that there was no firm understanding of just what complexity was.

At the 16th International Conference on Thermodynamics and Statistical Mechanics, in Boston in August 1986, he said, "We are faced with the puzzle that no accepted measure of complexity could, e.g., corroborate that music written by Bach is more complex than the random music written by a monkey."[6]

The only generally accepted measure of complexity Grassberger could refer to at the time was Kolgomorov complexity. This is a notion that came from one of the three gentlemen who appeared in the previous chapter with their algorithmic information theory.

In the 1960s, Andrei Kolgomorov suggested that the complexity of an object could be measured by looking at the length of the shortest description of the object—i.e., the shortest possible string of binary digits able to represent the object. Kolgomorov suggested that the longer the shortest description, the more complexity the object possesses. But of course this just means that a random string has the greatest complexity, for randomness is what cannot be expressed more concisely.

Kolgomorov had equated complexity with randomness, and thereby complexity with information. This is not a good idea, as it makes the monkey's mad pounding at the keyboard more complex than the inventions of Johann Sebastian Bach.

So there was something very wrong with Kolgomorov complexity.

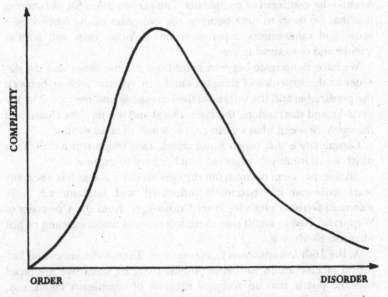

Complexity is found between order and disorder: With this image Bernardo Huberman and Tad Hogg demonstrated a simple, but important, connection.

But at the same time it was the most familiar measure. So in 1986 there was a problem. "The intuitive notion of complexity of a pattern does not agree with the only objective definition of the complexity of any specific pattern that seems possible (namely Kolgomorov's definition)," Grassberger explained. "[It's] a conundrum probably known for some time to many, although it seems to have appeared in print only recently."[7]

Bernardo Huberman and Tad Hogg, scientists at the Rank Xerox Palo Alto Research Center in California, had pointed out in 1985[8] that complexity must lie somewhere between order and disorder, and could therefore not be measured as algorithmic complexity or information. They proposed another measure of complexity, which meant that complexity was greatest in systems that have neither too much nor too little order.

Grassberger realized later that Huberman and Hogg's approach was not new; in fact, it had been expressed in 1962 by Herbert A. Simon,[9] one of the founders of research into artificial intelligence.

Nevertheless, we do not have to go back further than 1986 for a leading international physicist such as Peter Grassberger to regard as a complete novelty the notion that complexity lies between order and chaos, and that it is quite different from the randomness measured by Shannon's information.

However, before his 1986 lecture was printed, Grassberger, one of the nobler personalities of physics, imbued with great courtesy and modesty, added an apology at the proof stage: "While writing this, unfortunately I was unaware of C. H. Bennett's notion of 'logical depth.' "[10]

For the great breakthrough in the study of complexity had occurred the previous year.

"I have a criterion for meaning," Charles Bennett said bashfully during a dinner at Pasqual's in Santa Fe in April 1990. Bennett and his close colleague from IBM, Rolf Landauer, had been asked to explain what studies of computation theory could tell the rest of us about our everyday lives.

"A series of coin tosses has high information content but little value; an ephemeris, giving the positions of the moon and planets every day for a hundred years, has no more information than the equations of motion and initial conditions from which it was calculated, but saves its owner the effort of recalculating these positions," Charles Bennett wrote in 1985 when he introduced his criterion for meaning. "The value of a message thus appears to reside not in its information (its absolutely unpredictable parts), nor in its obvious redundancy (verbatim repetitions, unequal digit frequencies), but rather in what might be called its buried redundancy—parts predictable only with difficulty. In other words, the value of a message is the amount of mathematical or other work plausibly done by its originator, which its receiver is saved from having to repeat."[11]

Logical depth. This is the name of Bennett's criterion: the logical depth of a message is the measure of its meaning, its value. The more difficulty the sender experiences in arriving at the message, the greater its logical depth. The more "calculating time" he has spent—in his head or on a computer—the greater its value, as he saves the recipient the trouble of doing the work himself.

Whether the result takes less or more time to explain is not so important (to anyone but the telephone company). The important thing is the time spent arriving at the message that is to be transmitted.

In 1985, Bennett proposed that complexity could be measured as logical depth. It can also be used as a criterion by which we may determine how much meaning a message contains. Complexity is to be measured not by the length of the message but by the work carried out previously. The meaning does not arise from the information in the message but arises from the information discarded during the process of formulating the message, which has a specific information content.

What matters is not saying as much as you can. It is thinking before you speak.

"Informally, logical depth is the number of steps in the deductive or causal path connecting a thing with its plausible origin," Bennett writes.[12] But a more precise definition is possible.

We start with algorithmic information theory: A message can be compressed to the shortest form possible, the shortest description that can enable a Turing machine to formulate the message. The shortest form is a measure of the actual information present in the message. But it takes a certain amount of time for the Turing machine to formulate the message itself based on the shortest possible description—for example, when the laws governing planetary motion are to be translated into a table of solar eclipses. The compressed information has to be unfolded. This takes time. This time is what is measured as logical depth.

There is a bus every seven minutes. The buses depart from the bus station twelve minutes before they get to my bus stop. The first bus leaves at five. It is now half past six. When is the next bus? At 17:34.

The information content of "17:34" is not very great—on the face of it. But the computing time taken can be considerable, especially if I am just on my way out the door. Whoever has worked out the result can help someone else by telling him. This help saves the receiver a certain amount of computational time. It gives meaning.

Logical depth is a measure of the process that leads to a certain amount of information, rather than the amount of information that is produced and can be transmitted. Complexity or meaning is a measure of the production process rather than the product, the work time rather than the work result. The information discarded rather than the information remaining.

The notion of logical depth is thus perpendicular to information content. Everything has a certain face value as regards information content. But the face value does not necessarily tell us very much about its depth: how difficult it was to generate.

There may be an enormous amount of work or thought behind a given message or product. Yet it may be invisible. Making things look easy is hard. Clarity requires depth.

Nonsense, on the other hand, is not deep—baloney is random twaddle that cannot be expressed more concisely, because it possesses no order. There is therefore no difference between the shortest possible program for its repetition and full-length twaddle. So no computational time is involved, apart from the time taken to utter it.

A mess has no depth, either, because a mess cannot be described more concisely than the way it describes itself by simply being a mess.

The idea of Bennett's proposal is that any meaningful or complex quantities must be capable of being described more concisely but are not necessarily so; they can be compressed into a brief recipe.

A living organism can be specified in a few genes, but it takes time to decompress the creature concerned. A great opera can be written using just a few notes, but staging it requires a lot of work. A table of the phases of the moon throughout the year can be computed from a simple algorithm. But it takes time.

Disorder, baloney, and slips of the tongue cannot be put more concisely, however. The shortest program is equal to the entire rigmarole.

Bennett's notion indicates that complexity is something which takes time to arise. Time in which order is created. Time in which information is discarded so there is less to manage. Computational time on a computer, or evolutionary time on earth.

Thermodynamics permits living creatures to organize, for example. They have to burn up a lot of food, certainly (thereby exporting entropy), but then they can grow so complex that they can read books. As long as it happens slowly: It takes time to organize the living. Biological evolution has taken time, just as it takes time to grow big enough to read books. Bennett has formulated a "slow growth" law[13] for complex systems. It takes time for things to organize themselves into living creatures, for example. A long time. But it can be done. On earth it happened over the course of a few billion years.

Death and destruction, on the other hand, can be managed in an instant and produce copious quantities of information in no time at all. We can create an awful lot of information by tossing a coin or smashing plates in the kitchen. To describe the result costs a lot of information. But it is not very interesting; it does not have much depth.

The notion of logical depth is epochmaking. It implies that it is not the face value of the information but the prior process of discarding information that is central to understanding complexity. What is important is the information that was once present but is no longer there.

Most of what we find worth talking about comprises things and thoughts of great complexity: great depth but perhaps not so much surface area. A lot of information has been discarded along the way, and there may not be that much left. A state with a rich history. The interesting things in life may be not the ones that take long explanations to describe but those that take many experiences to get to know.

But there are also serious problems in the notion of logical depth. It presupposes that what we talk about can be equated with the result of a calculation. That may be meaningful, even for many material quantities, animate as well as inanimate. For lots of physical and biological systems can be understood as the result of a series of laws that have operated through processes described in these laws. In other words, we can simulate the evolution of a system on a computer. Then we can ask how long the computational time was. The longer the time, the greater the depth of the system.

A biological creature is the result of a very long evolutionary computation. An ingenious scientific law may be the result of a very long mental calculation. A "yes" or a "no" may be the result of a whole mass of hard-won experience.

But the world does not consist merely of calculators, let alone Turing machines. The most interesting calculations in the world take place inside a "computer" that works completely differently from a Turing machine: the brain. Perhaps all the symbolic, mathematical calculations the brain performs can be simulated by a Turing machine. But Turing machines cannot compute everything: As Gödel has shown, human beings know the truth of statements we cannot prove by mathematical symbols. In the final analysis, we discard information in ways the Turing machine does not. Ways we do not know.

So there is something intuitively unsatisfactory in having to regard all objects as the results of a computer calculation. Famous authors and composers cannot like it at all (although the idea of logical depth does recognize their superiority to monkeys and other keyboard acrobats).

Another problem is the anchoring of Bennett's notion in algorithmic information theory and its notion of the shortest possible program.[14] For what is the shortest possible program? The work of Chaitin, which rests on Gödel's theorem, says that we can never know whether we really have arrived at the shortest possible description of the way to make an object. So the computational time may be way out of line if we have got hold of an incorrect algorithm. Unreasonably short or unreasonably long.

Folklore all over the world is full of examples about the way people can perform something very simple in a highly complicated way. Modern society is full of professionals who are experts in arriving at simple solutions in highly complex ways: bureaucrats, academics, and soldiers, for example. Math problems also tend to be drawn up by teachers who are all too good at making intuitively simple sums difficult to work out.

We then tend to ascribe high degrees of complexity to matters one would have to be a public employee to find complicated.

This fundamental problem in the Gödel-Chaitin experience does happen to be very deep. We can never decide through formal means if pretend depth is real depth. It is a fundamental problem in our description of the world—and we should not be frightened by a notion just because it ends in such a problem. But it is partly because Bennett's notion needs to make a detour via a computer that this problem arises—and the idea of making a detour via a computer is of course to make the notion very precise. Nevertheless, it does not become so, because Turing's halting theorem shows that the computational time for a program cannot be calculated except by carrying out the calculation.

But the central point of Bennett's notion of logical depth is not the way it is calculated. The central point is to work out how much information has been discarded along the way. It is the idea itself that is revolutionary, rather than the definition of the notion of logical depth.

For many years, Hans Kuhn, a German chemist from Göttingen, has championed a related line of thought applied to biological systems. In an attempt to understand the origins and evolution of life, he has focused on the discarding of information along the way. According to Kuhn, biological evolution consists of a series of choices where an organism relates to its surroundings. These surroundings subject it to pressure, and it must choose to act in order to survive. Its genes contain experience in survival—otherwise there would be no organism, and no genes.

The more the organism survives, the more it experiences. And the more valuable its genes become. So the interesting thing is not how many genes it has—i.e., how long its DNA is. The interesting thing is the wealth of experience deposited in its genes.

The information an organism contains in its genes has a value that is proportional to the mass of experiences compressed there. What's interesting is not the face value of the information—i.e., the size of the genes—but rather the information discarded. "This quality constitutes knowledge, where 'knowledge' is measured by the total number of bits to be discarded,"[15] Kuhn wrote. Biological knowledge, then, is defined simply as discarded information.

This also disposes of a problem that bothered many scientists when it was discovered. Lilies have far more DNA than human beings. They are beautiful, yes, but surely they are not wiser?

The actual model for the origins and evolution of life Kuhn proposes is problematical, but it's closely related to the more promising models developed by Manfred Eigen and his assistant Peter Schuster.

There is tremendous depth in Kuhn's vision of biological evolution, a depth that is independent of his model.

A vital difference between Bennett's and Kuhn's perspectives is the theoretical status. Kuhn's notion is historical and factual, whereas Bennett's is logical and theoretical. In principle, Kuhn is talking about the information thrown away in the actual process, whereas Bennett is talking about the information that must be discarded in a theoretical reconstruction of the process. This difference does not necessarily have anything to do with the fact that Kuhn is talking about biology and Bennett primarily about physics. Kuhn's approach avoids the difficulties inherent in the computer-bound model. It would thus have obvious application to a more physical approach—and that is precisely what is behind the notion of thermodynamic depth.

"It was a thesis that was published too early, but unfortunately those were the circumstances," Seth Lloyd says of one of the most promising treatises published for many years. "Complexity as Thermodynamic Depth" appeared in *Annals of Physics* in 1988.

It was written by Lloyd and his Ph.D. supervisor at Rockefeller University, Heinz Pagels—the author of *The Dreams of Reason*, the book that in 1988 disseminated an understanding of the need for a theory of complexity; a book that combined tremendous scientific expertise on the physical problems with a sense for the philosophical aspects of the subject rare among natural scientists. Moreover, the extremely well-written and easily accessible account is spiced with informally autobiographical anecdotes. A rarely complex book that follows beautifully in the wake of Pagels's previous successes in putting physics across to a wide range of readers—books such as *The Cosmic Code* and *Perfect Symmetry*—it is a worthy conclusion to a great writing career.

Heinz Pagels died in summer 1988 while climbing with Seth Lloyd in Colorado.

This is why the results of Lloyd's Ph.D. thesis on complexity, which Pagels had supervised, were published too early and under pressure. A fact that may affect the very history of science, for the world of physics comes down hard on any idea launched before it is mature enough to become physics; physicists are interested not in what matters in the world but in what can be made the object of physical theories. Science is the art of the possible. So it is unpopular to float theories before it is completely obvious that they are fruitful and can be developed into a formal description other people can carry further. In this light, the idea of thermodynamic depth was published too early.

For obvious as it is that the notion of thermodynamic depth looks like just the notion for describing complexity, it is equally obvious that the treatise from *Annals of Physics* does not contain a satisfactory solution as to how the notion is to be formulated theoretically.

Thermodynamic depth is simply *the idea of defining complexity as the amount of information that is discarded during the process that brings a physical object into being.* A historical, rather than a logical, notion.

The problem is how to define this depth. How do we work out how much information has been discarded during such a process? For any but the most trivial objects, this is no simple matter. We do not know the history of a thing. We were not there when it came into being.

Lloyd and Pagels try to solve the problem by indicating the most likely history. Rather than looking for the shortest program capable of reconstructing an object (understood as a description in bits), we should look for the most likely way an object has come into being. This history rests on existing scientific theories about the processes that can lead to such an object. The amount of information discarded during the process is measured not in computational time but in the thermodynamic and informational resources that have probably been utilized.

This immediately provides a solution to an important problem in any definition of complexity: A natural requirement of any description of complex systems is that the presence of two specimens does not mean twice as much depth as one specimen alone. Lloyd and Pagels wrote, "Complexity must be a function of the process—the assembly routine—that brought the object into existence. If physical complexity is a measure of the process or set of processes whereby a set of initial states evolves into a final state, then seven bulls need not be much more complex than one bull. It took billions of years for the earth to evolve one bull; but one bull and a few compliant cows will produce seven bulls relatively speedily."[16]

The problem is turning these intuitively convincing ideas into clear, measurable quantities. It has not been solved.

In their 1988 article, Lloyd and Pagels tried to determine thermodynamic depth as the difference between two versions of the entropy of an object: entropy measured coarsely and entropy measured fine-grained. Coarse entropy is the ordinary thermodynamic entropy which tells us that there is a lot we do not know when we simply describe macrostates such as temperature. Fine-grained entropy is the entropy Maxwell's demon possesses: The demon knows more about the molecules of a gas than we know when all we know is the thermodynamic states such as temperature and pressure. The demon knows—and changes—a series of microstates and thereby removes the gas from the state of balance described exhaustively by its coarse-grained entropy.

As thermodynamic depth is a function of the difference between fine-grained and coarse-grained entropy, it tells us how far a system is from balance. If a system is in equilibrium with its environment, it must be "just as warm" as its environment. No work can be done by allowing the system to cool down. Conversely, no energy need be added to the system to keep it in its present state. Dead matter is in equilibrium with its surroundings, whereas living creatures are far from equilibrium: they all need something to eat in order to live.

According to Lloyd and Pagels, then, a system is complex only if it is not in equilibrium, for when it is in equilibrium the coarse-grained quantities tell us all we would want to know about the system: We are not interested in knowing any more about the molecular motion than the temperature tells us when the motion is random heat motion. The fine-grained entropy is just as great as the coarse-grained entropy. This corresponds completely to our intuitive expectation that disorder is not complex.

Similarly, a highly ordered system does not possess much depth, either. For it is also a characteristic of order that there is no loss of information in its description in superior terms. An orderly system can be described exhaustively from above, in broad terms. After all, order means that each macrostate corresponds to very few microstates. Total order means one microstate for every macrostate. In a crystal lattice, the atoms are located exactly where they are meant to be located. So there is no entropy involved in describing them by their macrostate. Again this means that totally ordered states have no depth.

This is a very profound idea. The distance from equilibrium is what matters. Anything wholly ordered or wholly disordered is stable by definition. A salt crystal changes only in solution; the only changes in a gas with the same temperature occur through movement at the microscopic level, but that is of no interest to us—at the macrolevel, nothing happens.

The thermodynamic depth of an object tells us that it has a history. Something happened to it that brought it out of a state it could maintain by itself, whether this state was trivial and motionless order or total chaos about which there was no more to be said than the temperature that characterized it.

Elegant ideas, but unfortunately nobody knows how to measure the difference between fine-grained and coarse-grained entropy.

Discussions on how to define thermodynamic depth always end in talk of the number of computational cycles in a computer;[17] this is really the thinking that lies in Bennett's notion of logical depth. Thus the whole point of thermodynamic depth vanishes—that the notion is determined by actual physical history rather than a logical reconstruction. What's more, all of Gödel's tribulations reappear: we can never know if we have obtained the shortest possible description.

The strength and weakness of the notion of thermodynamic depth is that it is historical. This means that we avoid the problem of never being able to know the shortest programs. Because the Gödel-Turing-Chaitin problem vanishes in principle when we have to provide not the shortest possible program but only the actual process undergone. The problem then is only to find out how things actually came into being. Then we know how deep they are.

(But this means that processes that "go round in circles" have great depth even though the tremendous amounts of information discarded have not really had any effect on the result. Processes that discard information in a superficial way can acquire great depth—and processes that happen to involve other processes, of greater depth, may suddenly acquire a whole load of depth without its actually meaning anything. As Rolf Landauer has put it, "Stone fragments known to be the result of human intervention are burdened with the whole history of human evolution by this approach, and are assigned a much greater complexity than the same fragments would have as the result of a natural geological event."[18] In 1989, Wojcieh Zurek tried to define a "minimal thermodynamic depth"[19] where it is not the actual history that is included in the depth of an object but the shortest possible history. As soon as this method is applied, we move from the historical to the logical level, but the gain is obvious: The thermodynamic depth becomes identical with the difference in algorithmic complexity between the starting point and the result. We lose the historical-factual perspective but gain a clarity that promises a possible eventual quantitative honing of the notion of thermodynamic depth. Zurek's results are important because imprecision is the Achilles' heel of this notion.)

The publication of complexity theory as thermodynamic depth in incomplete form in 1988 has had its costs. In theoretical physics, the sanctions are harsh if you have not got your sums up to snuff. The problem of quantifying these notions has caused many physicists to shrug their shoulders at them, despite their intuitive clarity. Today we have no quantitative notion of complexity—i.e., a notion that allows us to measure complexity. So it is not yet an area that counts for anything among physicists.

Seth Lloyd and his colleagues have taken only the first bite of the apple.

"There is some danger that the concern with the formulation of a definition comes at the expense of clearer questions,"[20] wrote Rolf Landauer in 1988, commenting on the development of Bennett, Kuhn, and Lloyd-Pagels's notions of depth and complexity: The basic idea of depth as a measure of the volume of discarded information is very promising. A clearer formulation may also emerge if a few silly questions point to new or astonishing aspects of the notions of depth and complexity.

Definitions very easily become tautologies, or statements that really say nothing at all ("Either it will rain or it won't"; "All bachelors are unmarried"). In *Nature*, Landauer writes about Bennett, Kuhn, and Lloyd-Pagels: "These definitions are, in a sense, tautologies. They all roughly say: that which is reached only through a difficult path is complex. Tautologies, however, are welcome if they replace nonsense. Darwin cleared the air by telling us that the survivors survive."[21]

So let us follow Landauer's advice and forget the problems physicists have with their defining and quantifying. Perhaps the problem is just that their world is too simple to address the right questions to the notion of depth. Let us forget the difference between logical and thermodynamic depth and stick to the clarity inherent in the very idea of depth: that it is the amount of information discarded during a process which tells us the complexity of the product. A clear idea however you measure it.[22]

Shannon's notion of information is a measure of surprise, unpredictability, unexpectedness. The depth of an object is a measure of the amount of information discarded as it came into existence. That is to say, depth is a measure of how many surprises the object has been subjected to in its history.

Depth shows that something has interacted with the world. It has changed, but it is still itself; out of balance, but not out of itself. It has known surprises in its time. But it is still here. It has marked the world, and the world has marked it.

It has grown deep.

PART II

≈

COMMUNICATION

CHAPTER 5

THE TREE OF
TALKING

The shortest correspondence in history took place in 1862. Victor Hugo—famous for writing *The Hunchback of Notre Dame*—had gone on holiday following the publication of his great novel *Les Misérables*. But Hugo could not restrain himself from asking how the book was doing. So he wrote the following letter to his publisher: "?"

His publisher was not to be outdone and replied fully in keeping with the truth: "!"

As *The Guinness Book of Records* says of the publisher's reply, "the meaning was unmistakable."[1] Certainly to Victor Hugo; *Les Misérables* was a great success as a novel, and popular now as movie and as musical.

It is fun to guess at what preceded the formulation of the two letters. At his holiday destination, Victor Hugo was surely wondering whether his great work would be understood and appreciated by the public. Countless concerns and considerations led him to contact his publisher, but instead of writing, "Come on, damn it, tell me if my book is selling!" he made do with that discreet question mark. On the other hand, his publisher was presumably ensconced in sales figures, reviews, and accounts, from which he could have served up endless statistics, but he was tactful enough to know that they would not have helped. What Hugo wanted to know was simple. An answer such as " " could have ruined his holiday.

Undoubtedly, considerable thought preceded the letter writing itself. Measured in bits, a question mark isn't much for a letter home. If there are thirty-odd characters in the alphabet (letters plus a few punctuation marks), each of them contains about five bits on average. So the entire correspondence consisted of about ten bits. But it worked; it worked very well.

It was not the number of bits transmitted that was decisive, but the context of that transmission. For Hugo and his publisher, the fate of *Les Misérables* was foremost in their minds during those initial weeks. It filled their consciousness. Both messages represent many considerations— thoughts, feelings, and facts—which are not present but nevertheless are. Information that is not there yet nevertheless is. The correspondence refers to a plethora of information—otherwise it would not be full of meaning.

This applies to any correspondence, of course. Before the words are written, a considerable amount of mental work takes place. Not all of it is present in the words, yet it is so nevertheless. The actual information in the correspondence at face value refers to a mass of information that is merely not present.

In writing his question mark, Victor Hugo is referring explicitly to information the publisher is not told about in any way apart from the reference itself. Before the question mark is put on the paper, Hugo discards a mass of information that has flown through his consciousness. He refers explicitly to this information without including it in his letter.

Hugo's question mark is the result of an explicit discarding of information. Not merely a discarding of information: He has not simply forgotten it all. He refers explicitly to what he has discarded, but from the point of view of the correspondence it is still discarded. For the purposes of this book, we will call such explicitly discarded information *exformation*.

A message has depth if it contains a large quantity of exformation. If, during the process in which the final message is formulated by a specific person, a mass of information that was present in the consciousness of that person is discarded, and thus absent from the message, we have exformation.

From the information content of the message alone, there is no way of measuring how much exformation the message implies. Only the context can tell us that. The sender fashions the information in the message so it refers to information he had in his head.

The puzzle of communication is how it can be possible: How can we refer, in some information that we pass on, to a quantity of information that we discard? How can we chart our mental state in the form of some information? This is remarkable in itself. But of course it is made no less remarkable by the fact that others have to be able to use this chart in order to picture the terrain for themselves.

A good communicator does not think only of himself; he also thinks about what the receiver has in his head. It is not enough for the explicitness of the information to refer to some information in the sender's head if that information does not somehow lead to the correct associations by the receiver.

The idea of transmitting information is to cause a state of mind to arise in the receiver's head that is related to the state of mind of the sender by way of the exformation referred to in the information transmitted. The idea of sending information is that the mind of the receiver must contain some inner information related to the exformation the sender has in his head. The information transferred must elicit certain associations in the receiver.

Take the word "horse," for example. When an author writes "horse," he draws on a huge amount of personal experience. He has seen horses, he has read about horses, he has watched horses on television; he knows that people variously associate horses with beauty and sensuality, pari-mutuel wins, and horse manure. From his memory he can summon up a vast amount of information related to horses.

Out of context, he cannot expect that what is in his mind when he writes "horse" will have very much to do with what you think when *you* read the word. But if he uses the word in a passage about the history of horse racing, he can be pretty sure that he and his readers will have the same thing in mind.

"Cow." It is already apparent that we are not talking racetracks or symbols of wealth. We are talking about domestic animals. Big, fascinating, frightening, nuzzling, amiable animals.

The author has excited a space of association in your head. The result would not have been the same if he had written "Horse. Cow." But almost. It does not take much for him to spark off associations in your head.

But he has to think about what he is doing; and so do you. The transfer of exformation requires attentiveness.

Of exformation . . . ? Can we transfer exformation?! Has it not been discarded prior to communication? So surely it cannot be transferred during communication? How can something by definition not present in the information nominally transferred *be* transferred? By writing "I did it my way" and "Frank Sinatra," how can an author strike up a very specific mood in your head and set the emotions flowing through your mind and body? "Yesterday." "Christmas." "Tax return."

He can do so only because he shares a vast number of experiences with his readers. They have all heard the same hits on the radio, taken part in the same rituals, and filled in their tax returns. They are part of a context communicated through language. When the author writes a word, it is the result of an inner activity where lots of experiences flash through his consciousness. The reason he selects that word in particular is that he senses it will arouse some of the same associations in you.

But he cannot be certain. Nor do you know what was in his mind when he wrote "Christmas." Perhaps he was just looking for a word he was fairly sure most people would respond to. Perhaps there was not much depth, not much exformation, in the word at all.

That is the risk of communicating. The receiver never knows how much information the sender has discarded. You never know how much exformation a given piece of information implies. It could be a bluff—or intellectual snobbery. Or indifference. Or the nine o'clock news: There is no guarantee that people listen to what they themselves say. Volumes of words can churn forth from people's lips (or fingers) without their "being there." If you make considerable effort to listen to them, you soon get cross. Not necessarily because what they are saying is uninteresting; after all, snobs always try to say something interesting. But because what you really wanted was to obtain a picture of what was going on in these people's heads, and you cannot do that when they supply information but no exformation.

The least interesting aspect of good conversation is what is actually said. What is more interesting is all the deliberations and emotions that take place simultaneously during conversation in the heads and bodies of the conversers.

The words are merely references to something not present. Not present in the words—but present in their heads. The idea of conversation is to elicit related states in each other's minds and then exchange the events that take place. You don't believe it, you sympathize, you oppose, you are carried away, you remember, you love it, you love them, you miss them, you get ideas . . .

≈

Exformation is perpendicular to information. Exformation is what is rejected en route, before expression, Exformation is about the mental work we do in order to make what we want to say sayable. Exformation is the discarded information, everything we do not actually say but have in our heads when or before we say anything at all. Information is the measurable, demonstrable utterances we actually come out with. The number of bits or characters in what is actually said. That is why there is no link that says "The greater the information, the greater the exformation."

The information content of a conversation is demonstrable, expressed, explicit. But the whole point of this explicitness is to refer to something else, something implicit, something unexpressed. Not just not present, but explicitly not present.

There is no conflict between information and exformation. But neither is there a link. A very brief message can contain enormous depth. A very long chat can contain enormous depth. But brief and extended messages can also be very superficial.

As concepts, though, they are linked. Exformation is the history of the message, information the product of that history. Each is meaningless without the other; information without exformation is vacuous chatter; exformation without information is not exformation but merely discarded information.

In most contexts, it is very difficult to decide what the exformation in a piece of information actually is. We can tell in the case of very precise messages: "I know somebody who has a rotary cultivator." In this case, the sender is obviously thinking about a digging job that would be easier if done by mechanical means and about a person who might be prepared to lend his implement. There is no reason to say a great deal about the person concerned; as long as the other digger understands that this person is sufficiently friendly to lend his rotary cultivator, that will do.

But we have no idea of the exformation in most of the messages we hear. We guess and sense and suspect—but we do not know. On the phone, it is harder to judge someone we don't know than it is face-to-face. But it can be done.

Conversation bears a veil of ignorance and uncertainty reminiscent of the problems physicists encounter in defining depth.

Thermodynamic depth can be hard to define because it contains the history of an entire process. Perhaps it does not matter that a lot of information has been discarded en route. Correspondingly, what does it mean when somebody says he has given a matter a great deal of thought? We do not know, unless we know him. Logical depth can be hard to define because it is unclear whether the computational time required to arrive at a message is meaningful—was the point of departure the clearest possible?

It is not particularly strange that such difficulties also appear when the subject is conversation. Actually, that is what makes conversations fun.

If we view them from without, as information being exchanged, they are not especially rich. But if we see them from within, as exformation, they can be tremendous fun. If you do not know the context, they can be dull. It is very boring to listen to people talking about someone you do not know. Such conversations tell you very little. But it is fun to talk about people you do know, whether personally or as public figures.

Information is not very interesting. The interesting thing about a message is what happens before it is formulated and after it has been received. Not its information content.

So perhaps it was not so dumb after all when, in 1948, telephone utility engineer Claude Shannon defined information as something completely meaningless, something closely related to disorder.

One may decide to reject Shannon's notion of information with disdain and annoyance; after all, it is a notion that deals with something quite unlike what the rest of us understand by the everyday word "information"—meaning, content, overview, order.

If one chooses this view, one has quite a lot of philosophers behind one. For decades, shoals of humanities professors and social scientists have criticized Shannon's notion for its narrowness.

For example: "Classical information theory is not really about information," the German philosopher Sybille Kramer-Friedrich wrote in 1986. "Information is not so much a scientific concept as a mythical one."[2]

Indeed, there are plenty of grounds for a conspiracy theory of the most devious kind: that the notion of information was invented and developed by engineers from big private corporations who then made a profitable business out of having the rest of us talk about truth, beauty, meaning, and wisdom—on the phone.

For not only was information theory developed by an engineer at AT&T's Bell Laboratories, but Claude Shannon originally published his theory in the telephone corporation's very own scientific periodical, the *Bell System Technical Journal,* in collaboration with none other than Warren Weaver, perhaps the most important *éminence grise* behind science this century.

Warren Weaver worked for the Rockefeller family, the most famous of all the wealthy American dynasties. Weaver was a physicist and adviser to the Rockefeller Foundation, which allocated massive sums to research. One of the classic themes of the social history of science is Weaver's influence on biology. In the 1930s, Weaver decided that he wanted a more "physical" biology, one that involved not the systematic classification of butterfly species but rather molecules and other physical quantities: molecular biology—a branch of science that brought biotechnology and genetic engineering into play half a century after Weaver's decision, firmly anchored in information theory. Indeed, modern molecular biology is based in its entirety on concepts drawn from information and computation theory.

Warren Weaver was behind the theory of information that was developed by an engineer from AT&T.

So it definitely looks like a seizure of power by industry that robs the man in the street of the everyday word "information," and gives him in return a totally meaningless notion about the way signals are spread through electronic apparatus—and then goes on to re-create the very genes of living nature in the image of this notion.

It's not all empty talk, either. Theodore Roszak, the American cultural historian, one of the most gifted critics of modern technological civilization, writes of the practical successes of information theory in computing and telecommunications: "Achievements of this astonishing order were bound to shift our understanding of information away from people (as sources or receivers) toward the exciting new techniques of communication."[3]

Attention was moved from the senders and receivers of information to the carrier of that information. Most of us tend to mix up the message and the medium anyway.

In 1876, the last emperor of Brazil, Pedro II, was on a visit to the United States. In Philadelphia, the head of this Portuguese-speaking country attended a great exhibition at which a teacher of the deaf, Alexander Graham Bell, demonstrated a new invention of his, the telephone. The emperor was permitted to try it. Tradition has it that he burst out, "My God! It speaks Portuguese!"[4]

The concept of information is a very bad one if it is taken at face value. If you suppose that the information in information theory is about meaning, the way you might think that energy is about what the rest of us mean by energy (namely, something we use when we want to keep warm), you are in for a disappointment.

But if we are prepared to accept that what we mean by information differs from the information information theory talks about, the gain may be that there is a lot of insight to be harvested from information theory.

Because our analysis of conversations earlier shows that it is no good merely saying that our words contain more than can be measured in bits. Because it is not what we say to each other every day that establishes all the meaning and beauty and truth our everyday conversations contain; it is everything we think before we speak.

Perhaps we should count ourselves lucky that information theory has demonstrated so clearly that information is not particularly important. For it thereby becomes clear that there must be something else that really counts: the real source of beauty, truth, and wisdom.

The ironic thing is that this "else" can be described as the information we have got rid of: *exformation.*

Meaning is information that has been discarded: information that is no longer present and no longer needs to be.

Information and meaning are rather like money and wealth. Real value, real wealth, is a matter not of money but of the money you have spent, money you used to have: utility values you have obtained by paying for them. Only Scrooge McDuck can use money itself, money as a concrete quantity, when he swims around in his money tank. The rest of us want money because we want to get rid of it again.

Likewise information: It is only when you have got enough of the stuff that you realize it has no value in itself.

≈

However mad you may get at the paucity of the concept of information in information theory, it is no good complaining about a lack of intellectual honesty on the part of Claude Shannon, Warren Weaver, or the other founding fathers of information theory. They make their case extremely clearly.

Oh, there has been plenty of confusion about the concept of information, because the word "information" has been used as a synonym for order and meaning. But this use of the word does not come from information theory, it comes from cybernetics—the science of communication and control. The father of cybernetics, Norbert Wiener, and pupils such as Leon Brillouin commingled "information" with plus words like "order" and "organization." In Chapter Two, we saw how this gave rise to half a century of confusion surrounding Maxwell's demon. But this confusion is not to be found in the original wording of the theory of information.

In his presentation of the theory, Claude Shannon wrote that "These semantic aspects of communication are irrelevant to the engineering problem."[5] Warren Weaver from the Rockefeller Foundation was even clearer: "information must not be confused with meaning."[6]

Weaver emphasizes that there are three levels in a communication theory: a technical level, a semantic level, and a behavioral level.

The technical involves the transmission of symbols of communication—i.e., the practical application of what Shannon's mathematical theory describes. The semantic level involves the question as to how far the symbols actually convey the desired meaning. Finally, the behavioral level describes the extent to which a communication actually affects the receiver's conduct in the desired way (if such a desire in fact exists).

Weaver makes it very clear that Shannon's theory tells us only about the first level: "Two messages, one of which is heavily loaded with meaning and the other of which is pure nonsense, can be exactly equivalent, from the present viewpoint, as regards information."[7] He adds, "The word 'information' in communication theory relates not so much to what you *do* say, as to what you *could* say."[8]

Information theory is a very cold theory. It ignores all the meaning-related aspects of communication simply in order to work out how thick telephone cables need to be to carry all the conversations. Information measures conversations from the outside—as physics, not psychology. But the point is, this really need not bother us.

In reality, the coldness of information theory saves the rest of us from a series of problems that would arise if we ascribed a meaning to an oral message on the basis of its exterior characteristics: Much of what is communicated via conversation (with or without modern aids) is nonsense. Humans have a need for interplay wherein we sometimes utter nonsense, sometimes speak profundities, but mostly keep our traps shut.

If we could go by the exterior characteristics of a message alone and still perceive its meaning—i.e., what was really being communicated—we would not be able to distinguish snobs from people who speak from experience. We would not be able to tell something learned parrot fashion from insight, bluff from genuine contributions to understanding.

Of course, doing so can be difficult at the best of times, but such difficulties are not something that appeared following the advent of AT&T. That words and gestures cannot be taken at face value is a fundamental condition of human intercourse and conversation.

On the contrary, we must stick to our guns and say that we, and not the telephone utilities, are the ones to decide how much meaning there is in the phone calls we receive.

The history of information theory is pervaded with numerous attempts to sneak a little *meaning* into the coldness of its conceptual universe. The American philosopher Kenneth Sayre divides these attempts into two categories: those asserting that information theory really is about meaning, and those maintaining that the demand for a little less precision in the concepts involved will bring in meaning.

Sayre regards Donald MacKay, a British information theorist, as the progenitor of the first version, where it is claimed that information theory in itself describes meaning. This is not quite fair, although Sayre is able to show that MacKay's insights led to just such a trivialization when other scientists took the idea further.[9] But MacKay's idea, launched in 1950, is not that far from some of the ideas about depth formulated in the 1980s. For example, MacKay writes that the information content is a numerical expression of the complexity of the fabrication process.[10] This is similar to the idea that the meaning associated with some information consists of the amount of information discarded during the process leading to this information (Charles Bennett's idea of logical depth, very much rephrased).

The other reaction Sayre identifies is the tendency to relax or adjust the concepts. "If we can solve a few problems in behavioral science by going beyond the usual use of the concepts, or by adjusting them, we should simply go ahead and do so," Wendell Garner wrote in 1962.[11] The most influential modern version of an adjusted information theory that includes meaning comes from Fred I. Dretske, an American philosopher, who concludes, however, with a concept of information that has very little to do with Shannon's.[12]

Kenneth Sayre's own approach to the problem is very reminiscent of what we are doing here: classical information theory as a perfectly orthodox point of departure but with interest focusing on the way the information disappears.[13]

Although philosophers such as Dretske and Sayre did stimulate discussion on information theory and meaning in the 1970s and 1980s, they epitomize what we might call the "impatience tradition": If theoretical concepts cannot describe all the phenomena of real life, just rearrange the concepts. Conversely, Shannon and Weaver belong to the "arrogance tradition": If the phenomena of real life cannot be described through the theoretical concepts, just forget the phenomena of real life.

Maybe a combination of the two is the most fruitful.

"The concept of information developed in this theory at first seems disappointing and bizarre," wrote Weaver in 1949. "But one should say, at the end, that this analysis has so penetratingly cleared the air that one is now, perhaps for the first time, ready for a real theory of meaning."[14]

It took nearly half a century, however, for the dust to begin to settle. Perhaps Shannon and Weaver cleared the air, but decades were to pass before the issue of meaning appeared seriously on the agenda in the context of information theory, when Charles Bennett expressed his idea of logical depth in 1985.

The fascination with all the information we could send flowing around our communities via technology was so great that we forgot what we wanted it for. Even critics of the information society were so absorbed by information theory that they thought the theory was where the problem actually lay.

But the modern information society is really good only at moving information about. It has become massively easier to converse over vast distances: Gigantic quantities of bits can be transmitted via satellites in orbit around the earth and cables deep down on the ocean floor. A myriad of information is constantly on the move worldwide. But all these channels fail to answer the vital question: What are we to say to each other?

Is there really anything interesting in being able to move information about? Does it mean anything in itself that communicating has become easier?

If communication overcomes sociological barriers, it does actually mean something—to society. The dissolution of Eastern Europe and the former Soviet Union is closely related to the way modern means of communication created numerous noncentralized connections between people inside and outside what used to be such closed societies. Means of communication are vital in societies where communication is in short supply.

These are sociological issues, which are important in themselves. However, there are also more theoretical, conceptual questions: At the purely physical level, thermodynamically speaking, things are different. It has only recently become clear that measured as a *physical* phenomenon, the moving of information about the place need not have any significance at all. From the thermodynamic point of view, the transport of information is a nonevent.

In *Nature*,[15] Rolf Landauer was able to correct an error in Claude Shannon's information theory. He did so not because he is critically disposed toward Shannon, whom he more or less regards as the Einstein of information,[16] but because Shannon made the same kind of mistake Leo Szilard had made in his analysis of Maxwell's demon: He took a special case and elevated the result to a general law.

Szilard investigated the way the demon measured molecular motion and discovered that certain measurements always had thermodynamic costs attached: that one always had to produce some entropy when one measured. But the special case Szilard and a large number of physicists after him had investigated did not hold up. It is not generally necessary to discard information when one measures. One can merely copy it, without creating entropy, without losing access to the energy one applied when one performed the measurement.

What Shannon analyzed was something else: the transfer of information. Communication. He studied how much entropy is created when we transfer information using wave signals in cables. It turned out that in this case you always create entropy—and the example is faultless.

But Shannon's students interpreted this special case as a law and believed that all transmission of information means the creation of entropy (noise, new information we can't be bothered to explain).

They were wrong. You can easily transmit information without creating new entropy. For example, by handing a book to someone (and then recycling the kinetic energy by receiving it back).

Ordinarily, communication has nothing to do with the creation or removal of information. Communication is merely transport.

Does this mean anything to those of us who could not care less about the specifications for the physical dimensions of telecommunications links? No, not in everyday practice, because the amounts of entropy involved in special cases are very small, far smaller than the noise generated on the telephone line or TV screen by other means.

But it means something *conceptually*. It shows that if we think that the discarding or creation of information is what matters, then in principle communication is of no importance at all: Information is created or discarded in communication for purely practical reasons. So that is not where we should look for what really matters: the *meaning* of it all.

"How Much Does Information Weigh?"[17] was the title of one lecture at the 1990 Santa Fe seminar. The speaker, Ben Schumacher, from Kenyon College in Ohio, looked quite capricious as he introduced "The Poor Student's Channel."

The scenario is this: A poor student goes off to a college far from home. His parents wonder whether he will be able to manage. They know they cannot help worrying. So they ask him to phone home every Sunday at four to tell them he is well. The student complains that he has almost no money and that spending all those coins calling home will be an expensive business. So he would rather not. But they agree on a solution: He will phone on Sundays at four only if he is having problems. If he does not phone, it is because everything is going well. So he rarely calls. But he sticks to his side of the deal.

He thus transfers a message to his parents every Sunday without having to spend a cent—assuming, that is, that the phone system is working. You can transmit a message without spending money and without any physical representation at all. Assuming that there is a connection.

If the lines are not intact, lack of a phone call will not tell you anything.

At this point, Schumacher was interrupted by Charles Bennett of IBM, who exclaimed, "It seems to me that the telephone company ought to be able to charge people for using the phone this way."

When you think about it, you will see that most of us use the phones like that quite a bit. "I haven't heard from her for ages, so she must be doing OK."

But the phone utilities know that very well. If you want to know how much it costs people to use the network like that, just try not paying your bill. Few things in modern life are as worrying as having your phone cut off; just who was trying to reach you?

So there are stacks of messages in a phone that does not ring. As long as you have paid your bill.

It does not require any information at all to transmit exformation. The student thinks, "I've no news. This week has been normal, no problems. I'm not going to call them." His parents think, "He must have been doing his assignments and getting out on the football field."

The exformation has been transmitted without the use of any information other than that agreed on.

Victor Hugo and his publisher have been overtaken: There is plenty of message in *not asking at all.* The world's shortest phone conversation takes place all the time: It consists of *not* phoning somebody you might otherwise have phoned. (The phone call you do not make contains no message if it is to somebody you do not know; it is only the absence of a call that *might have come* that contains a message.)

Rolf Landauer summarized his insight into the difference between communication and discarding of information in two sketches. Simple ones, the way physicists like them. Sketches containing a concept but not a bunch of finicky details.

One sketch shows how communication takes place. It consists merely of two parallel lines. Nothing really happens; it is just a pipe, a link.

The second sketch shows a computation: $2+2=4$. Two tracks converge at a point. The point is that two separate states, 2 and 2, are brought together into a combined state: 4. Something happens. You can go one way but not the other. From the point of departure—i.e., the states of 2 and 2—you can get to 4. But once you are there you cannot go back again, even if you know you moved from two states to the one you know. For 4 could have derived from many different states, even though there are only two of them: $1+3$ or $213-209$ or $-2+6$.

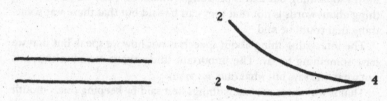

Communication and computation according to Rolf Landauer

Computation is a process in which information is discarded. Something real, irrevocable, and irreversible takes place. It does so because a computation discards information: There is less information in 4 than in $2+2$. So it is when the problem $(2+2)$ is replaced by the result that irreversibility occurs.

If you do not throw the starting point and intermediate computations away, thereby retaining only the answer, the computation is not irreversible. Computations can be made reversible so we can return to the starting point. But that means keeping the intermediate computations. Such reversible computations are most interesting from the theoretical point of view but not in practical terms. The whole point of computations is to reduce information. Unless we discard something along the way, any computation is a waste of time. We can distinguish between two types of computation: reversible ones and irreversible ones. The latter are irrevocable, and they are the ones that are interesting in practice: computation as the irrevocable discarding of information, where one can never guess one's way back to the starting point just because one knows the result.

But communication is not irrevocable. It is the same at both ends of the process. You can turn it around as you please. In fact, that is the whole point of communication: Information can be copied, transferred, moved, repeated, duplicated. Backward and forward are equidistant: In principle, communication can always be reversed.

Computations cannot. Nor can the production of exformation. Because when one discards information, one cannot go backward. One forgets which microstates led to the known macrostate. Forgetting is irrevocable. Communicating is revocable and reversible.

The irrevocable bit happens before and after communication, not during it. The interesting thing about communication is not that it moves something but that something is made movable. The interesting thing about words is not that they can be said but that there was something that could be said.

The interesting thing about speech is not how we speak but that we have something to say. The important thing about communication is not what one says but what one *has to say*.

That is why there are many things best said by keeping one's mouth shut.

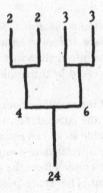 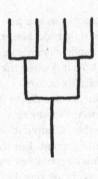

Binary tree

We can try making a slightly longer calculation than the one Landauer showed by his little fork. We can make a long sum: $(2+2) \times (3+3) = 24$. The sketch shows a double branching. Each branching branches again. The fork has become a small tree. With more complicated calculations we get trees with many branchings.

A tree like this is called a binary tree, because it branches by doubling. Binary trees are extremely useful in many areas of modern math and physics. Trees like these were used by Bernardo Huberman and Tad Hogg in 1985 in their first attempts at defining and putting numbers on complexity (an idea Herb Simon had suggested back in 1962). They are included in modern information theory too, because they explain why it is the logarithm for the number of microstates we cannot be bothered to hear about that yields the number of bits.

Let us toss our coin again. We toss it a large number of times and obtain a random series of binary numbers, where 0 means tails and 1 means heads: 001011101110. This binary string could be a lot of things besides the result of tossing the coin. It could also symbolize a number of choices made at a number of crossroads: right or left. So it is meaningful to draw a tree diagram that represents the entire volume of possibilities—the road network—and not just the route in fact chosen. In such a tree diagram, the actual route chosen is described by the

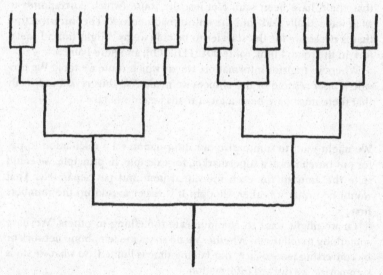

Tall binary tree

string of binary numbers—0 means right, 1 means left. The length of the string shows how many choices one has made: how many times one has had to choose.

The longer the string, the more choices one has made. But the number of roads one could have chosen, but did not choose, grows much faster than the number of choices. After seven decisions, one could have turned down $2 \times 2 \times 2 \times 2 \times 2 \times 2 \times 2$ roads. Two times itself seven times, or "two to the seventh." There is an enormous number of possible routes. Obviously it is not very interesting to be told that "two to the seventh" means 128. It is easier to remember that seven choices have been made. Eight choices means 256 roads, while four means 16.

The "binary logarithm" expresses the number of choices made. The logarithm tells us how many branches the tree has, how many levels the tree has sprouted.

The treetop expresses all possibilities. The number of choices is expressed by the "depth" of the treetop, the number of levels.

This is the figure information theorists are interested in: everything that could have been said. Not just the route (which corresponds to what was actually said) but the entire road network. The infrastructure that is necessary for the traveler to be able to say, "Eight times I met a fork in the road; I took route 001011101110, and here I am."

When we transfer information, we say which route we took. We provide a brief résumé of the choices we made. We thus reveal indirectly that there must have been a lot of roads we did not take.

We might want to summarize our information via a calculation to pay for our purchases at a supermarket, for example. In principle, we could state the amount for each individual item and pay separately. That would be rather a bother, though. It is easier to add up the numbers first.

Or we might want to communicate something to others. We have something to tell them. Whether we do so via the telephone network or by conversing face-to-face, our talking time is limited. So what we do is summarize: we discard information.

The misunderstandings regarding the information concept—Norbert Wiener and Leon Brillouin's notion of information as order and negentropy—probably originate from this: Certainly there is information in disorder, but what we human beings regard as information is what we might like to impart to one another—typically, something that is already the result of a computation, a summary. What we call information in everyday life is really more like exformation: In everyday language, if something contains information, it is the result of the production of exformation, it is a summary, an abbreviation suitable for communicating or guiding a transaction such as paying for our shopping.

So when we say "information" in everyday life, we spontaneously think of information-as-the-result-of-a-discarding-of-information. We do not consider the fact that there is more information in an experience than in an account of it. It is the *account* that we consider to be information. But the whole basis of such an account is information that is discarded. Only after information has been discarded can a situation become an event people can talk about. The total situation we find ourselves in at any given time is precisely one we cannot provide an account of: We can give an account of it only when it has "collapsed" into an event through the discarding of information. Only then can we say "I am sitting reading" without mentioning everything that went before and comes afterward and is present in the room.

Similarly, the things we want to talk about are things with a certain depth, things that have discarded information. A thing can be organized in a way we feel like talking about. So we say it contains information. We tend to believe that it is this organization that means the thing has information. But the fact is, a thing not structured and organized contains more information, because it is more difficult to describe. We just cannot be bothered to talk about it in detail, so we call it a macrostate, such as heat, a mess, or the dishes to do.

There is far less information about the kitchen in saying that the plates are clean and stacked in the cupboard than in saying that they are on the counter waiting to be washed. The clean, stacked plates are a macrostate that corresponds to very few microstates (generally speaking, the order of the plates in the stack is all that can be varied without provoking comments from the rest of the household), whereas dirty dishes can be arranged in the most incredible ways. As we all know.

But the information in a pile of dirty dishes is not very interesting. Actually, we happily discard that information. We do so by washing. When we have done so, the dishes are organized, which is a good thing and one we would think involved lots of information. But the opposite is true, and it is this conflict between the everyday concept of information and the scientific concept that led Wiener and Brillouin astray.

Our everyday concept of information is more like the concept of exformation than it is like Shannon's notion of information. There is considerable wisdom in our everyday language: All we can be bothered to talk about are things and situations characterized by a lack of information—organization, order, or simplicity manifested by stability in time. Things that contain the most information do not interest us, for they are a mess.

If we then add the human ability to apprehend—to compress experiences into briefer descriptions—it becomes obvious that what is interesting is whatever can be described in very little information: An anthill is more interesting than a heap of pine needles, but both consist of the same thing, and the information content is greater in the latter.

Information is a measure of disorder or randomness in messages we use to describe things not characterized by order and randomness. A message contains information because it is unpredictable. A message is interesting because it is about something that is, to a certain extent, predictable.

Our everyday concept of information knows this; but it is precisely therefore that the concept becomes so ambiguous. It is really more a matter of exformation than of information; when we say "information," what we really mean is closer to exformation. But not quite.

Let us therefore try to understand communication between human beings through a model that describes the transfer of information and the production of exformation that takes place prior to transmission. This may help to explain the discrepancy in our everyday notion of information.

We combine trees and tubes in a sketch based on the standard concepts of the mathematical theory of information but specially designed to tell us something about exformation. This is a map of how people talk to each other. Let us call it the *tree of talking.*

First, the person on the left has to think. She has to summarize an experience, an emotion, or a memory. Lots of information gets discarded, just as in a computation. (There is no other link to computation apart from the discarding of information—we are not saying that the creation of exformation corresponds solely to computation.) When her mental state is summarized through the discarding of a whole load of information, there are some words left that can be said. They are transferred via the tube. No discarding takes place there. At the other end of the tube, the words are received and are unfurled to reveal their meaning.

The movement proceeds from the left-hand treetop down to its root, through the forest floor and up the right-hand tree. On the left, a lot of information is compressed via the discarding of information, the production of exformation. Thoughts are composed into words. We can call this *incitation*. On the right, the limited information in the words is received. This is unfurled into more information. We can call this second process *excitation*.

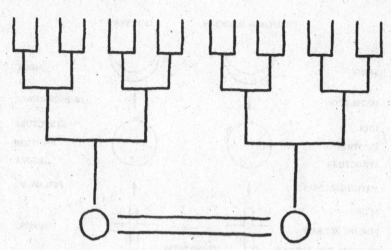

The tree of talking

A large quantity of information has been compressed via the production of exformation into a small quantity of information that is then transmitted. The information possesses depth because exformation has been created along the way.[18]

At the other end, the information is unfolded again. The recipient thinks about the horses she has seen in her life. She associates to experiences, thoughts, memories, dreams, emotions, horses. Excitation takes place.

A tiny amount of information has been transferred, but it has aroused a whole gallery of horse images at the other end. Incitation, communication, excitation. The discarding, transfer, and evocation of information.

This model does not apply merely to speech and writing. In fact, it was originally inspired by a Danish musician's description of what happens when one listens to music. In his book *Ind i musikken,* Peter Bastian describes the way the composer converts something spiritual/intellectual into a score that can be played by fingers on keys, leading to sound waves that are sensed, experienced, and transformed into music in the ears of the listener.[19]

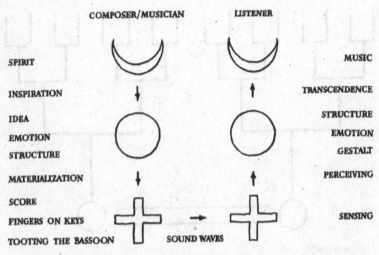

Musician Peter Bastian's sketch of the way music is conveyed from the musician to the listener. The symbols are irrelevant here. Note the structural kinship with the tree of talking.

The main thing in music is not the sound waves. It is that the composer/player converts a number of mental states into a pattern which evokes the same (or different) mental states in the listener. If we want to understand Bach or the Beatles, what we need to look at is not so much the information that is conveyed by the notes but the exformation that led to them, and thereby the exformation the notes evoke in the listener.

This line of thought is widespread in the study of the perception of music. David Hargreaves, a psychologist, has developed a theory of musical preference, described in *New Scientist* as follows: "The theory has its base in information theory, but the important insight comes from the distinction between this conception of 'information' and its psychological counterpoint. Fundamentally, the coding of physical information contained in a musical composition, as in information theory, predicts very little of interest, but coding the information in 'subjective' terms predicts quite a lot. Whether a person likes a particular piece or not depends on the information they are able to take out of it, rather than the information that is already 'in there.' "[20]

When we listen to music, certain states are created in our minds. They may be related to the state of the composer's mind when he wrote the music, but not necessarily.

Music can provide access to happy states. Not necessarily because "they're playing our tune"; it may simply be that this kind of music or tune happens to put us in a good mood.

Blood pressure readings and measurements of the electrical conductivity of the skin show that we really are affected by music: Studies undertaken in the wake of Hargreaves's theory have even demonstrated that the same places in a score affect different people the same way.

Listening to music is not a matter of knowing the name of the bass player or which Italian folk song the composition is a variation of. We do not need to know the score or the name of the vocalist's lover in order to enjoy the music. In fact, we need no details or knowledge at our fingertips in order to enjoy it. But we have to know ourselves—and have the courage to stand by what we know.

Music arouses mental states of which we may prefer not to be reminded, either because they are unpleasant or because we get depressed when we think about them. Music can arouse wonderful states: It can inspire energy, calm, eroticism, pensiveness, freedom, rebellion, sorrow, presence, the urge to dance, pride, laughter, a feeling of belonging, and irritation.

Music is a method of conveying emotional states from composer/player to audience via sound.

During live performances, the transfer goes both ways. An interplay takes place between player and audience. The emotional states evoked in the audience affect the player (because, for example, the breathing, postures, and facial expressions of the audience change). For rare, glowing moments, a reverse coupling can thus take place in which the player expresses his state of mind through the music and sparks states in the audience related to his own state, which is thereby enhanced and expressed with greater clarity.

So music has its tree, just like talking. But are these trees not sheer guesswork, based on the notion that there must be more information present in communication than that which is communicated explicitly?

Clinical Physiology and Nuclear Medicine is the name of a department located in the basement of the Bispebjerg Hospital, north of Copen-

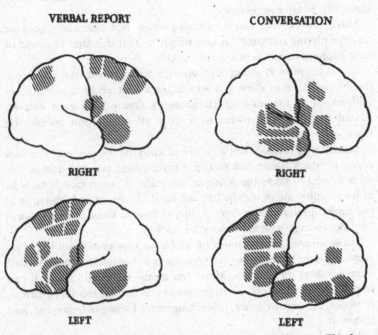

VERBAL REPORT   **CONVERSATION**

RIGHT   RIGHT

LEFT   LEFT

More goes on in our heads when we converse than when we merely report. This figure shows how much blood circulates through areas in the two halves of the brain. (After Friberg and Roland)

hagen. The name tells us that studies of human physiology—the way the organism functions—are carried out using radioactive chemicals. Over the last thirty years, a number of the most important details we possess about the way the human brain functions have been discovered there. The head of the department, Professor Niels A. Lassen, worked with his colleague David Ingvar, from the University Hospital at Lund, Sweden, on developing methods for studying blood circulation in the brain.

The foundations for their methods were laid in the United States in the 1940s and 1950s, but it was not until the 1960s that Lassen and Ingvar demonstrated that the way the blood circulates in the brain could be measured in detail.[21] It thereby became possible to show which parts of the brain are active when we perform specific actions. There are language centers, motor centers, planning centers, and hearing centers in the brain.

The existence of such centers had been known for over a century, primarily from studies of war casualties who had suffered partial brain damage. But the new methods for studying blood circulation made it possible to explore cerebral activity in far more everyday contexts. For example, there are major differences between simply talking and conversing. There are differences in blood flow in the brains of people merely describing their living rooms and people conversing (about, for example, how they spend Christmas).

Of course, we cannot see the individual thoughts, but we can see whether somebody is conversing or merely talking. Similarly, monitoring reveals whether a person thinks before he speaks: There are differences in the activity pattern when a person merely repeats a word given to him by the experimenter (chair, table) and when he is required to think before he speaks because of the association he may have to make to a given word (sit, eat).

In 1985, Lars Friberg and Per Roland, both pupils of Lassen and Ingvar, published a study of blood circulation during thought.[22] There are very big differences in the blood flow pattern during mental arithmetic, rhyme repetition, and visual memory operations, three different types of thinking.

For mental arithmetic, the test subjects had to subtract 3 from 50 and continue subtracting 3 from the result. For rhyme repetition, they had to omit alternate words in the nonsense rhyme "okker-gokker-gummi-klokker-erle-perle-pif-paf-puf," the Danish equivalent of "eeny, meeny, miney, mo." In the visual memory exercise, the subjects had to imagine that they stepped out of their front doors and alternated between turning right and turning left at every corner.

After they had performed one of these tests for a minute, the scientists noted where the blood flow was particularly pronounced. It turned

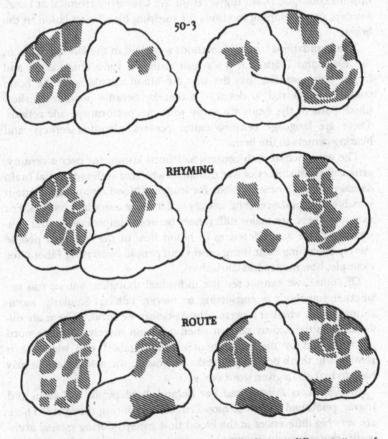

50-3

RHYMING

ROUTE

Mental arithmetic, rhyming, and visualizing a walk lead to very different patterns of activity in the brain: One can see what people are thinking about. This figure shows blood circulation in the two brain hemispheres. (After Friberg and Roland)

out that there were major differences between the three types of thought. The last of the three is by far the most demanding, and indeed it demanded the most blood.

The amounts of blood concerned are not insignificant. Cerebral blood flow is increased more by thought than by tasks consisting of sensual perception or movement (although the blood flow in the body is of course increased during movement). In a study of how much cerebral metabolism increases during mental activity, Roland and his colleagues demonstrated that the oxygen metabolism of the brain (which is closely related to blood flow) could be increased by ten percent by thought.[23]

That is a very high percentage, because the brain already appropriates a large proportion of the body's overall resources: a fifth of its entire energy consumption.

No wonder we so often feel like a snack when we start pondering over a really tricky problem!

Lars Friberg has shown that there are major blood flow differences when people listen to tapes of spoken Danish played forward and backward. When the tape is played forward, the listening and language centers are activated along with other relevant centers in order to understand the message in what is being said. But when the tape is played backward, the entire brain is activated![24]

It is harder to understand a tape being played backward than one being played forward—indeed, we cannot understand the former. So the brain draws on much more energy in order to digest a backward tape. Because when the tape is played forward, we simply hear words understood in a particular context. The code is clear. Backward, and all you get is nonsense, very difficult to make any sense of.

But how does this relate to information theory? Surely the number of bits is the same whether you play the tape backward or forward? Well, that depends on who is listening.

If the listener understands the tape when it is played forward, he experiences only the bits the language is code for. That is far fewer bits than the total number present in the aural image.

But if he does not understand the tape, the number of bits is the same whether it is played backward or forward, because there are an equal number of differences in the aural image.

If you know that the tape is intelligible when it is played forward, there are fewer bits on the tape when it is played forward than when it is played backward. Knowing that the language on the tape is Danish means that there are fewer surprises in the aural image—less information. That is, if you happen to speak Danish.

More brainwork is required to digest the enormous quantities of information in a sound recording that yields no meaning than for a sound recording with meaning. There is more information in experiencing a mess than in experiencing order. Not because all the messy bits are not present in the clear message, but because the brain knows very well that it does not need to relate to all the messy bits when it hears ordinary speech. It has to relate to the words, and nothing else.

When we hear a message and in the everyday sense of the word perceive it as information, what this really proves is that there is not so much information present in the message as there might be: The pipe or channel we listen through contains far more details than we perceive when we perceive the message. But we ignore these details, because we know that what we have is a message and not some kind of cryptic code where we don't know what anything means.

The everyday notion of information is actually about discarded information: In everyday life we perceive messages as being rich in information because we do not need to note all the details, all the physical information, but can make do with a handful of differences.

The tape played backward, on the other hand, is not perceived as being rich in information in the everyday sense: It is just a collection of sound differences that has not been structured through the discarding of information. We perceive it not as information (even though in the physical sense there is stacks of it) but as a mess. Mess is so rich in structure as to appear structureless.

Our everyday notion of information bears upon the question "Is there a macrostate that will allow us to ignore a whole bunch of microstates?" If so, we understand the message we receive and do not need to expend so much brainpower digesting it. Less blood flow is required.

The concept of *understanding* is thereby linked to an objective physiological process. Lars Friberg and his colleagues have invented a method that, through the study of blood flow patterns, can decide objectively whether people understand Danish! Or, if you prefer, Navajo.

At a conference on blood flow studies in Copenhagen in 1990, many of the veterans of these studies discussed how this metabolic activity was to be understood. What actually causes the blood to flow to an area of the brain where something is going on?

Louis Sokoloff from the U.S. National Institute of Mental Health, a pioneer in the field, summarized that it is not the function of the nerve cell itself that sparks metabolic activity and thus a need for blood. It is the nerve cell's work in preparing for the next task that requires metabolism. That is to say, it is not the function the cell is performing that demands blood—it is preparation for the next task: being relieved of its waste products.

"The metabolic activation appears, therefore, to be associated not directly with the functional activity but with the recovery from the consequences of that activity," he explained.[25]

Just as the real problem for Maxwell's demon is not how to acquire knowledge of the whereabouts of the molecules but how to get rid of all that knowledge again.

Blood flow is actually a measure of all the information that has been discarded during a process. It is the necessary metabolism required to allow the nerve cell to forget what it just did.

Studies of cerebral energy metabolism are studies of the *work* the brain does. It is very important to realize that even internal mental activity, such as recalling the way a room is furnished, is a genuine physical and physiological activity, with clear links to perfectly tangible factors. Thought is a material event in the body that is in every way reminiscent of corporal activities such as movement.

There is no reason to consider thought as being different from the rest of what the body does. Thought requires calories just like tennis. So it is perfectly sensible to say there is a kind of tree in our heads when we are talking; we can measure and prove that something goes on in the heads of people who are talking to each other.

Perhaps the exformation concept is far less well defined than that of information; perhaps many years will pass before we can measure exformation. But it is very obvious that there are measurable physiological phenomena that involve the same states as those we refer to when we talk about a big tree or a small one (a lot or just a little exformation) behind a message.

There is meaning in talking about how much one has thought before one speaks. Concrete, physiological meaning. The time factor is still very poor in studies of blood flow in the brain, even though a range of methods have evolved. It is difficult to measure precisely events less than a minute long using these methods, so it is still difficult to study conversations and the thought process in detail. But in due course there can be no doubt that methods like these will assume the same high resolution in time as they currently enjoy in spatial terms, and it

will thus become possible to study when and where the blood flows
through the brain when we think, talk, and troll.

Yet although there is good physiological sense in maintaining that we
must think before we can speak, that does not answer the question as to
how we ever learn to talk in the first place. Where does it come from,
this ability to reconstruct information not actually present in the information we receive?

Children learn to talk—and to understand. It takes a few years, and
nobody has any idea how they do it. But we have all done it. We have
learned to understand what a horse is. We have learned to listen to stories about horses and to be able to picture what they are about.

Fairy tales are a good example. Children love having stories read to
them. They love hearing them again and again. While the grown-ups sit
with them, reading.

Children love hearing the same stories over and over again because
they are practicing understanding. Along with the grown-up they are
learning the noble art of associating. Of guessing at the mental state of
the author, packed with horses as it was, when he wrote the words.

It takes years of training to learn the peculiar maneuvers shown in
the sketch of the "tree of talking."

A tree shows how the narrator compresses a lot of information into
very little information. It passes downward on the left-hand side. Much
information becomes little information. Exformation is generated.
Then the little amount of information is transferred through the horizontal "pipe" and is received unchanged. The next problem is how to
associate outward and up the tree, and obtain all the associations
needed to picture the princess and the prince on the white horse.

Association tracks are laid down, patterns of recognition, which the
child loves practicing again and again.

But how can this be possible? How can the child guess its way to more
information than that present in the narrative? How can a tiny bit of
information set off an avalanche of the stuff? How can exformation in
the sender become the recollection of old information by the receiver?
Information (from previous experiences of horses) not present in the
receiver's consciousness here and now but which is then recalled?

How can information previously discarded from the consciousness
during association to an idea be excited again so that the narrator's

exformation provokes memories of previously discarded information in the receiver? How can one couple the sender's information to recalled, excited exformation in the receiver?

The only real answer is "go ask the kids." They are the only people capable of carrying out the unfathomable process of acquiring this ability. But we have all done so. We were all kids once. So even if we have forgotten how we acquired it, just as we have forgotten how we learned to ride a bike (but not how to ride one!), perhaps we can reconstruct part of what must have happened.

At any rate, we can say this much: There must have been more information present during the process than that in the words that were actually spoken. Otherwise we would never have been able to guess what we were meant to think about upon hearing words. After all, we surely cannot produce information in our heads just because we hear a word we have never heard before—such as "erecacoexecohonerenit"—can we?[26]

But children do learn. There must be something else present, something more than just the text, when it is read aloud. And indeed there is: a grown-up.

Little children can learn from grown-ups. Over and over.

There must, then, be something else present, something more than just words, in a context that can teach a child to speak. More than mere verbal information.

This leads to the question: Are there channels between the trees other than the oral one, and if so, how much information do they contain; is a conversation really only a stage setting for a far greater, far more real drama? Is talking the smallest part of conversation?

If this is so, we must prepare to face another unpleasant question: When we talk to one another, the talking is what we are aware of. It fills our consciousness. But if most of a conversation takes place beyond the talking, and the rest takes place in our heads, why are we not aware of it? How do our thoughts get sorted out before they emerge as speech? Is there a demon for sorting information?

Is consciousness only the tip of a mental iceberg? Is consciousness just as heartrendingly meager, and in all its self-importance just as helplessly comical, as information?

The answers must lie in the bits.

NEWSPAPER PRODUCTION

In every journalist's office, newspapers pile up: foreign papers, competitors, trade papers. Piles of them. Every single journalist reads stacks of newspapers every day. Or should do so but does not always get around to it, because information also has to be gleaned from other sources: meetings, phone calls, interviews, wire services.

Many articles from the other newspapers are condensed into one article for tomorrow's edition of the journalist's own newspaper. Oceans of information pass through his head but are rejected en route before he writes his own article.

An editorial team converts piles of newspapers into one newspaper. Mountains of printed matter are discarded in order to create one more for the pile, one that now contains enormous amounts of exformation, a wealth of discarded information. All this exformation is represented in the information in tomorrow's paper.

When the first copy of today's paper has been written and laid out, it is photographed so that the plates can be prepared. Then thousands of identical copies are printed from the plates. Information multiplied. Exformation expressed in information that can be copied.

The work of the journalist does not concern the number of copies printed. His work concerns only the number of other newspapers discarded along the way.

One copy of each of many different newspapers is condensed into many copies of one newspaper—that is what newspaper publishing is all about. But sometimes it is not true. Sometimes the journalist has not read the other newspapers. He has been lazy and guessed at what happened in Sri Lanka; he has read just a single paper. No need to check the story. His article will still run to the same number of column inches. His newspaper will be printed in just as many copies.

It is easy to see how much information a newspaper contains. One can simply count the letters. It is hard to see how much exformation is present. Terribly hard. But if one follows the newspaper over a period—and perhaps even reads other newspapers at the same time—one can begin to assess whether all the foreign newspapers the journalists discarded were actually read before they discarded them.

Information is visible. Exformation becomes visible only in a context: It is hard to measure complexity.

ROAD SIGN

A bend is approaching. The sign shows that in a moment the road will swing sharply to the left. It would be wise to slow down. Useful information which reflects the fact that an accident has occurred here: Last year a businessman ended up in a shopkeeper's garden because the road was too slippery for him to steer around the bend. A chicken was run over. But we do not wish to know all that; we simply assume that the easily digested information provided by the sign refers to a mass of information that is not present. We would not be able to take it in as we sped past, anyway. But we perceive the sign.

The figure on the sign is a map of the bend—highly stylized. Practically all that is left of the bend is that it bends. But that is enough in this context.

The road sign tells us very clearly that the person who had the sign put up knows a lot more about the bend than the sign reveals. There has been knowledge: This is announced by the fact that it is an authorized road sign. The sign tells us explicitly that it has come into existence during the conversion of information that is no longer present. That is what makes it a sign and not just a sheet of metal covered in paint.

CHAPTER 6

THE BANDWIDTH OF CONSCIOUSNESS

Of the thirty-four chapters in *Human Physiology*, Springer-Verlag's 825-page textbook for medical students, there is one whose final four and a half lines are set in italic type. It is unusual for such heavyweight textbooks to finish off a review of technical matters with a conclusion emphasized so markedly. Nevertheless, Professor Manfred Zimmermann, from the institute of physiology at Heidelberg University, did so in his chapter "The Nervous System in the Context of Information Theory." Not without reason; for the conclusion contains a fact that has been known for almost forty years, yet remains relatively unnoticed, even though it constitutes one of the most important testimonies we have about what it means to be human. Zimmermann writes:

"What we perceive at any moment, therefore, is limited to an extremely small compartment in the stream of information about our surroundings flowing in from the sense organs."[1]

In another textbook, Professor Zimmermann concludes a chapter on the same topic with the following words, this time not in italics:

"We can therefore conclude that the maximal information flow of the process of conscious sensory perception is about 40 bits/s[ec]—many orders of magnitude below that taken in by receptors [nerve endings]. Our perception, then, would appear to be limited to a minute part of the abundance of information available as sensory input."[2]

An astonishing number of textbooks in physiology and neuropsychology fail to mention this. Not because Zimmermann's analysis is original; it most definitely is not. It simply repeats a conclusion that was reached at the end of the 1950s and has been repeated sporadically in the literature of medical, psychological, and information theory ever since, though without making much of a mark either on physiology and neuropsychology or on our culture as a whole.

The fact is that every single second, millions of bits of information flood in through our senses. But our consciousness processes only perhaps forty bits a second—at most. Millions and millions of bits are condensed to a conscious experience that contains practically no information at all. Every single second, every one of us discards millions of bits in order to arrive at the special state known as consciousness. But in itself, consciousness has very little to do with information. Consciousness involves information that is not present; information that has disappeared along the way.

Consciousness is not about information but about its opposite: order. Consciousness is not a complex phenomenon; it is what consciousness is *about* that is complex.

It is presumably this fact that is the reason many scientists over the decades have tended to perceive information as something involving order and organization. Because consciousness is about an experience of order and organization. But consciousness is a state that does not process much information—consciously. Consciousness consists of information no more than a person who consumes large amounts of food can be said to consist of food. Consciousness is nourished by information the same way the body is nourished by food. But human beings do not consist of hot dogs; they consist of hot dogs that have been eaten. Consciousness does not consist of hot dogs but consists of hot dogs that have been apprehended. That is far less complex.

The thesis is extremely simple, at least when expressed in numbers. We can measure how much information enters through the senses. We do so simply by counting how many receptors each sensory organ possesses: how many visual cells the eye has, how many sensitive points the skin has, how many taste buds the tongue has. Then we can calculate how many nerve connections send signals to the brain, and how many signals each connection sends a second.

The numbers are vast. The eye sends at least ten million bits to the brain every second. The skin sends a million bits a second, the ear one hundred thousand, our smell sensors a further one hundred thousand bits a second, our taste buds perhaps a thousand bits a second.

All in all, over eleven million bits a second from the world to our sensory mechanisms.

But we experience far less: Consciousness processes far fewer bits. Over the decades, scientists have measured how much information the human consciousness can take in per second. This has been done in all kinds of ways, one of which is by measuring how many linguistic bits we can process when we read or listen. But language is not the only aspect studied. The ability to see and distinguish flashes of light, sense stimuli to the skin, tell different smells apart, and much more besides can be used in calculating that we consciously perceive about forty bits a second with our consciousness. A figure that may even be exaggerated.

Our sensory perception admits millions of bits a second; consciousness two score. The flow of information, measured in bits per second, is described as the *bandwidth* or *capacity* of consciousness. The bandwidth of consciousness is far lower than the bandwidth of our sensory perceptors.

In 1965, Dietrich Trincker, a German physiologist, gave a lecture on the occasion of the three hundredth anniversary of the founding of the University of Kiel, in which these figures are summarized in a useful rule of thumb: A million times more bits enter our heads than consciousness perceives.

"Of all the information that every second flows into our brains from our sensory organs, only a fraction arrives in our consciousness: the *ratio* of the capacity of *perception* to the capacity of *apperception* is at best a million to one," Trincker writes. "That is to say, only *one millionth* of what our eyes see, our ears hear, and our other senses inform us about *appears in our consciousness.*"

"Metaphorically," he continues, "consciousness is like a spotlight that emphasizes the face of one actor dramatically, while all the other persons, props, and sets on the vast stage are lost in the deepest darkness. The spotlight can move, certainly, but it takes a long time for all the faces in the chorus to be revealed, one after the other, in the darkness.

"It goes without saying that this newly discovered fact has the greatest practical significance for all areas of human life," Trincker writes.[3] He continues with a technical analysis of the background to the insight that only "an incredibly insignificant fraction" of our sensory experiences and memories can pass through our consciousness at any given moment.

Consciousness consists of discarded information far more than information present. There is hardly any information left in our consciousness. Or we can put it another way: Information is not a particularly good measure of consciousness. Information tells us no more about consciousness than the number of food calories required tells us about a ballerina's pirouettes.

But there must be information before consciousness can arise, just as the ballerina needs her breakfast.

It is peculiar that this fact, known so long, has gone so unnoticed. Presumably this is because of the spontaneous feeling of indignant huffiness that arises in our consciousness when we are made conscious of how little we are conscious of.

Precisely because from one instant to the next consciousness can switch from one object to another, it is not perceived as limited in its capacity. One moment you are aware of the lack of space in your shoes, the next moment of the expanding universe. Consciousness possesses peerless agility. But that does not change the fact that at *any given moment* you are not conscious of much at all.

Right now you may be aware of the words on this page, or your posture, or the phone call you are expecting, or the room you are sitting in, or the situation in Central Europe, or the noise in the background. But only one thing at a time. You can switch back and forth between events, processes, and facts that are widely disparate in time and space. The flow of what goes through your consciousness is limited only by the scope of your imagination. But there are limits to the volume of flow at any given moment, even though the next moment something quite different may be passing through.

No matter how simple these facts may appear, they do run counter to our intuitive perception of the capacity of consciousness as vast.

There are therefore good grounds for a thorough inspection of the knowledge that leads to the limited capacity of consciousness; for one thing, such an inspection leads to the conclusion that our consciousness processes far less information than forty bits a second. The correct figure is probably from one to sixteen bits a second. But this is so contraintuitive and confusing that it will take many chapters to unravel all the threads: *To be aware of an experience means that it has passed.*[4]

Close your eyes—no, not until you have read all the instructions—close your eyes, turn your head slightly so you are not looking down at the page. Then open your eyes for a fraction of a second, no more than a wink, and then close your eyes again and recall what you saw. Try it!

With practice, you can get pretty good at "capturing" the image for a moment while your consciousness "reads" it.

You can also try with your head turned in different directions. Try again.

The point is this: When you open your eyes for an instant, you see something. You see the lamp, for example. Or your rubber plant. Or a pile of books. Immediately. But while your eyes are still closed, you can also recall other things that appeared in your field of vision. Even though you no longer "see" the image, you can direct your consciousness around in it.

In other words, you see far more in that wink of an eye than you can be immediately aware of. You need lots of seconds, lots and lots of "moments," in order to read the image you captured in that wink of an eye. Consciousness cannot read the entire image while you are looking at it. You just manage to see "lamp"—it is only when you examine the picture in your mind's eye that you also see "plant" and "table" and "the other lamp."

Consciousness works slowly. It takes time to identify the various objects we have observed in a single glimpse. Consciousness cannot perceive all that we see at once.

Another experiment: Close the book, with your thumb marking this paragraph. Look at the front cover for a second or two. Note it. Look back at this paragraph. Try it!

What were you thinking about when you did this exercise? Remove your gaze from the book and consider what you thought about in the couple of seconds you were looking at the front cover. Do not think about the front cover (it could have been the plant too)—think about what you thought about. Reconstruct your thoughts. Take your time. Think hard!

It is true, is it not? You managed to think quite a lot in that couple of seconds! "What is he getting at?" "Why won't he let me read in peace?"

"This is like dissecting a play you've just seen!" "I don't like that front cover!" "I could do with an apple right now."

What you thought about is not what matters. The important thing is that it took you much longer to explain to yourself what you thought than it did to think it.

Consciousness is far slower than your inner mental life. More happens in your head than you know, unless you stop and think about it.

One last experiment: Close your eyes, and listen. When you've listened for a bit, try and hear how many sounds there are around you. Start by identifying them by source. Try it!

There were lots of sounds—traffic, people, birds, computer monitors, planes, radios, neighbors—or it was very quiet, just your own breath.

But there were sounds, and you could hear them all the time. When you "catch ear" (as in "catch sight") of them, you can hear that they have always been there. You just did not notice them. Most of the time, far more enters your ears and your head than you realize.

These experiments are ordinary, simple self-observations. You can come up with more like them.[5] (Notice how the body senses your leg position, the tightness of your waistband, the room temperature, the taste in your mouth, the elevation of your eyebrows, the declension of your lower jaw, the rounding of your shoulders, the smell in here; and how are your feet today?) All these exercises require no more of you than moving your attention around your body or your surroundings or the inside of your skull.

The point of the experiments is simple: There is a lot more experience available to you than you immediately experience. You can elect to move your attention about and thus become aware of something you have always sensed was there. You can see the light, hear the noise, notice your clothing, register your posture, smell the odor, or sense the heat. If you want to. Or not, as the case may be. You can direct your attention where you like.

There is certainly plenty of choice. Your consciousness is not identical to what your senses perceive. You sense far more than you are conscious of. Whether you want to or not.

So it is perhaps not so surprising that consciousness takes in far fewer bits per second than the senses. Imagine having to think about everything all the time! We would not be able to notice anything at all! There is a character of unity about consciousness. We are conscious of one thing at a time, or we are conscious of one sensory modality at a time—one kind of sense: hearing, seeing, feeling, or tasting.

When we are aware of an object outside ourselves, we use all our senses at once and combine information from them all, without being aware of the individual sensory modalities. But if we have to *listen* for a moment, we shut our other senses out of our consciousness. We close our eyes in order to listen hard. We can direct our attention and consciousness at an object or at a sensory modality: all our senses at one thing, or one sense at everything.

But surely we can be conscious of more than just one thing at a time?

The measuring of the number of bits that flow through our consciousness every second started from questions like this. It began a few years after Claude Shannon proposed his theory of communication and information. Wendell Garner and Harold Hake, two psychologists from Johns Hopkins University in the United States, published a study of our ability to distinguish stimuli—such as light or sound—measured in bits.[6] In the years that followed, a whole series of studies emerged on how much information the human consciousness can process.

Some of the results were summarized in 1956 by the formulation of the key concept of "the magical number seven"—a number we have known about for ages.

In the last century, Sir William Hamilton, the Scottish philosopher, wrote, "If you throw a handful of marbles on the floor, you will find it difficult to view at once more than six, or seven at most, without confusion."[7]

In March 1956, the psychologist George A. Miller published an article in *Psychological Review* in which a large number of anecdotes and scientific observations were summarized into an elegant presentation entitled "The Magical Number Seven, Plus or Minus Two: Some Limits on Our Capacity for Processing Information." Miller began as follows:

"My problem is that I have been persecuted by an integer. For seven years this number has followed me around, has intruded in my most private data, and has assaulted me from the pages of our public journals."[8]

The integer Miller found everywhere was seven. Seven plus-or-minus-two. The expression "plus-or-minus-two" is scientific jargon for a number subject to some uncertainty: seven plus-or-minus-two means a number somewhere between five and nine.

Humans can keep seven different words, numbers, terms, sounds, phonemes, impressions, or thoughts in their head at once. When they really put their mind to it.

It is not difficult to keep four different items in our head at once; five, and it gets difficult; six ... seven ... We find ourselves in a real mess once we get to ten.

"There seems to be some limitation built into us either by learning or by the design of our nervous systems, a limit that keeps our channel capacities in this general range," Miller wrote.[9]

Of course, this does not mean we cannot digest more than seven things at a time. But it does mean that if we do, we cease to understand them as individual items and start perceiving them as an entity.

E-n-t-i-t-y. You did not read the word the way you did when you first learned to read. You read the word "entity" as an entity. As a composite picture. Otherwise you would not be able to misspell at all—or ignore typos in a manuscipt. (Did you notice there was a typo before you noticed which letter was missing?)

This phenomenon is called "chunking," and it is necessary in order for us to be able to read, for example—or take in a crowd. Or tell the wood from the trees.

We do not have to go further than a handful of items before we perceive them as one mass. With all the thermodynamics we have already been through in this book, it is natural to say that seven microstates is enough for us to prefer to make a macrostate.

Conversely, if we say "that marble"—and we know that it is one of the seven we are thinking about—we can say how many bits the observation contains. After all, if we can distinguish among seven marbles, it means we have seven different states in our head at once. How many bits is that?

The bit is the unit of measurement for information that expresses our ability to distinguish among differences. Information is defined as the logarithm of the number of microstates combined in a macrostate. Since we can perceive seven objects or seven different states, let us take the logarithm for seven. We are talking about the so-called binary logarithm used in information theory, so the question we must now ask is: "How many times does two have to be multiplied by itself to make seven?" Two times two is four, as we know, while two times two times two is eight. So log 7 is somewhere between two and three; more precisely, it is 2.8.

Miller argued that our ability to process information is therefore great enough for us to be able to keep 2.8 bits in our consciousness at once. Now, that is not much!

After all, we could have had seven binary digits in our head: 0100101. That is seven bits. (But you have to practice a little before you can keep seven binary numbers in your head at a time.) That is to say, we can have more than 2.8 bits in our consciousness at once if we remember seven binary digits.

Or seven letters: TIYRFIO. Each letter in the alphabet contains an average of almost five bits, because it is one of twenty-six possible letters, so seven items can easily be more than 2.8 bits. In this case, seven times five bits, or thirty-five bits. (Strictly speaking, this is true only if the string of letters is random, as in the above example. If we take a normal word, the bit content is lower, because there is redundancy in the language.)

In other words, symbols are smart. They help us remember masses of information, even though we can keep only seven things in our minds at once. Symbols are the Trojan horses by which we smuggle bits into our consciousness.

"Our memories are limited by the number of units or symbols we must master, and not by the amount of information that these symbols represent. Thus it is helpful to organize material intelligently before we try to memorize it," Miller wrote.[10]

But there is an alternative to the intelligent organization of material: learning parrot fashion, by rote memory. Plenty of people are able to memorize the most impressive amounts of numbers, words, and train times, even outside the exam season. In order, and almost without stopping to breathe.

But the existence of such mnemonic techniques does not conflict with Miller's magical number seven. These techniques consist of forming chains of units so that one unit can pull the next one behind it, and so on. An actor can use a prompter even though the prompter does not read the entire play for him. A key word is enough—then the chain starts moving again.

A combination of intelligence and learning by rote is especially useful when you make a speech, for example. An overall structure of what you have to remember leads down to the individual elements, organized into a tree of ever-increasing detail. But this presupposes a certain "temperature"—tolerance—in the details: It is far harder to memorize a text one understands perfectly well *completely* by heart, so that you do not put so much as a comma wrong, than to memorize it sufficiently to relate it without every single word being exactly where it was in the original.

If you have to memorize only a few overall ideas and sequences but not every single word, you need to retain fewer units in your head. But if every single detail has to be correct, it is harder. The larger the number of permissible microstates consistent with the seven main points of your speech that you can remember (and seven subheadings you can remember when you are on each main point), the easier it will be. It is important to have entropy in the macrostates: They must permit many different microstates.

An outline is good if it contains macrostates with high entropy: lots of possible microstates for each macrostate. An outline is bad, brittle, if it can be implemented only by a single correct flow of words, because every single transition has to be formulated correctly in order to work.

Intelligence is thus not about remembering lots of microstates at once in sequence. Intelligence is about being able to see which macrostates best combine all the microstates.

The trick with intelligence is not to be able to account for a load of information but to be able to account for a load of exformation: information deliberately discarded, compressed into notions encompassing the vast exformation.

Such compressions of large amounts of information into a few exformation-rich macrostates with small quantities of nominal information are not only intelligent; they are often very beautiful; yes, even sexy. Seeing a jumble of confused data and shreds of rote learning compressed into a concise, clear message can be a real turn-on.

The laws of nature are examples of such compressions. Maxwell's equations are perhaps the most beautiful of them all.

Beauty, elegance, ease, and laid-backness are linked: Saying a lot in a few words or signs or movements or looks or caresses—now, *that* is beautiful, clear, and cathartic.

The headiness of attaining high, clear awareness is a matter of this simplicity of beauty: everything that is not present, but is not gone either. Consciousness as it breathes information and exformation.

Miller's magical seven from 1956 was the result of a combination of many investigations carried out in the wake of Shannon's formulation of information theory in 1948. Now that we have the unifying concept, we should look at just what it sums up. Lots of different kinds of distinguishing were measured in order to find out how much information the human consciousness could process. Distinguishing between points on a line, musical intervals, volumes, and tastes. There is no reason to go into all the details, so we will summarize in a small table the results of widely different experiments, to see how small the differences really are:

EARLY PSYCHOPHYSICAL MEASUREMENTS OF THE ABILITY TO DISTINGUISH[11]

YEAR	SCIENTISTS	DISTINGUISHING BETWEEN	BITS/DISTINCTION
1951	Garner & Hake	Points on a scale	3,2
1952	Pollack	Pitch	2,2
1953	Garner	Loudness	2,1
1954	Eriksen & Hake	The size of little squares	2,2
1954	McGill	Points on a scale	3,0
1955	Attneave	Pitch/Orchestra leader	5,5
1955	Beebe	Sugar concentrations	1,0
1953	Klemmer & Frick	Points on surfaces	4,4
1954	Pollack & Frick	Musical pitch, dynamics	7,0

We can see Miller's magical number seven (of which the logarithm is 2.8) in the table. Apart from the orchestra leader, people can distinguish only about four to eight things from each other (two to three bits)—apart from cases where several dimensions are involved: By finding points on a surface, one expresses more information than by finding a point on a line. But it is also harder, so there are not twice as many bits in the ability to distinguish. There are more bits in distinguishing between the pitch of notes and their volume simultaneously than pitch alone. This corresponds to the fact that telling marbles apart is not the same as distinguishing among binary numbers or letters.

But it also gets more and more difficult the more dimensions there are that describe the states one has to distinguish between. It is really only when we know the context that these figures mean anything: Someone who had never heard of the Roman alphabet would probably not distinguish between an A and an Å.

Karl Steinbuch, a German engineer, points out that six letters can form part of a word and thus not much more than ten bits (because each letter in the language contains one–two bits); six letters may also be six signs from the alphabet irrespective of their semantic meaning, and if so, we would have five bits per letter for an alphabet consisting of twenty-nine letters, such as the Danish—i.e., thirty bits in total; but one could also read the letters as ink spots on the paper—and then, Steinbuch calculates, one would see two hundred dots, yielding twelve hundred bits for the six letters.[12]

But it does not take equal lengths of time to study six letters in those different ways. There is a difference between reading the word as the entity "entity"; reading the letters constituting it: "e-n-t makes ent, i-t-y makes ity . . ."; and, rather than reading, studying the typographical details such as the stem thickness of the t.

So we have to combine the study of how many signs we can keep in our heads at one time with the time factor: What we are really looking for is the number of bits consciousness can process per second.

But this, too, was studied in the wake of Shannon's 1948 theory.

In 1952, Edmund Hick, from the Laboratory of Applied Psychology in Cambridge, England, undertook a study of a subject acting as a communication channel. The subject looked at a number of flashing lights and had to press one of several keys in order to indicate which lamp was flashing. How quickly could the experimenters send information through such a subject without his making mistakes? They found that 5.5 bits per second could be transmitted without errors resulting.

In a variation of the experiment, the subject was asked to react more rapidly even if it meant mistakes. This resulted in more decisions per second: The keys were pushed more frequently. But errors crept in. Speed increased, but so did the error rate. The increase in errors balanced out the time gain.

The speed of 5.5 bits a second was constant, irrespective of whether it occurred slowly and error-free or rapidly with errors. The 5.5 bits a second seem to be a ceiling to the speed with which a human being can transfer information in Hick's experiment.[13]

Many years later, Hick's experiment received this comment: "There is, however, a deep problem for this or any other technique for measuring the bit rate for the human nervous system—for we are never quite limited to the alternatives provided by the experimenter." So Richard Gregory, a prominent English experimental psychologist, wrote in his *Oxford Companion to the Mind* (1987). He continued, "Thus, the subject in Hick's experiment (actually the editor of this *Companion to the Mind!*) was not deaf, or blind, to everything except the lights to which he was responding, so that his range of possibilities was always greater than the experimenter knew, or could take into account."[14]

Perhaps humans can process more than 5.5 bits a second, but not if it involves something as boring as flashing lights!

Piano playing was the subject of a study carried out by an American, Henry Quastler, and published in 1956. It turns out that the piano player can manage about 4.5 hits a second, or twenty-two bits (there were thirty-seven keys). "Informal estimates of the rate of information transmitted by a good proof-reader and by a good tennis player gave the same result, about 25 bits/sec," Quastler wrote. His study was presented at an information theory symposium in London in September 1955. The minutes indicate that after Quastler's paper, Benoit Mandelbrot, the mathematician who achieved world fame decades later for his work on fractals—mathematical objects of sublime beauty—put a question to him: "Is there any estimate of the capacity of a human being while searching his own memory?" Quastler's reply: "We tried [such] a study using as data performances in a quiz programme where subjects had to name a tune as fast as they could. They processed about 3 bits/sec, counting from the moment the music started to play."[15]

"I have read a good deal more about information theory and psychology than I can or care to remember," wrote the Bell Labs engineer John R. Pierce in his book *Symbols, Signals and Noise.*[16]

John Pierce does not like the extensive literature attempting to measure bit rates. But after summarizing the measurements of Hick and others, he presents his own ideas on the issue. By really squeezing the guinea pigs till they squeak, in a series of studies undertaken with J. E. Karlin in 1957, Pierce ends up on forty-four bits a second. But he needs letters to do so.

"These experiments gave the highest information rate which has been demonstrated,"[17] Pierce writes, but he is not satisfied. "What, we may ask, limits the rate?"

To the communications engineer, these results are very disturbing. A TV channel can transmit four million bits a second. A telephone four thousand. John Pierce and his employer make their living by selling people telephone systems capable of transmitting thousands of bits a second, but the human consciousness cannot perceive more than 40 bits/sec!

Are we using a sledgehammer to crack nuts when we put up our telephone poles?

"Now, both Miller's 7 plus-or-minus-2 rule and the reading rate experiments have embarrassing implications," writes Pierce. "If a man can transmit only about 40 bits of information per second, as the reading rate experiments indicate, can we transmit TV or voice of satisfactory quality using only 40 bits per second?

"I believe the answer to be no. What is wrong? What is wrong is that we have measured what gets out of the human being, not what goes in. Perhaps a human being can in some cases only notice 40 bits a second worth of information, but he has a choice as to what he notices. He might, for instance, notice the girl or he might notice the dress. Perhaps he notices more, but it gets away from him before he can describe it."[18]

The telephone engineer is forced to realize that there is more to man than consciousness is aware of; otherwise there would be no reason to make such high-quality telephones. The human consciousness can express the experience of only very few bits a second. But that is not to say we do not experience more than that. Consciousness is a measure of but a very small portion of what our senses perceive.

In the late 1950s and early 1960s, Karl Küpfmüller, a professor at the technical university in Darmstadt, made a number of reviews of how much information goes in and out of people. His measurements of what goes in lie between 10 million and 100 million bits/sec, while what goes out through consciousness is far lower.

Based on the studies mentioned above and estimates from German scientists, Küpfmüller arrived at the following table of what consciousness can handle:

CONSCIOUS PROCESSING OF INFORMATION[19]

ACTIVITY	BITS/SEC
Silent reading	45
Reading aloud	30
Proofreading	18
Typewriting	16
Piano playing	23
Multiplying and adding two numbers	12
Counting objects	3

Küpfmüller's figures correspond to the use of normal speech. People making radio programs use as a rule of thumb that it takes 2.5 minutes to read a page aloud. A page contains forty lines, each sixty characters long. That is 2,400 characters in 150 seconds, or an average of sixteen a second. On average, a character contains two bits, so that is 32 bits/sec. Reading aloud entails more than just characters, so if we round up the number of bits to account for rhythm, intonation, pitch, etc., we arrive at a figure like Pierce's 40 bits/sec. Always supposing that it is meaningful to measure the flow of information according to its letters.

Karl Küpfmüller sums up the numbers: "All the instances in the human organism that take part in processing messages seem to be designed to the upper limit of 50 bits/sec."[20]

It is remarkable that roughly the same number of bits can go in and get out of the system: Whether we are reading or writing, the bandwidth of language is about the same.

Simultaneously with Küpfmüller, Professor Helmuth Frank, from the Institute of Cybernetics at the Pädagogischen Hochschule, Berlin, also published studies of the capacity of consciousness.

Frank based his work on a more theoretical point of view and arrived at a slightly lower figure, *sixteen bits a second.* The major difference between the two Germans was that Küpfmüller collected empirical data, while Frank used the idea that "the maximal central information flow" should be regarded as a general property expressed through the various skills. Frank's image is of a fixed capacity of consciousness, which finds expression in the skills that can be measured by various psychophysical methods.

Helmuth Frank has very elegant arguments in favor of a capacity or bandwidth of consciousness of 16 bits/sec: He operates with a subjective time quantum, or *SZQ (subjektives Zeitquant),* which denotes *a psychological moment.* It is the smallest space of time we can experience: the temporal resolution ability in human perception.

Frank points out that the human ear picks up pulses of sound that arrive at a frequency of under sixteen a second as ... pulses. But if there are more than sixteen a second, the ear hears something completely different: a continuous tone. The same goes for images: If fewer than sixteen frames a second flicker past the eye, we see flickering images; when more than sixteen–eighteen frames are presented each second, we see not flickering but moving images.[21] There are twenty-four frames in a second of film, twenty-five or thirty in TV.

Against the background of observations like these and many others, Frank considers he can define an SZQ with a duration of exactly one-sixteenth of a second. In other words, we experience sixteen SZQs a second when our mental functions are at their peak in late adolescence. With age, the moments grow longer, and there are fewer of them per second.

The duration of an SZQ also varies from organism to organism: A snail is said to have an SZQ of a quarter of a second.[22]

The capacity of consciousness is thus established in simple fashion: One can process exactly one bit per SZQ. So a person at his true prime has a bandwidth of 16 bits/sec.[23]

Frank's views have been further developed by his pupil Siegfried Lehrl and are being applied today in research into intelligence as linked to concepts like reaction time and mental agility. For decades, besides Lehrl, two of the most controversial personalities in the debate linking intelligence to genetics and surroundings have been trying to couple the notion of intelligence to reaction time: H. J. Eysenck from London and Arthur Jensen from California.[24]

In 1985, Siegfried Lehrl, from the Psychiatric University Clinic in Erlangen, and Bernd Fischer, from Baden, listed the differences be-

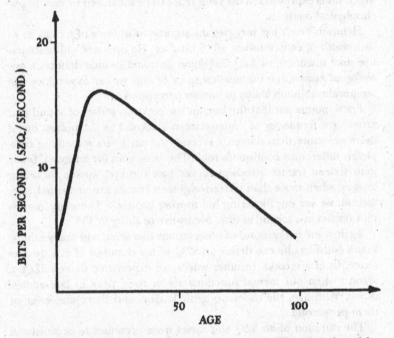

The bandwidth of consciousness compared to age. The bandwidth peaks in late adolescence, where we experience 16 SZQ (subjective time quanta) per second. (After Frank and Riedel)

tween the views we find in Küpfmüller and Frank, with the excitable criticism characteristic of closely related academic traditions. Since they're pupils of Frank, there is little doubt as to whose side they are on, even though the title of their article in *Humankybernetik* restricts itself to raising the question "The Maximal Central Information Flow According to Küpfmüller or Frank: Is It 50 Bit/s or 16 Bit/s?" But as early as the subtitle of the article, we see the temperament that one often encounters in academic debate: "On the Use and Harm of Küpfmüller's Assessments for the Spreading of Information Psychology." The two scientists conclude, "The tragedy of Küpfmüller's publication consists in its initial positive effect on psychologists because their interests were drawn to the fact that cognitive variables are quantifiable by information theoretical methods. On the other hand, however, it implicitly presented arguments against the generality of bandwidth of information flow. By this the use of the conception has been made dubious. Thus Küpfmüller probably has contributed considerably to the later decreasing interest of psychologists in information psychology."[25]

Research into this matter practically came to a halt. Neither the British nor the American analyses from the 1950s or Küpfmüller's and Frank's analyses from the early 1960s were followed up. In a 1969 summary, E. R. F..W. Crossman, a British psychologist, wrote, "These procedures were exploited energetically in the decade after Shannon's work first attracted notice. However, once the main areas had been mapped out the impetus seems to have subsided."[26]

Very few studies of any significance have been published since the early 1960s. Considering the importance of the profoundly shocking insights these studies revealed, it is a mystery why the field has been allowed to die out.

This is hardly something for which we can reproach Küpfmüller or other individual researchers in the field. But it is a mystery worth keeping an eye on. We will be returning to it in the next chapter.

But there are good grounds for believing that many assessments of the capacity of consciousness actually put the figure too high: Skills are measured that process information, but not in a conscious fashion. A typesetter can set a passage of text flawlessly, even if he has no idea what it is about. One can play the piano without being aware of what one is doing. Indeed, there are many skills that we best exercise when we do not think about what we are doing.

In August 1975, three Cornell University psychologists, Elizabeth Spelke, William Hirst, and Ulric Neisser, presented a study to the American Psychological Association. Two young adults, Diane and John, recruited via the student job exchange, had had to read short stories while taking dictation—that is, they had to simultaneously read a text and write down words that were dictated to them. Initially they were not very good at it, but after a few weeks of practice the picture was quite different. "Diane and John appear able to copy words, detect relations among words, and categorize words for meaning, while reading as effectively and as rapidly as they can read alone. What accounts for their surprising abilities?" Spelke, Hirst, and Neisser asked.[27]

The explanation is that many fairly advanced activities can be carried out "automatically"—i.e., without summoning awareness. But a learning period is required. We can render our skills automatic, but we have to practice first. Or as Spelke, Hirst, and Neisser wrote, "People's ability to develop skills in specialized situations is so great that it may never be possible to define general limits on cognitive capacity."[28]

When you have acquired a skill to the degree that it has become automatic, you can process very large quantities of information in a nontrivial way without your consciousness being involved. This is something familiar to most of us from everyday life—driving in traffic, for example.

This goes to show that we must be careful not to overestimate the quantity of information processed when we study the capacity of consciousness. Just because an automatic skill means grappling with large quantities of information in a meaningful way, this does not mean the information has been present in our consciousness.

Many of the measurements of the capacity of consciousness come from activities that are acquired skills performed partly automatically and from the recognition of patterns in pictures of letters and numbers. So lots of bits creep into the behavior of the subjects even though they are not present in consciousness.

Studies of consciousness therefore overestimate the abilities of consciousness if they fail to take account of such Trojan horses, where bits are smuggled through the person without being discovered by his consciousness. So the figure for the capacity of consciousness is presumably far lower than 40 bits/sec. A better figure would be 16 bits/sec, but this may also be exaggerated. In reality, the normal capacity of consciousness may be only a few bits a second.

But it really does not matter. What matters is that we admit far more bits to our heads than we ever become conscious of.

Richard Jung, a prominent German neuropsychologist, from Freiburg University, summed up the lessons from Frank, Küpfmüller, and others as follows: "All these numbers are approximations. . . . Although the authors differ in one or two log units they all agree about the reduced information of consciousness."[29]

We can apply Manfred Zimmermann's summary of the figures from his textbook *Human Physiology*:

INFORMATION FLOW IN SENSORY SYSTEMS AND CONSCIOUS PERCEPTION[30]

SENSORY SYSTEM	TOTAL BANDWIDTH (BITS/S)	CONSCIOUS BANDWIDTH (BITS/S)
Eyes	10,000,000	40
Ears	100,000	30
Skin	1,000,000	5
Taste	1,000	1
Smell	100,000	1

A pretty powerful computer is required: Every single second, many millions of bits have to be compressed into a handful. This allows us to be conscious of what is going on around us without necessarily being distracted by it if it is not important.

But how big does the computer actually have to be in order to undertake the enormous discarding of information that ends in a conscious experience? It must necessarily be able to process more information than just the eleven million bits we take in through our senses. After all, it has to do the bodily housekeeping too—and create all the weird and wonderful images and ideas we have inside us. Measurements of the channel capacity of the brain are harder to undertake experimentally, but we can estimate the magnitude.

Karl Küpfmüller arrives at a figure of ten billion bits a second, or far more than we take in from our surroundings. He calculates the number of nerve cells at ten billion, each of which can process one bit per second. His figures are very conservative: There are more like a hundred billion nerve cells, each equipped with an average of ten thousand connections to other nerve cells and thus able to handle more than one bit/sec. But no matter how high the precise figure, these figures really are what you could call astronomical. There are maybe a hundred billion stars in the Milky Way—and for each of them we have a nerve cell in our head. The number of connections is beyond comprehension: a million billion links between these hundred billion cells.

From this massive array we receive a conscious experience containing maybe ten–thirty bits a second!

From the brain's point of view, just as much goes in as comes out again: There are roughly as many nerve connections *from* the sensory organs as there are nerve connections *to* the motion organs. Küpfmüller puts the figures at three million nerve connections sending information to the brain (from the senses and the body), while one million go the other way. They all end up in motion aimed at ensuring quality of life, including survival.

If we try to measure how many bits there are in what people express to their surroundings, we get a number lower than 50 bits/sec. The value of what we do is greater, but seen from the point of view of human consciousness, we cannot talk, dance, or shout our way to more than 50 bits/sec.

An overall picture of the information flow through us, drawn by Küpfmüller in 1971, looks like this:[31]

The remarkable thing is that the brain receives an enormous amount of information at a high bandwidth but is nevertheless able to process far more information than it receives. It then releases another quantity of information to the rest of the body, of roughly the same size as the amount it takes in. Fair enough. But our consciousness does not get told much at all about what is going on!

These figures express a number of fairly mundane everyday experiences in a way which may seem pretty disturbing:

Most of what we experience, we can never tell each other about: We experience millions of bits a second but can tell each other about only a few dozen.

Even if we talked nonstop (which some of us tend to do), we could not recount very much of what our senses actually take in.

But we can recount everything we are conscious of. All we can do is hope it is the most important bit.

As far as our conscious linguistic togetherness is concerned, we are all in a state of radical solitude. But all of us are in the same boat; we are not alone in our solitude. This solitude is a condition that applies to us all, and one we can talk about. We share a heartrending silence—we can share the experience that through language we are unable to share most of what we experience.

The tree of talking is an attempt to express these relationships. We can now quantify what happens when we talk. Our actual conversation takes place at a very low bit rate, but the mental and sensory processes

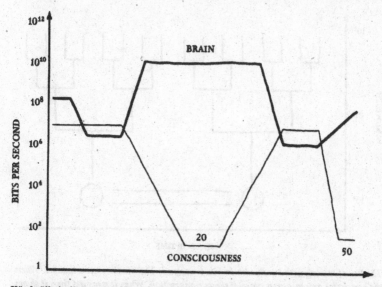

Küpfmüller's diagram of the information flow through a human being: from the senses through the brain (and consciousness) to the motor apparatus. The thick line shows how many million bits from the senses are sent via nerve connections to the brain, which has a very high bandwidth. From the brain the information is sent to the body, which manages about the same amount of information as the senses receive. The thin line shows how consciousness processes only a very little proportion of this information.

we are talking about take place at a far, far higher rate. In some way or other, we can summarize, map, or compress all these experiences in our speech—a compression that is already necessary for consciousness to exist at all.

A child having a story read to her does not make use solely of her linguistic channel. Words and their pronunciation are not all that enter her brain. She also experiences her parent's whole body and its expression: smells, sights, and sounds that tell her how her parent is experiencing the story. There is a vast amount of nonverbal communication present.

The body reveals a great deal that the words do not necessarily express. Thus the child can learn what *tension* is, whose side to be on,

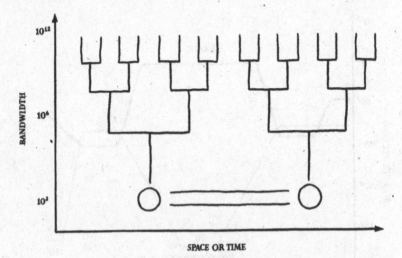

The tree of talking with bandwidth in bits per second. The numbers are estimated. When the horizontal axis measures space, it shows conversation. When it measures time, it shows recollection.

express. Thus the child can learn what *tension* is, whose side to be on, that there are good guys and bad guys, rescuers and jailers.

Children love repetition. Not because they think there is much information in a story; after all, there is not. There is far less information in a children's book, measured in letters, than in a book for grown-ups. Children love repetition because it allows them to relive the real drama of the text: the *excitation* of information in the listener's head. Again and again they can *imagine* the prince, the princess, and Donald Duck. They can think their way to what is going on in the story.

Fairy tales train attractors—meaning-magnets, notions that draw stories into them. The child learns a whole range of basic plots, learns the significance of heroes and villains, helpers and opponents, minor roles and major ones, action and wisdom, tension and release. But the best thing of all is doing so with an adult! Being able to sense the change in his breathing when the action intensifies, the slight sweat as the dragon breathes fire. Again and again! Information processed to exformation: the nominal value of the text processed into the parent's inner exformation—information about real events now discarded and forgotten but that nevertheless left strange traces in the mind, which are roused when you hear the story of the bold prince.

Great storytellers like Hans Christian Andersen or Karen Blixen are masters of knowing precisely which attractors are to be found in the mind: at playing on precisely those inner pictures that are the most fundamental, archetypal, and dynamic in any mind, young or old.

They are masters at staging plots that use very small amounts of information to make the entire register of previously produced exformation grow forth in people's heads—in children and adults alike. Their mastery links the story to the archetypal imaginings we have in our heads. Such primordial pictures were first discussed by the psychoanalyst C. J. Jung. A Danish pupil of his, Eigil Nyborg, pointed out in a pioneering analysis of the fairy tales of Hans Christian Andersen in 1962 that "Any viable work of poetry (and work of art in general) rests on archetypal foundations."[32]

Fairy tales are not meant only for children, you see. If they were, they would not work. For the true power of the fairy tale comes because children and grown-ups can together experience the wonder of the narrative: that a text with so little information can raise a tree of empathy in the mind of the reader or the listener.

Children's books only for children are not good for reading aloud. They do not give the child the opportunity to experience the parent as a control of what can be experienced through such a story. Having them repeated is no fun, because they do not inspire the parent: They do not excite anything in the adult mind. (The problem of comics like Tintin and Donald Duck—which many adults do not enjoy reading aloud—is presumably of another kind: There is so much information in the illustrations that it is hard to coordinate trees.)

Similarly, adult art and adult popular art are well suited to "inspiring" our mental activity. Going to the cinema with someone we want to get to know is a good idea. Not that the film needs to be anything special, but because it is good to see whether you "swing together" in the darkened auditorium: whether trees grow in our heads capable of strengthening each other, whether we can sense each other's inner mental state and feel togetherness around an experience—wretched as it may be—of stars on a silver screen.

The dramatic increase in our use of media may distance people and lead to impoverishment. But it also gives us new opportunities to share nonverbal experiences, to sense each other's physical reactions to a text or a movie. To perceive each other's trees.

Stories read aloud are a matter not of words but of what words do to people. Live concerts are not about music but about what that music does to people. Football matches watched at the stadium are not about football but about what football does to people.

Television isolates us during the act of experiencing. But it also creates a vast fellowship: the knowledge that millions of people are feeling that same headiness at the very same instant. However, something is lacking if one sits alone in front of one's television set and never talks to anyone about what one sees. A physical experience is lacking: the recognition of other people. A sense that information takes on meaning only when it is perceived by a human being.

If we combine Küpfmüller's graph with the tree of talking from the previous chapter, this is what we get:

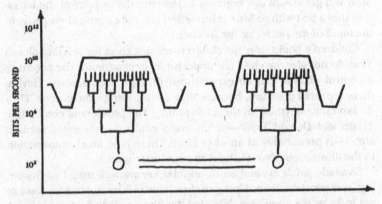

The tree of talking incorporated into Küpfmüller's diagram. Two people converse over a low bandwidth, but each has a tree in his head. The tree grows toward the high bandwidth given for the brain in Küpfmüller's diagram.

Remarkably, there may be other communications channels present, not just that of language or the communications channel of consciousness with such a low capacity. Why can we not communicate at higher rates—through eye contact, for example? Well, we can—and that is really what makes conversation possible at all.

The American anthropologist and cyberneticist Gregory Bateson, the originator of the saying "Information is the difference that makes a difference," has also described the limited bandwidth of consciousness. Bateson talks of a paralinguistic domain, *kinesics*, which involves bodily communication: We say a great deal not said in words.

"As mammals we are familiar with, though largely unconscious of, the habit of communicating about our relationships," Bateson wrote in 1966 in an article on the difficulties of communicating with dolphins. "Like other terrestrial mammals, we do most of our communicating on this subject by means of kinesic [movement] and paralinguistic signals, such as bodily movements, involuntary tensions of voluntary muscles, changes of facial expression, hesitations, shifts in tempo of speech or movement, overtones of the voice, and irregularities of expression. If you want to know what the bark of a dog 'means,' you look at his lips, the hair on the back of his neck, his tail, and so on. These 'expressive' parts of his body tell you at what object of the environment he is barking, and what patterns of relationship to that object he is likely to follow in the next few seconds. Above all, you look at his sense organs; his eyes, his ears, and his nose."[33]

The problem is that in practice we humans do not wish to admit that we are animals: We think our consciousness is identical with ourselves. So we tend to believe that everything we say lies in the words. We take ourselves very literally. We think information is the important part of a conversation.

In the 1950s, Gregory Bateson's pioneering studies of the many levels of communication led to a series of insights, the most important of which was the double-bind theory for schizophrenia, the group of psychiatric disturbances where the patient experiences a loss of control over his mental processes and will (a "split personality," for example). A schizophrenic often takes a statement *very* literally:

"If you tell a schizophrenic to 'clear his mind' before making a decision, for example, he may well go and stick his head under the tap," the psychologist Bent Ølgaard writes in a book on Bateson's communication theory, "and a schizophrenic patient is quoted as sitting on his bed with his feet on the floor for several days because he was afraid of losing his grounding."[34]

In the language of this book, schizophrenics have trouble with exformation. They cannot guess at the exformation implicit in a message: They understand the message literally and take the information at its face value.

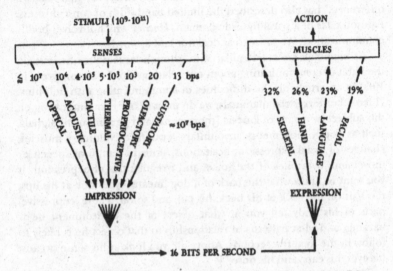

An overview of the information flow through a human being, drawn up by the Erlangen School (Frank, Lehrl, et al.). A so-called organogram. Just as Küpfmüller's diagram it shows that more information goes in and out of humans than consciousness perceives.

Bateson's idea is to explain the origin of such schizophrenic behavior in the double bind of childhood: With his body, the parent says the opposite of the words he speaks. Over and over, the child experiences the grown-up's lying. This puts the child in an impossible situation: If he takes the words at face value, he must lie to himself, because he clearly senses the parent's contradictory message. Maybe the message in words is that the child should go to bed for his own sake, but what the grown-up is expressing through his entire body and manner of speaking is that the kid should go to bed for the *grown-up's* sake.

The impossible situation in which the child has to choose between believing the grown-up's words and trusting his own feelings can lead to a dilemma in which the coherence in the way the child perceives his own feelings begins to crumble. According to Bateson's model, this may end in schizophrenia.

Bateson's double-bind model is a fundamental element in many traditions of psychotherapy—and more or less relevant to the description of most people's childhood. The characteristic experience that it is just as difficult to lie to children on emotional matters as it is easy to lie to them on intellectual ones indicates that children have not "grown out of" a fundamental knowledge that the body speaks more than words. (However, they have not discovered that many intellectual assertions take place only in consciousness and so do not find expression in body language.)

But it is not only a phenomenon with relevance to our understanding of psychiatric diseases. It is true of everybody that the languages our bodies and faces speak say a great deal that does not always accord too well with the words we use.

Another American anthropologist, Edward T. Hall, described in the 1950s and 1960s how different cultures use the movements of the body in space and time to express messages that are not apparent in the words. This causes severe difficulties at multinational companies, because a German and an American mean pretty much the opposite by an open door to an office: The German thinks doors should be closed at first and then opened, while the American perceives the closed door as a rebuff.

But doors are mere details. The real drama is the language of the body, which says far more than the language of speech. "This notion that there are significant portions of the personality that exist out of one's own awareness but which are there for everyone else to see may seem frightening," Hall wrote. "The unconscious is not hidden to anyone except the individual who hides from himself those parts which persons significant to him in his early life have disapproved."[35]

Others know more about us than we know ourselves. Because through our body language, others have access to a knowledge of the millions of bits in our brains that never reach our consciousness. After all, language is a rather new invention in our biological evolution. Long before it became important to find out if other people could express themselves in well-bred fashion, it was considerably more important to figure out if they would behave themselves.

Exformation is more important than information. It is more important to know what is going on in people's heads than to understand the words they speak.

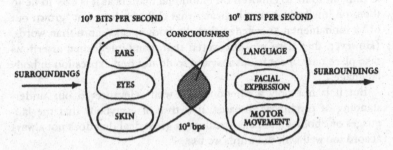

10⁹ BITS PER SECOND · CONSCIOUSNESS · 10⁷ BITS PER SECOND
EARS · EYES · SKIN · SURROUNDINGS · LANGUAGE · FACIAL EXPRESSION · MOTOR MOVEMENT · SURROUNDINGS · 10² bps

Consciousness between impression and expression, sketched by W. D. Keidel of the Erlangen School.

But if there is a contradiction between what is said and what is meant, in the long run you go mad. It is good for you to *get* mad at people who say one thing verbally and the opposite with their bodies. For the alternative is to *go* mad yourself.

Conscious language manages very little of what goes on in a social situation. Far too much information is discarded before we get to the information.

People who do not understand this make fools of themselves. Gangs of boys are forever poking fun at anyone who does not understand the codes, does not grasp the exformation in the information. Snobbery, cliquishness, clubbiness, prejudice, and the persecution of minorities all involve mocking those who do not understand the exformation in the information.

The weapon to deal with such vulgar information fascism is humor. Jokes prove that the information is not consistent: that the words meant the opposite of what seemed to be the case at the start of the joke; that there was another context, which could reveal the paucity or incorrectness of the first one. A good joke gets this across with a real punch.

But in order to do so, it must be built up consciously to allow for the punch line to yield a *sudden* and radical reinterpretation of everything said up to that point.

An example is a footnote from the book that founded information theory—Claude Shannon and Warren Weaver's *The Mathematical Theory of Communication*, in which Weaver cites the neuroscientist Karl Lashley for the following story:

"When Pfungst (1911) demonstrated that the horses of Elberfield, who were showing marvelous linguistic and mathematical ability, were merely reacting to movements of the trainer's head, Mr. Krall (1911), their owner, met the criticism in the most direct manner. He asked the horses whether they could see such small movements and in answer they spelled out an emphatic 'No.' "[36]

Generous laughter is the linguistic consciousness's awareness of its own paucity. Mean humor is proof of the paucity of other people's semantic or mental information.

In the words of the Italian semiotician and author Umberto Eco, the devil is "faith without smile," while "the mission of those who love mankind is to make truth laugh."[37]

"I am lying." In 1931, this statement led to Gödel's theorem, which set off the collapse of the belief that the world can be described exhaustively by formulae and semantic systems, the central theme of the century. In science, philosophy, and thought, it has become clear that the world cannot be captured in the net of thought or language.

The problem is that language and the formal systems tend to seem as if they can cope with everything: describe everything. The semantic paradoxes such as the liar are the reluctant admission by language of the fact that it is a map of the terrain and not the terrain itself. Gödel's theorem is the admission by the formal system that it is a formal system. The philosophical paradoxes are the intellectual world's version of children's pain as they witness adults saying one thing while showing with their bodies that they mean another.

The possibility of the lie is one cost of consciousness. "Consciously one can lie, unconsciously one cannot. The lie detector, for example, is proof of this,"[38] Karl Steinbuch, of the Technical High School in Karlsruhe, writes in his *Automat and Man*, 1965. The possibility of the lie arises precisely because of the low information content of consciousness; the possibility of negation derives from the fact that there are so few bits to move around. An individual who is one with one's body cannot lie—as children know very well.[39]

But the ancient Greeks had come so far with civilization and the belief that consciousness is identical with man that they discovered the paradox of the liar: "I am lying."

In mathematics in this century, the liar paradox was rediscovered by Bertrand Russell, who tried to get rid of it again by drawing up rules for *logical types*. His central thesis was that we should ban concepts from talking about themselves: ban the combination of concepts with what the concepts were about.

Russell's attempt was at once an admission of the existence of the problem and an attempt to learn how to limit the problem to a corner of mathematical logic.

Gregory Bateson's description of the peculiar logic of schizophrenia is reminiscent of the liar. Indeed, Bateson draws his epistemological starting point from the paradox of the liar and in Bertrand Russell and A. N. Whitehead's *Principia mathematica*, 1910–13. Bateson refers to Russell again and again.

Some of Bateson's contemporaries have found this strange. In 1980, the science historian Stephen Toulmin wrote in connection with the publication of Russell's final book, *Mind and Nature*, that "In many ways Russell is the last philosopher one would have expected Bateson to choose as an ally."[40] Russell does not exactly stand for the kind of envelope-pushing epistemology Bateson formulated. So Toulmin cannot understand why Bateson was enthusiastic about Russell. However, there was a profound inner connection between Bateson's ideas on schizophrenia—and in a wider sense all communication between people—and Russell's rediscovery of the paradox of the liar.

This does not mean that at the ideological level Toulmin is wrong in considering Bateson's enthusiasm for Russell strange. Because Russell wanted something quite different in his studies of the liar than did Bateson. To Russell, the paradox of the liar was the pathological thing: a kind of disease in the foundations of mathematical logic, a misfortune to be got rid of. In 1931, when Gödel showed that Russell's paradox was merely a pointer to far deeper matters now being discovered, Russell could not have cared less.

To Bateson, the liar was the entry to an epistemological description of phenomena from everyday language: that we cannot take spoken words at face value, and that we have to know the context if we want to understand them.

In fact, what Russell and Bateson wanted out of their mutual interest in the paradox of the liar was in direct contradiction to each other. What they did have in common was that neither of them showed particular interest in Kurt Gödel's work.

With Kurt Gödel and Gregory Chaitin later, it was proved clearly that the consequences of the paradox of the liar are present anywhere we try to describe the world in a limited, formal language.

Any language, any description, any consciousness, consists of information that is the result of exformation. Enormous amounts of information have to be discarded before we can be conscious. So in the final analysis, this consciousness and its expression can be understood and grasped only when it is anchored in what discarded all that information: the body.

We never perceive most of what passes through us. Our conscious *I* is only a tiny part of the story. When children learn to say "I am lying," they already know that the biggest lie is the *I* that in all its incredible pomposity thinks that the body allows it to lie.

THREE MEDIA

Making a newspaper, making radio, making TV. Three media, three worlds. But often with the same starting point: an interview with a person- who knows more about the issue than you do; a conversation that lasts for hours but is condensed to something that is consumed in two minutes. Information is discarded. Two hours of conversation become two minutes of reading the newspaper, listening, or viewing.

The amount of freedom granted varies a great deal. When an interview has to be edited into a short text for a newspaper, statements that arose at widely different times during the interview can be shuffled around. Two half sentences can be joined together without its mattering much. For there is not much information in the text. Very little of the character of the conversation is conveyed. All the body language, background noise, and facial expressions vanish. Only the words are left. The journalist's editorial task is easy.

Compared to the radio journalist's, anyway. He cannot cut in mid-sentence without it sounding very strange. There is tempo and rhythm in the language; the interviewee warms up, and you cannot cut backward and forward in the conversation. The intonation reveals whether you are at the start of an argument or the end. There is far more information in a taped reproduction of an interview than in a conversation reproduced as words on a page. It is harder to edit a radio program than a newspaper article. But not as hard as editing a TV interview.

Television reveals gestures and eye movements; the face shows very clearly how the speaker relates to what he is saying. When an interview is edited, the journalist has to respect certain rules as to what viewers are prepared to watch. Nobody can stand an interview where the interviewee leads up to his vital point with his hands and eyebrows—only to be edited out of the picture. Maybe the sound track does not reveal this, and one would never be able to tell from a transcript. But the man was about to say something significant. Even if the journalist happens to be right, and it is not significant to the viewers, it feels bad to see a man being cut off. That is why it is harder to edit television than radio.

There is far more information in a TV reproduction of an interview than in a radio reproduction—and far more than in a written reproduction of an interview.

We can measure the difference by examining how much the three media can convey: how many bits per second can be transmitted: the bandwidth. Television has a bandwidth of more than a million bits/sec. Radio more than 10,000 bits/sec. A text read aloud, about 25 bits/sec.

This does not necessarily mean that the journalist can control all these bits or that the receiver can. But the chance of the body language saying something other than that which the journalist is listening for means that a sequence edited very reasonably according to a tape transcript fails entirely to communicate when screened.

CHAPTER 7

THE BOMB OF PSYCHOLOGY

Why did research into the capacity of consciousness run out of steam in the 1960s? Why was the revolutionary view of man invited by these results so completely ignored?

An explanation may be found in events that took place in another branch of science, closely related in its experimental methods to the studies into the capacity of consciousness: the study of subliminal perception.

When the study of human perception was founded at the end of the last century, one central concept was the idea of a threshold defining the smallest stimulus perceptible to the organism. The existence of a threshold means that stimuli above that threshold can be registered, while a stimulus weaker than the threshold cannot.

For example, a certain volume is required before we can hear a sound, and a certain amount of light before we spot that star in the sky.

Subliminal perception means sensing stimuli below the threshold (*limen* is the Latin word for threshold). The interesting thing about subliminal perception is that it is the conscious awareness of a stimulus that has defined the threshold. Anything perceived subliminally is a stimulus that has been picked up even though it is so weak that it was not perceived consciously.

In 1911, Harald Høffding, a Danish philosopher and psychologist, described how a number of mental activities that are normally conscious can occur unconsciously: "An activity which would otherwise take place with consciousness can, when consciousness is absorbed in something else simultaneously, occur below the threshold of consciousness."[1]

The notion that human behavior can be influenced by perceptions which do not lead to consciousness but merely remain in the organism has always been associated with considerable fear. "Few hypotheses in the behavioural sciences have occasioned so much controversy as the suggestion that people may be affected by external stimuli of which they remain wholly unaware," according to Norman Dixon,[2] the English psychologist who has published two books on subliminal perception and the ensuing controversy.

In the first book, published in 1971, Dixon uses a graph to show the degree to which people have believed in the existence of subliminal perception throughout history.[3]

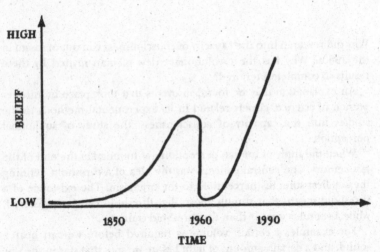

Belief in the existence of subliminal perception in recent times. (After Dixon)

Belief is on the increase, but there is a very pronounced dip around 1960: a dip that did not only mean that people stopped believing in subliminal perception; it also meant that scientists stopped researching the subject.

The cause of the big dip has been described as the atom bomb of psychology.

$\approx$

In 1957, an enterprise named Precon Process and Equipment Corporation, in New Orleans, started offering the placement of subliminal messages in advertisements and movies—messages not perceived by consciousness but containing sufficient influence to get somebody to pay for their being there. Messages that work unconsciously or *preconsciously*, hence Precon.

Another enterprise based on the same idea called itself the Subliminal Projection Company and kicked off with a press conference in New York. Radio and TV stations from all over the United States began to sell commercial airtime in which subliminal perception was used. The companies behind the technique claimed they could generate massive improvements in sales because viewers unaware that they had seen or heard a given commercial were induced to acquire the product being advertised.

Psychological studies had proved that very brief images which consciousness fails to pick up can influence people's behavior. These observations were what led to commercial exploitation.

Naturally, public reaction was fierce. Here was a method capable of sneaking messages into people, and they would not have any chance of knowing they had been stimulated! A storm of protest led to a suspension of subliminal messages in commercials in the United States and most of the Western world. Consumers refused to be so thoroughly manipulated.

This solved the immediate problem. But another problem remained unsolved: Just what is subliminal perception? How important is it in our everyday lives?

"The announcement of a commercial application of long-established psychological principles has assumed nightmarish qualities, and we find ourselves unwillingly cast in the role of invaders of personal privacy and enemies of society," three American psychologists wrote in a summary article on the subject in 1958. J. V. McConnell, R. L. Cutler, and E. B. McNeil went on: "The highly emotional public reaction to the 'discovery' of subliminal perception should serve as an object lesson to our profession, for, in the bright glare of publicity, we can see urgent ethical issues as well as an omen of things to come. When the theoretical notion $E = mc^2$ became the applied reality of an atom bomb, the community of physicists became deeply concerned with social as well as scientific responsibility. Judging from the intensity of the public alarm when confronted with a bare minimum of fact about this subliminal social atom, there exists a clear need for psychologists to examine the ethical problems that are part of this era of the application of their findings."[4]

The three psychologists acknowledged their responsibility as scientists to be aware of how their findings could be used to affect society. But the strange thing is that the community of psychologists did not accept this responsibility. They pretended the whole thing was a misunderstanding. Norman Dixon described it as follows:

"This scare in the late fifties had a remarkable effect upon the profession. Erstwhile proponents of subliminal perception began to change their minds. A vigorous reappraisal of earlier researches and conclusions got under way." Dixon continues with the following assessment of his fellow psychologists: "Since those in the forefront of this reassessment were psychologists and the object of their obloquy [was] rather less dramatic than the explosion of an atom bomb, their solution of the 'ethical problems' referred to by McConnell et al. was less difficult than that being demanded of physicists. Whereas the latter could hardly deny the reality of nuclear fission, psychologists were not similarly handicapped by subliminal perception. Instead of saying (as perhaps they should have done), 'Yes, there is sufficient evidence to suggest that people may be affected by information of which they are unaware,' and then trying to allay public anxiety by suggesting ways in which commercial or political exploitations of the phenomenon might be prevented, they chose the easier path of using arguments to prove that since subliminal perception could not occur there was nothing to fear."[5]

Norman Dixon's verdict is a harsh one: The psychologists simply ran away, tails between their legs. The climate was not pleasant, either. One of the opinionmakers who considerably influenced the debate at the end of the 1950s was Vance Packard. In a book published in 1978, the American writer looked back at the effects of the debate that caused subliminal perception to disappear from the front pages. "As a matter of fact interest in subliminal perception has continued, but much more quietly. I have reports on fourteen studies that have been made in recent years, and references to quite a few more. The psychologist James McConnell in his new, widely adopted textbook, *Understanding Human Behavior*, devotes a chapter to 'Subliminal Perception.' "[6]

What bothered Packard was that research in this field was being done at all. He'd have preferred that the psychologists would stay out of it.

Decades later, the problem has become classic: Is society to control technological progress by banning research or by banning technology? Are we to stop while still at the research stage, or should we ban the use of the knowledge we obtain?

In the case of subliminal perception, the scientific community chose self-censorship. But that works only for a time—and that time is up.

Research into subliminal perception continued throughout the 1970s, and in the 1980s in particular it became clear that most of the information that passes through a person is not picked up by consciousness, even when this information has a demonstrable effect on behavior.

This presents the now paradigmatic dilemma: The research can be abused—not only for advertising but for all kinds of opinion forming and manipulation. So it is a dangerous thing.

But there is another possibility: that it is of vital importance to humanity's ability to survive in civilization that we realize we do not possess awareness of very much of what goes on inside us. The insight that consciousness plays a smaller role in human life than most of us would believe may be vital because it is the only insight capable of transforming a culture that now has serious viability problems.

If this view—to be argued more closely in later chapters—has any justification at all, a ban on research into subliminal perception might prevent abuse by the advertising agencies in the short term, but in the long term it may block the path to vital self-knowledge.

That is the dilemma for all notions of scientific censorship. But research has not stopped. On the contrary, the 1990s is the decade of a breakthrough in the scientific acknowledgment that man is not transparent to himself. The germ of this breakthrough lay in knowledge that has been apparent for the last thirty years: that the ratio of what we sense to what we perceive is 1,000,000 to 1.

But once that discovery had been made, research into the topic ceased, only to come alive again decades later.

≈

Research into the human mind has undergone many somersaults over the centuries. The significance of consciousness has been lent very different weights during different periods.

Modern philosophy started in the Renaissance, with a view of consciousness as central to man. In 1619, René Descartes concluded after considerable doubt that there was one thing he knew for sure—that he doubted: "I think, therefore I am." Consciousness was the real token of existence: Consciousness itself was the only thing one could not doubt.

In England, John Locke published his *Essay Concerning Human Understanding*, in which man's self-awareness and ability to see himself were the central issues. This became the view that affected most thinking about the human mind, especially in English-speaking countries: Man is transparent.

At the end of the last century, the notion of the transparent man was severely challenged. Hermann von Helmholtz, the German physicist and physiologist, began studying human reactions around 1850. On the basis of his technical data, he concluded that most of what took place in our head was unconscious. Sensing is based on inferences that are inaccessible to consciousness. Even if the conscious mind understands and knows these inferences, it cannot change them. Helmholtz pointed to the fact that one can invoke an experience of light by gently pressing the closed eye. The cells in the eye that have been constructed to pass on a message when they receive light receive something (which is not light) and passes on the message that something was seen; since all these cells know about is light, they report light when they are stimulated by pressure. Even though one knows that the pressure has nothing to do with actual light as radiation, there is nothing one can do about it. "It may be ever so clear how we get an idea of a luminous phenomenon in the field of vision when pressure is exerted on the eye; and yet we cannot get rid of the conviction that this appearance of light is actually there at the given place in the visual field," Helmholtz wrote.[7]

The idea of unconscious inferences was definitely unpopular at the end of the last century; it roused a furor that anticipated the invective that the founder of psychoanalysis encountered at the turn of the century when he introduced the idea of the unconscious—an idea that was a full-scale rebellion against Locke's notion of the transparent man. Sigmund Freud asserted that many of man's actions are due to drives that are often unconscious. These urges are repressed by a range of cultural causes that are rooted particularly in our upbringing. The sexual drive is the most important of these—and the most repressed.

But the ideal of psychoanalysis was still the transparent human being who did not repress his unconscious drives. Psychoanalysis is a science that was developed during studies of sick people who repress far too much. Insight into the patient's history should enable the patient to overcome the repression.

Helmholtz's clash with the absolute control exercised by consciousness was more radical than Freud's: Helmholtz not only points out that conscious decisions can be influenced or changed by unconscious drives. He maintains that consciousness must necessarily be a result of unconscious processes, whether we like it or not.

Psychology then went off in a peculiar direction. Helmholtz's and Freud's analyses had clearly demonstrated that introspection is a dubious method of studying the human mind. Introspection simply means self-observation: looking at one's own mind. As introspection is by definition our only source of information about our own consciousness, the difficulties with introspection meant serious problems in studying consciousness.

But at the beginning of the century, this led to a new movement that refused to apply notions such as consciousness or methods such as introspection.

Behaviorism, as this movement was called, dominated British and American psychology from the 1920s to the 1950s. It advocated the study of human beings in strictly objective terms: environmental factors; behavior; stimulus, response. There was no need for notions such as "consciousness" or "state of mind"; they were nonsense. Either there was a law associating impression with expression (in which case it was unimportant how the facts appeared from within) or there was no law (in which case it was unimportant how they appeared from without). The behaviorists banned the problem of consciousness and thereby a range of other concepts, such as attention, and naturally any discussion of subliminal perception.

The radicality of the behaviorist opposition to any kind of introspection and self-observation is perhaps best demonstrated by the joke about the two behaviorists who have intercourse. Afterward one behaviorist says to the other, "That was fine for you, but how was it for me?"[8]

After the Second World War, behaviorism died out and was succeeded by the so-called cognitive revolution in the 1950s. "Miller's magical number seven" is one of the fundamental insights in cognitive psychology, which views man as an information-processing creature. Central elements in the cognitive revolution were drawn from the study of languages and computers. Computations became the central concept in the describing of man—computations of the type that could be carried out by the computers of the day: series of computations, all controlled by a central monitoring unit in the computer.

Cognitive science is not particularly concerned with the unconscious. It attempts to understand which logical rules and algorithms are needed in order to describe the human mind. It assumes that there are clear, logical rules, not incomprehensible quantities of unconscious calculation.

In 1958, Donald Broadbent, a British psychologist, proposed the "filter theory." Broadbent started out from the knowledge that far more information enters a person than enters consciousness. He thought that the sensory information was stored in a short-term memory, whereupon a filter very quickly determined what would be expedited to consciousness. His theory was revolutionary because it sought to address the problem of the big sensory bandwidth versus the little conscious bandwidth. But trouble quickly arises: Broadbent's theory means that most of the information is discarded unprocessed. It disappears if it is not needed at the conscious end. If the long-term memory has told the filter what one wishes to hear during a cocktail party, the filter simply throws the rest away. One hears what one hears—and what the ear does not hear, the heart cannot grieve for.

But this is precisely the view that is disputed by the perspective of subliminal perception. Information that has not entered consciousness can also influence the content or decisions of consciousness, or so the notion of subliminal perception tells us.

In the 1980s, cognitive psychology was renewed or replaced by a new perspective: parallel distribution processing, or PDP. A formidable phrase, and indeed it involves computers: but where cognitive psychology took as its point of departure the existing computers, in which a central processing unit (CPU) controls everything, the PDPers chose a kind of computer built on the pattern of the human brain: parallel computers with no CPU monitoring everything. Parallel processors are being developed rapidly nowadays, but the major problem is how to coordinate all the parallel activities.

In a PDP model, there is no particular filter that discards everything except what is shown clemency by the higher levels of consciousness. With PDP, the function of the entire brain is regarded as an extensive computation resulting in a state that is consciousness. The unconscious processes in the mind handle information rapidly and in parallel, while the conscious processes are slower and serial—they take one thing at a time, like an old-fashioned computer.

So apart from the bizarre behaviorist interlude, psychologists have always admitted that consciousness is not the whole story of man. But in the last decade or so, the picture has slowly changed. Now it is the unconscious, parallel and inscrutable, that is easy to understand, while human consciousness has become almost incomprehensible.

The American philosopher and cognitive psychologist Daniel Dennett has described the process as follows: "We have come to accept without the slightest twinge of incomprehension a host of claims to the effect that sophisticated hypothesis-testing, memory searching inference—in short, information processing—occurs within us even though it is entirely inaccessible to introspection. It is not repressed unconscious activity of the sort Freud uncovered, activity driven out of the 'sight' of consciousness, but just mental activity that is somehow beneath or beyond the ken of consciousness altogether."

Dennett adds with barely concealed disquiet, "Not only are minds accessible to outsiders; some mental activities are more accessible to outsiders than to the very 'owners' of those minds!"[9]

Which is disturbing in general and is particularly so in a society where many people's jobs consist of enticing the rest of us to do things we cannot afford to do.

Sigmund Freud and psychoanalysis made the Western world take the unconscious seriously. For much of this century, the natural sciences have looked down on the psychoanalytical tradition, with all its talk of unconscious drives. Both scientists and philosophers have considered psychoanalysis as something a bit to one side. So it may seem unfair that psychoanalysis is again being subjected to criticism today, when the nonconscious processes are taking center stage in psychological and natural science–oriented studies of human beings alike. As the end of the twentieth century approaches, our knowledge of the significance of the unconscious for the functions of the human mind has reached the stage where the psychoanalytical tradition is criticized for allowing the unconscious too small a part. Now the critics are saying, "Psychoanalysis taught us to take the unconscious seriously, sure. But not seriously enough!"

Some of Freud's pupils developed a psychoanalytically based view of man that allowed plenty of room for the unconscious mental processes. Carl Gustav Jung developed the idea of a self superior to the conscious I and containing conscious and unconscious processes alike. Wilhelm Reich developed the idea of the body's functions as a direct manifestation of the unconscious processes.

Jung criticized Freud for underestimating the importance of the nonconscious. In *The Ego and the Unconscious*, Jung writes by way of introduction, "As we know, the various contents of the unconscious are limited, according to the Freudian view, to infantile tendencies that are repressed because of their incompatible nature. Repression is a process that begins in infancy, under the moral influence of the child's surroundings, and continues all life long. In analysis, the repression is removed and the repressed desires are rendered conscious. According to this theory, the unconscious should, so to speak, contain only the parts of the personality that might just as well be conscious and are basically suppressed only through upbringing." Of his own views, Jung wrote, "We emphasize that in addition to the repressed material, the unconscious also contains all the mental material that has become subliminal, including subliminal sensory perceptions."[10]

In recent years, modern ideas on unconscious cognitive functions have also found expression in the modern psychoanalytical tradition— and as so often happens when a theoretical father image is rejected, it is accompanied by the claim that all the *other* psychoanalysts read only *parts of* Freud's oeuvre, whereas a new school can be created from the *last* of Freud's writings.

The American psychoanalyst Joseph Weiss and colleagues at the Mount Zion Psychotherapy Research Group in San Francisco have proposed a revised interpretation of psychoanalysis in which the unconscious is assigned an important role in "higher" mental functions such as thinking, planning, and decisionmaking.

Weiss criticizes the traditional psychoanalytical view of the unconscious as the domicile of a series of mental experiences repressed in childhood because they could not be tolerated by the conscious self. These experiences include sexual and aggressive impulses kept in check in adults by repressive forces. This view, according to Weiss, basically originates "from Freud's early writings and assumes that people have little or no control over their unconscious mental life."[11]

The alternative view, which Weiss proposes, is based on Freud's later writings and emphasizes man's ability to relate to the unconscious: It is not repression and suppression that keep the unconscious impulses down but decisions made unconsciously. These decisions are not always appropriate but can be changed through therapy. The core of this therapy deals with the patients'-unconscious decisions as meaningful. The unconscious mind must be helped to realize that, say, there is no risk in sex.

"It seems that the cognitive capacities of the unconscious mind have been underappreciated and that human beings can unconsciously carry out many intellectual tasks, including developing the executing plans for reaching certain goals," Weiss writes.[12]

The unconscious is not merely a morass of repressed sexual desires and forbidden hatred. The unconscious is an active, vital part of the human mind.

The capacity of consciousness is simply not big enough to allow much of what happens in our heads to appear in our conscious minds. So repressed sexual desires and death wishes are not the only things to be found in our unconscious; also present, and dominant, are the undramatic and familiar.

But remarkable activities do take place in the unconscious. The study of subliminal perception has indicated in definitive fashion that many of Freud's ideas are correct.

In 1917, the neurologist O. Pötzl discovered that in dreams people can recall subliminal stimuli to which they had been exposed while awake.

They were shown a picture, but so briefly that they could not make anything of it consciously or remember it while awake. But the image reappeared in their dreams.

Undeniably an insight that can contribute to interpreting one's dreams! Pötzl's phenomenon, as it is known, has been repeated in many experiments, not just dreams. Daydreams, free associations, and free image generation (techniques used in psychoanalysis) can also provide access to subliminally perceived images.

The experimental technique behind studies of Pötzl's phenomenon recurs in many studies of subliminal perception. The apparatus used is a tachistoscope, a tool central to many disciplines within experimental psychology. The tachistoscope allows an image to be shown to the subject for a period—e.g., one-hundredth of a second—too brief for consciousness to perceive. (A TV program is made up of twenty-five or thirty image frames per second, and you have to be very attentive and used to videotape editing to be able to catch a single frame as it flies past. We perceive TV images as "moving pictures" because we cannot discriminate between such brief intervals.)

Pötzl proved by experiment that unobtrusive images of archaeological digs resurfaced in his subjects' dreams even though the subjects could not remember the pictures while awake. The phenomenon has been confirmed by numerous control studies since, but naturally it has also been contested.[13]

Pötzl's phenomenon is the oldest example of subliminal perception studied by modern methods.

On 17 October 1884, a lecture on small differences of sensation was delivered at the U.S. National Academy of Sciences. The lecture was later published by the academy. Its authors, the mathematician and philosopher Charles Sanders Peirce and the perception psychologist Joseph Jastrow, had performed a little experiment together: an experiment that effectively and elegantly did away with the idea of thresholds of perception.

Their point of departure was the idea that there had to be some difference between two sensations before one could distinguish between them, an *Unterschiedschwelle*, a threshold for distinction. Jastrow and Peirce investigated whether the human organism could discriminate between two sensations that consciousness could not tell apart.

By experimenting with pressure on the skin exerted by tiny weights, Jastrow and Peirce were able to demonstrate that they could distinguish between sensations where they did not consciously experience any difference. Their ability to "guess" which stimulus was the stronger was far too good to allow them to say that their conscious ability to discriminate defines the limits to what humans can tell apart.

"The general fact has highly important practical bearings," Peirce and Jastrow wrote, "since it gives new reason for believing that we gather what is passing in one another's minds in large measure from sensations so faint that we are not fairly aware of having them, and can give no account of how we reach our conclusions about such matters. The insight of females as well as certain 'telepathic' phenomena may be explained in this way. Such faint sensations ought to be fully studied by the psychologist and assiduously cultivated by every man."[14]

Charles Sanders Peirce developed the term "abduction" to describe the process in which one "draws on unconscious powers" in drawing up a scientific hypothesis or perceiving something from everyday life. Many years before the experiments with Jastrow, Peirce had had a valuable chronometer stolen from him during a voyage by riverboat from Boston to New York. Peirce was able to identify the thief but unable to say how he had done so. As Peder Voetmann Christiansen, a Danish expert on Peirce, comments, "That Peirce was able to identify the thief with certainty was due not primarily to logical reason but to an ability to stop the inner semantic dialogue and put himself into a state of passive receptivity to the non-semantic signs that normally drown in noise from the cortex."[15]

One of the most convincing and irrefutable examples of man's ability to sense and act on the basis of information from his surroundings that his conscious mind knows nothing about is the phenomenon of *blindsight*. It was discovered in the 1970s in patients with serious damage to the part of the brain that processes visual stimuli, so that they could not see anything in large parts of their field of vision.

Or could they? When shown objects in the blind area of their field of vision, they could point at them, seize them, manipulate them correctly, and describe their orientation. But they said they could not see them. The confused doctors and psychologists subjected the patients to a series of tests in which they had to determine which way a stick was pointing, for example. The presumably blind patients always guessed correctly, while maintaining that they could not see anything.

One patient, D.B., was examined by L. Weiskrantz, a psychologist. In his book *Blindsight*, he says, "After one such long series of 'guesses,' when he made virtually no errors, he was told how well he had done. In the interview that followed, and which was recorded, D.B. expressed considerable surprise. 'Did you know how well you had done?' he was asked. 'No,' he replied, 'I didn't—because I couldn't see anything; I couldn't see a darn thing.' 'Can you say how you guessed—what it was that allowed you to say whether it was vertical or horizontal?' 'No, I could not because I did not see anything; I just don't know.' Finally, he was asked, 'So you really did not know you were getting them right?' 'No,' he replied, still with something of an air of incredulity."[16]

The explanation proved to be that optical information from the eye is treated in different areas of the brain—and in different ways. Only the normal way leads to awareness. The other links between the eye and the brain do not lead to awareness. So when the normal route for processing optical information is destroyed because part of the brain is not functioning or has been removed, the patient does not experience seeing anything. But he can see it anyway. His behavior proves it.

One can hardly imagine a more unequivocal example of perception without conscious awareness.

Around 1980, intense research commenced into a phenomenon known as "priming," which is of interest mainly because it involves clearly "cognitive" processes: not only ordinary perception but the recognition of words and other meaningful objects.

A priming experiment could consist of two presentations with the tachistoscope, for example. The first presentation runs so rapidly that the subject does not pick up what is shown. The second presentation consists of an object (a word or an image) that the subject has to relate to: Is it a real word? Is it a possible object? If there is a link between the two images, subjects are much better and much quicker at figuring out what the second picture shows.

In other words, one can learn something from a stimulus that is so brief that one does not perceive it. The subjects do not know why they are so clever.

This is interesting, naturally, as a scientific result. But it is no less interesting as regards our everyday lives.

In 1987, the psychologist John F. Kihlstrom wrote in *Science* about the perspectives of priming and other examples of subliminal perception: "Such information-processing activity would be nonconscious in a double sense: neither the stimuli themselves, nor the cognitive processes that operate on them, are accessible to phenomenal awareness. Such doubly nonconscious processes nevertheless exert an important impact on social interaction. Through the operation of routinized procedures for social judgement, for example, we may form impressions of people without any conscious awareness of the perceptual-cognitive basis for them."[17] And further: "A large number of social judgements and inferences, especially those guiding first impressions, appear to be mediated by such unconscious processes."[18]

We are not just talking about love at first sight. This goes for many of the quick assessments we make of other people—not always voluntarily. How often do we find that we cannot rid ourselves of the first impression of a person we would like to like but with whom we have got off on the wrong foot? How often do we realize to our dismay that we simply cannot get the chemistry to work in a situation where we wish very much that we could?

A phenomenon like priming provides almost direct evidence of the existence of the high bandwidth channels in the tree of talking, faster than language and consciousness. Information that enters through the eyes influences our ability to read words and images via the conscious channel.

In 1990, two psychologists, the Canadian Endel Tulving and the American Daniel Schacter, wrote in *Science*: "We still know relatively little about priming at this early stage of research. Nevertheless it seems clear that it plays a more important role in human affairs than its late discovery would suggest. Although priming is typically observed only under carefully controlled experimental conditions, similar conditions frequently occur naturally, outside the laboratory. It is reasonable to assume, therefore, that priming represents a ubiquitous occurrence in everyday life.

"One remarkable feature of priming is that, unlike other forms of cognitive memory, it is nonconscious. A person perceiving a familiar object is not aware that what is perceived is as much an expression of memory as it is of perception. The fact that people are not conscious of priming probably accounts for its late discovery. It is difficult to study phenomena whose existence one does not suspect."[19]

Lots of the experiences we undergo in everyday life may involve our recognizing something we are not conscious of recognizing. Not only when we have a déjà vu experience (when we know we recognize but do not know what) but also when we like a house, a woman, or a chocolate cake at first sight.

A new bout of interest may be expected from the advertising industry—and a new debate on ethics by the psychologists.

But it is not only subliminal perception proper that tells us consciousness is not in on much of what happens inside us. A number of the skills we use in everyday life are not conscious when we use them. We can train automatic processes that we perform best when unaware of them. We may call this being good at our jobs or our sport.

We can cycle, but we can't explain how. We can write but not explain how while we are doing so. We can play musical instruments, but the better we get, the harder it is for us to explain just what is going on.

The learning of these skills is controlled by consciousness, but the application is not. When we learn to speak a foreign language, play a new game, or find our way around town, initially we feel our way forward, fumbling and stuttering, awkward and confused. Suddenly a change occurs, and we start performing the activity best if we do not think about what we are doing. As soon as we think that we are now speaking a language we really cannot speak, we grow conscious of what we are attempting—and right away we are not so good at it.

Sleepwalking is an activity that may imply an unequivocal perception of our surroundings (children do find the bathroom in their sleep, even when there is a chair in the way) but is accompanied by a total lack of awareness as to what is going on.

Finally, the body senses a great deal in relation to its surroundings that it relates to without our being conscious of the fact: temperature, oxygen pressure, and traffic. If we consider for a moment our chances of survival in modern society *without* the use of unconscious perception and choice of behavior, we soon realize that a massive amount of subliminal activity must be taking place in our heads.

"One thing is now clear," John Kihlstrom wrote in *Science* in 1987. "Consciousness is not to be identified with any particular perceptual-cognitive functions such as discriminative response to stimulation, perception, memory, or the higher mental processes involved in judgement or problem-solving. All of these functions can take place outside of phenomenal awareness. Rather, consciousness is an experimental quality that may accompany any of these functions."[20]

The picture is very clear: Plenty happens inside us that we are not aware of. But there is still criticism and argument. As recently as 1986, the Belgian psychologist Daniel Holender proved that there were problems in some of the studies that led to the belief in the existence of subliminal perception and the automatic application of skills.[21]

The methodological difficulties of proving that people are influenced by something they are not aware of are naturally considerable. Precisely because subliminal perception is such an important part of being human, it is essential that we study it as thoroughly and honestly as possible; and precisely because there are such colossal, almost indescribable possibilities of applying this facet of human beings for purposes of manipulation and control, it is vital that the public ensure that the phenomenon is studied by independent scientists. It is no good burying our heads in the sand the way psychologists did around 1960. Subliminal perception is a reality that it is very important to be aware of.

From the point of view of common sense, it is really quite obvious that subliminal perception must take place. Remember that the capacity of consciousness is vastly smaller than that of our senses. If all the information that thunders in through our senses is merely discarded, apart from the bit we are aware of, how can we tell that the bit we are aware of is the right one?

If consciousness and awareness are not just a luxury for people who have time to read books, there must be some reason—a biological reason. Why do we possess a body and sensory apparatus that gathers such an incomprehensible amount of information from our surroundings even though we are not aware of it? We do so because we have to know about the jungle fauna, and the way traffic lights change, if we are to survive. But if consciousness selects at random from what comes in, it really is not much use.

There must necessarily be a degree of "wisdom" in the sorting that takes place—otherwise we would just go around conscious of something random, with no connection to what really matters.

Consciousness is based on an enormous discarding of information, and the ingenuity of consciousness consists not of the information it contains but of the information it does not contain.

It is most practical to be able to remember a telephone number by heart the moment we need to make a call. But it is not particularly clever to remember a hundred phone numbers and the shopping list the moment we want to make that call. It is super to be able to spot a berry in a wood when out for a stroll, but it is not too smart if there is a tiger after you.

Consciousness is ingenious because it knows what is important. But the sorting and interpretation required for it to know what is important is *not* conscious. Subliminal perception and sorting is the real secret behind consciousness.

Everyday examples are legion. Just take the local main street: Is there a fabric shop or not? Many people have lived near a specialist outlet for years and never known it was there—until the day they need just such a store and either are directed to it or spot it themselves. Afterward they cannot imagine how they managed to wander along that street so many times in ignorance of the shop's existence.

"Consciousness is a much smaller part of our mental life than we are conscious of, because we cannot be conscious of what we are not conscious of," the American psychologist Julian Jaynes wrote in his landmark work from 1976, *The Origin of Consciousness in the Breakdown of the Bicameral Mind*, which we shall be returning to in a later chapter. He continues: "How simple that is to say; how difficult to appreciate! It is like asking a flashlight in a dark room to search around for something that does not have any light shining upon it. The flashlight, since there is light in whatever direction it turns, would have to conclude that there is light everywhere. And so consciousness can seem to pervade all mentality when actually it does not."[22]

Jaynes points out, for example, the problem of how much of the time we are conscious. Are we conscious throughout our waking day? "Yes," we would reply automatically. But then comes the counterquestion: How can you be conscious about the moments when you are not conscious but merely *are*? Just like the flashlight that can see only when it is lit, we can only know we were conscious at a given moment if we were conscious. If we simply *were*, we could not know we were not conscious. "We are thus conscious less of the time than we think, because we cannot be conscious of when we are not conscious," Jaynes writes.[23]

We could object that this might apply when we are out for an evening stroll or picking our noses. But there are times when we are always conscious of what is going on—when we think or when we read, for example.

"The fact that you can recall the meaning but not the words of the last sentence is a commonplace observation," write the British psychologists Richard Latto and John Campion. They go on: "As you read this sentence it is actually very difficult to describe just what you are conscious of, although you are clearly conscious of something."[24]

Or are you? But thinking . . . Surely thinking is a conscious activity. Don't you think?

"I insist that words are totally absent from my mind when I really think," wrote the French-American mathematician Jacques Hadamard in his famous *Essay on the Psychology of Invention in the Mathematical Field* in 1945. "Even after reading or hearing a question, every word disappears at the very moment I am beginning to think it over; words do not reappear in my consciousness before I have accomplished or given up the research. . . . I fully agree with Schopenhauer when he writes, 'Thoughts die the moment they are embodied by words.' "[25]

Hadamard's book is based on a questionnaire in which he asked a number of the greatest mathematicians of his day if they were conscious when they were thinking. One of those who replied was Albert Einstein, who wrote, "The words or the language, as they are written or spoken, do not seem to play any role in my mechanism of thought. The psychical entities which seem to serve as elements in thought are certain signs and more or less clear images which can be 'voluntarily' reproduced and combined."[26]

One might object that consciousness and words are not the same thing. One can be conscious of what one is doing even though one does not express it in words at the time.

When did you last have fish for supper? No, there is nothing to be ashamed of, even though fish is good for you. On Friday? On holiday? Today?

You are certainly conscious of the question; you are also conscious of the answer. But what did you think about while you were considering when you last had fish? What were you looking for? It is possible that you acted the politician and said/thought, "Er . . . on the basis of the information available, I would estimate that it could possibly be . . ."

But *bang!* Suddenly you've got it. "It was last week, we had trout, it was delicious."

"Er" is a word we use to pretend we are conscious while we are thinking. But in reality, thinking is highly unconscious. As Julian Jaynes puts it, "the actual process of thinking, so usually thought to be the very life of consciousness, is not conscious at all. . . . Only its preparation, its materials, and its end result are consciously perceived."[27]

A good thing, too. Imagine if the question about when we last had fish sparked off a *conscious* review of all the meals of the last few weeks; or a *conscious* recollection of all the meals we did not like, or a *conscious* review of the traditional dishes served in the festive seasons? Thinking would be quite unbearable.

How about more advanced questions than eating habits? Jaynes proposes the following experiment:

○△○△○△○ . . .

What is the next figure in the sequence? *Bang!* The answer is there the moment you spot it. Perhaps you thought, "Er, this is difficult," but the instant you saw the answer, you saw it—and it had nothing to do with your "Er."

Thinking is unconscious—or as the great French mathematician Henri Poincaré put it at the turn of the century, "In a word, is not the subliminal self superior to the conscious self?"[28]

In 1890, William James published *The Principles of Psychology*, an influential work that, thanks to equal portions of theoretical clear-sightedness and clarity of expression, became the cornerstone of a century of psychology. Many passages in James's great work have a powerful contemporary ring, even after a hundred years. Against the background of the fertile period of the birth of psychology in the second half of the nineteenth century, James was able to describe a number of facets of the human mind that behaviorism and positivism removed from the psychological agenda for half a century.

In what may be the most famous chapter of the book, "The Stream of Thought," James emphasizes that consciousness always chooses: "It is always interested more in one part of its object than in another, and welcomes and rejects, or chooses, all the while it thinks."[29]

Consciousness consists of selection: rejection. Discarding. James provides this remarkable conclusion to his chapter on the stream of thought:

"The mind, in short, works on the data it receives very much as a sculptor works on his block of stone. In a sense the statue stood there from eternity. But there were a thousand different ones beside it, and the sculptor alone is to thank for having extricated this one from the rest. Just so the world of each of us, howsoever different our several views of it may be, all lay embedded in the primordial chaos of sensations, which gave the mere matter to the thought of all of us indifferently. We may, if we like, by our reasonings unwind things back to that black and jointless continuity of space and moving clouds of swarming atoms which science calls the only real world. But all the while the world we feel and live in will be that which our ancestors and we, by slowly cumulative strokes of choice, have extricated out of this, like sculptors, by simply rejecting certain portions of the given stuff. Other sculptors, other statues from the same stone! Other minds, other worlds from the same monotonous and inexpressive chaos! My world is but one in a million alike embedded, alike real to those who may abstract them. How different must be the worlds in the consciousness of ant, cuttle-fish, or crab!"[30]

A hundred years later, the eminent German neurophysiologist Hans H. Kornhuber expressed the same fact, though a little less poetically: "Thus, there is a great deal of information reduction in the nervous system. Most information flow in the brain is, by the way, unconscious. The soul is not 'richer' than the body; on the contrary, most of the processing in our central nervous system is not perceived. The unconscious (which was discovered and elucidated long before Freud) is the most ordinary process in the nervous system. We just look at the results, but we are able to direct the focus of attention."[31]

So let us take a closer look at the way our consciousness is built on unconscious processes. It becomes disturbingly clear if we take a look at sight.

CHAPTER 8

THE VIEW FROM WITHIN

"It is difficult to explain to a layman that there is a problem in how we see things. It seems so effortless," the eminent biologist and neuroscientist Francis Crick wrote in 1990. "Yet the more we study the process, the more complex and unexpected we find it. Of one thing we can be sure: we do not see things in the way common sense says we should."[1]

Our insight into how advanced human vision really is derives not least from the attempts in recent decades to get computers to see. Since the end of the 1950s, research into so-called artificial intelligence has tried to create machines capable of taking over mental activities from humans. Not merely the physical functions, the way bulldozers and loudspeakers have done; and not mere sums and double-entry accounting, the way computers have done. But genuine advanced functions, such as diagnostics, pattern recognition, and logical reasoning.

Artificial intelligence has not got very far. In fact, it has been rather a fiasco. The computers and robots we can come up with today are still pretty unintelligent. But the attempts to imitate man have revealed a great deal about what man is—or, more correctly, is not. Artificial intelligence perceives man as a creature that functions according to a set of specific rules and recipes: algorithms. Man is regarded as specifiable, comprehensible, transparent. This view is repeated in the cognitive psychology discussed earlier, which is closely related to the attempts to create artificial intelligence.

But the historical irony is that this research has refuted its own basis: man as a conscious, rational being, able to explain what it is doing.

The peculiar thing is that the very attempts to create artificial intelligence have indicated the central role in the human mind played by the unconscious processes.

It is not that difficult to build computers capable of playing chess or doing sums. Computers find it easy to do what we learned at school. But computers have a very hard time learning what children learn *before* they start school: to recognize a cup that is upside down, for example; navigating a backyard; recognizing a face; *seeing*.

Early on, people thought that teaching computers to see would be a piece of cake. "In the 1960s almost no one realized that machine vision was difficult," one of the most perceptive scientists in the field, the late David Marr, wrote in his visionary but sadly posthumous work, *Vision* (1982).[2]

Marr's close associate, Tomaso Poggio, from the Artificial Intelligence Laboratory at MIT, wrote in 1990: "It is only recently that research in Artificial Intelligence has illuminated the computational difficulties of many visual and other perceptual tasks. We do not have a subjective introspection into it, so it has been easy to underestimate the difficulties of perception. If seeing seems effortless, it is because we are not conscious of it. Chess, on the other hand, seems hard because we have to think about it. I would argue that we tend to be most conscious of the things our intelligent brain does least well, the recent things in evolutionary history such as logic, mathematics, philosophy, in general problem-solving and planning, and we tend to be quite unconscious of its true powers—say, in vision."[3]

It is everything we *cannot* figure out that we think about. After all, we have no reason to puzzle over what we are really good at. We just do it. Without consciousness.

Attempts to reconstruct humans as machines have made this fact very clear. But it is nothing new.

◆ Close your left eye and direct your right eye at the little diamond left of the line. Move your index finger along the line, away from the diamond. Keep staring at the diamond, but let your attention follow your finger. Try a couple of times (it is hard not to move your eye). Then you will observe a phenomenon: Your fingertip will disappear as you approach the right-hand margin—i.e., where the line ends. It reappears a couple of centimeters later.

When you have found the point where your fingertip disappears, move your finger back and forth a few times to convince yourself that there really is a blind spot in your field of vision.

It is not something we needed computers to figure out. The blind spot has been known for centuries and has a very sensible explanation: Somewhere or other on the retina, there must be an area where there are no vision cells, allowing for optic nerve fibers and blood vessels to exit from the eye. That is why there is a "gap" in our field of vision, the so-called blind spot.

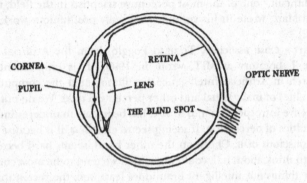

The blind spot

But the existence of the blind spot is not the interesting thing. What is interesting is that we do not see it. In normal circumstances, we use two eyes, which are constantly in motion, so it is not so strange that we do not see a blind spot. But even when we use only one eye, we do not see the blind spot: The relevant area of the retina simply gets filled in by something reminiscent of the surroundings. We have to move a finger across a page of a book in order to notice it. If there is no finger but just the page, the gap in the picture gets filled up with page.

In fact, it is not a blind spot at all. It is, as the psychologist Julian Jaynes puts it, a "non-spot."[4] Even if we have no information from that spot about what is going on, we do not experience a gap but merely experience a smoothing, an average of the immediate surroundings. We do not know that what we are seeing is a trick. What we are seeing has been cosmeticized.

Look at the figure opposite. It is the oldest, most famous example of a visual illusion. It was created by the Swiss Louis A. Necker, in 1832.

Known as the Necker cube, it is a beautiful example of the fact that consciousness cannot control what it experiences, however it wishes to.[5]

Can you see that it looks like a cube? Which side is closest to you? Try looking at the edge that is farthest away—i.e., deepest beneath the surface of the paper. And presto! Now this edge is the closest.

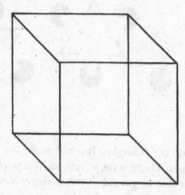

The Necker cube

There are two ways of regarding the Necker cube. There are two different three-dimensional images but only one drawing, which consists of lines on the two-dimensional surface of the page. You supply the rest—all the spatial aspects. You interpret the sketch as a cube.

But there *is* no cube, even though it is impossible to regard it as anything else. We can vacillate between the two different versions of the cube (and to some extent control which one we want to see, by directing our attention at the farthest corner). But we cannot get rid of the cubes. Nor can we see the two different versions simultaneously.

However conscious we are of the fact of lines on a piece of paper, we can't miss seeing a cube. Our consciousness can select one of two possibilities, but it cannot discard them both.

We can try marking the cube by putting a dot on one surface and saying, "This is the nearest." But when the cube changes spatially, the dot moves too!

We do not see the lines and then interpret them into a drawing of a cube. We see the interpretation, not the data we interpret.

Look at the figure below: Can you see the triangles? They are known as Kanizsa triangles, after the Italian psychologist Gaetano Kanizsa, from the University of Trieste.[6]

There are no triangles but what are known as subjective contours. Look at the page; look closely: it really does look as if the paper is a

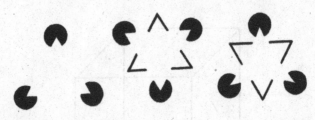

Kanizsa triangles

touch lighter inside the triangles. But no! Study the sides of the triangles, their very edges. There is no transition. It is pure illusion.

But it is not possible to get rid of the triangles simply by convincing oneself and one's consciousness that "they are not really there." One sees them anyway.

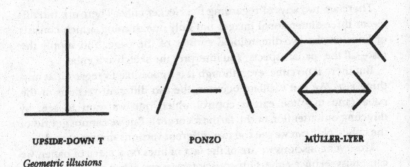

UPSIDE-DOWN T **PONZO** **MÜLLER-LYER**

Geometric illusions

The figure above contains geometric illusions: We see geometric figures of a different length or size than they appear to be. The two lines are of equal length in the upside-down T, just as they are in the Müller-Lyer illusion. In the Ponzo illusion, the horizontal lines are of equal length, but we "read" a perspective into the drawing and think the upper line is farthest away—so it must be longer than the lower one when they both look the same length. Even though we know it is not true.[7]

The upside-down T explains why the moon looks biggest when it is closest to the horizon: We perceive distances in an upward direction differently than we do distances horizontally away from us. The same phenomenon applies to constellations, which also look biggest when they are low in the sky, for then they are not so far away. Consider how huge the difference is between moving 100 meters upward and 100 meters along the ground. So it is understandable that we have got used to perceiving something as farther away if we view it in an upward direction. Doing so also means that we perceive it as smaller. The funny thing about the moon is that its diameter is always half a degree in the sky, no matter whether it is high or low. The image on our retina (or a photograph) is the same size whether the moon is high or low. But there is a huge difference in our perception of the size of the moon

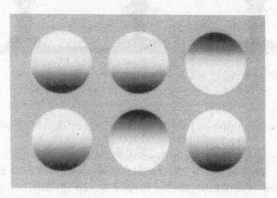

Depth illusions

when it is high in the sky, and looks tiny and far away, and when it is hanging there, brooding and gigantic, just above the horizon, so close you could almost touch it.

Look at the figure above. It shows that we are living on a planet that orbits a star! Well, observe the depth in the images: Are they globes or hollows, concave or convex? You probably see four of them as globes and two as hollows. Turn the book upside down. See? The scene changed. This tells us that our vision assumes that the light comes from above. If the shadows are topmost, the images must be hollows. If the shadows are lowest, they must be protrusions.

When there is light on our planet, it comes from the sky, not from earth. Our vision knows this perfectly well, even though it was not until a few years ago that the psychologist Vilyanur Ramachandran, from the University of California, San Diego, came up with these splendid examples. The actual effect of the direction of light determining whether we

Rubin's vase

see shapes as concave or convex was described by David Brewster in the 1800s.[8]

We can thank the Danish psychologist Edgar Rubin for the figure above, or, more correctly, the American photographer Zeke Berman's elaboration of Rubin's vase,[9] a double image initially conceived by Rubin in 1915. You can choose to see black vases—with the white faces as background. Or you can see the faces—and then the black vases become background. You choose to see one as the shape, the other as the background. But you cannot choose both of them simultaneously. You distinguish between signal and noise. Again it is not the raw data that you see; you see an interpretation, and only one interpretation at a time. Berman's version of the Rubin vases is not a drawing. He used silhouettes of real faces. The figure above is a drawing inspired by Berman.

When you have spent a moment looking at the figure below, your age can be guessed: If you see a young woman with her face averted, you are probably young yourself; if you see an old woman, you are probably no spring chicken.

That, at any rate, is the consensus from the Exploratorium in San

Young or old?

Francisco, where this picture, originally conceived by E. G. Boring, an American psychologist, is on display.[10] As a rule, it takes a while to switch views. But the effect is dramatic once you do so. (When you are familiar with the picture, it is quite easy to control which one you want to see. Just direct your gaze at the place in the picture where the eye of the desired figure will appear—then you can spot the whole woman at once.)

≈

The British neuropsychologist Richard L. Gregory has spent a lifetime collecting visual illusions like these. For they reveal a great deal about our way of seeing. Gregory has formulated his understanding of the illusions thus: Our sight really consists of a hypothesis, an interpretation of the world. We do not see the data in front of our eyes; we see an interpretation.

In his widely used textbook on the psychology of sight, *Eye and Brain* (1966), Gregory wrote: "The senses do not give us a picture of the world directly; rather they provide evidence for the checking of hypotheses about what lies before us. Indeed, we may say that the perception of an object is an hypothesis."[11] Further, " 'ambiguous figures' illustrate very clearly how the same pattern or stimulation at the eye can give rise to different perceptions, and how the perception of objects goes beyond sensation."[12]

These visual illusions have played an enormous role in our understanding not only of sensation and experience but also of science and philosophy. The challenge by philosophers such as Ludwig Wittgenstein, and scientific historians such as Norwood Russell Hanson and Thomas Kuhn, to the positivist belief that we could explain knowledge without reference to who was doing the knowing took such illusions as its starting point.[13]

Many of the illusions were studied and investigated early in the twentieth century as part of the program for Gestalt psychology.

Gestalt psychologists such as Edgar Rubin insisted that we could not divide sensation into arbitrarily small units that could be studied independently. There is a wholeness about human sensation, which cannot be done away with. We see either one Necker cube or the other, even though we are looking at only one drawing. We experience a wholeness before we perceive the parts, we see a configuration (in German: *Gestalt*) before we see the elements of which it is made up.

Gestalt psychology had a tough time of it during the domination of the behaviorists at the start of the century, but today it is recovering its honor and dignity, because it has become clear that sight can be understood only along lines of wholeness and hypotheses.[14]

We do not see what we sense. We see what we think we sense. Our consciousness is presented with an interpretation, not the raw data. Long before this presentation, an unconscious information processing has discarded information so that what we see is a simulation, a hypothesis, an interpretation; and we are not free to choose.

In the case of Necker's cube we can choose between two possibilities, but our consciousness cannot choose the two possibilities it wants to choose between. Or that there should *be* two possibilities.

The interesting thing, of course, is that the visual illusions (Necker's, Ponzo's, etc.) are carefully refined and researched examples of some of the few cases where we can in fact make a choice, or realize that our sight does deceive us.

What about all the situations where we can see only a single interpretation, or fail to see that we are distorting a geometric perspective? Surely there must be some unconscious discarding of information before we perceive?

Of course there is, but we cannot see it. The illusions are the special cases which tell us that any seeing and any experience is based on a vast mass of decisions, discards, and interpretations that take place long before we become conscious of what we are experiencing.

We do not experience the world as raw data. When our consciousness experiences the world, the unconscious discarding of sensory information has long since interpreted things for us.

What we experience has acquired meaning before we become conscious of it.

It is not solely the arrangement of our nervous system that gives rise to these illusions. Cultural factors play a very large part; for example, many non-Western cultures do not use perspective in their illustrations. Many of the illusions thus involve cultural conventions as to how we "read" pictures. But this does not make such conventions less unconscious. It is hard to set oneself apart from one's own background, because one discards copious quantities of information long before one begins consciously to "see" a picture.

One example of the information that gets discarded when one looks at a visual illustration is from anthropologists' investigation of image perception in the Me'en people of Ethiopia. The anthropologists gave them a picture and asked what it was. "They felt the paper, sniffed it, crumpled it, and listened to the crackling noise it made; they nipped off little bits and chewed them to taste it."[15] The pattern on the paper did not interest the Me'en, because pictures as they knew them were painted on cloth. (Presented with Western pictures on cloth, the Me'en had trouble seeing what they were meant to see by our standards.)

The anthropologist Colin Turnbull studied the Pygmies in the Congo, who spend their entire lives in the forest and thus have no experience judging the size of objects at great distances. Turnbull once took Kenge, his Pygmy guide, out of the forest.

"Kenge looked over the plain and down to a herd of buffalo some miles away. He asked me what kind of insects they were, and I told him buffalo, twice as big as the forest buffalo known to him. He laughed loudly and told me not to tell him such stupid stories. . . . We got into the car and drove down to where the animals were grazing. He watched them getting larger and larger, and though he was as courageous as any pygmy, he moved over and sat close to me and muttered that it was witchcraft. When he realized they were real buffalo he was no longer afraid, but what puzzled him was why they had been so small, and whether they had really been small and suddenly grown larger or whether it had been some kind of trickery."[16]

Westerners, too, can have trouble with Western pictures, especially if they are disguised as art.

Pablo Picasso was once asked in a train compartment by a fellow passenger why he did not paint people "the way they really are." Picasso asked what the man meant by the expression. The man pulled a snapshot of his wife out of his wallet and said, "That's my wife." Picasso responded, "Isn't she rather small and flat?"[17]

What we see is not a reproduction of the raw data. So what is it a reproduction of?

Color vision provides interesting evidence. As we know, fire engines are red. Morning, noon, and night. Everyone would agree that fire engines are a splendid red and that they remain so round the clock. In principle, they are the same color in the dark; it is just that nobody can see them as such.

But the light is not constant throughout the day. In the morning and evening, the light is considerably redder than at midday. When the sun is low in the sky, lots of blue light gets scattered away, because the sunlight has to penetrate a greater quantity of air when it passes through the atmosphere "at an angle."

Yet fire engines are equally red all day. But the light our eyes receive from fire engines is not the same. This is known as color constancy: We see the same color, even though the information we base our color perception on changes. This is extremely expedient. It would be highly impractical if fire engines changed color throughout the day (and even more inexpedient if the poison mushroom fly agaric did so).

The colors we see are the result of computations that are performed by the brain. The electromagnetic rays that reach us from an object are compared to those coming from other parts of the scenery. Against this background the color of the object is computed. This means that the same object takes on the same color even if the information the eye receives from the object changes: color constancy. Color is a property of the brain rather than of the object.

We can create visual illusions from colors. Colored shadows, for example, in which yellow and white light create a blue shadow. Or mixed colors, where a red spotlight and a green spotlight create a yellow patch of light. If we add a blue spotlight, we get a white patch.

Colors are the result of computations: The colors we see do not exist in the outside world. They arise only when we see them. If the colors that we see were a property of the outside world, we would not be able to see the illusion of colored shadows.

The expediency of this lies in its constancy: An object is seen as the same color regardless of the light conditions. What we experience when we see a red fire engine is the result of a computation in which the brain tries to ascribe the same experience to the same object, even if the information it receives changes.

This computation is performed by the brain on the basis of information from three different kinds of visual cells. Each kind is best at "seeing" its own particular wavelength. A similar system is used in video cameras, which register three different colors. The colors are then combined into a TV picture. But a video camera is rather less adroit than a human, so it cannot work out what the surroundings look like by itself. We have to tell video cameras what the light is like. Otherwise we end up with color flaws in our picture. This often occurs on TV news programs when a person is interviewed by a window. If the camera is adjusted for artificial indoor lighting, which is very yellow, daylight looks very blue. If the camera is set for daylight, electric light looks very yellow.

In practice, this problem is solved by showing the camera a piece of white paper before recording starts. Knowing what white is meant to look like, the camera can then "calculate" the lighting for the given situation.

It is this white balance that human vision carries out every time it sees a fire engine. By looking at something expected to be white, like a house, it has figured out in advance what white looks like. So our sight can correct for what is in this context an utterly irrelevant detail: the actual composition of the reflected light the eye receives from the fire engine.

White balance adjustment happens unconsciously. We do not perceive that this is a red fire engine in the midday sun; we perceive a red fire engine.[18]

But the white balance can be influenced by consciousness—or, more accurately, by the knowledge we have of the situation, as the following experience shows:

There was lots of room on the clothesline in the dim basement. There was only a woman's white sweater hanging there when he entered with his white wash. As he hung his undershirt on the line, he could not help noticing that the sweater was not quite white but pinkish. He thought somewhat absentmindedly that somebody must have put a red sock in with that load. Such things do happen.

A few moments later, the owner of the sweater came into the basement. Before he could extend his sympathy, she burst out, "Goodness, your clothes are all bluish!"

Indeed, he was the one who had been sloppy and had put something blue into his white wash, turning everything ice blue.

This man's personal white balance had unconsciously been adjusted on the basis of the white wash, which by definition results in white laundry. So he defined the slightly bluish hue as white and, thereby, the white sweater as pink. The remarkable thing is that once he was conscious of this, he could see it easily.

Even though colors arise in our heads, they are not too subjective or arbitrary to allow us to sort out who put the wrong sock into the washing machine.

No palette on the planet is more fascinating than the sky. What an orgy of deeply shimmering colors and fragile shades plays above the horizon when clouds, sunset, and sea collude to form a scene we can watch for hours! The changes in the light from day to day and region to region can be a balm to the vacationing soul released from the monotonous, ergonomically correct artificial light of the office. Just a glimpse of the sky, and one's head feels alive. Why? Perhaps because seeing colors is an active process, a computation, a discarding of information, which leads to an experience. A new sky is a new challenge; a new light is a new experience, quite irrespective of what is seen in this new light. Are the colors of nature not deep, inexplicably fragile and complex, richly shaded and varying from second to second in the restless surface of the ocean? Do we not rejoice when our eyes are put to work, when there is information to be discarded, when the reduction of sensation to experience is visual digestion, as pleasurable as crispy vegetables and fresh fish? The sky is seldom listless and easily absorbable, like fast food. The older we get, the greater our delight at a rare sky.

Richard Gregory is a great man. In physical stature he is a big man, a tall, broad Brit with pronounced features. A suitable appearance for an experimental psychologist who is an expert in visual illusions and regards experience as a hypothesis—a view Gregory bases on a long life of experimental work. It is not a great step from regarding experience as interpretation to regarding the entire reality we experience as an interpretation rather than a reproduction of a reality.

When, for the purposes of this book, Gregory was asked his idea of what reality was, he beamed as he replied, "Reality is a hypothesis. That's what I call it—a hypothesis." A statement that sums up much of Gregory's contribution to experimental psychology.

When the laughter at the possibility of obtaining a better hypothesis had faded, the next question was: "How about regarding reality as a *simulation*?"

"Oh, that's probably a better way of putting it,"[19] he replied promptly. A great man.

A simulation is a reconstruction, a replica, a crib of something. If you can simulate a process, it means you can reproduce important facets of it so that, without necessarily carrying out the process itself, you can work out where the process will end. A simulation is a dynamic interpretation, a hypothesis, and thus a prediction. Our experience of reality is in a sense an experience of our simulation of what goes on *out there*.

The dramatic insight the visual illusions provide is that we never experience things directly; we see them as an interpretation. We cannot help seeing Necker's cube as three-dimensional and have to make an effort to experience it as lines on a page. First we experience the interpretation, the simulation: not what we sense but our simulation of what we sense.

We do not sense, then experience, and then simulate, interpret, assess, and surmise.

We sense, simulate, and *then* experience. Maybe. For sometimes we sense and simulate—and then we act, because there is not enough time to experience first.

That is the lesson of the visual illusions: sense, simulate, and only then experience. A very radical lesson.

"What the Frog's Eye Tells the Frog's Brain" is the title of a remarkable scientific paper published in the *Proceedings of the Institute of Radio Engineers*. The article was about how frogs see the world, and no more than that, despite the fact that the U.S. Army, the U.S. Air Force, and the U.S. Navy were all credited with providing funding for the project (which was also supported by Bell Telephone Labs, Inc.). "This work has been done on the frog, and our interpretation applies only to the frog,"[20] wrote its four authors, Jerome Lettvin, Humberto Maturana, Warren McCulloch, and Walter Pitts, all of whom worked at MIT.

But the consequences were to affect the worldview of people, not frogs. Not because of defense funding (in the 1950s, the armed forces were a standard source of finance for pure research) but·because of the perspectives for epistemology. The four authors had proved the existence of "the synthetic a priori," genetically built into frogs.[21]

The synthetic *a priori* was Immanuel Kant's term for the preconditions for knowledge that we cannot get rid of. Kant revolutionized philosophy in the 1700s by pointing out (as described in Chapter Three) that human knowledge must necessarily have certain preconditions, certain *a priori*, that precede experience, such as time, place, and causation. Without such preconditions we cannot know anything at all, but when we have them, we do not know the world itself; we know a world seen through the spectacles the *a priori* constitute. We can never know the world as it is, know only the world as it is for us. So Kant distinguished between things as they are, *Das Ding an sich*, and things as we know them, *Das Ding für uns*.

And now, on defense funding, the four scientists had come across *Das Ding für frogs*.

A frog's eye tells the frog's brain only four things about the world—namely, where in its field of vision there are: (1) clear lines of contrast (which reveal the whereabouts of the horizon, for example); (2) sudden changes in illumination (which reveal that a stork is approaching, for example); (3) outlines in motion (which reveal the stork's movements, for example); and most important of all, (4) the curves of the outlines of small, dark objects. The authors write that they are tempted to call the latter bug perceivers.

The frog's brain does not get informed about the view—or it does, but only about the part of the view that is of interest: friends, enemies, and the surface of the water. The froggy brain is not concerned with forming a "realistic" image of the surroundings. It is interested in getting something to eat without getting eaten.

This characteristic of the frog's way of seeing the world is built into its anatomy. The nerve fibers from the eye to the brain are each connected to lots of vision cells, so they do not only say whether there is light or not in a particular cell. They reveal a pattern. The brain receives the result of a computation. As the four scientists put it:

"What are the consequences of this work? Fundamentally, it shows that the eye speaks to the brain in a language already highly organized and interpreted, instead of transmitting some more or less accurate copy of the distribution of light on the receptors."[22]

That is why it is only when you kiss it that the frog realizes you are a princess.

The four scientists were not the first to study frog vision. Horace Barlow, a British scientist, published a study of frog vision in 1953. Twenty years later, he wrote, "The result makes one suddenly realize that a large part of the sensory machinery involved in a frog's feeding responses may actually reside in the retina rather than in mysterious 'centres' that would be too difficult to understand by physiological methods."[23] Further, "each single neuron can perform a much more complex and subtle task than had previously been thought. . . . The activities of neurons, quite simply, are thought processes."[24] The frog's unconscious resides in its eyes.

Since then, similar information discarding in the eyes has been proved in animals with more advanced feeding habits than frogs. In cats, monkeys, humans, and many other creatures, corresponding divisions of information from the surroundings have been found.

In man, nerve impulses are led from the eyes to the brain via a complex route. The signals pass through a structure deep in the brain, the thalamus, from where they are conveyed to the visual areas of the cortex. There are a hundred million nerve cells in the first visual area the impulses reach. That is quite a lot, because there are only a few million visual cells in the eye. In the 1960s, an American, David Hubel, and a Swede, Torstein Wiesel, who was working in the United States, showed that the cells of the cortex have special tasks: They can discover some special property of the field of vision—an edge, a line, a contrast, a direction, etc.

Hubel and Wiesel's work created considerable belief that we would be able to explain how human beings see. Their contribution was a clear successor to the work on frogs done by Barlow and others.

Initially there was great enthusiasm at the discovery that every cell in the visual area of the cortex could take part in interpreting what we see. But gradually the scientists began to lose heart. During the 1970s, it became obvious that something vital was missing.[25]

In 1990, for example, Horace Barlow wrote as follows about the hundred million nerve cells in the visual centers of the cortex, each of which interprets a particular characteristic of the field of vision:

"This is an interesting way to represent an image, and the fact that each individual nerve cell conveys an important piece of information makes us feel that we have made some progress in understanding how images are 'digested.' But there is also something profoundly unsatisfactory about it: what earthly use is an array of 100 million cells, each of which responds to some rather specific characteristic of a small part of the visual field? The images we are familiar with in our heads have a unity and usefulness that this representation, fragmented into a vast number of tiny pieces like a jigsaw puzzle, seems to lack. Why is it represented like this? How is the picture on the jigsaw puzzle detected, or rather what neural mechanisms carry the analysis of the image further, and what is the goal of these further steps? I want to suggest that the main obstacle here is that we have not grasped the true problem."[26]

Perhaps the true problem is that there is no image, only a jigsaw puzzle. Barlow tacitly assumes that there is an image first, and this image is then divided among a hundred million nerve cells, before being put together again and seen/experienced.

There *must* be an image, one might object, because what we see is the world. Our eyes compose a picture of what the world looks like. All right, but who has ever seen the world unless it has been through the hundred million pieces in our jigsaw? After all, you only see *Das Ding für you*—you have never seen *Das Ding an sich*, the thing in itself.

You cannot see unless through your eyes, and you can see through your eyes only via the hundred million nerve cells in the primary visual center of the brain (which happens to be located at the back and not just behind your eyes). You see colors and edges and shapes and flies and frogs. But what you see is the result of computation and simulation.

There is not the remotest reason to believe that what we see resembles what we are looking at.

But, you might object, we all agree on what we see. We see the same tree, the same bus, the same red fire engines. Well, yes, as far as we can talk our way into agreement. But our talk will take place at a very low bandwidth. A few bits per second, the capacity of consciousness. This capacity is incapable of conveying the quality of experiencing red. It can only point and make itself agree with other conversers about fire engines, treetops, and buses.

We can draw pictures of what we see. Surely then we can see that we see the same thing? Yes, unless we are dealing with Me'ens or with Pablo Picasso, for they tend to raise questions that we more or less have to relate our entire life story to answer.

We agree on what things look like, but do we also agree on what red is? Is your red the same as mine?

This is a classic philosophical problem, which the American philosopher Thomas Nagel put very succinctly: "How do you know, when you and a friend are eating chocolate ice cream, whether it tastes the same to him as it tastes to you? You can try a taste of his ice cream, but if it tastes the same as yours, that only means it tastes the same *to you*: you have not experienced the way it tastes to *him*." Nagel continues: "If we go on pressing these kinds of questions relentlessly enough, we will move from mild and harmless skepticism about whether chocolate ice cream tastes exactly the same to you and your friend, to a much more radical skepticism about whether there is any similarity between your experiences and his. . . .

"How do you even know that your friend is conscious? How do you know that there are any minds at all besides your own? The only example you've ever directly observed of a correlation between mind, behavior, anatomy, and physical circumstances is yourself," Nagel writes.[27]

This is known as "the problem of other minds." Are there any other minds out there?

It is a contumacious problem, because of course there are other minds. If you did not think so, you could not be bothered to read this book.

But the interesting thing is not that there are other minds; because there are. What is interesting is that even though philosophers have been discussing this problem for centuries, they have still not come up with convincing logical arguments to prove that there *are* other minds. A small, obdurate, and generally youthful group of philosophers always maintains the idea of solipsism: that one is the only person in existence. "I alone am." Which is of course rubbish. "If I were a solipsist I probably wouldn't be writing this book, since I wouldn't believe there was anybody else to read it," Nagel writes.[28]

The problem of other minds is closely related to the problem of the existence of the external world. How can we say there even is one? A Danish philosopher, Peter Zinkernagel, has solved this problem by pointing out that we cannot say there is no external reality: Language breaks down totally if we assert that language does not have anything to talk about.[29]

Correspondingly, we can state that communication breaks down totally unless we acknowledge that there are other minds. All communication is based on the premise that whoever we are communicating with are people, that they have a tree of talking inside them. Without this premise, conversation is meaningless.

But this is not proof that there are other minds (or an external reality, for that matter). It is merely a stating of the fact that here is a problem we cannot discuss. Because the discussion itself presupposes that the answer is yes, there is somebody else to talk to.

So unless you acknowledge the existence of other minds, you have nobody to talk to about this point of view of yours.

Let us look at the route the optical impulses take from the eye to the cortex again. Why is there a relay station at the thalamus, deep inside the brain? The special structure of the thalamus, which acts in the transference of the impulses down the optic nerve, goes by the formidable name of *corpus geniculatum laterale,* which translates as lateral geniculate and is abbreviated as LGN.

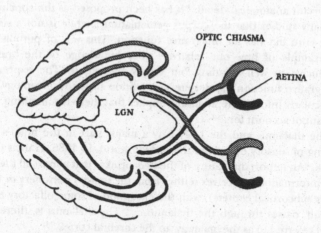

Information from the retina passes through the LGN in the thalamus before it reaches the visual centers of the brain, which are located at the back of the head.

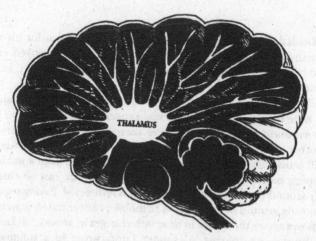

The thalamus is deep inside the brain and acts as a gateway to the cortex. Almost all the information from the surroundings passes through the thalamus before it reaches the cortex.

Danish medical students are told the following about this very important anatomical detail: "It has been proposed as the conclusion of many studies that the corpus geniculatum laterale is not a simple relay core but has an integrative function. This way of putting it is an example of how our relatively poor knowledge of the brain is conducive to well-sounding but empty statements. The expression 'integrative function' is, despite its tradition in neurophysiology, not particularly informative; it almost implies that there is something here we cannot account for."[30]

The thalamus and the LGN play a major part in the brain's processing of sensory data from the outside world. In 1986, Francis Crick wrote, "An important feature of the neocortex is that almost all the outside information it receives (either from the sensory periphery or from other subcortical centers), with the exception of some olfactory information, passes through the thalamus. . . . The thalamus is, therefore, often referred to as the 'gateway' to the cerebral cortex."[31]

The thalamus is not just a gateway; it also receives feedback from the cortex. An intense to-ing and fro-ing takes place between the thalamus and the "higher" functions of the cortex. There are many centers or nuclei in the thalamus that take part in this interplay. In the case of sight, it is the LGN.

The Russian neurophysiologist Ivan Pavlov is best known for his early-twentieth-century experiments on dogs, in which he provoked conditioned reflexes by ringing a bell every time they were to be fed, until in the end they salivated merely at the sound of the bell.

Pavlov pointed out the importance that structures deep inside the brain have for the cortex itself. Actual processing of information from our surroundings takes place in the cortex, but the activity level of the cortex is regulated by deeper structures, such as the thalamus. The overall activity level of the cortex (tonus) can change from a waking to a sleeping state; similarly, activity in the waking state can be changed locally around the cortex as our attention is redirected. Pavlov regarded this moving around of attention as "a mobile, concentrated searchlight that moves across the cortex in time with changes in activity," as another great Russian neurologist, Alexander Luria, wrote in a summary of Pavlov's idea.[32]

Luria continued Pavlov's line of thought by dividing the brain into three blocks: that which regulates wakefulness/tonus/attention (deep structures); that for processing sensory data (the back of the cortex); and that for planning and cognition (the front of the cortex). The thalamus plays a leading part in the first block.

We may regard the first block, then, as a searchlight that determines

SENSORY CORTEX   **PLANNING CORTEX**

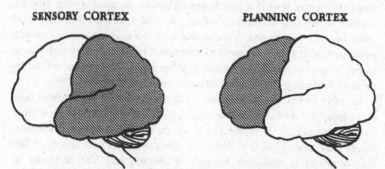

The departments of the brain according to Luria: The whole is shrouded by the cortex. The thalamus and a number of other vital centers are located deep inside the brain. The cortex is divided into a hind section, which mainly processes sensory input, and a fore-brain, which handles plans and ideas in particular.

where the cortex is to be illuminated—and thereby where our attention is directed. An anatomical version of the metaphor for consciousness we encountered earlier as the spotlight moving around in the dark room. In the mid-1980s, Francis Crick tried to define this model by indicating a particular area, the reticular complex on the outside of the thalamus, as the operator that controls the searchlights of consciousness.[33] Crick went on to realize that this idea was too simple.

But the metaphor is good enough as a metaphor: attention and consciousness are a searchlight that picks something out on a stage where a great deal is going on at the same time.

Humberto Maturana was one of the authors of "What the Frog's Eye Tells the Frog's Brain." In recent decades, he and another Chilean, Francisco Varela, have become the leading proponents of the view that our experience of the world around us does not imply a representation or reflection of our surroundings. Reproductions do not come into it, argue the two biologists. A subtler truth is at play.

In 1987, Varela wrote, "The LGN is usually described as a 'relay' station to the cortex. However, at a closer examination most of what the neurons in the LGN receive comes not from the retina (less than 20%), but from other centers inside the brain. . . . What reaches the brain from the retina is only a gentle perturbation on an ongoing internal activity, which can be modulated, in this case at the level of the thalamus, but not instructed. This is the key. To understand the neural processes from a nonrepresentationist point of view, it is enough just to notice that whatever perturbation reaches from the medium will be informed according to the internal coherences of the system."[34]

In other words, the fact that we see is not primarily the result of messages from the retina (which are more than just the light received there in the first place). It is the result of an extensive inner processing, where data from outside is linked to inner activities and models.[35] But this summary is distorted, because Maturana and Varela refuse to acknowledge that anything comes in from outside. The whole thing is a closed circuit, they say; the nervous system does not gather information from the surroundings.[36] The nervous system consists of a self-regulatory whole where there is neither an inside nor an outside, only coherences between impression and expression—sensation and behavior—in order to ensure survival.

This is a highly radical epistemology, and what is more, the two Chileans define it as a closed system. Humberto Maturana in particular is well known for spurning any discussion as to how his views relate to the couple of thousand years' tradition of thought to be found in epistemology. He has come up with a complete theory, and it cannot be debated.

But how does Maturana view the discussion of Kant in the article on the frog's eye? He is not enthusiastic. "The description of the outside world is not about the outside world at all, it's about *us*," he explained in 1991.[37] "There is only experience to be explained. Epistemologically speaking there is nothing else," says Maturana, who thinks it is nonsense to talk of a world without us, *an sich*, for how can we talk about it at all?

A metaphor for Maturana and Varela's point of view is that we perceive the world in the same way as does a crew that spends its entire life on board a submarine. The crew members can manipulate knobs and register the effects of their interventions, but they have no direct experience that there is a world outside the submarine. The world could be completely different from what they thought, as long as it is consistent with all the experiences the crew has gleaned.[38]

Maturana and Varela's standpoint is extreme in the sense that it is not shared by the majority of scientists in their field. But it is consistent, it hangs together. In its logical structure it is entirely reminiscent of what is known as the Copenhagen interpretation of quantum mechanics, the physics of atoms: an interpretation propounded principally by Niels Bohr. "It is wrong to think that the task of physics is to find out how nature is. Physics concerns what we can say about nature,"[39] Bohr said, emphasizing that we cannot describe the world without including in our description the fact that we are describing it.

The spokesmen for the Copenhagen interpretation today are no more interested in Maturana's ideas than Maturana is interested in the ideas of quantum mechanics, but the similarity is striking: The big problem in describing our own description is that we would so very much like to think of the world as something we describe, reflect, reproduce, copy, represent in our heads.

But perhaps it is not possible to speak clearly and unambiguously in that way. (It is definitely also very difficult to talk clearly and unambiguously in terms of "there is no world out there at all"; in this chapter, we have more or less constantly assumed the traditional view that there is a world—otherwise we could not talk about illusions as illusions.)

Indications are that the very idea of an inside and an outside is heading for a fall. From physics and neurophysiology we are getting the same message, perhaps most elegantly put by John Wheeler as quoted in Chapter One: "There is no *out there* out there."

It is worth noting that the link between the Copenhagen interpretation and the Maturana/Varela point of view raises a question: Are these descriptions complete? If we accept that they are consistent, we are forced to ask if they include everything. They do not. They cannot. Kurt Gödel proved as much: His theorem says that a perfect, rounded theory cannot be consistent and complete. If it is consistent, there will be statements in it the truth of which cannot be determined, even if we know by other means that they are true.

In 1935, Albert Einstein, for years Gödel's best friend, posed the following question of quantum mechanics: Is it complete? He tried to prove by a cunningly devised example that it was not. This resulted in a lengthy discussion, where his opponent was Niels Bohr, who insisted that quantum mechanics was complete. Experiments carried out in the 1980s finally proved that Einstein's example did not hold water.

Quantum mechanics is complete: We cannot know more about the world of atoms than it tells us. As far as we know.[40]

We can put the same question to Maturana and Varela's point of view: Is it complete? Certainly not! It is a complete and total description of life on a submarine, but this description presupposes that there is a world outside the submarine, and only that. Otherwise it does not hang together.

Maturana and Varela's point of view can account for any experience inside the submarine, but it presupposes that there is a world outside; otherwise it is sheer nonsense. But you cannot see this from inside the submarine.

It is not enough to demand of a point of view that it is consistent, for there are loads of consistent but uninteresting points of view in life. For example, the solipsism: I alone am.

Maturana and Varela's point of view may be *correct*, but in a sense it is not particularly *important*.

The neurosciences face a major problem today, one sometimes known as *the binding problem*. Information from our surroundings is split up and analyzed in many different centers of the brain. Not only do impulses from the various sensory modalities such as sight and hearing go to different parts of the brain to be analyzed; the input from the individual modalities also gets split up among myriads of nerve cells, each of which sees an edge or a shape or a movement or a color or an amount of light or a contrast or a direction or a spatial location.

Not only do all these aspects have to be analyzed and then reassembled into a composite picture of the horse one is riding; and not only does this visual image have to be associated with smell, hearing, feeling, and pleasure—it has to happen simultaneously, and before one falls off the horse!

The human brain has to cope with coordinating the processing of more than eleven million bits that arrive every second and are divided among hundreds of millions of nerve cells, so that all these different impulses are composed into one conscious picture of what is going on.

It has to do so constantly, for up to sixteen hours a day. Without the experience going out of sync.

This is the binding problem. We could also call it the figure/ground problem.[41] In the ambiguous figures like the vase/faces on page 184, how does the brain figure out what is vase and what are faces in the data it processes? How do all the various aspects of an object get assembled? Indeed, how is it decided at all in the first instance which part of the scenery is the figure and which the ground?

The binding problem is a very profound problem, whether there is a world out there or not.

In 1989 and 1990, there was considerable enthusiasm for an idea that seemed for the first time to bring the phenomenon of consciousness into the realm of the natural sciences. The cause of this enthusiasm was partly that the idea mooted a mechanism for solving the binding problem.

It was the joint idea of a young German physicist, Christof Koch, who heads the laboratory for computation and nervous systems under the institutes of biology at the California Institute of Technology, and the British physicist, biologist, and neuroscientist Francis Crick, who works at the Salk Institute in La Jolla, California. The idea is so embracing, bold, and simple that it would scarcely have been taken seriously, had it not been for two remarkable circumstances.

One was Francis Crick—one of the most legendary scientists of the twentieth century, who came to fame in 1953 through the solution of the mystery of inheritance when he and the American James Watson discovered the structure of the DNA molecule: the famous double helix, which has become a symbol of our time. Time and time again since 1953, Crick has put forward simple, cheeky, and—now and then—correct ideas that have totally changed the scientific debate.

The other remarkable circumstance was that there seemed to be experimental backing for Crick and Koch's idea. In 1989, a group of German scientists discovered that nerve cells in cats oscillate in synchrony when the cells see the same object. These oscillations take place forty times a second and apparently express agreement by the cells that they are seeing the same object.[42] When Wolf Singer and his scientific colleagues in Frankfurt published the extent of their findings, the respected American journal *Science* reported the news under the headline "The Mind Revealed?" and introduced the article by asking, "Has Wolf Singer uncovered the cellular basis of consciousness?"[43]

Crick and Koch's idea is that the oscillations Singer found are the basis of consciousness. All the cells that receive stimuli originating from the same object "lock into" synchrony, which they maintain for a brief period.

This theory applies initially to conscious sight, but the two scientists do not hide their belief that it may explain the basis of all consciousness.[44] Originally, the idea of oscillations that express nerve cells collaborating was mooted by a German, Christoph von der Malsburg, in 1986.[45]

The enthusiasm was great in the summer of 1990 when, for the first time in many years, Singer's results and Crick and Koch's bold speculation gave the scientific community the sense that it was coming to grips with the riddle of consciousness. Since then, experiments have provided less encouraging results. It turns out that it is very difficult to repeat the same effect in monkey brains, so the optimism that surrounded the idea a few years ago has cooled markedly. Scientists could find only weak signs of the same oscillations in simian brains—only five–ten percent of the cells participate in such activity—and it has not been possible to even begin studies on human subjects.[46]

But the elegant aspect of the idea is that at the same time it explains *attention*, the essence of consciousness of the outside world. When a number of nerve cells oscillate in synchrony at forty hertz—forty times a second—this *is* attention. Different groups of nerve cells oscillate in synchrony about different objects in our surroundings (the desk, the chair, the book, the manuscript, the horse), and one of the oscillation patterns wins. *That* is consciousness.

The oscillation pattern that dominates for a moment when we are aware of something couples myriad nerve cells together and forms consciousness. We can be conscious of only one thing at a time (or, more accurately, seven plus-or-minus-two things), because one of the oscillations dominates.

Each time a thing has become the object of such 40 Hz oscillations, we have been aware of it—and we can remember it. Oscillation patterns that correspond to something we can remember win more easily than brand-new oscillations representing new objects, because then you have a pattern of neurons that have never oscillated together before.

The plethora of objects that stimulate oscillation but do not win at any given moment can either become objects of attention later, when the oscillations win—or never become so.

At any given moment, the brain contains a very large number of nerve cells oscillating in synchrony. Very few of them ever become amplified into the dominant 40 Hz oscillation for even the tiniest instant. None of these oscillations will ever become the object of attention.

They represent the unconscious processing of information by the brain.

"There is also much neural activity in the visual system that does not reach full awareness," Crick and Koch wrote. "Much of this corresponds to the computations needed to arrive at the best interpretation of all the incoming information that is compatible with the stored, categorical information acquired in the past. It is this 'best interpretation' of which we become aware."[47]

The strength of this theory is that it makes it intuitively understandable why consciousness is able to alternate so rapidly and efficiently between such widely differing objects: There is constantly a vast army of nerve cells oscillating in synchrony. But only one of the sets of oscillations wins and becomes consciousness. The rest compete for consciousness's favors.

In this way, 40 Hz oscillations can convey a kind of searchlight that peruses the various activities of the brain. But note that the metaphor is no longer just spatial, like a searchlight. The coherence between the nerve cells is expressed *in time*, not only in space.

"If there are several possible interpretations of the incoming information," Crick and Koch write, "then it may take some time for the one particular interpretation to dominate its rivals and establish itself. In the case of 'rivalry,' when the percepts alternate, as in the well-known case of the Necker cube, we assume that the oscillations that first became established eventually habituate somewhat so that the other interpretation gets the upper hand by establishing the oscillations relevant to it and in doing so pushes down its rival. After a delay it is then itself pushed down, and so on."[48]

So we return to the visual illusions and the Gestalt psychologists' studies of human sight.

"The roles we are suggesting for the 40 Hz oscillations bring to mind some of the ideas of the Gestalt psychologists. What we have referred to as an 'object' would be better termed a 'gestalt,' " Crick and Koch write. They go on, "What to a psychologist is a particular gestalt would, to the neuroscientist, be expressed by a particular set of phase-locked oscillating neurons."[49]

Crick and Koch's idea is unlikely to be the right one. Neither was it ever (almost) meant as more than a thought model, an existence proof that thinking about what consciousness is is meaningful.

The effects of their proposal will presumably be felt for years to come, even if their actual theory does not hold water.

Crick and Koch introduce the presentation of their theory with the words: "It is remarkable that most of the work in both cognitive science and the neurosciences makes no reference to consciousness (or 'awareness'), especially as many would regard consciousness as the major puzzle confronting the neural view of the mind and indeed at the present time it appears deeply mysterious to many people. . . . We suggest that the time is now ripe for an attack on the neural basis of consciousness."[50]

The way is paved for a study of consciousness and attention—a subject that in general the "hard" sciences have hitherto ignored and that the human sciences have not tried to juxtapose with the natural science view of the world.

But perhaps the most important aspect of the Crick-Koch theory is that it will make neuroscientists take the binding problem seriously. The natural science–oriented neuroscientists tend to ignore problems as "complicated" as the Necker cube and Rubin's vase. The idea of the forty-hertz oscillations shows that Gestalt psychology's research into the world of human experience may be central to a "hard" science theory of nerve cells. Irrespective of whether one wants to grasp at radical solutions, like Maturana and Varela, and declare the outside world irrelevant, or whether one wishes to maintain a more traditional epistemology, one must inevitably face the fact that in the binding problem there is a very big problem indeed.

Most of all, perhaps, the time problem is a grave one: How can all these processes oscillate in synchrony, allowing us to experience the various aspects of an event simultaneously, when their analysis has taken place in so many different areas of the brain? Taste, smell, sight, balance, and hearing have to hang together pretty well when you are on horseback. How does this coordination take place in time?

Consciousness is a very *deep* phenomenon: Vast quantities of information have to be discarded during its making. How can all these processes occur in coordination? And how long do they take? Halfway into this account, let us pause and sum up. In the next chapter, we will come upon the answer to the question of consciousness in time. A rather disturbing answer—so let us convince ourselves that it was inevitable.

Maxwell's demon told us that knowledge involves the world. That information is a notion which is based on thermodynamics, an understanding of heat and steam engines. It costs to possess knowledge of the world: not necessarily because it costs anything to obtain this knowledge, but because it is difficult to get rid of it again. Pure, clear consciousness is the true cost—and we cannot know anything about the world without this clear consciousness, which, on the other hand, we cannot possess unless we have discarded all the information we had in our consciousness a moment ago.

Computation and cognition consist of discarding information: picking what matters from what does not. The discarding of information is the thermodynamic *proper*, that which *costs*.

Information is interesting once we have got rid of it again: once we have taken in a mass of information, extracted what is important, and thrown the rest out. In itself, information is almost a measure of randomness, unpredictability, indeterminacy. Information is more related to disorder than to order, because order arises in situations where there is less information than there could have been. Information is a measure of how many other messages could have been present than the one actually present; of what we could have said, not what we said.

The complexity of the physical and biological world can be described as *depth:* the amount of discarded information. What interests us in life is not that which contains the most information and thus takes longest to describe, for it is identical with disorder, untidiness, chaos. Nor is it the extremely well ordered and predictable, for there are no surprises there.

What interests us are things that have a history, things preserved in time not because they are static and closed but because they are open and concurrent, because they have discarded quantities of information on the way. That is why we can measure complexity or depth as *thermodynamic depth* (the volume of information discarded) or the closely related notion of *logical depth* (the computation time spent discarding the information).

Conversation involves exchanging information, but that is not the important thing. For there is very little information in the words of a conversation. Most important is the discarding of information that takes place before anything is put into words. The sender collapses a mass of information into a very small amount of information in the form of what actually gets said. From the context, the receiver excites a mass of information that had actually been discarded. This way, the sender can create exformation by discarding information, transmit the resulting information, and see a corresponding amount of old exformation provoked in the receiver's head.

So the bandwidth of language—the capacity for transmitting bits per second—is very low: about fifty bits per second or less. As language and thought are capable of filling up our consciousness completely, the capacity of consciousness cannot be greater than that of language; experiments in psychophysics in the 1950s revealed that the capacity of consciousness is very small. Less than forty bits a second, presumably less than sixteen bits a second.

This figure is incredibly small compared to the volume of information we take in through our senses, about eleven million bits per second. The conscious experience constitutes a very small portion of the information constantly admitted by our senses.

This means that our actions in the world must necessarily be based on a mass of information that enters through our senses but never reaches our consciousness. For a few bits a second is not enough to explain the wealth of behavior we see in human beings. Indeed, psychologists have revealed the existence of subliminal perception (even though research into the subject demonstrates peculiar historical gaps that can be explained by concrete fear that this knowledge would be exploited for commercial purposes and abstract fear of man's inscrutability).

Consciousness cannot tell itself about this subliminal perception precisely because it is subliminal. But observations of illusions and other everyday phenomena prove that what we experience is a simulation of what we sense. A discarding of information and thereby an interpretation of sensory input has taken place long before it reaches consciousness. Most of our mental life takes place unconsciously—not only as the result of Freudian repression but as the normal way of functioning.

Consciousness can be understood from within, but if so, it is a closed, partly mendacious system, which claims that what we experience is what we sense. The illusions show that the truth cannot be so simple. Consciousness can also be regarded from without, but then it is hard to understand how the enormous amounts of information offered to consciousness end as a coherent, complete picture of an experienced reality. The relationship between consciousness seen from within and without is a very fundamental problem.

Human consciousness possesses a high degree of complexity. It is a phenomenon of considerable *depth*. A great deal of information is discarded in its making. Characteristic of consciousness is its high complexity but low information content.

Charles Bennett, the physicist, defined logical depth by the computation time that accompanied creating anything. The longer the computation time, the greater the depth, because depth is an expression of a mass of information that has been discarded. Discarding information takes time, just as releasing a beautiful sculpture from a block of marble takes time.

We must therefore now ask: "Does creating consciousness also take time? Does discarding most of the sensory information before we experience also take time?"

Well, it *must*. So the real question is how long it takes. A very urgent question it is, too, because we sense constantly and we are conscious—almost—all the time. *So if consciousness takes time, it must constantly lag behind!*

A pretty weird notion: We do not live in real time at all; we experience the world with a delay. This of course allows us time to keep track of all the illusions and solve all the binding problems: to coordinate the many different sensory data that are processed in numerous ways via numerous channels in the brain into one world, one experience, one object. But nevertheless it means that what we experience is a lie. Because we do not experience the fact that our conscious experience lags behind.

Subliminal perception does not reduce the problem of the computation time required, because it tells us that a much greater portion of sensation than that of which we are conscious is capable of influencing our consciousness in the final analysis. If Donald Broadbent's filter theory were true, the problem would not be so large: Then it would just be a question of discarding all the sensory data apart from the tiny bit that ends up in our consciousness. But the whole perspective of subliminal perception is that Broadbent's filter theory does not stand up. The bulk of the million bits that thunder into our heads do actually get processed in some way or other. In fact, consciousness has access to a great deal of what we sense—when it can be bothered to pay attention. Not that it gives the senses much notice—we can change the object of our attention in an instant. So there is loads of information to be processed constantly and immediately.

It must cost computation time on our inner computer. There is no way around it: Consciousness lags behind.

The only question is by how much. A pretty disturbing question.

The brain and its method of discarding information have not yet been sufficiently well understood to allow us to work out the answer to this question. It can not yet be answered theoretically.

But another scientific tradition than the one that gives us occasion to raise the question has actually provided an answer, an answer known since 1983. The answer is no less disturbing than the question.

How much does consciousness lag behind? *Half a second!*

PART III

≈

CONSCIOUSNESS

CHAPTER 9

THE HALF-SECOND DELAY

The question raised by the American neurophysiologist Benjamin Libet was an unusually good one.

It arose from what was an astonishing discovery in its own right by the German neurophysiologist Hans H. Kornhuber and his assistant Lüder Deecke, who included the results in his doctoral thesis. Kornhuber and Deecke had applied modern methods for collecting and processing data in order to study "bio-electrical phenomena preceding 'spontaneous' events within the nervous system,"[1] as they called it: the link between ordinary voluntary hand movements and the electrical pattern around the brain.

In 1929, the Austrian psychiatrist Hans Berger discovered that knowledge of cerebral activity could be obtained by placing electrodes on the subject's head, thus measuring the electrical activity on the outside of the skull. This method, electroencephalography, or EEG, traces alpha waves and other patterns in the brain: alpha rhythms, for example, reveal that the subject is at rest.

Kornhuber and Deecke wanted to see whether it was possible to study more defined phenomena than general states like wakefulness and sleep. They investigated whether an EEG could reveal that a subject was performing an action.

Nerve cells work electrically: The state of a nerve cell, or neuron, is defined by the electric potential across its surface—that is, the difference in voltage between the inside of the cell and its surroundings. When the cell is stimulated, the potential can change. This change spreads through the cell and out along the nerve connections to other cells. Actual communication from one neuron to another is mainly chemical, while the language of the neuron itself is mainly electrical.

But EEG is a very rough measure, because there has to be activity in a large number of nerve cells before there is a change in the electric field around the brain. Further, what is being measured has to be measured through the cranium.

Kornhuber and Deecke succeeded by adding a huge number of events together. They asked their subjects to repeat a simple action— such as flexing a finger—again and again. Then they added up all the EEG measurements: If there was a special EEG event at the time the action took place, the signal would be amplified if lots of measurements were added together. The noise that almost drowns the signal

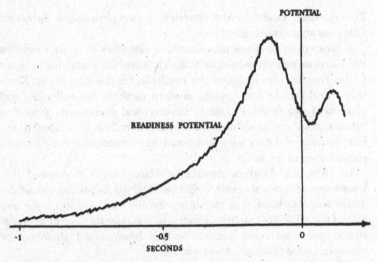

The readiness potential. A change in the electrical field around the brain that sets in a second before an act. (After Kornhuber and Deecke)

would not be amplified by adding lots of events together, because noise is random.

This technique allowed Kornhuber and Deecke to show that a simple action like moving one's hand or foot is presaged inside the brain. The brain displays what Kornhuber and Deecke called a *Be-*

reitschaftspotential, or readiness potential: a shift in the electrical potential, which shows that an action is being prepared. The change in the electrical pattern reflects an activity in the nerve cells of the brain, in this case in the so-called secondary motor area of the cerebral cortex.[2]

This readiness potential is logical: The brain prepares an action by calculating how it is to be performed. The only strange thing was the timing.

Obviously, the readiness potential must precede the act it is preparing. But it was not so obvious that preparation would take so long as Kornhuber and Deecke proved it took: *a whole second.* (The average is actually 0.8 second, but cases of up to 1.5 seconds have been recorded.) That is a long time.

Kornhuber and Deecke were recording not reactions but actions initiated by the subjects themselves. The subjects decided to flex their fingers. But a second before they did so, their brains indicated that they were getting ready for the act.

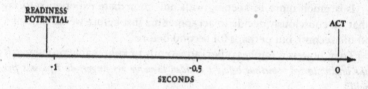

READINESS
POTENTIAL   ACT

-1   -0.5   0
                  SECONDS

The readiness potential sets in a second before an act.

"I began thinking along these lines in the 1970s,"[3] Benjamin Libet says of the question he put against the background of Kornhuber and Deecke's discovery of the readiness potential. The question was part of Libet's research as professor of neurophysiology at the University of California Medical Center in San Francisco.

Many years later, after he had studied and settled the issue, he put the question thus: "The long time interval (averaging about 800 ms) by which RP [readiness potential] onset preceded a self-paced act raises the crucial question whether the conscious awareness of the voluntary urge to act likewise appears so far in advance."[4]

In other words: If such a simple act as moving a finger starts in the brain a whole second before the muscle activity, when do we consciously decide to initiate the act?

Just the slightest pause for thought—easy now that Libet has raised the question—reveals that if we compare the readiness potential with our own experience of everyday life, something is completely crazy.

A second does not pass from the decision to flex a finger or wiggle a toe until we actually do so! No way! A second is a very long time—we can easily feel a second going by. If we put out our hand for something or kick the cat, a second does not pass between decision and action. We would notice.

So the conscious decision cannot take place at the same moment the readiness potential starts. Because that would mean that it did take a second from the moment of decision to the moment we acted. (Of course, it often does. It often takes years. But here we are talking about the decision to snap our fingers, voluntarily and because we feel like it.)

So on the basis of self-observation, we can exclude the possibility of the decision to act coming at the same time as the start of readiness potential.

It is much more in keeping with our immediate experience to say that we consciously decide to act sometime just before we do so. Not a whole second, but perhaps 0.1 second before.

That, however, implies other, apparently unfathomable problems: *If the brain started sometime before I decided to move my finger, do I possess free will?*

The show starts before we decide it should! An act is initiated before we decide to perform it!

This is apparently no good either. As Benjamin Libet puts it, "If a conscious intention or decision to act actually initiates a voluntary event, then the subjective experience of this intention should precede or at least coincide with the onset of the specific cerebral processes that mediate the act."[5]

Anything even close to an everyday, normal perception of the notion that we consciously determine our actions when we exercise our free will surely requires that the execution of decisions is not initiated a second before we make them.

So there is no apparent answer to the question as to when the conscious decision comes into play. The kind of question you cannot answer, but that makes you feel extremely confused, is a good basis for a scientific experiment—and that is what Libet embarked upon.

His experiment was as simple as its outcome was epochmaking. He asked his subjects to perform a simple act: flex a finger or move a hand when they felt like it. So they did.

To discover what went on, Libet and his colleagues Curtis Gleason, Elwood Wright, and Dennis Pearl set up quite a few pieces of apparatus. They could record when the hand or fingers moved by measuring electrical activity in the hand. They could record the moment when the readiness potential started via electrodes attached to the subject's head. Finally, they could ask the subject to tell them when he or she consciously decided to perform the act.

With the three categories of data in their hands, they could compare them—determine when consciousness makes up its mind compared to when the readiness potential starts.

The final measurement, as to the moment of conscious decision, is controversial—and it is vital. For Libet was no newcomer to research into consciousness. In fact, he was one of the very few neurophysiologists in the world who had undertaken serious experiments on the subject.

Since the mid-1960s, when he commenced his studies of consciousness, Benjamin Libet has had a very clear sense that consciousness is a primary phenomenon. We cannot reduce consciousness to anything else—for example, some kind of measurable property in the brain. A person experiences a conscious decision, and it is this person and this person alone whom we can ask about that experience. We cannot study consciousness by relating it to something "objectively" measurable.

Consciousness is consciousness, Libet realized. "Conscious experience, understood as awareness of a thing or an event, is only accessible to the individual who has the experience, not to an external observer." The consequence of this knowledge is that "any behavioral evidence that does not demand a convincing introspective rapport cannot be assumed to be a sign of conscious, subjective experience." So we can never know whether there is a conscious experience unless the person tells us so.

"This is the case quite irrespective of the appropriateness of the act or the complexity of the cognitive and abstract problem-solving processes involved, for they can all take place—and often do so—unconsciously, without the subject being aware of it." It is not enough for an act to seem conscious. The person who performs it must experience it consciously before consciousness can be said to be present.

So we cannot learn anything about the subject's consciousness except through the subject himself. We have to ask. The problem is that if we ask when someone decided to flex his arm, we do not get a particularly precise answer. Certainly not as regards time. It takes time to formulate a "Now!"

So Libet came up with something else. He put his subjects in front of a television screen that showed a revolving spot, just like the second hand of a clock. The only difference between an ordinary clock and Libet's was that the spot took 2.56 seconds, not sixty, to complete a circuit. This allowed Libet to pinpoint a time by asking where the spot was on the clock face when the event happened. Accuracy would be considerable, as the distinction between "one o'clock" and "two o'clock," which would be five seconds on an ordinary clock face, would correspond to 0.2 second here.

A series of control experiments was undertaken to prove that pinpointing the time this way was meaningful. A control stimulation of the skin showed that the method was indeed pretty accurate.

The rotating spot is a classic method in experimental psychology. A German, Wilhelm Wundt, used it in the nineteenth century to study reaction times; it is known as Wundt's complexity clock.[6]

The experiments themselves went like this: The subject was seated in a comfortable lounge chair and asked to relax. Upon a given signal, he or she would look at the center of the clock face, let the spot make a circuit, and then flex a finger or move a hand as he or she pleased. Subjects were urged to wait until they felt like acting: an urge, a decision, an intention.[7] They should wait until they actually felt such an urge, and then follow it. At the same time, they were to note where the spot was on the clock face when they felt the urge to make their movement.

This provided Libet with three pieces of data: when the person made a conscious decision to act; when he or she acted; and when the readiness potential began.

The experiments were carried out in March and July 1979 on five subjects, all students in their twenties.

"I was surprised at the accuracy," Libet explained years later. The results matched nicely; the figures yielded meaning when analyzed. Both the control experiments involving skin stimulation, control experiments involving pinpointing the time when an act was experienced as happening, and the figures for the time of the conscious decision hung together statistically.

The results were very clear: The readiness potential starts 0.55

second before the act, while consciousness starts 0.20 second before the act. The conscious decision thus takes place 0.35 second *after* the readiness potential commences. That is, 0.35 second passes between brain start-up and the conscious experience of making a decision.

If we round the figures out, which is reasonable when they arise from a concrete experiment, the conclusion is that consciousness of

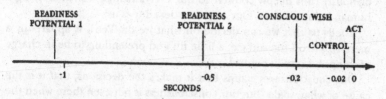

Benjamin Libet's measurement of the delay of consciousness: The act takes place at time 0. A control stimulation of the skin to control the subject's timing ability is experienced at on average -0.02 second. For acts that require preprogramming, the readiness potential is seen a second before the act. In simpler acts the readiness potential appears 0.5 second before the act: at a time of -0.5 second. But the conscious decision to perform an act only appears at -0.2 second. Thus more than 0.3 second passes before consciousness discovers that the brain is already implementing the consciously chosen act! (After Libet)

the will to carry out an act decided on by ourselves occurs almost half a second after the brain has started carrying out the decision.

So three events take place: First the readiness potential starts, then the person becomes conscious of initiating the action, and finally the action is carried out.

The desire to carry out an action becomes a conscious sensation long after the brain has started initiating it. But consciousness does occur *before* the action is performed.

"The brain evidently 'decides' to initiate or, at the least, prepare to initiate the act at a time before there is any reportable subjective awareness that such a decision has taken place," Libet and his colleagues write in the report on their findings. They go on: "It is concluded that cerebral initiation even of a spontaneous voluntary act of the kind studied here can and usually does begin *unconsciously.* "[8]

Or as Libet put it a few years later, "This leads me to propose that the performance of every conscious voluntary act is preceded by special unconscious cerebral processes that begin about 500 ms or so before the act."[9]

Our actions begin unconsciously! Even when we think we make a conscious decision to act, our brain starts half a second before we do so! Our consciousness is not the initiator—unconscious processes are! If the reader is not jumping up and down in his eagerness to present his objections to these conclusions, something is up. Because this result obviously runs deeply counter to our everyday image of what being a human being involves. Our consciousness dupes us!

It tells us that we can decide on what we do. Yet it is apparently a mere ripple on the surface, a little tin god pretending to be in charge of things beyond its control.

Our consciousness claims that it makes the decisions, that it is the cause of what we do. But our consciousness is not even there when the decision is made. It lags behind, but it does not tell us that. It dupes itself—but how can my consciousness dupe itself without duping me? Is the self-duplicity of consciousness not my own self-duplicity?

But let us not get carried away. There must be lots of murky, dubious aspects to such a series of experiments. Before we begin to conclude that our entire perceived existence is built on self-deception, we should examine the questions that can be raised.

For example, we could, *firstly*, object that all that is involved here is the experience of when we became conscious. Of course our consciousness starts the process! We simply do not get told until later.

Sure. But what do you mean if you say you make a conscious decision you are unconscious of? After all, the interesting thing about consciousness is that it is primary: If we were not conscious we had made a decision, but we had indeed made it, how could we say it was a conscious one?

We have to face the fact that precisely because consciousness is a primary phenomenon, which cannot be weighed or measured except through conscious experience, the criterion for consciousness is quite simply consciousness. If you are not conscious of something, you are not conscious of it (as Julian Jaynes said, we cannot know how much of the time we are not conscious). Actually, that is a very good rule of thumb one should try to remember whenever one considers the notion of consciousness: *Only the conscious is conscious.* Which is not very much, when one considers the capacity of consciousness.

But we could, *secondly*, object that it took the experimental subjects about 0.3 second to spot the spot once they had felt the urge to act, and that surely explains the phenomenon. Then, however, we have to explain that the subjects were pretty good at pinpointing a skin stimulus in time, and the muscle movement itself. In Libet's concrete case and in the history of experimental psychology, Wundt's complexity clock is a thoroughly studied method, which yields reliable results. The control stimuli on the skin were indeed recorded at precisely the instant one would expect from studies of skin stimulus awareness Libet had previously undertaken (about 0.02 second after physical stimulation).

Thirdly, there is certainly something peculiar here, we might object. Human reaction times are a lot shorter than 0.5 second. It does not take half a second to snatch your fingers away when you burn them! So how can it take half a second to move them of your own free will? How can it take longer to do something oneself than to do it as a reaction to something from outside? Well, it can, because reactions are *not* conscious. We snatch our fingers away, and then we think "Ouch!" Not the other way around. Our reaction time is much shorter than the time it takes to initiate a conscious action.

Fourthly, we could object that consciousness is mainly about clever things like going to the theater and reading books—and we can certainly decide to do things like that well over a second in advance! This objection is quite right: Most major decisions are indeed taken after lengthy consideration. When we decide to go shopping, we easily have time to be conscious of our decision before we set off. Libet's experiments only tell us something about whether the immediately conscious decisions that we make the whole time (such as to put out our hand) really are conscious after all. But if they are not, how do we get to the stores?

OK, we could say, *fifthly*, "What is so strange about all this anyway? *If consciousness is itself a product of cerebral activity, surely there is nothing odd about cerebral activity starting before consciousness appears.*" In fact, it must necessarily be thus, we could add. To which the answer would be yes, exactly; unless consciousness just hovers freely in the air, it must be linked to processes in the brain, and they must necessarily start up before consciousness appears. It is not our consciousness that initiates, for only the conscious is conscious.

This point indicates an important fact. If we want to perceive consciousness as a materially based quantity caused by activity in the brain, consciousness can never come first. *Something* must have started before consciousness can commence. The only peculiar thing is that our conscious decision is experienced so long after it was made; and this takes us back to our first objection: How can the consciousness be in charge when it is not the initiator? As only the conscious is conscious, and consciousness has to be the result of cerebral mechanisms so boring that we are unconscious of them, consciousness can never be in charge.

This is a point that tells us there are problems in our notion of consciousness. If we assume that body and mind hang together (and that the mental and the physical do not belong to widely separate worlds, as the dualistic view of the relationship between body and soul would claim), it is clear that consciousness cannot come first. Libet's experiments do not concern a holistic theory of body and mind or the logical consequences of it. They tell us that awareness of performing an act is experienced half a second after the brain starts moving. Of course, it is amusing to realize after performing an experiment that its outcome was predetermined: that consciousness cannot come first. But did it really have to be so far behind?

Sixthly, we could—like Nobel laureate and dualist John Eccles— object that man is simply incredibly clever: The readiness potential does not start the action at all; our consciousness does. But consciousness always elects to do so just after a readiness potential has started a second earlier. With this theory Eccles rescues his dualism, his belief that mind and matter are two widely different things. Rather like when the timetable decides when the passengers will arrive, but *not* that they take the train. The problem with Eccles's explanation is that it implies a series of assumptions that we are currently unable to put to the test.

For example, one would have to assume there must be some kind of rhythmic variation in the electrical field inside the brain that makes it favorable to start an action just as the field changes, the way it does in the readiness potential. If such a rhythmic variation exists, our consciousness could choose to ride the wave of electrical changes in our head, thereby getting a free ride on the brain waves. So an act is initiated to match precisely a wave that started a second before. Consciousness surfs the brain waves.

An elegant theory, which leads John Eccles to conclude, "There is no scientific basis for the belief that the introspective experience of initiating a voluntary action is illusory."[10] Our consciousness does not decide on when but decides only *that* it shall happen. Oh, it does not inform its owner that this is so, but it does at least issue the order, even if it does not choose the precise fraction of a second.

This theory explains Libet's findings, but it does so by explaining away the entire readiness potential as a false phenomenon arising because our consciousness always elects to act when just such a variation occurs in the brain.

This is an objection that could in principle prove correct. The point would be that the day we become more closely acquainted with the background noise of the brain waves (we cannot measure them today), we will see that consciousness always chooses to initiate actions when there is a wave to ride. So we cannot conclude that just because there is a wave before every decision, the decision comes after.

But again the problem is that this does not bring the consciousness into play unless it monitors all these waves before it acts. "The consciousness has to monitor all these waves. There is an incredible amount of noise in the brain, an incredible number of waves to keep track of, so this cannot be so," Libet says. If it is our consciousness that decides, our consciousness must be conscious. Not even in the simplistic experiment in which a subject has only to flex a finger can we see this background. So how is the consciousness meant to keep track of all the waves amidst the hurly-burly of everyday life? After all, we are talking about a whole second.

John Eccles's explanation is in practice hair-raisingly complicated: rather like the medieval explanations of the planets' motion through the sky in terms of epicycles—a system that was swept aside once Copernicus proposed that the sun, and not the earth, was the center of the universe.

It is not unusual to see a logically impeccable objection like Eccles's directed at a scientific experiment. Actually, it is the usual situation in the history of science. There are always loopholes. So evaluation of an experiment is based partly on a logical analysis and partly on further observations, which are in line with the experiment. What is more, there are other, very powerful arguments in favor of the theory that most of what goes on in people's heads is unconscious. For exactly half a second.

Many of the counterarguments above come from an extensive discussion of Benjamin Libet's results that took place in 1985 in *The Behavioral and Brain Sciences*.[11] This journal is a gold mine. A review article of an important field is followed by a series of responses by other scientists in the field. This allows outsiders to get an overview of discussions that are not normally conducted particularly openly in scientific literature. The rest of us can gain an insight into the climate in which it is taking place. The discussion on Libet's experiment is one of the most exciting *The Behavioral and Brain Sciences* has ever carried. It included everything from enthusiastic acclaim to vexed irritation.

As mentioned earlier, Lüder Deecke and Hans H. Kornhuber made the great discovery that laid the foundations for Libet's experiment: a readiness potential. Deecke's commentary on Libet contains the following remark: "A 'preconscious' appearance, if there is any, of the SMA BP [the readiness potential] does not particularly disturb the neurologist, who is familiar with the various infraconscious brain operations and . . . asks himself why phylogenesis (biological evolution) may have invented consciousness: for the sake of data reduction. That's why the method of introspection is limited. Introspection may fail, but this does not mean that all that is not accessible to it is supernatural."[12]

Now, there is nothing supernatural about Libet's results, though perhaps there's something strange. But Deecke wanted to remove the *metaphysics* from Libet's results.[13] Libet himself denies that there is anything metaphysical about them. (Among scientists, as a rule, "metaphysics" is a term of abuse for everything they cannot study by applying scientific methods but can only surmise.)

From the tone of Deecke's response, it is not hard to conclude that he was irritated by Libet's results.

Well, it *was* a good question Libet asked himself on the basis of Kornhuber and Deecke's study. Since then, others have wondered why many more people did not think of it.

Of course, they did. But nobody else followed up the question with an experiment. Or did they? As so often before in the history of science, the vital experiments were carried out many times. But not everyone dared take the matter seriously enough to end up in scientific literature with their results.

In the 1985 debate, the Finnish psychologist Risto Näätänen, for many years a noteworthy scientist in the field of evoked potentials, posted the following account: "First of all, I am convinced of the soundness of this data-base from some of my own pilot work of over a decade ago. Puzzled by the long duration of the RP before the actual movement compared to the fact that even unwarned motor responses in reaction-time experiments occur within a much shorter time from stimulus onset . . . , I, in pilot experiments with T. Järvilehto, tried to 'fool' the cerebral RP generator by concentrating on reading a book and suddenly acting on movement decisions occurring 'out of nowhere' by pressing a response switch. In this way we tried to produce a movement with no preceding RP or with only a very short one. Nevertheless, much to our surprise, RPs of quite a long duration were still there although the subject felt he had (immediately) followed a sudden, spontaneous urge to press the switch."[14]

Another astonishing precedent to Libet's experiment was reported to Libet by the prominent American psychologist Arthur Jensen (who achieved notoriety in the 1960s for his theory that for genetic reasons black Americans are less intelligent than white ones). Jensen had carried out a series of reaction time experiments in which subjects demonstrated reaction times of about 0.25 second, which is very normal. However, he was in doubt as to whether some of the subjects were deliberately cheating by being too slow. Apparently they did not quite trust what Jensen would do with the results. To find out whether they were cheating, Jensen asked them to gradually increase their reaction time. But none of them could! As soon as they tried to increase their reaction time to more than a quarter of a second, it leaped to at least half a second. Jensen was astonished. Until he heard about Libet's experiment.

"He came to me and said, 'You have explained my crazy result,'" Libet says.

Libet is happy to tell this story. Because it shows very clearly that human beings can react tremendously quickly but they cannot voluntarily react *a little* more slowly. If they want to react *a little* more slowly than they do instinctively, they have to react consciously—and that takes *a lot* longer.[15]

So things that need to happen quickly happen subconsciously. Consciousness cannot do them a little more slowly. Only a lot more slowly; for consciousness is something we use when there is not such a hurry.

Libet's experiment has been repeated with the same outcome by other scientists; even scientists who are not particularly enthusiastic about his conclusions. In 1990, the neuropsychologists I. Keller and H. Heckhausen from Munich published a study that reproduced Libet's results. The conscious decision appears 0.267 second after the readiness potential.

Keller and Heckhausen are not happy with Libet's interpretation of the experiments. They think the explanation may be that the subjects have become aware of something that normally takes place subconsciously. "It was the advice to introspectively monitor internal processes which led the subjects to perceive a feeling of 'wanting to move.' "[16] So according to Keller and Heckhausen, the consciousness present in Libet's experiments is not "genuine" at all, but a pseudoconsciousness that doesn't count.

This argument is based on a departure from a vital, fundamental principle behind Libet's experiments: You cannot begin to discuss with people what they are conscious of—nor can you take their consciousness away from them. If people say they have a conscious experience of an urge to flex a finger, you cannot claim that this conscious urge is invalid. Consciousness is a *primary* phenomenon, which the experimenter has no right to argue with.

Less technically, we can express this argument as follows: It does not really matter if anyone says that it was the advice of the experimenter that made people perceive a feeling they would not normally be aware of (and very few of us are particularly conscious of many of the times we flex a finger). What matters is that the subjects perceive that they are performing a conscious act—and that we can then relate this conscious experience to other measurements. But no matter which scientific theory we may have, we cannot start taking people's experiences away from them. Because then we would be studying not consciousness but something else.

But even though Keller and Heckhausen's objections are not that important, the results of their experiments are very important: Libet's results have been *reproduced*. In practice, this means that no sneaky detail cheated Libet during his investigation, a detail that meant Libet came up with false results. When others can repeat the experiments with the same results, there are grounds for trust.

Fairly powerful experimental arguments exist for the delay of consciousness. Without a doubt, this raises considerable philosophical problems for common sense. But before we bring such airy matters into it, perhaps we should turn the clock back three decades and ask what put Benjamin Libet on the scent of the question as to how far consciousness lags behind.

"I was not looking for anything in particular, but when I found the half-second delay I knew instantly that it had to be important," explains the now septuagenarian Benjamin Libet about a discovery he was given the chance of making in the 1960s. "So I decided to pursue the matter."

It turned out that a human being feels something only after the cortex has been stimulated by electrical impulses for at least half a second. Shorter stimuli are not experienced at all.

Of course, human beings are not designed to be stimulated by electric current in their heads. If there is anything evolution has equipped us to avoid, it is having our brains tampered with.

But our shield against such stimuli can be penetrated; our skulls can be opened. Neurosurgery is not something anyone does for fun. In the 1960s, neurosurgeons had developed methods, which we would now regard as pretty crude, for reducing chronic pain and serious uncontrolled tremors caused by Parkinson's disease. They opened up the skull and inserted a heating element into the brain. When the temperature reached 60 degrees centigrade, a group of nerve cells could be destroyed, thus alleviating the patient's chronic pain or other serious afflictions.

One of the leading practitioners of these brain operations was the late Bertram Feinstein, a surgeon and physiologist at Mount Zion Hospital in San Francisco. Feinstein agreed to allow the opportunities created by his operations to be utilized for studying the way we function. He admitted his good friend Ben Libet from the department of medicine at the University of California, San Francisco, to the operating theater.

"I would not have been given this chance by any other surgeon but Feinstein," Libet explains. "Most neurosurgeons are only concerned with opening and closing people's heads. They are not interested in looking at what's inside."

But Feinstein let Libet look. "I wanted to find out what I'd have to do to the brain to make the patient say, 'I can feel that!' "

Benjamin Libet subjected the exposed brains of Feinstein's patients to brief electric shocks. The experiments were carefully prepared so they meant only a minimal increase in the length of the operation. The patients were fully conscious during the operation and the experiment. They had fully consented, and there was no bleeding or pain.

Nevertheless, it does not sound like a particularly pleasant kind of research. What business have we going into people's heads? Could we not do the same experiments on animals instead?

"There is one thing you can do to patients that you cannot do to animals: ask questions," Libet explained one afternoon in spring 1991 in the small office he has at his disposal at the University of California Medical Center on Parnassus Avenue in San Francisco. Benjamin Libet was now a professor emeritus, a retired professor, but he continued to pursue the clues he found via his work with Feinstein and his patients. For he received some pretty interesting answers when he asked, "What does the sensation feel like to you?"[17]

This was the central issue: not only to observe objectively how patients reacted but to find out what they themselves thought, what they themselves had to say about it. To compare the brain from within and without.

The desperate difficulties in understanding man's functions through introspection or self-observation discovered by pioneers like Helmholtz and Freud in the nineteenth century have caused many scientists to lose interest in introspection. Subjects such as consciousness and awareness were struck off the agenda, because one cannot trust what people say about themselves. The mind cannot understand itself from within, so many scientists elected to study it only from without, by observing objective signs of the activities of the mind.

But just because we cannot rely on subjective experience does not mean that it disappears from people's lives. Few things are more important in life than the subjective experience of what is going on (one might even wonder whether *anything* is more important).

So a vital question is going unstudied: the relationship between the function of the mind viewed from without and viewed from within. *What is the relationship between an event as it is recorded objectively and as it is experienced subjectively?*

Raising this question without wanting to use the one to judge the

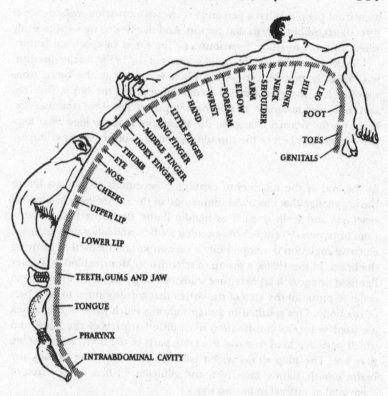

The brain's map of the body: The cortex receives information from the body. But not all parts of the body require equal space in the cortex. (After Penfield et al.)

other was Benjamin Libet's true stroke of genius. That is also why animals will not do, for they provide no feedback, or very little, about their subjective experience.

As early as 1965, Libet considered carefully and methodically how one could measure the relationship between the mind seen from within and without. His main focus was the mind seen from within: The conscious experience is a *primary* phenomenon, which cannot be reduced to anything else. "The subjective or introspective experience of awareness of something is the primary criterion of conscious experience,"[18] Libet wrote in his account of the thinking behind his study of Feinstein's patients. In other words, he did not want to take experience away from people: What a person perceives as a conscious experience is directly accessible only to that person. And *that* is what we want to study when we want to study consciousness: the mind viewed from within.

Viewed from without, the mind consists of the brain. So the question was, What is experienced within when we stimulate the brain from without? Not the eyes, ears, or spinal column, but the brain. Directly, and in its own language of electrical impulses. For if we stimulate the brain via the normal channels, the senses, we have no idea what happens on the way before the stimulus becomes a subjective experience.

At the end of the nineteenth century, observations of patients led to the knowledge that electrical stimulation of the cortex leads to physical reactions and feelings such as itching limbs. From the first barbaric (and unpopular[19]) studies of wounded soldiers and laboratory animals, electrostimulation developed into a very important method of studying the brain. In the 1930s, a group of scientists in Montreal led by Wilder Penfield undertook an extensive study of a large number of patients in order to pinpoint the area of the cortex that corresponded to each part of the body. This resulted in a map showing which parts of the cortex are used to receive information from different parts of the body, and which parts are used to move the same parts of the body, and how big they are. The map shows which parts of the body most occupy the brain: mouth, hands, face, feet, and genitalia. In that order. Each of them vital to survival in its own way.

Electrical stimulation of the areas of the brain concerned with the body's sense of touch leads to the feeling that *the body* is being affected. We have no sense of touch that tells us about stimuli to the cortex. For under normal circumstances, the skull protects the brain from such stimuli. They never occur, so there is no biological point to sensing them. If your brain is open, you have more important things to worry about than whether stimulation of the sensory cortex results in a tingling of the toes.

There is no sensation in the cortex, so perceptually, any stimulation is projected onto the body. We experience the stimulus as if the body were being stimulated, not the brain.

The effect of an electrical stimulus of the cortex corresponds to the activity in the cortex nerve cells that is unleashed by a sensory experience. The brain cannot tell the difference between a skin prick or an electrical current applied to the brain itself: It perceives both as a skin prick (if the part of the brain being stimulated is the one that contains the center for experiencing skin pricks). Electrical signals are the language of the brain.

Electrical stimulation allowed Benjamin Libet to stimulate the brain from without, while asking conscious patients who had had their skulls opened what they felt when he did such and such.

The patients were subjected to brief pulses of electricity, or shocks, to the part of the cortex concerned with the skin's sense of touch. Each pulse was very brief, less than a thousandth of a second, but the patients received "trains"—i.e., a series of stimuli up to several seconds in duration.

"I simply wanted to find out what happened. I was not looking for anything in particular," Libet explained. But he received an important surprise. If the cortex was stimulated for less than half a second, the patient felt nothing. "They explained that they didn't feel anything," said Libet, "even when the strength of the individual pulses was great enough to make them feel something if the train lasted longer than half a second. I realized immediately that I was onto something important."

Because of course it does not take half a second of skin pricking before we feel something. A stimulation of the senses is felt even though it is very brief. So why should the sensory cortex require so much time before we experience anything?

Libet came up with an explanation: It is only when the cortex has been stimulated for half a second that the feeling becomes a *conscious* sensation. A sensory stimulus leads to a cascade of neuronal activity in the cortex. It is this cascade that leads to a conscious sensation half a second later.

The theory is weird, for a stimulation of the skin leads immediately to a conscious sensation. How come it takes half a second of brain activity before we become conscious of the sensation?

Stimulating the skin leads to electrical activity in the brain. This electrical activity corresponds to the stimulus to which Libet subjected Feinstein's patients (and they could not tell the difference). How can an electrical stimulation of the brain correspond to a neuronal activity arising from a sensory experience, if the electrical stimulation has to last half a second before it is felt? Stimulation of the skin *immediately* results in sensation, but the activity in the cortex required to mediate the sensation has to be at least half a second long.

"This result had a disturbing implication," physiologist Bruce Bridgeman wrote. "If we do not report conscious sensation until the cortex has been stimulated for half a second, how does consciousness remain in 'real time'? Clearly, we do not live half a second behind events in the outside world."[20]

In 1979, Libet and his colleagues published a study[21] in which they compared direct stimulation of the sensory cortex to stimulation of the skin. The question was, *When* do we sense stimulation of the skin? When it happens? Or when the nerve cells in the sensory cortex have had their half-second time for reflection so the sensation can be a conscious one?

The astonishing answer was that yes, it may take half a second of activity in the sensory cortex before consciousness occurs, but the subjective experience is assigned to an earlier point in time—namely, the moment at which stimulation actually occurred! Consciousness lags behind, but our subjective perception does not lag!

The background to this remarkable finding was a study Libet and his colleagues had published in 1967. The brain displays *evoked potentials* when the senses are stimulated. These are changes in the electrical field around the brain, and they are revealed by an EEG. Normally, an EEG is a fairly peaceful affair, because the electrodes are attached to the outside of the skull. But to record evoked potentials after very small stimuli, Libet placed his electrodes directly on the surface of the brains of Feinstein's patients.

It turned out that very weak stimuli to the skin, which did not lead to conscious sensation, could result in evoked potential. This means that the brain has registered the stimulation but consciousness has not been informed. A more powerful stimulus also leads to evoked potential, of course, but it also leads to awareness.

This is very powerful, direct evidence that subliminal perception can take place: Libet was able to demonstrate that the brain registered stimulation of the skin, but that consciousness did not register it.

Nor were the patients able to report any conscious sensation when Libet drew their attention to the stimulation. But their evoked potentials showed that their brains had registered the stimulus. "This fact may be taken to indicate that a possible physiological basis could exist for so-called 'subliminal perception,' "[22] Libet and his colleagues wrote in *Science* in 1967.

In these experiments, Libet was also able to stimulate the sensory cortex directly. This demonstrated that brief trains of stimuli there were not felt consciously, while longer stimulations were; this was consistent with the first findings from his studies of Feinstein's patients.

Libet thus detected two components of the brain's way of receiving a message from the outside world: (1) a change in the EEG, which takes place without awareness, and (2) an electrical activity, which, after half a second, can lead to awareness.

A stimulus that leads only to a change in the EEG does not necessarily lead to awareness. A stimulation powerful enough or long enough to result in electrical activity of at least half a second leads to awareness.

The original stimulation of the skin may be very brief, but it leads to a cascade of activity in the sensory cortex, which, half a second later, results in awareness.

So the stage was set for an interesting question that could be investigated in Feinstein's operating room: When do we experience the stimulations of the skin that, after half a second of activity in the brain, lead to awareness? Do we experience them when they happen, or after the half second has passed?

To settle this question, Libet introduced an elegantly designed experiment, which led to his 1979 discovery. He stimulated the sensory cortex so the stimulus was felt as a tingling in one hand, while simultaneously he stimulated the skin of the *other* hand.[23]

This meant that he could simply ask the patient, "What did you experience first—your left hand or your right?" The patient could answer, "Left first," "Right first," or "At the same time."

The experimental setup allowed Libet to vary the order of the stimulation—sensory cortex or skin—and the interval between them.

During the experiment, neither the patient nor the observer knew which stimulus was applied first. After a huge number of such attempts, Dennis Pearl, a statistician, was able to analyze how long the individual stimuli took to lead to awareness.

The elegance of this design is that Libet asked the patients for only one bit—right or left (1.5 bits really, because there were three possibilities, simultaneity being the third). The experience was boiled down to something consciousness is good at: recognizing a sequence and talking about it. The impossible problem of pinpointing the time of an experience was solved by comparing the sensation of pins and needles in the two hands human beings are equipped with.

Libet expected to be able to show that half a second's activity was required in the sensory cortex before a stimulation was experienced, irrespective of where it came from—the skin or the sensory cortex.

If a stimulus was applied to the left hand while the cortex was being stimulated in a place corresponding to the right hand, the experience of skin stimulation would be expected to come last. After all, it would take half a second for the experience to reach consciousness.

But this proved not to be so. Even when skin stimulation of the left hand did not start until 0.4 second after the sensory cortex was stimulated in a place corresponding to the right hand, the patient said "Left first." A peculiar result: It takes 0.5 second for us to become conscious of stimulation of the sensory cortex. Something similar would be expected of skin stimulation, because some neuronal activity is required before the stimulus can be felt. In just 0.1 second, a stimulation of the skin can sneak in front of a stimulation of the sensory cortex.

Libet had to amend his theory. Either he could drop the idea that it takes half a second of activity for a stimulus to be felt if applied to the skin—and he did not want to do that—or he would have to apply a more extensive theory.

He was not too keen on changing his view that half a second of brain activity was required before a conscious experience occurred. There was powerful support for this view. Libet had already demonstrated that powerful stimulation of the cortex 0.2 second after a stimulus was applied to the skin meant that the patient never became conscious of the stimulus to the skin![24] If there was not a half-second hesitation before the skin sensation became conscious, it is hard to see how a later stimulus applied to the sensory cortex could lead to the skin stimulus never being felt at all.

So Libet developed his theory: There are two elements in recording skin stimulation. One notes the time, and the other leads to consciousness.

The 1967 study showed that the brain reacts with an evoked response in the EEG pattern, also when awareness of a skin stimulus is not attained, for example because it is very weak. This evoked response does not in itself lead to awareness, but it appears very soon after the skin is stimulated: roughly 0.02 second after.

The theory, then, was this: Awareness occurs half a second after skin stimulation. But it is experienced *as if* it occurs when the brain puts out an evoked response. A subjective relocation in time occurs, and the

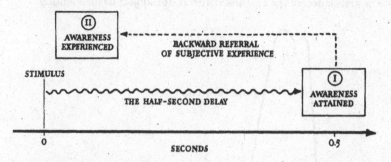

The half-second delay: Stimulating the skin leads to activity in the cortex, which, after half a second, leads to consciousness. But consciousness is experienced as if it set in very shortly before the stimulus, because the subjective experience is referred back in time. (After Libet)

skin stimulation is consciously experienced as if it occurred at a moment when awareness has not set in but the brain has unconsciously reacted. This moment is closer to the moment of skin stimulation than to the moment at which we become aware of it.

The subjective experience is put back in time so that it is experienced as if awareness set in at the moment when the brain EEG displayed an evoked response. This happens about 0.02 second after the stimulus is actually applied to the skin, much earlier than the 0.5 second it takes for awareness to occur. The event used as a time marker, the change in the EEG, cannot itself result in awareness. Only after half a second of electrical activity does awareness set in.

In other words, *the conscious experience is projected back in time in exactly the same way as a stimulation of the sensory cortex is projected out onto the body.*

What we experience is a lie, for we experience it as if we experienced it before we experienced it. But there is a good point in this fraud, because what we need to know is when our skin was pricked, not when we became conscious of it.

Stimulation of the sensory cortex, on the other hand, is not equipped with such a relocation in time. It is experienced when half a second has passed, and half a second after it started. What is moved around in subjective time is only a real (and biologically speaking realistic) stimulation in our senses, on our skin. Something as unnatural as a stimulation of the cerebral cortex is not subject to such editing.

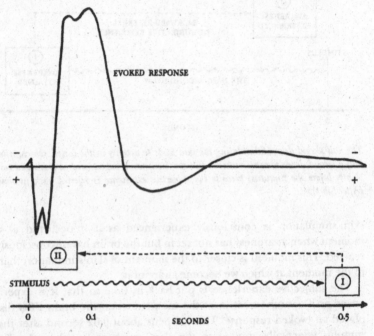

EVOKED RESPONSE

STIMULUS

0   0.1   SECONDS   0.5

The electrical field of the brain shows an "evoked response" very shortly after stimulation of the skin. It cannot lead to consciousness by itself, but is used to determine the time of the skin stimulus. (After Libet)

That was Libet's theory. But theory is one thing, observation another. Libet conceived an extremely elegant experiment to see whether the theory held water. "I would never have dared publish these results if it hadn't been for the result of the control experiment," he explained many years later.

Mammals have two very different paths by which signals reach the cortex. One system is very old and is shared by many other creatures.

The other is younger and is found primarily in humans and monkeys. The old system is known as the unspecific system, while the other is called the specific system, because it connects signals from one kind of sensory modality with a specific area of the brain.[25]

The idea of Libet's experiment was as follows: If we stimulate an area of the thalamus, which is just beneath the cortex, through which the specific system passes, how long does it take before we experience something—and when do we experience it?

The cunning thing about this method is that a stimulation of the

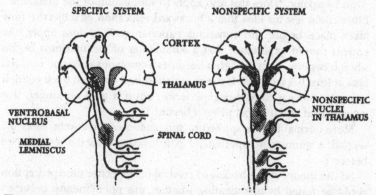

SPECIFIC SYSTEM   NONSPECIFIC SYSTEM

CORTEX

THALAMUS

NONSPECIFIC
NUCLEI
IN THALAMUS

VENTROBASAL
NUCLEUS

MEDIAL
LEMNISCUS

SPINAL CORD

The specific and nonspecific nervous systems. The specific nervous system links specific parts of the body to specific areas of the cortex. On the way, the system passes through an area of the thalamus known as the ventrobasal nucleus. The nonspecific system gathers information from the whole body in the thalamus, which transmits the information to the whole cerebral cortex.

relevant area of the thalamus is just as unnatural and strange as a stimulation of the cortex. It also takes half a second of stimulation before anything is experienced. But a stimulation of this area also results in the appearance of an evoked response in the EEG pattern of the cortex.

In other words, a stimulus to the special area of the thalamus through which the specific system passes looks like a skin stimulus on the EEG but a cortical stimulus as regards the requisite half second of stimulation.

Libet now expected that a thalamic stimulus would resemble a skin stimulus also as regards the subjective experience of the timing. At the same time, we are talking about an unnatural stimulus that cannot be experienced at all if it is less than half a second long.

This overcame the incomparability of stimuli to the skin and cortex: Libet's idea was that both required half a second of neuronal activity before they became conscious. But the stimulus to the skin can itself be very brief, even if it unleashes a cascade of activity that is half a second long.

A stimulation of the thalamus resembles a stimulation of the cortex, apart from the fact that it also has the same effect on the EEG pattern as the skin stimulation.

So by asking, "Does this also apply to stimulation of the thalamus?" Libet could test his idea that a backward relocation of subjective time takes place before the conscious experience. If it does apply, the patient should experience that a stimulation of the thalamus begins when it begins—even though it becomes a conscious sensation only if it lasts at least 0.5 second.[26] If the stimulation lasts less than 0.5 second, it never becomes a conscious experience, but if it goes on longer, it is experienced as if it began when it began!

More normal factors applied to stimulation of the cortex. After 0.5 second, a stimulus is experienced as if it began after 0.5 second. Not before.

So the theory of the backward referral of subjective time perception could be tested by investigating whether this phenomenon occurred for stimulation of the thalamus the way it did for skin. It did.

Feinstein's patients experienced a stimulation of the thalamus at the time it occurred—that is, corresponding to the moment of their evoked response, 0.02 second after the stimulus itself.

The backward temporal referral was proved.

The neurologist Sir John Eccles and the philosopher Sir Karl Popper write in their magnificent work, *The Self and Its Brain*, "This antedating procedure does not seem to be explicable by any neurophysiological process."[27] Eccles and Popper were not the only ones who were astonished. Many philosophers have tried to refute the results of the 1979 study.

Patricia Churchland writes in her *Neurophilosophy* (1986) that "According to Eccles and Libet, the data show that a mental event precedes in time the brain states causally responsible for it."[28] But Libet does not claim this. He claims only that it is experienced as such.

Others have called the results self-contradictory,[29] irrelevant,[30] or proof that man does not possess free will,[31] as everything is predetermined. But these are not objections strong enough to liberate us from Libet's weird experience.

Among the attempts to actually interpret Libet's results is the view that consciousness cannot be pinpointed in time at all. This has been proposed by Roger Penrose, the physicist, in his book *The Emperor's New Mind*, where he summarizes Libet's 1979 results and then writes, "I suggest that we may actually be going badly wrong when we apply the usual physical rules for time when we consider consciousness!"[32] But Penrose does not provide a recipe for how we should deal with the phenomenon of consciousness. He just indicates that there may be fundamental problems.

Another researcher who has suggested an interpretation that includes dropping the idea of the unity of time experienced by consciousness is the American philosopher Daniel Dennett, from Tufts University in Massachusetts. In June 1992, Dennett presented an article for debate in *The Behavioral and Brain Sciences*. He and his colleague Marcel Kinsbourne proposed the Multiple Drafts Model,[33] which says that there is no unequivocal flow of time in consciousness but there are lots of different drafts present concurrently. Dennett thinks that this model, which is also presented in the book *Consciousness Explained*,[34] explains Libet's results better than Libet does. A viewpoint Libet quite naturally disputes.[35]

But the main problem with Dennett's model is that the notion of lots of drafts for consciousness existing in parallel does not explain the clear sense of unity one experiences subjectively in being conscious. Nor, then, the real problem: How are all our experiences and thoughts coordinated into an illusion that consciousness does the deciding?

Dennett and Kinsbourne's view takes as its point of departure the binding problem discussed in the previous chapter. Their work, particularly because Dennett is one of the dominant figures in the philosophy of consciousness in America, is a sign that the binding problem really is on its way onto the agenda for philosophers and physiologists alike. How on earth are all the impressions from outside, which cannot take exactly the same amount of time to process in the brain, added together into the experience of a smoothly synchronized reality that we all take for granted—every one of life's two billion seconds?

The delay of consciousness Libet has demonstrated *gives us time* to solve this problem: It takes a little time before we experience the outside world, but we just relocate the experience backward in time, so we experience that we experience the world at the right moment. Mammals have a method of transporting signals from the outside of the body to the "experiencer" so they know when things happen, even though they actually experience them a little later.

It is like the blind spot in the eye: There may be flaws in the way we sense the world, but we do not experience them. Our consciousness lags behind and does what it can to hide the fact—from itself. Consciousness deceives. Consciousness is self-delusion. Which is very expedient. When there is time, anyway.

Anyone who has ever sat on a thumbtack knows that we do not take half a second to react. But then most of us get up from the tack before we have had much time to think it over. Consciousness is not something people use as much as they think—and certainly not when they are sitting uncomfortably.

Benjamin Libet's exploration of consciousness and its basis in the brain came in two parts. First, the studies of Bertram Feinstein's patients led to the astonishing knowledge that it takes half a second of brain activity before consciousness occurs. These studies led later on to the even more astonishing realization that consciousness performs a temporal readjustment backward, so that awareness of an outer stimulus is experienced as if it occurred immediately after the stimulus, even though in fact half a second passes before we become conscious of it.

After Dr. Feinstein died, in 1978, Libet adopted other methods: studies of normal EEG in healthy patients. These studies took the peculiar readiness potential as their point of departure and showed that conscious experience of the conscious decision to undertake an act appears about 0.35 second after the brain has started.

Together, the two sets of studies produce a remarkable picture: Almost half a second of brain activity is necessary before consciousness appears. This goes for sensory experiences and decisions alike. In the former, the subjective experience is put back in time, so it is experienced as if it occurred at the time the sensory stimulus occurred. In conscious decisions to act, the conscious decision is experienced as the first step in a process. The activity that has been going on for almost half a second is not experienced.

In 1991, Benjamin Libet and a number of colleagues published a study in *Brain*,[36] which in one fell swoop confirmed both the theory that it takes half a second to generate consciousness and the existence of subliminal perception.

The study involved patients who had had electrodes inserted into their heads to reduce pain—similar to Feinstein's patients. When asked whether this was not a most macabre way of doing science, Libet responded that the patients were pleased to have a bit of diversion during their treatment.

In fact, the studies the patients participated in were quite entertaining. They had to guess whether they were getting electric shocks! But it had nothing to do with pain; it dealt with sensation on the very edge of subliminal perception. The patients were given short and long series of weak electrical stimuli via an electrode in the thalamus. The short ones lasted less than half a second, the others somewhat longer. Only the long trains of stimuli led to conscious experience. The patients then had to guess *whether* they were receiving a stimulus at a given moment.

If they were receiving a long train, they had the conscious experience of being stimulated, so it is hardly surprising that they could "guess" yes. But if they were receiving a shorter train, they could still make the right guess. In a way they were not conscious of, the patients' organisms could pick up the stimulus and lead to a "correct" guess.

A quarter second of stimulus was enough to enable them to guess correctly without knowing why. Half a second of stimulus was enough for them to be conscious of why they could make the correct guess.

A result that confirmed Libet's idea that it takes half a second to become conscious and that the difference between nonconsciousness and consciousness is whether or not there is a process involved that lasts half a second.

Consciousness presents its possessor with a picture of the world and a picture of himself as an active player in this world. But both pictures are heavily edited: The picture of a sensation is edited in such a way that consciousness does not know that other parts of the organism have already been affected by this sensation for perhaps half a second before consciousness occurs. Consciousness conceals any subliminal perception—and reactions to it. Similarly, the picture of the subject's own actions is also distorted: Consciousness portrays itself as the initiator, but it is not, as events have already started by the time consciousness occurs.

Consciousness is a fraud, which requires considerable cooking of the temporal books. But that of course is precisely the point with consciousness: Enormous quantities of information are discarded; what is presented is precisely that which is relevant. For normal consciousness, it is utterly irrelevant whether a readiness potential starts half a second before consciousness occurs. What matters is knowing what one has decided to do. Or has felt on one's skin. What things look like when we open patients' skulls or get students to flex their fingers is pretty unimportant; the important thing is that consciousness occurs when we have discarded all the information we do not need.

In fact, Benjamin Libet's half-second delay is really most convenient for the purposes of this account. After all, Charles Bennett's notion of logical depth indicated that consciousness must be something that costs a certain amount of time to attain, and now Benjamin Libet has given us half a second to play with. Half a second with the most powerful computer in the world (the brain), where we have to reduce eleven million bits of sensation to ten–fifty bits of consciousness—and erase the traces. Surely that is plenty of time. A brilliant theoretical challenge to the field that calls itself computational neuroscience:[37] We have a thousand billion neurons and half a second, and the task is to reduce eleven million bits to sixteen bits so that the sixteen bits can be used as a map of the eleven million. In principle, a task that may be solved in a few decades' time. The half second is a boundary condition of the computational problem, which makes it intuitively clear that the problem can be solved. So all is well.

But what about free will? Never mind our getting up from the thumbtack without a lot of discussion; do Benjamin Libet's findings mean we do not possess free will? For what but the consciousness can exercise free will? If the brain is already in action when we think we decide to reach for the relish, there is not much free will in us.

If we return to Libet's experiment with the readiness potential, there is a very important detail we have not discussed yet: Consciousness may occur after the *brain* has gone into action, but it also occurs before our *hand* does so.

From the conscious experience of making the decision until it is carried out, 0.2 second passes. Can our consciousness manage to stop the act before it is carried out?

This is Benjamin Libet's own salvation for free will: the veto. Consciousness has enough time to veto an act before it is carried out. Libet even had experimental backing to show that such a veto mechanism works: When his subjects reported that they had aborted an action they had decided to carry out, they did have a readiness potential. But it looked different toward the end (as action approached) from when the action had been carried out. The subjects could interrupt themselves. So they possessed free will: *Consciousness cannot initiate an action, but it can decide that it should not be carried out.*

Libet had developed a veto theory for free will and the function of consciousness: "Processes associated with individual responsibility and free will would operate not to initiate a voluntary act but to select and control volitional outcomes."[38]

This point of view is particularly interesting, not least historically: Free will operates through selection, not design. Free will corresponds more to the way the surroundings mold the evolution of biological organisms through natural selection than consciousness corresponds to the design, the blueprint, most of us spontaneously picture when we imagine how we make conscious choices in life.

Consciousness is not a superior unit that directs messages down to its subordinates in the brain. Consciousness is the instance of selection that picks and chooses among the many options nonconsciousness offers up. Consciousness works by throwing suggestions out, by discarding decisions proposed by nonconsciousness. Consciousness is discarded information, rejected alternatives—no, thanks!

The notion of consciousness as a veto is a very beautiful, very rich one. Its kinship with Darwinism and natural selection is not its only parallel in the history of thought.

Veto principles have always been common in human morality.

"Many ethical strictures, such as most of the Ten Commandments, are injunctions not to act in certain ways," Benjamin Libet wrote in 1985. He added, "If the final intention to act arises unconsciously, the mere appearance of an intention could not consciously be prevented, even though its consummation in a motor act could be controlled consciously."[39]

Libet distinguishes between the action as a physical act and the urge to act as a mental phenomenon. We can control our actions but not our urges, he concludes.

This is a very profound distinction. For there is a very great difference between a perception of morality that tells you *what you may do* and one that tells you *what you may have the urge to do*.

As Libet says, "How else could Freud's suppressed urges act? If there were no difference between the urge to act and the act, suppressions could not work at all. There *has* to be time for suppression!"

But Freud is not the only one Libet can back up with his findings. There is also his own religion. Benjamin Libet is a second-generation American Jew. His parents, originally called Libetsky, immigrated from the Soviet Union to Chicago, and thence moved to San Francisco, where Benjamin could better keep his asthma under control.

There is a very big difference between Judaism and Christianity regarding what you may and may not do. Judaism talks in vetoes. You must not kill, steal, fornicate, etc.: The Ten Commandments, from the Old Testament, are the moral foundations of the Jewish faith.

Christianity, however, talks of disposition—it condemns the very urge to do some of what the Ten Commandments forbid. It is sinful to want to do something you must not, even if you do not do it.

"Have you heard of Rabbi Hillel?" Benjamin Libet asked me when we were discussing his veto theory. "He said, fifty years before Christ, 'Do not do unto others what you would not have them do unto you!' That is a much clearer rule than the Christian 'Do unto others what you want them to do to you.' When you think about it, it does not yield meaning," Libet says.

True indeed: A man might know quite a few women who would not like him to do unto them what he would like them to do unto him!

Benjamin Libet refers to the American philosopher Walter Kaufmann, from Princeton, and his book *The Faith of a Heretic*.

Kaufmann points out the huge problems Christian theologians have had down the ages in trying to turn the idea of do as you would be done by into a practical moral precept. "Anyone who tried to live up to Jesus' rule would become an insufferable nuisance," he writes. "Try, for example, to derive a sexual ethic from Jesus' rule."[40]

Rabbi Hillel came up with his formulation when a pagan declared that he wanted to learn the whole Torah—the law—" 'on condition that you teach me the whole Law while I stand on one leg.' Hillel said to him: 'What you don't like, don't do to others; that is the whole Law; the rest is commentary; go and learn!' "[41]

Hillel compresses every one of Moses' Ten Commandments into one formulation, which preserves the logical structure of the commandments and their proscriptive nature. Morality is a question of what one may *not* do. Again, this means that morality is not a question of what one may feel like doing; morality is a question of what one *does*.

The origins of Christianity are closely connected to a rejection of this way of thinking. In the Sermon on the Mount, Jesus says, " 'Ye have heard that it was said by them of old time, Thou shalt not kill; and whosoever shall kill shall be in danger of the judgment. . . . Ye have heard that it was said by them of old time, Thou shalt not commit adultery: But I say unto you, That whosoever looketh on a woman to lust after her hath committed adultery with her already in his heart. . . . Therefore all things whatsoever ye would that men should do to you, do ye even so to them: for this is the law and the prophets.' "[42]

The Sermon on the Mount introduces a mental ethic: Not only may you not lie with your neighbor's wife; you may not even feel like it. You cannot even fancy her.

"That gave Jimmy Carter a few problems." Benjamin Libet erupted with a laugh at the thought of one of the crazier episodes in U.S. politics: Presidential candidate Carter was asked during an interview for *Playboy* whether he had ever been unfaithful to his wife. He had not, but he had wanted to, he replied. That is no good in a Christian culture, and his statement unleashed a flood of protests.

The second point in the Sermon on the Mount is the Golden Rule that one should do as one would be done by—i.e., a direction as to how to act rather than a ban on acting.

Christianity says that we must do the right thing and not even feel like doing anything wrong. Judaism says you may not do what is wrong. Christianity's interdiction concerns the urge to do wrong, Judaism's concerns the act of wrongdoing. Christianity then adds that you must do the right thing.

In the light of Libet's veto theory, the difference between Judaism and Christianity stands out very clearly. If our consciousness has no possibility of controlling the urge to act (because it is not even informed when the urge arises), it is difficult to see how we can be responsible for our urges and dreams. The Christian precepts not to desire your neighbor's wife and not to feel like doing away with your boss imply problems if the knowledge Libet gained by experiment is correct. For our consciousness cannot control our desires.

You might say we did not need scientific experiments to tell us that, but would that not just be flippancy on your part? The story of Christianity is very much a story of sin and salvation: of people laboring with their sinful minds in an eternal struggle not to be led into temptation. As Walter Kaufmann put it, "Christianity failed morally not because Christians have not been Christian enough, but because of the very nature of Christianity."[43] Christianity has always managed to make people feel that their sinful thoughts were their own individual problem.

Yet a Jewish neurophysiologist comes along and tells us that according to his theories, it is not even possible for the conscious *I* to control the urges it is presented with.

Benjamin Libet and his experiments indicate with tremendous precision the difference between the Old Testament and the New, between Judaism and Christianity. The difference between what we may do and what we are allowed to want to do is an old tradition in European culture.

If the conscious *I* has no possibility of controlling its urges to act, how can we condemn people who experience lust every time they see their neighbor's wife? But that is exactly what the Sermon on the Mount says we must do.

Conversely, Libet's findings also point the finger at *the problem of Judaism:* that people have the right to think and feel whatever they like about each other, as long as they do not act it out. "Only the actual carrying out of a volitional movement can be of practical significance for other people," Libet says of the moral effect of letting people think whatever they like about each other: It is not your disposition but your actions that mean something in practice—the essence of the ethics of Judaism. But is that true? And what are the consequences if it is not?

Judaism easily becomes a spiritual license to entertain cruel—

indeed, evil—feelings and hopes vis-à-vis other human beings. As long as you do not act in a way you would preferably not be subjected to yourself (or that contravenes the Ten Commandments), whatever you think or feel is OK. The absence of a code of mental ethics in the Jewish tradition can lead to the form of inner cruelty and evil Shakespeare portrays in *The Merchant of Venice*.

All this is acceptable because it is only actions that affect other people, says Judaism. *But this is simply not true,* even though, seen from a scientific point of view, there may have been grounds for believing it until a few decades ago.

The problem is that if there are such things as subliminal perception and priming, we actually know more about what other people think and feel than our consciousness does. So what we think and feel about each other does matter, even when our conscious common sense tells us that it will not harm anybody if deep down we think they deserve to be spanked.[44]

If it was only what we said and did that affected others, we could think and feel however we liked and it would not matter. But this is not a realistic view of man. In fact, Libet's own findings are like a boomerang for Jewish moral perception: Precisely because our consciousness lags behind, it is hard to control how many of our thoughts do become actions.

The problem with Judaism is that it permits an inner cruelty that the consciousness cannot really control, because it lets out more from inside than we are conscious of. For example, through body language. The problem with Christianity is that it demands an inner goodness but demands it of our consciousness, which has no ability to manage what happens inside a person's mind.

Together, the two problems indicate that a radical revision of fundamental moral issues will come onto the agenda in the wake of the recently emerging understanding of the significance of consciousness.

But the veto theory is not interesting just in relation to grand-scale highbrow moral discussions. It is also extremely interesting in relation to perfectly routine questions.

Libet's veto is a very beautiful description of the way consciousness functions, but also, perhaps, a fundamentally misleading picture of what it means to be human in everyday life.

Remember the fundamental rule: *Only the conscious is conscious.* In this context, that means a conscious veto can be imposed only by consciousness. One can impose unconscious vetoes on all kinds of unconscious desires, sure, but doing so just does not have anything to do with consciousness.

A conscious veto is a veto we are conscious of. So we can ask ourselves how often we veto a decision 0.2 second before it is carried out.

The answer is surely that there are certain situations in which we consciously veto our urges all the time. But otherwise we seldom do so. Vetoes appear frequently only in situations that are themselves not frequent.

For example: when we are bashful and nervous and trip over our own two feet, stammer, sit down, get up, gesticulate in a peculiarly abrupt manner, perform peculiarly half-completed deeds, say, "Yes, of course . . . no, I didn't mean it," and insult and confuse others with the oddest of utterances.

Or when we learn something new that we find difficult: a language, a game, a dance. We are awkward and clumsy, we are painfully conscious of what we can do and what we cannot, we catch ourselves midmovement and stand there looking like the sheepish novices we are.

Or when there is something that really is important to us and for that reason—precisely for that reason—we make complete fools of ourselves and screw up good. Like Woody Allen, in his movie *Play It Again, Sam,* displaying inappropriate self-interruptions while trying to make contact with women.

In other words, it is the highly unpleasant situations in which we are conscious of ourselves and conscious of the fact that we keep interrupting our impulses to act.

It is not only when we fear divine sanction that it is unpleasant to veto our impulses to act. It is simply an unpleasant process. Clumsy. Awkward. Strained.

We keep interrupting ourselves because we may be uncertain of our ability to perform or fear the judgment of others. We are afraid of being laughed at. When we are conscious, we tend to judge ourselves, to view ourselves from without, to see ourselves through other people's eyes.

A conscious veto is necessary only because there are differences between what the conscious will and the nonconscious urge are after. A veto applied to something nonconscious reflects that there are differences between what the consciousness and the nonconsciousness *would like*.

There are no limits to what people pour into themselves by way of cocktails, tranquilizers, and other drugs in order to transcend these conscious vetoes. We so much want to get away from situations where we veto ourselves—and this is not remotely related to whether we are Jews or Christians.

But it fits in nicely with Libet's way of thinking. In a letter on vetoes in everyday life, Libet writes, "I think your point about the conscious veto coming in more often with unpleasant situations is a good one. But I would not minimize its importance for many at least neutral situations—say in vetoing an urge to say something to a person (about his/her look, or behavior), or in veto of an inclination to stop a child from what he may be about to do (if it is really better for his development to go ahead) etc. But your point about vetoes in conflicts between conscious will and the unconsciously initiated urge etc. is not trivial and worth making."[45]

In the early twentieth century, the Danish philosopher and psychologist Harald Høffding formulated this point very clearly, even though of course he had no knowledge of veto theory or the idea of vetoes as associated with discomfort. The italics are Høffding's:

"As long as the unconscious tendencies to act pull in the same direction as the conscious thoughts and feelings, they are not easily remarked. . . . Their strength most often coalesces with that of conscious motives, which are given the honor or shame for the whole act."[46]

In other words, we notice the nonconscious only when it goes against the conscious. Because our consciousness prefers to believe that it is identical to the person and does not happily make way for nonconscious urges.

Perhaps this mechanism explains why the Freudian tradition has particularly emphasized the subconscious quality of *suppressed* experiences: Precisely because the nonconsciousness is not conscious, our consciousness prefers not to acknowledge it—and the only situations in which the consciousness is forced to acknowledge that there is more to man than his consciousness are those where there is a conflict between the conscious and the nonconscious. So all that can be seen, paradoxically enough, is the (almost) suppressed.

That the veto process is usually associated with discomfort does not mean that we cannot impose such a conscious veto. The veto exists, even if we do not use it. But that means only that we do not enjoy doing so; and this again means that we feel most content when our consciousness does not exercise free will.

People are happiest when it is not their consciousness that selects the nonconscious urges to act. People feel most content when they just act.

But the consequence of this observation is that we must face the fact that it is not our consciousness that is in charge when we're feeling good.

So we must ask: Do we possess free will only when we are feeling bad? Or do we also possess free will when we feel good? And if so, who possesses it?

CHAPTER 10

MAXWELL'S ME

Michael Laudrup had half the enormous expanse of green at Wembley Stadium in London to himself. Allan Simonsen had made an ingenious pass, which tricked the England defense and sent Laudrup away unimpeded in midfield. Apart from their goalie, Peter Shilton, all the England players were in the Danish half, so nineteen-year-old Laudrup had a clear run.

The soccer match on 21 September 1983 was not even a minute old. Michael Laudrup's free run toward the England goal was a bit of a shock for the 82,000 spectators, for England had always been one of the world's great teams, and Denmark had not. Oh, the Danish Vikings had boasted before the game, saying that Denmark was on her way to her international breakthrough. But to defeat England—at home—was some undertaking. It had to be done, though, if the true goal was to be reached: qualification for the final round of the European Soccer Championships in France in 1984. It was Denmark or England.

After just fifty seconds of play, the Danes had forged a chance of the kind you seldom receive in an away international.

Peter Shilton ran out toward Laudrup, but the elegant Dane dummied past him. All that was left was Laudrup, a ball, a lot of grass, and an open goal.

Michael Laudrup had veered toward the side of the goal area and was very close to the dead ball line on his way around Shilton, but the goal was empty. All he had to do was give the ball one last poke.

"I had plenty of time. I thought about what I should choose to do; I screwed up,"[1] Laudrup explained when he was asked if a player has time to be conscious of what he is doing when he does it. Michael Laudrup sent the ball into the side netting. Denmark did not take a first-minute lead. Laudrup had had time to become conscious before he acted. The result was a miss that millions of TV viewers remember to this day.

But thirty-five minutes later, Laudrup was brought down in the England penalty area. Allan Simonsen scored, Denmark won 1–0, and the "Danish Dynamite" team went on to enjoy considerable success in France in 1984 and at the World Cup Finals in Mexico in 1986. Michael Laudrup would become one of the greatest stars of world soccer.

A soccer player does not have time to think consciously while he is on the field. Things just move too fast. But when you watch a player like Michael Laudrup, you can see him thinking. Thinking plenty.

There is a great deal to think about. The ball, the players, the state of the field. Modern soccer has become an ever more complicated game. In the old days, when the game was young, it was about positions. You passed to a teammate because he was standing in the right place. Then movements were added and had to be grasped: where your teammate was moving, relative to the opposition's movements. In the last twenty years, the game has become all about acceleration. You no longer have to keep track of movements alone but must watch how these movements change in time.

But in particular, a Michael Laudrup has to form a highly complex pattern in his head: Players and ball move around, and what he has to do is read the play and predict it. And then do something nobody expected.

Modern soccer is characterized by many well-practiced patterns. The true geniuses, like Pele, Cruyff, Netzer, Maradona, and Laudrup, keep breaking the mold. That is why they are so good.

When Laudrup is going to pass to a teammate, he has to grasp the movements and acceleration of a handful of players from each team while keeping the ball under control himself and remembering that the simplest, most obvious solution is the one the others are waiting for and planning to counter.

But there is not much time to think. A key player gets tackled at once unless he passes.

From outside, the rest of us can see that the calculation Laudrup performs in his head must be complicated. But we can also see that it happens quickly. So we may ask, "Can one be conscious of one's game while one plays it?"

Laudrup's very clear answer is no. "It is just something you do, just like that!"[2]

Soccer players are not conscious while they are playing. But nobody who knows anything about the game would claim that a superb, original mental process does not take place when a player like Laudrup makes an ingenious pass. A number of advanced computations take place, but they are not conscious.

Except, that is, in unique situations where there *is* time to think things over. And where things go wrong as a result.

Benjamin Libet's eyes beamed behind his unusually thick glasses. "Joe Montana says the same thing!" Libet declared enthusiastically when he responded to the story of a European soccer player with a story about one of the greatest personalities of American football. "Joe Montana is the best quarterback ever. He also said in an interview that he is not conscious while he is playing."

Sports are an area of human behavior worth a closer look if one wants to consider the significance of the half-second delay. The same goes for theater, dance, music, and children's games.

Half a second is quite a long time when you are playing soccer or playing with children. But it is not much when you are behaving like an adult. Most decent, civilized activities occur at a very slow pace. Half a second does not mean much in a conversation, because it takes place so slowly. You can almost always work out how a sentence will end at least half a second before it ends. So you can keep up and reply quickly in a conversation, even though it takes half a second to become conscious of what you hear.

But that is no good during a soccer game. Most reactions displayed by human beings come much more quickly than half a second. Reaction time is typically 0.2–0.3 second. So you see why a defender can intervene quickly and instinctively to get the ball out of the danger zone. He is merely performing a trained reaction.

Michael Laudrup, on the other hand, is a player of genius. This means that he not only does what he has learned but comes up with new, astonishing things all the time. He does actually think while he plays. He just does not know it. He is just as unconscious of his cognitive processes as Albert Einstein said he was of his.

But how on earth is it possible to react before one becomes conscious?

In 1990, the Australian physiologists Janet Taylor and D. I. McCloskey published the results of a very elegant study of human reaction times. They took as their point of departure a technique developed for studying subliminal perception: masked stimuli.

You subject people to a masked stimulus by showing them two different things, such as two flashes of light, close to each other in time and space. By showing a very bright flash and a very weak flash one after the other, you can mask the weak flash so the subject does not notice it. This is also true when the weak flash precedes the bright one! This reverse masking can be used to erase sensory input so it never reaches consciousness.

Taylor and McCloskey then investigated the following: If subjects are asked to carry out an action in response to a stimulus, but the stimulus is masked, can they react nevertheless? The answer was yes. We can react to a stimulus we are not conscious of. A reaction does not necessarily have anything to do with a conscious perception of what we react to.

The reflexes Taylor and McCloskey studied were not instinctive reactions such as getting up off a thumbtack. They were more complicated reactions, which required a certain mental coordination. The subjects had to move both arms in a coordinated pattern that ended in both arms meeting. But this coordination was acquired by practice so it could be performed without bringing the consciousness into play.

"Thus it can be concluded that one can pre-program, and then trigger without further conscious decision, simple movements . . . as well as more complex movements."[3]

This conclusion is interesting in its own right if we wish to understand how people can play soccer and undertake other activities that require rapid but complex reactions. Such as riding a bike or having a fight.

But it is also a disturbing insight: We can act before we become conscious of why we act. Not only do we not know what the idea of acting is; we have no idea what made us act.

Taylor and McCloskey put it this way: "Almost all motor reactions and many other motor performances must occur before conscious perception of their triggering stimulus. Furthermore, a stimulus, having triggered a motor reaction, might never achieve neuronal adequacy for conscious perception."[4]

In other words, a stimulus can be so short that we never become conscious of it yet react to it nevertheless. So we can react to something we never become conscious of. We do not know what we reacted to!

This situation is reminiscent of the phenomena psychologists have discovered during studies of subliminal perception. Here, too, input occurs that never becomes conscious but nevertheless decisively influences behavior.

Taylor and McCloskey refer in their account of the occurrence of such reactions to Benjamin Libet's theory that it takes half a second for consciousness to be attained.

The consequence of these observations is considerable: It takes longer to decide on an action than to react unconsciously to a stimulus. It is possible to react without being conscious of why. It is possible to preprogram complicated patterns of action that are sparked off without our knowing why. Perhaps many of our reactions and responses occur without our consciousness being informed about what happened.

This may be disquieting if you think it is important for us to be conscious of everything we do. But on the other hand, it explains certain paradoxes. For example, the fact that in westerns it is always the hero who wins the gunfights.

The hardworking theoreticians of the fertile international physics community that throve in the 1920s and 1930s at the Niels Bohr Institute, on Blegdamsvej in Copenhagen, often visited the cinema. Bohr himself, who had a weakness for bad westerns, also had a penchant for finding flaws in the logic in the often dubious plots, in which the heroes always won the shoot-outs.

Russian-American physicist George Gamow says about Bohr: "His theoretical mind was on display even during these visits to the movies. He developed a theory which explained why the hero is quicker and manages to kill the villain despite the fact that the villain is always first on the draw. The Bohrian theory was based on psychology. As the hero never fires first, the villain has to decide when he is going to shoot, and this hampers his movements. The hero, on the other hand, acts reflexively and snatches his revolver quite automatically the instant he sees the villain's hand move. We disagreed on this theory, and the next day we went into a toy store and bought two revolvers in western holsters. We shot it out with Bohr, who played the hero. He 'killed' all his students."[5]

But where does that leave free will? Actions can be initiated and implemented without involving consciousness. Indeed, it can be argued that many of our everyday actions happen that way.

There are large areas of our behavior of which our consciousness does not have control. But the concept of free will is closely linked to the concept of consciousness.

Can my conscious *I* not determine at all what I get up to, then? We cannot see how we can define an *I* without its involving consciousness. The *I* is characterized by its responsibility and coherence. The ability to account for its acts and to occasion them is a very considerable part of the idea of an *I*. But the *I* is a spectator to many of its owner's actions.

He was late as usual. As he jumped on his bike, he knew he would be late for the meeting, so all he could hope to do was reduce his lateness as much as possible on the way, which usually took just under half an hour.

As he crossed Strand Boulevard on his way down Østerbrogade, he was way in front of the bus behind him and would have no trouble passing the bus stop before the waiting passengers swarmed out onto the cycle path to catch the bus. So he thought.

A boy suddenly stepped out onto the cycle path a few meters in front of him. The cyclist was moving fast. Very fast. There was nothing he could do. As if in a dream or a drug-induced high, he saw time reduced to a snail's pace, while his I *was reduced to a spectator to his own actions. A decision was required: either run into the boy or turn his bike over deliberately and take a fall. There were no other alternatives, because to his left was the rush-hour traffic and to his right even more people waiting for the bus. Like someone watching a movie, he saw the decision come out in the boy's favor: The bike was thrown sideways, sending him sliding the last few meters along the tarmac. It hurt, but that was all. He got a few grazes and a good excuse for being late for the meeting—and a story to tell (had the decision gone the other way, he would hardly have told the story, would he?).*

Who made the decision? Not his I. *His* I *was a spectator. But neither was it the boy—or Michael Laudrup.*

Something inside him made the decision, but the experience was clear and unequivocal: It was not his I, *for his* I *was an observer, outside the door, suspended. Overruled in advance, because there was no time to begin to think.*

His I *did not have any free will in that decision. But he was the one who made the decision.*

The situation is perfectly analogous to the situations studied by Benjamin Libet: It is not a person's conscious *I* that really initiates an action. But it is quite clearly the person himself.

There is a difference between the *I* and the person as a whole. "I realize that I am more than my *I*."

But the *I* does not want to accept this. The thinking, conscious *I* insists on being the true player, the active operator, the one in charge. But it cannot be. Not if we take Libet's findings seriously. These show quite clearly that the conscious *I* does not initiate our actions. In many situations where time does not allow a conscious veto, the *I* is simply put out of play. The *I* may think it is doing the acting, but this is an illusion.

So free will seems to disappear into the blue: The *I* is merely a piece of will-less driftwood, an innocent victim of wind and weather; and, what is more, a piece of driftwood that constantly reassures itself, "I am keeping my course!"

We might interpret Libet's experiments as the ultimate argument that man does not possess free will,[6] but that would be a misinterpretation. For the premise that would allow us to take the nonconscious initiation of volitional acts as proof of the nonexistence of free will is belief in the *I*. If we insist that the *I* can account exhaustively and definitively for what a person is, we will get into hopeless trouble with free will—in the light of Libet's delay. If we want to say that everything decided by a person is decided consciously, or that everything a person does is done consciously, things will go wrong with our idea of free will, simply because the bandwidth of consciousness is far too low for consciousness to control everything a person does.

The point of Libet's delay is *not* that it is not people themselves who decide when to undertake an action: The point is that it is *not people's consciousness* that begins the process but something else, nonconscious. It is still my self who disposes, but it is not my *I* that has the power to dispose. It is Me.

This allows us to formulate a solution to the problem of free will: *I possess free will, but it is not my* I *that possesses it. It is* Me.

We must distinguish between the *I* and the *Me. I* am not identical with *Me. Me* is more than my *I.* It is *Me* who decides when I do not.

The *I* is the conscious player. The *Me* is the person in general. The *I* is not at the wheel in many situations; when urgency is required, for example. The *I* is in charge of lots and lots of situations where there is time for thought. But there is not always time.

The term *Me* embraces the subject of all the bodily actions and mental processes that are not initiated or carried out by the *I,* the conscious *I.* The term *I* embraces all the bodily actions and mental processes that are conscious.[7]

Empirical evidence from measurements of the bandwidth of consciousness, subliminal perception, and Libet's experiments shows that the *I* does not decide nearly as much as it thinks it does. The *I* tends to take the credit for decisions, computations, realizations, and reactions carried out by the *Me.* In fact, the *I* refuses to acknowledge that there is a *Me* not identical to the *I* itself. The *I* cannot account for the *Me* but just goes on pretending.

This is not a new interpretation of Benjamin Libet's findings. When asked how he viewed the possibilities of solving the problem of free will in the wake of his experiments, Libet referred to a remark by the American philosopher Thomas Nagel (quoted in Chapter Eight). In 1987, Nagel wrote an essay for the *London Review of Books* in which he described Libet's work and its consequences. "The brain appears to have made the choice before the person is aware of it. A philosopher to whom I described this experiment said wryly that the implication was clear: 'Our brains have free will but we don't.' "[8]

Nagel is not quite comfortable with the situation, though. "An experiment like this seems to raise the disquieting possibility that what we take to be free actions are just things that happen to us, and that our conscious sense of choice is an illusion of control after the fact."[9]

Still, we may ask why we cannot just use Nagel's philosopher's formulation: "Our brains have free will but we don't."

Because the concept of *Me* covers more than the brain. First and foremost, it involves the body. Not for nothing do we say that our emotions originate in the heart or gut. Very few of us would enjoy being identified with our brains.

So it seems unwise to declare too hurriedly that the brain is the active operator, when it cannot be the consciousness and so not the *I*. It is wiser to limit ourselves to saying that it is the non-*I;* the part of the person that is not the *I* but, in perfectly undramatic fashion, is still the person. To describe the non-*I* who is me, the word *Me* seems appropriate, because it does not imply any further assumptions.

Similarly, Freud's concept of the unconscious is included in the concept of the *Me*, though without saying anything else about the relationship than that both involve the part of the person that is not conscious and therefore not the *I*. In fact, the idea of the concept of the *Me* is not to say too much at all: If the *I* does not possess free will, another part of the person must—i.e., the *Me*. I possess free will, but it is not my *I* that possesses it. It is *me*.

This distinction between an *I* and a *Me* is considerably less "innocent" than it sounds. It summarizes the radical changes in perception of what it means to be human that are emerging at the end of the twentieth century: People are not conscious of very much of what they sense; people are not conscious of very much of what they think; people are not conscious of very much of what they do.

Man is not primarily conscious. Man is primarily nonconscious. The idea of a conscious *I* as housekeeper of everything that comes in and goes out of one is an illusion; perhaps a useful one, but still an illusion.

The realization of the impotence of the *I* and the potency of the *Me* can lead to a feeling of anxiety: Who am I, then? What might I do? The *I* is disturbed by the existence of something outside itself but inside the person whom it believes itself to be identical to.

At bottom, the *I* cannot accept that there are at work in the person powers that the *I* does not have access to. But if the *I* wants to maintain this view, it must face the fact that the person it is talking about does not possess free will.

If the *I* wants to maintain its omnipotence over the person, this implies the person's impotence: Then there is no free will.

Libet's delay forces us to choose between the *I* and free will. We have to face the fact that we are far more than we believe ourselves to be;

that we have far more resources than we perceive; that we leave our mark on more of the world than we notice.

In the traditions of the history of philosophy, the problem of free will is closely connected to the argument about determinism. Determinism, or fatalism, is the philosophical view that everything is preordained. There are laws governing the phenomena of the world. If you know the initial conditions, these laws will carry their way to the preordained result with relentless logic. To assume that such laws exist for man means that people merely do what the laws say they must do under the given circumstances.

The determinist says there is no free choice at all, for everything is preordained. The only reason we feel we have a choice is that we do not know the circumstances inside us or outside that determine what we will do. We are automatons, very stupid ones, who do not understand ourselves and so do not know we are automatons. Only our stupidity and lack of knowledge make us believe that we possess free will. (This stupidity is itself a consequence of conditions over which we have no control.)

The most powerful objections to determinism are expressed in existentialism. Founded by the Danish philosopher Søren Kierkegaard in the nineteenth century and developed in the twentieth by Karl Jaspers and Martin Heidegger from Germany and Albert Camus and Jean-Paul Sartre from France, existentialism emphasizes existential *choices:* Man is regarded as fundamentally a *maker of choices*, defined by his freedom, so to speak.

The two basic views can be said to regard man from two angles: Determinism sees man from without—as the result of a series of causes that work on him. Man is a creation of the laws of nature at work around and within him. Existentialism sees man from within, as his own cause, acting outwardly on the environment. Man is a chooser, who causes consequences to his surroundings.

But what is seen from without/within? Not the whole person, for if the whole person were "inside," only the most hard-line determinists would claim that causes acting from without totally determine behavior and mental life. Man would then be only a consequence of his surroundings. A deterministic view cannot but assert that what is inside us—from our genetic apparatus to our personal memories—plays a part. But as causes that help to determine what we choose to do.

It is more correct to say that it is the conscious maker of choices who is viewed from without or within. Viewed from without, this conscious player is a quantity who reacts to a series of influences stemming from the outside world and the inner, nonconscious world alike. Viewed from within, this player is, quite simply, the chooser.

But performing this differentiation between within and without is far from simple. That the difficulties are profound in nature is exemplified by the argument about the death of Alan Turing.

Turing, whom we met in Chapter Three, was a rare mathematical genius who developed Gödel's disturbing insights into a theory of computation. Turing held that we can never know when a calculation will halt unless it actually does so. This finding—*Turing's halting problem*—is of profound significance for the theory of knowledge.

On the evening of 7 June 1954, Alan Turing solved his private halting problem. Crushed by the prosecution and persecution he had been subjected to as a gay in the prudish England of the 1950s, he took his own life.

Or did he? He was found by the housekeeper on 8 June, in bed, with froth around his mouth. The cause of death was quite clearly cyanide poisoning. Beside his bed lay an apple, of which several bites had been taken.

In the house were several jars of cyanide; Turing used it in electrolytic experiments. The apple was never analyzed, but the picture was clear: It had been dipped in cyanide. One bite of the apple of knowledge, and Turing was released from further criminal proceedings as a homosexual.

The official investigation unequivocally pointed at suicide. But the circumstances did not reveal any planning: theater tickets, computer time reservations, and dinner dates were waiting.

Turing's hobby of silver plating and gilding objects by electrolysis, involving the use of cyanide, had worried his mother for a long time. "Wash your hands, Alan, and get your nails clean. And don't put your fingers in your mouth!" Turing's mother was always telling him, most recently at Christmas 1953.[10]

Andrew Hodges, the mathematician, writes in his biography of Turing, "Anyone arguing that it was an accident would have had to admit that it was certainly one of suicidal folly. Alan Turing himself would have been fascinated by the difficulty of drawing a line between accident and suicide, a line defined only by a conception of free will."[11]

Perhaps, Hodges writes, it was all arranged to protect his mother's feelings. She never accepted that it was suicide.

From without, it looked like suicide. But the circumstances were not clear enough to settle the matter for sure. From within, it must have been obvious whether it was an accident, suicide, or a game on the very cusp of death (Russian roulette).

But this very *within* disappeared when Turing died. All that is left is the *without*, which cannot show what happened. Was it free will, or was it a tragic accident? This can be determined from without only if there is a message from within—a letter, a sign, or an unambiguous scene.

Free will is, then, a quality unequivocally linked to a subjectivity experienced from within. A suicide committed by free will implies a will to die, which is different from accident or disease.

But if the *I*'s image of itself as the controller is a false one, how on earth can we talk of suicide—or of free will at all?

The problem of free will is not interesting because of extreme conditions such as suicide. It is interesting because it is a notion important for our understanding of everyday life.

When something has to be done very quickly because an accident is imminent, we become spectators to our own actions. We do not see ourselves from within as a creature of choice; we see ourselves from without as takers of action responding to a challenge.

To see oneself from within as a creature of choice is linked to having plenty of time to make decisions that do not need to be taken in under half a second. In emergencies, there is no time for experiencing free will.

The experience of free will is linked to situations where the *Me* dares to allow the *I* to make the decision. When more speed is required, the *I* and its free will are suspended. The *Me* simply reacts. The *I* experiences free will when the *Me* lets it.

We are often in situations where the *I* has asked the *Me* to suspend the *I*. When we go to our soccer club or onto the field to play, our *I* has made the decision to put the person into a situation in which the *I* has no say at all. We long for this experience of the now. We spend much of our spare time pursuing it, in sports, dancing, playing games, intense conversation, sex, and intoxication.

Another diversion consists of observing other people who have suspended their *I*'s to allow their *Me*'s to live to the full: We call it art, performance, or first-class athletics.

The theater is peculiar if regarded from the point of view of information theory. The bandwidth of the performance piece is very low. *Hamlet* consists of a text that can be delivered at various speeds but never faster than the bandwidth of the language allows. Indeed, the audience often knows the text beforehand; there may well be people present who know it by heart. Similarly, many concertgoers know the scores by heart. So what do they come for?

An actor has a much higher bandwidth than language does. There are gestures and gesticulations, intonations, movements, glances, and charisma: a series of nonverbal communications, which the audience perceives more or less consciously. Similarly, the musician does not wish merely to deliver a score but hopes to transform it into notes that supply it with pauses, accents, phrasing, and other goodies.

The director and the conductor work with the actors and musicians in converting the very low amount of information in text and score into the far greater amount of information present in the performance proper.

A good actor does not merely deliver the text but is himself the role being played: The actor contains a wealth of inner states corresponding to the one the character in the play presumably has in his given situation.

Vital to our experience of a performance is whether the actors themselves are *present* onstage. Whether they feel hatred when they repeat the hateful words of the text. Whether they feel joy when they play out the joyful words. Whether they feel love when they play it.

If an actor is himself present, being in the audience is a great experience. If the actor is not present, there is no reason for the audience to be. Everyone would have been better off staying home and reading Shakespeare.

The same goes for music and learned lectures. The great conductor Wilhelm Furtwängler put it this way: "The only indispensable prerequisite [for an audience to understand a lecture] is that the lecturer himself knows what he is saying and understands the meaning of his words. This sounds like a matter of course, but for the musician it is not at all so. Only when what is said is in accord with one's own understanding can it assume the right sound; only when what is sung or played is in accord with one's own feelings can it attain the right form that leads to other people's understanding."[12]

The difficulty of putting on a good play is that the *I* does not have access to the great quantity of information that is required to make the actor present with his entire personality during a performance. Because people mostly convert information in an unconscious way, the conscious *I* cannot automatically activate all the information required for a good performance. The *I* can repeat the text, but that is not enough. The *I* must allow the *Me* to "live" the part. To feel it as it develops.

Theater involves setting the *Me* free, so it can unfold. If the *I* does not set the *Me* free, we get a performance riddled with vetoes. The consciousness wants to control and monitor all the time. As a result, the performance is uneven and lacks credibility, because no emotion appears credible if it is controlled and hampered by the consciousness.

But the problem lies in giving the *Me* this freedom. It requires trust on the part of the *I*. A trust that comes through practice.

Training, rehearsals, and more training. In all performance, training and preparation are the key. This is by no means least true of performances where a sense of improvisation is desired. The most important thing about training is that the *I* comes to trust the *Me*. The *I* learns to believe that the *Me* can feel the emotion and carry out the movement.

Training creates a quantity of automatic skills that can be applied without the need for awareness that they are being so used. The *I*'s beady eye is there during training but not during the performance proper.

The same applies to ball games, cycling, and sex. We are allowed. We dare. We have faith in ourselves.

All performers are plagued more or less by an apparent paradox: shame at success. This is a curious but very real phenomenon. Performers find it hard to accept applause. Some even want to abolish it completely (the great pianist Glenn Gould wrote an essay in 1962 entitled "Abolish Applause!").[13]

In an interview at publication of his landmark book, *Inside Music*, Peter Bastian explained his own difficulties in accepting applause. "It is hard to have the courage to tell yourself 'You are good.' Sure, people clapped when I played, but deep down inside I thought I was bluffing."

But after considerable effort spent developing himself personally, Bastian found the courage to admit his own mastery—the ability to invoke inspiration at will—and thereby the ability to dare to accept praise from other people. As he formulated the attitude that allowed him to accept their applause, "I acknowledge that I have been putting myself to great effort: I acknowledge that I have practiced myself."[14]

This may sound like a psychological truism, but it is not: All the toil and labor behind a great performance is due to training, rehearsal, discipline. The conscious *I* has insisted on this training, which has given that same *I* trust in the *Me*'s ability to cope with the task. But it is not the conscious *I* that puts on the performance, any more than it is the director or conductor. It is the *Me* that performs. Without consciousness.

When the performance is over and the audience begins to clap, the consciousness and the *I* return as if from a trance and wake amidst the cheers. The shame comes because it was not the *I* that gave the performance, but the *Me*.

Language almost tells us this if we rephrase Peter Bastian's confession: "*I* acknowledge that *I* have been putting *Me* to great effort: *I* acknowledge that *I* have practiced *Me*."

Yet the *I* gets all the credit.

Performances live by this contradiction, this swinging back and forth between the *I*'s clear, disciplined awareness of technique, expression, and coherence on the one hand and the way the *Me* brings all these intentions to life in an unconscious, vetoless flow of empathy on the other.

These factors are not limited to the performing arts. They are present in everyday life. Peter Bastian writes, "We do not need to be musicians in order to know what I am talking about. I see the same state spontaneously appear in my everyday life. While I'm washing up! Suddenly everything glides along like in a ballet, the plates stop clattering, the washing-up brush describes infinitely satisfying arabesques across the china, like heavenly signs I understand instantly."[15]

Everyday life contains a plethora of examples of our ability to attain a sense of total, blessed unity with what we are doing. A spontaneous, direct feeling that the energy is flowing, that the force is with us.

This experience comes to us particularly often in conjunction with activities that are well prepared, such as at work or in close personal relationships that we have nurtured with discipline and perseverance for many years.

The American doctor and dolphin expert John Lilly started studying human consciousness at the end of the 1960s. For years, he had tried to achieve communication with the dolphins, which are highly intelligent creatures with brains easily comparable to ours in terms of ratio to body weight.[16] But Lilly had not succeeded in getting the dolphins to talk. So he concluded that the intelligence gap between man and dolphin was too wide: Dolphins were too clever. Instead Lilly threw himself into the study of man.

During an extensive odyssey through the many agents available in the 1960s for scientific studies of consciousness—drugs such as LSD—Lilly found himself in Chile, in the house of a magician named Oscar. He had a system for describing very good and very bad states of consciousness, and Lilly adopted it. There is no need to go into details; the important point is that Oscar and Lilly operate with a state they call "+24," or "the basic professional state."

This +24 state is a pleasant one, which Lilly describes as the state in which "we lose our self in practice" and "enjoy the working process and no longer have an ego." He writes, "The important part about +24 is the enjoyment and the automatic nature of what one is doing plus the loss of self, selfhood, and the absence of ego."[17]

In the language employed here, these are situations in which the *Me* is allowed to do what it does, automatically and without any control from the *I:* pleasurable situations not marked by vetoes and awareness. Experiences like these are not imbued with nervousness and shyness but possess familiarity, coziness, tranquillity.

It may seem strange that Lilly associates this state with *work.* After all, the term does not normally resound with self-transcending feelings of happiness. But there is a profound point here: Part of what gives us humans the greatest pleasure is doing things we do not need to control consciously the whole time, and such things are imbued with a feeling of familiarity, coziness, and trust.

At its best, work engenders just such a feeling, even when the pay is lousy and the boss tends to reject your brilliant ideas. When things are going well, they simply go. You are well prepared, and your skills are zinging.

Perhaps the tendency toward workaholism, so widespread in many segments of society, is really about the search for this state of nonconscious presence.

But it is not only at work and at home that we can feel great pleasure at being one with what we do. Religious practitioners have always talked of such feelings. Characteristically, religions also embody powerful traditions of disciplines to be followed—prayers, services, hymns, liturgy, ceremonies, rituals, repetition—states that can then be invoked to order, because they have become so familiar and routine. Even though this is precisely how they are not felt.

Really good experiences, whether they appear at work, at home, or while communing with nature or the Everything, may seem trivial from without—we're just doing what we usually do—but profoundly nontrivial from within.

The American psychologist Abraham Maslow came up with the term "peak experiences" to describe highs like these. Maslow describes as Taoistic (after the Eastern philosophy) the state of awareness in which you do not desire to change that of which you are aware: "The Taoistic approach to learning about the nature of things . . . is . . . an attitude to nature rather than a technique in the ordinary sense. Perhaps even it should be called an antitechnique," Maslow writes. "Real receptivity of the Taoistic sort is a difficult achievement. To be able to listen— without presupposing, classifying, improving, controverting, evaluating, approving or disapproving, without dueling what is being said . . . such listening is rare." Not that Maslow thinks we should use solely this strategy of noninterference in our awareness: "Science has the two poles of experiencing and comprehending concreteness and also of organizing the welter of concreteness into graspable abstractions."[18]

But how can one explain religious "highs" by saying that the conscious, verbal *I* gets pushed into the background? After all, characteristic of prayer and meditation is that words are spoken—whether in the form of the Lord's Prayer or a mantra. Why would that give access to the pleasures of the *Me*?

Overload is a central technique suggested in a book called *The Inner Game of Music*—one of countless guides on how to increase your ability to perform. In books on tennis, golf, and skiing, its author, W. Timothy Gallwey, has developed the idea of Self 1 and Self 2 and the problems this dualism gives rise to.

Self 1 more or less corresponds to the *I* in this account. The problem is that Self 1 wants badly to control and decide everything. But it is Self 2 that carries out the performance as a tennis player or music maker. It is Self 2 that knows how to perform a good forehand, while Self 1 is concerned with how you look, how the next shot should be carried out, the result of the last forehand, etc. Self 1 interrupts and confuses, while Self 2 is the reservoir of potential, of everything we can do.

The problem for the music maker, tennis player, or skier is the inner struggle between Self 1 and Self 2: If Self 2 is left to work in peace, the result may be great performances, but it is constantly disturbed by Self 1's "what if" way of thinking.

The goal is to attain "the non-judging state of pure awareness" that Self 2 represents. When it is allowed to.

Gallwey and his coauthor, the musician Barry Green, suggest a series of techniques for allowing Self 2 to unfold its talents. One of the most important is overload: "When you short-circuit the mind by giving it an 'overload' of things to deal with, it has so many things to attend to that it no longer has time to worry. Self 1 sometimes 'checks out,' and lets Self 2 'check in.' "[19]

The idea is simple. If you want to learn how to manipulate a violin bow, it can be a good idea to concentrate on something else as you try. "If someone had told me that a person with no previous experience of the instrument could be taught to play 'Mary Had a Little Lamb' on the bass with a full sound and correct position while smiling, singing the words and directing the audience to sing along—all in the first fifteen minutes—I simply wouldn't have believed them,"[20] Green and Gallwey write.

Overloading means that the conscious *I*, Self 1, does not have a chance. Another technique they propose is to "surrender to the ridiculous": think of oneself as a fish playing the double bass. One's self-importance disappears, and things are much easier.

One might ask whether it is not precisely this that is the cause of the indisputable effect on the human mind of prayer and meditation: precisely because a mantra or a text is being recited, the verbal channel fills up. The modest bandwidth of language is filled by the accustomed words, so the possibility of *thinking* is excluded. One of the main points of meditation is to avoid thoughts. Concentrating the language channel on something familiar, which does not make us deliberate, releases the rest of the mind to the object of our prayer and meditation.

Ritual words can be spells that block the "inner radio transmitter" and permit the free development of the *Me*.

The theater director Keith Johnstone has developed a series of techniques for training actors in the rare art of devotion that is the basis of all great performances, and particularly for free improvisation. The real problem is the necessity for personal courage, for openness. In his book, *Impro*, which is a gold mine of observations about the relation between self-control and self-development, Johnstone writes, "If you improvise spontaneously in front of an audience, you have to accept that your innermost self will be revealed." The problem is always whether you dare to trust yourself. Johnstone writes about actors that "if they are worried about failing, then they'll have to think first; if they're being playful, then they can allow their hand to make its own decision."[21]

The *I* can communicate and control its communication with others. The *Me* can also communicate, but it does not have the same awareness of what it communicates. The *I* is social and can enter into agreements with other *I*'s. The problem is whether the *Me* will abide by those agreements.

The social field is established through agreements, social contracts, entered into verbally. So the cohesive force in our social life is something with a very low capacity or bandwidth. There is not much information on the bandwidth of language, yet it has to direct our entire social life.

The problem of being social creatures who turn up for appointments and abide by the rules is also an individual problem: the relationship between the *I* who makes the appointments and the *Me* who has to initiate the actions. To put it another way: As people mainly function nonconsciously, whereas our social life is arranged through agreements made consciously, the problem is getting the nonconsciousness to abide by the agreements entered into by the consciousness.

The relationship between You and Me thus becomes an internal relationship between *I* and *Me*. Much of the drama that is played out between human beings is really a drama that is played out inside the individual person between the *I* and the *Me*. The *I* represents the social side of things in *Me*.

The relationship between *Me* and *I* is not easy. But it is a central theme in everybody's life. Professionals in music and the theater are not the only ones familiar with the problem. It is a basic theme in much of life.

The thing is that the *I* has to have faith in the *Me*'s ability to cope. Let us look at a few typical themes in modern life.

The dominant issue when one thinks about free will is one of legal

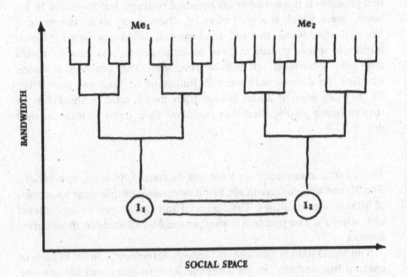

The social tree. Two Me*'s operating at a very high bandwidth have to keep to agreements entered into at the very low bandwidth of the* I*'s.*

philosophy: If there is just the slightest problem in ascribing free will to people, and thus free control of their actions, much of the basis for justice as we know it disappears. How can we punish people for what they have done if they themselves did not decide to do it? Won't any idea of a regulated society disappear if free will does?

This book does not assert that free will has disappeared. Instead it maintains that free will is exercised by the *Me* rather than the *I* (in the sense that it is the *Me* that determines which of the two is to make a decision). But it is the *I* that enters into social contracts and knows the limits for what is socially acceptable—and the *I* has only its wretched veto to work with.

The problem for the individual is therefore that the *Me* acts, while the *I* is accountable to society. The *I* has to take responsibility for things it is not fully in charge of. The law prescribes that the individual must learn the important lesson *I take the responsibility for my* Me.

Psychotherapy has become an important component of modern society. It is becoming increasingly difficult for the individual to administer the forces at work inside him. It is hard to accept all the hatred and anxiety that can well up from the subconscious. All the urges to act that appear. All the love we want to give but cannot unburden because others do not want it. Or all the antipathy to people around us. The theme of psychotherapy can be formulated as the *I*'s acceptance of the *Me*: the *I*'s acceptance of the fact that it cannot control the real subject of an act even though our entire culture tells us we can if only we try to be a bit pious and holy. The point of psychotherapy for the individual is the lesson *I accept my* Me.

Spiritual traditions, not necessarily religious or therapeutic, have emerged in the last few decades. One thing they have in common is the effort to get to know the essence of a person, the essence of oneself in all its complexity, ranging across the spectrum from divinity to senseless animal willfulness.

In a sense, spirituality merely involves taking your own life seriously by getting to know yourself and your potential. This is no trivial matter, for there are quite a few unpleasant surprises in most of us. Great spiritual personalities are characterized by an aura of experience, self-knowledge, and acceptance. The highest ideal for Buddhists is that nothing can surprise them. The point of spirituality can be said to be to get to know the terrifying truth *I know my* Me.

The problem of *daring*—even though almost forgotten in modern culture—is self-confidence's *I trust my* Me.

The list can be continued:

The philosophy of law:	I take responsibility for my *Me*.
Therapy:	I accept my *Me*.
Social relationships:	I accept you.
Personal relationships:	My *Me* accepts you.
Spirituality:	I know my *Me*.
Courage:	I trust my *Me*.

The relationship between the *I* and the *Me* also appears in contexts where they are less prominent. In medical care, for example, it is the general experience of (qualified) doctors that most pharmaceuticals are of dubious therapeutic value. The major infectious diseases were eradicated not by pharmaceuticals but by improved hygiene and living conditions. Better diets, housing, and sanitation eliminated diseases such as tuberculosis.[22]

But that does not mean that medical treatment does not work. It merely means that it is not necessarily the medicine that works. By far the most effective pharmaceutical known is the *placebo*, from the Latin for "I want to please." Placebos work, but not because of the pills or

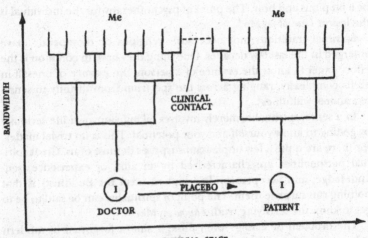

*The placebo tree. Clinical contact between doctor and patient (at the high bandwidths) secures the patient-*Me's *faith in its self-healing abilities. The patient's* I *is given a placebo and some medical Latin so the* Me *can be left to heal itself in peace.*

potions prescribed. They are effective because the patient believes they will work.

The good carer knows the value of clinical contact. The understanding and sympathy of a good doctor or nurse can inspire the belief that a patient will get better. In this context, it is less important which pharmaceuticals are employed, even though for many patients it is vital that a pharmaceutical *be* used.

What can happen when such a pharmaceutical is employed is that the *I* again begins to trust the ability of the *Me* to heal itself. Disease often involves crises in which we lose faith in our own abilities: overwork, disappointments, and unhappiness make the body say Stop, and send us to bed with a cold, say. This crisis-imbued starting point means that we no longer believe that we can cope with the situation and recover. The *I* does not want to let the *Me* have its way by giving in to the urge to go to bed and eat candy while we watch soap operas and read magazines. The *I* does not believe in the self-healing powers of the *Me*. So the relationship between treater and treated is really also—and maybe mostly—a relationship between the patient's *I* and *Me*.

The same applies to horoscopes. In 1991, *New Scientist* published an article discussing the various explanations for the inexplicable popularity of horoscopes in the modern world.

"The more plausible reason for the popularity of graphological and astrological interpretations, readings and the like is because, paradoxically, they are true,"[23] the psychologist Adrian Furnham writes. Horoscopes contain series of general, mainly positive, statements. In the 1950s, an American psychologist, Ross Stagnar, set a group of personnel managers a personality test. But instead of individual responses, each of the sixty-eight managers was given the same bogus list, containing a series of statements derived from horoscopes. When asked how accurate the assessment was, many felt they had been described very well by statements such as "While you have some weaknesses in your personality, you are generally able to compensate for them."

Who would not feel that this struck home? It is not difficult to come up with general statements that most of us would believe described us accurately. It is even likely that we would feel that our secrets had been revealed. A German psychologist, Kreuger, carried out a graphological experiment on students who were asked to assess reports based on an analysis of their handwriting. They were all enthralled by the individual precision of the reports. But they had all been given the very same one, which told every single one of them that they were fundamentally, deep down inside, weak and insecure but knew how to appear happy and strong.

Horoscopes tell the despairing *I*, which has to try and figure out all the multifarious, complicated, contradictory initiatives from the *Me*, that *this* is how we hang together. Not only do we feel they are accurate. We also feel a secret has been revealed—and that is a relief. We need not be so afraid of ourselves any longer.

Viewed in this light, horoscopes play an important role in modern culture. They give the *I* trust in the *Me*. What matters is not that there is no good reason to believe horoscopes provide any basis for this trust but that there are other reasons for this trust. Because the dominant psychological problem of modern culture is that its members do not want to accept that there is a *Me* beyond the *I*.

The problem for the *I* is that there is no alternative to accepting the *Me*. One is what one is, and one cannot escape the fact. But one can certainly enter into plenty of agreements with oneself and others that the *Me* refuses to accept.

Just as the central problem in legal philosophy is the management of the responsibility of the *I* for the *Me*, we could translate the central problem in existentialism as being the *I*'s choice of the *Me*.

Even though we have no alternative but to choose ourselves—and the *I* thus has no choice but to choose the *Me*—this choice does not come easy. For the *Me* is everything the *I* cannot accept: It is unpredictable, disorderly, willful, quick, and powerful.

Kierkegaard talked about three stages on life's way, three possible choices, which now and then, but not always, appeared sequentially. The first stage is the aesthete, who lives life in an effervescent preoccupation with sensory experiences. In a sense, this is the free, untroubled *Me*, living its life recklessly to the full. The second stage is the ethicist, who tends his marriage and his work diligently and peacefully, keeping to all his agreements. In a sense, this is the pure *I*. Kierkegaard's third stage is the religious one, which unifies the other stages in humility to God.

In Kierkegaard's successors, many of the same themes recur. Sartre emphasized the importance of seeing oneself from within. Heidegger talked about the angst at the way the world can be freely interpreted, but experienced only through interpretation: the anxiety of the *I* at not being the *Me*.

Existentialism is a grandiose attempt to put the fundamental problem of the *I*'s acceptance of the *Me* into words. The true, full existential gravity does not arise from what one chooses, but *that* one chooses. It is not the reflection by the *I* over which option is the right one; what is vital is that the *I* dare choose one option and stand by it as its own (even if it is not).

Angst, nausea, alienation, dislocation, *Unheimlichkeit*—all the discomfiting experiences of existentialism can be interpreted as the *I*'s lack of contact with the *Me*. This was perhaps expressed most dialectically by Kierkegaard, who talks of angst as a mixture of attraction and repulsion: "Angst is a sympathetic antipathy and antipathetic sympathy."[24] One of his examples is a walk along a North Zealand clifftop: You may fear tripping over a stone and falling off, but angst comes from a sudden urge to leap off.

This is the kind of thing the *Me* can come up with.

In *The Sickness unto Death*, Kierkegaard describes the feeling of despair, which comes at three levels, all concerned with the situation of the self, where the self is the spirit or consciousness: the relating of oneself to oneself. Relating to oneself can lead to despair in three ways: "The despair of not being conscious that one has a self; the despair of not wishing to be oneself; the despair at wishing to be oneself."[25]

There may be sense in "translating" this trinity in terms of the *I/Me* distinction, even though a translation reproduces only one aspect of what is translated:

The first form of despair relates to the fact that there is no relation between *I* and *Me*: the *I* is adrift.

The second form of despair involves an *I* that does not accept the *Me* it is *I* for. The *I* holds back but loses every time and so despairs. "I don't want to be *Me*."

The third level of despair in Kierkegaard involves an *I* who would like to be *Me* but cannot let go, abandon itself, and accept the *Me*, despite all its good intentions. "I would so much like to be *Me*. But I don't dare."

Of course, the *Me* does not contain only beautiful, wondrous dance steps and superb soccer passes. The *Me* contains large quantities of markedly negative characteristics, as psychoanalysis, by no means least, has made very clear. Similarly, the *I* contains not only vetoes and controls but also the ability to communicate and maintain thoughts through our lives and among friends. The two sides of man are definitely richer in things good and bad than the "phenomenological" analyses above would seem to indicate.

But before we throw ourselves into a closer study of just what the *I* and the *Me* are, there may be reason to point out that we have solved one problem along the way: Boltzmann's question as to who wrote Maxwell's equations.

You will recall that when James Maxwell lay on his deathbed, he said to his friend Professor Hort, "What is done by what is called myself is, I feel, done by something greater than myself in me."

It was not intended as such, but it was the answer to his fellow physicist Ludwig Boltzmann, who had asked in awe as to the origins of Maxwell's wonderful equations.

Boltzmann: "Was it a god that wrote these signs?"

Maxwell: "No, it was me!"

Something greater than myself in me.

CHAPTER 11
THE USER ILLUSION

"Two thousand years of Western thought has urged the view that our actions are the product of a unitary conscious system," writes the neuroscientist Michael Gazzaniga, from Cornell University: "This represents a rather substantive body of opinion, and there are many institutions and scientific beliefs built up around this assumption. To effectively challenge this view takes time, great effort, and always more supporting data."[1]

Through studying patients whose brains are split into two halves, Gazzaniga and his colleagues present a multitude of observations which will astonish anybody who thinks that consciousness is a single phenomenon in us.

Probably most dramatic is a series of studies involving a patient known as P.S.

P.S. was a sixteen-year-old boy who suffered from such incapacitating epilepsy that drastic steps were necessary. Medical treatment had not helped, so in January 1975, American neurologists decided to split surgically the two hemispheres of the brain. This operation had been in use since 1940, when it became clear that epileptic seizures can spread from one hemisphere to the other. It was a drastic procedure, but the result was a considerable improvement in quality of life—and astonishingly few side effects, which, however, were of considerable scientific interest.

Like anybody else, P.S. had a certain division of labor between the two halves of his brain, so that they performed different tasks. The American neuroscientist Roger Sperry discovered in the 1960s that the two hemispheres are good at widely differing things: The left hemisphere is linguistic, analytical, and rational (some would say "masculine"), while the right is more spatial, holistic, and intuitive (some would say "feminine"). This division of the brain soon became the object of a succession of myths about "the western" and "the eastern" brain hemispheres; myths that have a grain of truth in them, though the picture is not as black and white as they indicate.[2] Through studies of blood flow in the two hemispheres, the neuroscientists Niels A. Lassen and David Ingvar, from Copenhagen and Lund, have demonstrated that speech is not located only in the left hemisphere, for example; the right brain supplies the intonation, rhythm, and other

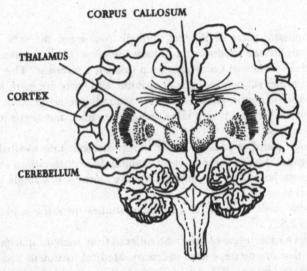

The two hemispheres of the brain as they look if one sections the brain vertically through both ears. The two halves are linked by the corpus callosum, which is surgically severed in some patients.

nonverbal sides of language: its melody, or *prosody*, as it is called. Cooperation between the right and left hemispheres provides the normal speech functions, but the image of the left brain as the linguistic one is broadly correct (in right-handed people; in the case of left-handed people, the picture is more complicated).

When a patient has the link between the two brain halves severed, one brain half loses its links with language. The phenomenon can be studied by showing such a patient two different pictures in the two areas of the field of vision. As our vision is arranged so that the right-hand side of the field of vision in both eyes is processed by the left hemisphere of the brain and vice versa, each hemisphere processes its own side of the field of vision (whereas both eyes see both sides).

If you show the patient a picture of a face composed of two different faces (a boy to the right and a woman to the left), you receive two different answers, depending on which hemisphere you ask. Ask the linguistic hemisphere—i.e., the left brain—that sees the right-hand side of the picture, and the answer you receive is that the picture is of a boy; if you ask the patient to pick a picture from a range of male and female faces, the patient's right brain will point out a picture of a woman.

What we have here are two perfectly valid, meaningful, sensible answers. But the patient does not know there is a difference. The two brain halves are independent, because the link has been cut.

But P.S. was special. He was the first patient to be studied who evidenced clear linguistic ability in the right brain: the ability not only to imbue his words with prosody but to express himself fluently. (His right hemisphere could not talk, but it expressed itself via letter cards.) This ability probably originated in left-brain damage long before the operation, which forced P.S. to use the right brain linguistically.

P.S.'s right and left hemispheres did not always agree. For example, his left brain would announce (through speech) that P.S. wanted to be a draftsman when he grew up, while his right brain spelled its way to "racing driver."

Such remarkable contrasts have led many pioneers in the study of the two brain halves to the view that a person can have two consciousnesses—if the link between the two halves has been severed. The two can disagree as to how much they like different words (names, terms), and the extent of this disagreement can change from test to test. P.S. was in his best moods on days when the two halves were in accord.

But the most incredible result of the study of P.S. is not due to the ability of the right brain to express itself linguistically. The cause was the classic pattern in patients with split brains: the way the left hemisphere dominates.

"It is hard to describe the spell-binding power of seeing such things,"

Michael Gazzaniga writes of a reply he received from P.S. in an experiment that has since been repeated hundreds of times.

P.S. was shown the usual composite pictures, where the right-hand field of vision contains one thing and the left-hand field another. P.S. was furnished with cards showing other objects. He then had to choose the cards that matched what he saw.

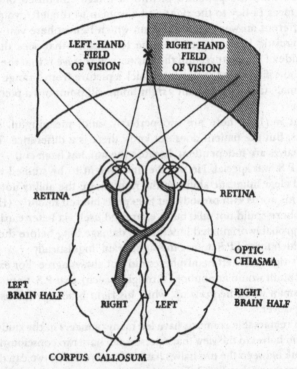

Optic paths crossing: The left half of the object is seen by the right-hand sides of both retinas. The information from the right halves of both eyes is processed in the right brain half. The other side of the object is processed in the left brain half.

The right brain saw a snow scene, while the left brain saw a chicken claw. With his left hand (corresponding to his right brain) P.S. pointed at a shovel, while his right hand pointed at a chicken. This is very logical, of course, for the right hand is directed by the brain half that sees something related to chickens, while the left hand is directed by the brain half that sees snow, which is removed by a shovel.

But then something happened that astounded Gazzaniga: "After his response I asked him, 'Paul, why did you do that?' Paul looked up and

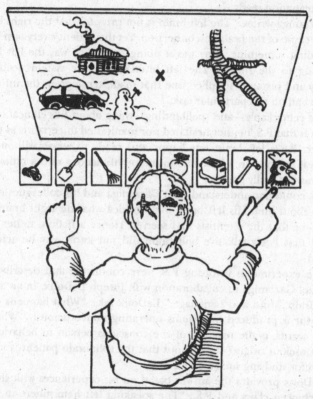

A patient with separated brain halves sees two different images: one with each brain half. He has to point at the relevant pictures below. But one hand does not know what the other is doing. The result is a verbal explanation that spellbound researchers. (After Gazzaniga and LeDoux)

without a moment's hesitation said from his left hemisphere, 'Oh, that's easy. The chicken claw goes with the chicken and you need a shovel to clean out the chicken shed.' "[3]

The left brain has heard and seen nothing to do with snow. It knows only about chickens. But it can see that the left hand (corresponding to the right brain) is pointing at the shovel. So the left brain readily—without hesitating—came up with an answer as to what P.S.'s left hand was doing.

One hand does not know what the other is doing, but the brain has an explanation ready.

Gazzaniga writes, "The left brain is not privy to what the right brain saw because of the brain disconnection. Yet the patient's very own body was doing something. Why was it doing that? Why was the left hand pointing to the shovel? The left brain's cognitive system needed a theory and instantly supplied one that made sense given the information it had on this particular task."[4]

The remarkable—and spellbinding—thing about this clinical observation is that P.S. neither hesitated nor manifested uncertainty as to his answer. P.S.'s left brain was happy and ready to weave without the slightest reservation a little tale to imbue his actions with a rationality that was not really present.

P.S. could not understand what Gazzaniga and his colleagues might know about him. His left brain had no idea what his right brain had seen—or that the scientists had seen it. Hence a fiction, rather than admit that P.S.'s talkative half brain did not know why he acted as he did.

The experiments involving P.S. were conducted and described by Michael Gazzaniga in collaboration with Joseph LeDoux. In an article on "Brain, Mind and Language," LeDoux asks, "What happens when behavior is produced by systems operating nonconsciously? What, in other words, is the reaction of the conscious person to behaviors of nonconscious origin? It turns out that the split-brain patient is ideally suited for studying such a question."[5]

LeDoux provides the answer based on his experiences with shovels and chicken claws and P.S.: "The speaking left hemisphere in these situations thus witnessed its body performing behavioral responses and it immediately incorporated these responses into its perspective on the situation. These observations of course are only relevant to the extent that it can be shown that in our daily lives the conscious self is confronted with behaviors produced by non-conscious systems. As we have seen, however, this is a reasonable suggestion if not a demonstrable fact."[6]

LeDoux wrote this in 1985. But today, when the consequences of Benjamin Libet's studies have begun to be obvious, it is very clear that even the most banal and trivial actions—such as flexing a finger—are the result of nonconscious processes that the consciousness thinks it. initiates but in fact does not.

The consequence of knowledge gained from P.S. and similar patients is thus the question as to how many of our everyday actions are explained in our consciousness by completely misleading rationalizations after the event. How often do we lie to ourselves about the motives for our actions?

In the 1950s, as quoted in Chapter Six, Edward T. Hall, the anthropologist, pointed out that other people often know more about what is going on in our heads than we do.

How often are we ordinary people in the situation split-brain patients can get into when their mute right brains are given the order "Walk!" and they instantly get up from the chair and leave the testing area? When asked where they are going, their left brain responds, for example, "Going into my house to get a Coke."[7]

LeDoux points out that we often come up with explanations like these when we have not been conscious about what we were doing. After a trip during which we haven't been conscious of driving a vehicle or of which route we took (a common occurrence for experienced motorists), we come up with deliberate excuses: the road was straight all the way, or we could do it in our sleep.

"Such thoughts are the result of the conscious self having been confronted with the fact that purposeful activities have been carried out without its sanction or assistance. The conscious self thus attempts to weave a tale that it can live with," LeDoux writes. He goes on:

"We are not consciously aware of all the information our mind processes or of the causes of all the behaviors we produce, or of the origin of all the feelings we experience. But the conscious self uses these as data points to construct and maintain a coherent story, our personal story, our subjective sense of self."[8] To LeDoux, the conclusion is obvious: "Weaving such tales about the self and its world is a prime function of consciousness."[9]

The lesson we learn from studies of split-brain patients is that the self or the *I* (as we call it in this book) lies like crazy to create a coherent picture of something it does not understand in the slightest. We lie our way to the coherence and consistency we perceive in our behavior.

But we do not lie to other people so much as to ourselves. They're not lies in the ordinary sense (where we know we are deceiving someone else) but lies in the special sense that is characteristic of consciousness: not deceit of others, but self-deceit.

"The subjective unity of self, of thought and of personal experience is an illusion created by the limited capacity of self-awareness systems,"[10] the psychologists David A. Oakley and Lesley Eames write in an attempt to summarize observations of the two brain halves, hypnosis, and hysteria (with repressed or exaggerated experiences of sensory input), among other things. Consciousness simply does not have the capacity to convey all the activity behind the conscious experience. Therefore the mental variety is concealed from us, so we experience a unity that is not particularly accurate. "Our unitary perspective of our own conscious processes is a consequence of the constraints imposed by our viewing them through the limited window of self-awareness," Oakley and Eames say.[11]

The *hidden observer* was discovered in 1973, reportedly by accident. A group of students were being given a demonstration of hypnotically induced deafness, where a subject had been told that on the count of three he would go deaf. His hearing would return when the hypnosis was lifted. The hypnosis worked, and the subject displayed no reaction to questions or unexpected loud noises behind his back.

Such demonstrations are routine, for even though the term "hypnosis" rings hollow in many people's ears, it is a straightforward, well-studied phenomenon of the human mind, and it played a central role for Sigmund Freud in his development of psychoanalysis.

But one student put a question to Ernest Hilgard, the scientist conducting the experiment. Was it possible that "part of" the subject knew what was going on, even during hypnosis?

Hilgard then told the hypnotized subject that there was another part of the person he was talking to who knew more than the part to whom he was talking. He used the following instructions (quoted from the account of a later experiment to confirm the "hidden observer"):

"Now I would like to tell you something interesting about your mind. When you are hypnotized as you now are, you can have many experiences where things appear different from the normal reality. You can fail to smell things or see or hear things that are actually there; you can imagine things that are not actually there; you can have a whole range of experiences that are different from normal reality. But while you are having these experiences and you are unaware of normal reality, you have a hidden part of you that knows reality, what is really going on. This is a part of your mind, a special part. Even though you in hypnosis are not aware of what is going on, your body knows, this hidden part of your mind knows. Now there are many regulators of body processes that do something just like this. You don't have to know of your breathing and yet your breathing goes on. Likewise there is this part of the mind that knows things that are going on. And it is possible while in hypnosis to reach this part of the mind. Now you will find that when I want to speak with this hidden part of your self, I'll place my hand on your shoulder like this. And when I place my hand on your shoulder I will be in communication with this hidden part. We can talk together. But the hypnotized part of you, the part to whom I am talking now, will not know that we are talking together."[12]

. During the demonstration to his students, Hilgard then asked the subject to raise the index finger of his right hand if one part of him heard what was going on. To Hilgard's amazement, the subject lifted his finger and then announced that he wanted to come out of hypnosis. He had just felt his finger move on its own and demanded an explanation![13]

Since then, the existence of a hidden observer has been demonstrated in other hypnosis contexts where the subject has pain inflicted on him but does not feel it (though it is felt by a hidden observer inside the person who is tolerating the pain). The same goes for patients under anesthesia.

The psychologist John Kihlstrom comments on the phenomenon: "The hidden observer is a metaphor for these nonconscious mental representations of stimulus input and the means by which they may be accessed. The success of the technique indicates that analgesic subjects may be unaware of stimuli that have been thoroughly processed by the sensory-perceptual system."[14]

The phenomenon also shows us how little we really know about what consciousness is: Even under anesthesia, we can sense and process the pain in such a way that the hidden observer feels it, even though "we" do not.

In 1991, two scientists from completely different fields, dentist John Kulli and neuroscientist Christof Koch, raised the following question: "Does anesthesia cause loss of consciousness?"

They introduce an article on the subject with this comment: "Although about 30 million operations carried out under general anesthetic are routinely performed each year in the USA alone, it is not possible to determine reliably whether or not a given anesthetized patient is conscious during surgery. As a result, some patients may be either partially aware during the operation or may be able to recall some aspects of it afterwards. It is therefore crucial to develop some experimental means to evaluate the state of consciousness of the anesthetized patient."[15]

Kulli and Koch cite a number of terrifying cases where things were not as the anesthetists believed. "The feeling of helplessness was terrifying. I tried to let the staff know I was conscious but I couldn't move even a finger nor eyelid. It was like being held in a vise and gradually I realized that I was in a situation from which there was no way out. I began to feel that breathing was impossible and I just resigned myself to dying."[16]

The patient did survive to tell the tale. But the account indicates that consciousness is a phenomenon we know far too little about. This does not mean, of course, that we would be able to define consciousness if only we knew what anesthesia was: We could not deduce from a rat's *not* being anesthetized that it possesses consciousness in the human sense. But it is nevertheless extraordinary that so many surgeries are carried out without our really being in control of whether patients are conscious or not.

Consciousness is a peculiar phenomenon. It is riddled with deceit and self-deception; there can be consciousness of something we were sure had been erased by an anesthetic; the conscious *I* is happy to lie up hill and down dale to achieve a rational explanation for what the body is up to; sensual perception is the result of a devious relocation of sensory input in time; when the consciousness thinks it determines to act, the brain is already working on it; there appears to be more than one version of consciousness present in the brain; our conscious awareness contains almost no information but is perceived as if it were vastly rich in information. Consciousness is peculiar.

But Benjamin Libet's studies have furnished us with half a second in which to produce all these peculiarities.

If we take as our point of departure Libet's discovery of the temporal backward shift of conscious awareness, the following picture emerges:

An external stimulus such as a skin prick is reported to the brain by two means: the rapid, specific nerve system, which does not trigger conscious awareness but date-stamps conscious awareness when it appears; and the slow, nonspecific system, which leads to half a second of activity that leads to conscious awareness.

If we think about a skin prick, it cannot be experienced without a context: Is it a mosquito or a caress? Is it a thumbtack we are about to sit on or a poke on the shoulder by somebody who wants to whisper a message? Are we doing the moving, or is the surrounding world moving in on us?

A skin prick is *experienced* in context. It is not experienced first as a skin prick and then interpreted. When we experience something consciously, we have already interpreted it (and perhaps already reacted by getting up off the tack on the chair).

It was late in the evening, and his stream of consciousness was running along somewhere out there among a bunch of highly abstract problems. His thought process had been in operation for ages, and he was in a kind of introverted daze on the sofa: awake but distant.

His arm jerked as if he wanted to protect himself, but its movement was instantly halted by the awareness that "it doesn't matter if the table gives a bit." Only then did he hear the sound: a tiny creak from the table as it settled in the cool evening air in a completely undramatic fashion.

The sequence of experiences, then, is: (1) he reacts; (2) there was no reason to; (3) he hears the sound that triggered (1) and (2).

"I have had similar experiences on the Fourth of July," says Benjamin Libet. "I sometimes jump before I hear the fireworks go off."[17]

A novel exercise that demonstrates dramatically how we fail to experience a sound until it has been interpreted can be carried out using a TV and a pair of headphones. It is a simple exercise: Watch and listen to the news or another program featuring people talking. Through the headphones, you will notice two different patterns of sound: (1) the speech of the person talking and (2) noise.

The interesting thing is to ask yourself where the sound is coming from—or more accurately, because of course it is coming from your headphones, where you experience it as coming from. Quite obviously it is coming from the box in which a man is sitting and talking (the sound is coming from the TV picture). But the noise is coming from your headphones! The sound of the noise is attributed not to the talking man on-screen but to the headphones you are wearing. The hearing experience automatically interprets and sorts the input contained into signal and noise: shape and background. The sound shape is attributed to the place where the corresponding visual shapes are experienced, whereas the noise does not get attributed but is experienced as coming from where the physical effect comes from.

(A VCR is the simplest way of creating this phenomenon, because there is a lot of noise on a videotape sound track; or you can adjust the TV controls to increase the amount of noise.)

Consciousness presents us with sensory data that have already been heavily processed, but it does not tell us that: Looking like raw data, they are encapsulated in a context without which they are not what we experience at all. After all, we experience a caress or a mosquito bite, not a general prick that we must then interpret.

The content of our consciousness is already processed and reduced, put into context, before we experience it. Conscious experiences possess depth: They have been put in context; lots of information has been processed but is not presented to us. A mass of sensory information has been discarded before conscious awareness occurs—and this sensory information is *not* presented. Yet the experience itself is based on this discarded information.

We experience sensation but do not experience that this sensation has been interpreted and processed. We do not experience the enormous mental work we do when we experience. We experience sensation as an immediate, direct sensation of the surface of things, but sensation is really the result of a process that gives depth to the sensory data experienced. *Consciousness is depth but is experienced as surface.*

The trick consciousness pulls is to combine two widely different approaches to the world: One approach concerns the stimuli we sense from the outside world; the other concerns the image we have in order to explain these experiences.

We do not experience the raw sensory data. We do not see the wavelength profile of the light but see different colors. We hear the newscaster not from the headphones but from the TV set. We do not feel a caress as a potential mosquito bite.

But the colors and the talking head and the caress are experienced as if they were happening here and now, and as if they consisted of precisely what we are experiencing. But in fact they are the result of a *simulation*.

We experience not the raw sensory data but a simulation of them. The simulation of our sensory experiences is a hypothesis about reality. This simulation is what we experience. We do not experience things themselves. We sense them. We do not experience the sensation. We experience the simulation of the sensation.

This view involves a very far-reaching assertion: What we experience directly is an illusion, which presents interpreted data as if they were raw. It is this illusion that is the core of consciousness: the world experienced in a meaningful, interpreted way.

Why do we not merely experience what we sense? Because we sense far too much, millions of bits a second. We experience only a fraction of what we sense—namely, the fraction that makes sense in the context.

But why do we not see that the data we experience have been processed, that masses of information have been discarded before we are presented with a scrap of information?

One possibility is this: because it takes time to achieve this depth, and because it is not particularly expedient to know that this time has passed. There are bundles and bundles of intermediate calculations that are not relevant to our actions in the world. We have to solve the binding problem before we can experience anything at all; we have to form a hypothesis about where the sound comes from before we hear it.

Benjamin Libet has shown how the specific nerve fibers from the sensory organs to the brain allow a fixing of the time of the sensation, which is not experienced until the nonspecific nerve fibers have led to half a second of activity that means the sensation can be experienced.

This way, a sensory experience can link input from lots of different sensory modalities receiving stimuli from the same object, even though the input from the various modalities (hearing or sight) may not need the same amount of time to be processed in the brain. If there were not half a second in which to synchronize the inputs, we might, as Libet puts it, experience a jitter in our perception of reality.

Our consciousness lags behind because it has to present us with a picture of the surrounding world that is relevant. But it is precisely a picture of the *surrounding* world it presents us with, not a picture of all the superb work the brain does.

The sequence is: sensation, simulation, experience. But it is not relevant to know about the simulation, so that is left out of our experience, which consists of an edited sensation that we experience as unedited.

Consciousness is depth experienced as surface.

Once in a blue moon, you come across an idea that immediately and instinctively seems very important to you, yet you do not understand why. Rather like when you meet someone you really like without knowing why. Just such an idea appeared several years before my interest in Libet's experiences made it fundamental for me. But the aha experience was there right away.

The idea stems from the design of computers. Called the *user illusion*, it involves considerable epistemological depth and is a superb metaphor for the picture of consciousness sketched above.

The notion of the user illusion appeared in an article by a notable computer scientist. Alan Kay used to work at Xerox PARC, the Rank Xerox Research Center at Palo Alto, in Silicon Valley, south of San Francisco. In the 1970s, PARC was home to the development of a revolutionary computer language called Smalltalk. Rank Xerox lacked the vision to realize the enormous potential of Smalltalk, so it was left to Apple to do so with machines like the Macintosh—a computer that is as easy to communicate with as a good friend over a cup of tea.

The basic idea was that a computer—which can of course be programmed to do anything at all—should present itself in polite and cooperative fashion. It is the computer that is meant to do the donkey work, not its user.

This may sound obvious, but it certainly was not so before Apple put its computers on the market. The dominant form of computer is based on principles developed by engineers who spend their entire lives working on computers. Naturally, they do not mind remembering all kinds of weird codes and acronyms for the inner state of the computer, since the computer is what interests these engineers, not what it can be used for.

For the rest of us, it is the other way around: If need be, a computer can be interesting in itself as a plaything or a status symbol, but what is important is not the computer but the use we make of it. These words are being written on an Apple Mac, which shows the words on the screen and a few symbols in the margin that allow one to scroll back through the pages. But as a user, one has no idea exactly how *this* word is stored in the computer. Nor does it matter, as long as the word appears on the screen when one wants it to.

Of course, hordes of engineers, software programmers, and designers have furnished the computer with a bevy of clever tricks that allow *this* word to be stored, but as a user, one could not care less about them. As long as they do the job.

In the old days, which in the case of computers means just a few decades ago, you could communicate with a computer only if you could write in a language that explained to the machine precisely what it was to do. You explained where in the computer it should store what. You had to have a mental picture of how the machine worked in order to make it work.

The great shift from the demanding computer to the helpful computer was Smalltalk and its application of the user illusion. This notion implies a radical change in the user interface—i.e., the part of the computer we communicate with: monitor, keyboard, etc. The engineers who developed the first computers did not put much thought into the user interface because all the users were professionals. So the computer looked cryptic and clumsy. Alan Kay writes:

"The user interface was once the last part of a system to be designed. Now it is the first. It is recognized as being primary because, to novices and professionals alike, what is presented to one's senses is one's computer. The 'user illusion,' as my colleagues and I called it at the Xerox Palo Alto Research Center, is the simplified myth everyone builds to explain (and make guesses about) the system's actions and what should be done next."[18]

The user illusion, then, is the picture the user has of the machine. Kay and his colleagues realized that it does not really matter whether this picture is accurate or complete, just as long as it is coherent and appropriate. It is better to have an incomplete, metaphorical picture of how the computer works than to have no picture at all.

So what matters is not explaining to the user how the computer works but the creation of a myth that is consistent and appropriate—and is based on the user, not the computer.

The computer currently recording *this* word presents the user with a sequence of texts organized into folders on a desktop. Lousy chapters get dragged into the trash can at bottom right. When the user wants to see if a chapter is too long, he can use the pocket calculator in the desk drawer.

But there are no folders, trash cans, or pocket calculators inside. There are just quantities of 0's and 1's in sequence. Indescribable quantities: A computer can contain many million 0's or 1's. But this is nothing that bothers the user; all he needs is to extract his work when he has finished it. The user can be completely indifferent to these enormous numbers of 0's and 1's. The user is interested only in what the user illusion presents: pages of a chapter, folders of completed chapters, folders of loose ends, correspondence, goofed sentences, and unorganized thoughts.

The user illusion is a metaphor, indifferent to the actual 0's and 1's; instead it is concerned with their overall function.

The claim, then, is that the user illusion is a good metaphor for consciousness.[19] Our consciousness is our user illusion for ourselves and the world.

Consciousness is not a user illusion for the whole world or the whole of oneself. Consciousness is a user illusion for the aspect of the world that can be affected by oneself and the part of oneself that can be affected by the consciousness.

The user illusion is one's very own map of oneself and one's possibilities of intervening in the world. As the British biologist Richard Dawkins puts it, "Perhaps consciousness arises when the brain's simulation of the world becomes so complete that it must include a model of itself."[20]

If consciousness is my user illusion of myself, it must insist that precisely this user *is* the user; it must reflect the user's horizons, not that which is used. Therefore the user illusion operates with a user by the name of *I*.

The *I* experiences that it is the *I* that acts; that it is the *I* that senses; that it is the *I* that thinks. But it is the *Me* that does so. *I am my user illusion of myself.*

Just as the computer contains loads of bits that a user is not interested in, the *Me* contains loads of bits the *I* is not interested in. The *I* can't be bothered to know how the heart pumps the blood around the *Me*—not all the time, at any rate. Nor can the *I* be bothered to know how an association occurs in the *Me:* the *I* would much rather know what it involves.

But it is not only the *I* experienced as our personal identity and active subject that is an illusion. Even what we actually experience is a user illusion. The world we see, mark, feel, and experience is an illusion.

There are no colors, sounds, or smells *out there* in the world. They are things we experience. This does not mean that there is no world, for indeed there is: The world just *is*. It has no properties until it is experienced. At any rate, not properties like color, smell, and sound.

I see a panorama, a field of vision, but it is not identical with what arrives at my senses. It is a reconstruction, a simulation, a presentation of what my senses receive. An interpretation, a hypothesis.

What would happen if we could experience the world directly, without simulating it first, without requiring half a second to digest the experience, which is then presented as if it were contemporaneous with the material being experienced?

Aldous Huxley described such an experience in his *Doors of Perception* (1954), which became a kind of omen for the massive upheaval in the perception of reality that has affected Western culture since the 1960s. Huxley, who had taken mescaline, gave the following account:

"I took my pill at eleven. An hour and half later I was sitting in my study, looking intently at a small glass vase. The vase contained only three flowers—a full-blown Belle of Portugal rose, shell pink with a hint at every petal's base of a hotter, flamier hue; a large magenta and cream-coloured carnation; and, pale purple at the end of its broken stalk, the bold heraldic blossom of an iris. Fortuitous and provisional, the little nosegay broke all the rules of traditional good taste. At breakfast that morning I had been struck by the lively dissonance of its colours. But that was no longer the point. I was not looking now at an unusual flower arrangement. I was seeing what Adam had seen on the morning of his creation, the miracle, moment by moment, of naked existence."

Huxley goes on: "I continued to look at the flowers, and in their living light I seemed to detect the qualitative equivalent of breathing—but of a breathing without returns to a starting-point, with no recurrent ebbs but only a repeated flow from beauty to heightened beauty, from deeper to ever deeper meaning. Words like Grace and Transfiguration came to my mind, and this of course was what, among other things, they stood for."[21]

During his mescaline trip, Huxley repeated again and again, "This is how one ought to see," when, for example, he looked at the creases in his trousers or the spines of books on the shelves. This experience led him to the following comments on what is here called consciousness as the result of the discarding of information:

"Reflecting on my experience, I find myself agreeing with the eminent Cambridge philosopher Dr. C. D. Broad 'that we should do well to consider much more seriously than we have hitherto been inclined to do the type of theory which [the French philosopher Henri] Bergson put forward in connection with memory and sense perception. The suggestion is that the function of the brain and nervous system and sense organs is in the main eliminative and not productive. Each person is at each moment capable of remembering all that has ever happened to him and of perceiving everything that is happening everywhere in the universe. The function of the brain and nervous system is to protect us from being overwhelmed and confused by this mass of largely useless and irrelevant knowledge, by shutting out most of what we should otherwise perceive or remember at any moment, and leaving only that very small and special selection which is likely to be practically useful.' According to such a theory, each one of us is potentially Mind at Large. But in so far as we are animals, our business is at all costs to survive. To make biological survival possible, Mind at Large has to be funnelled through the reducing valve of the brain and nervous system. What comes out at the other end is a measly trickle of the kind of consciousness which will help us to stay alive on the surface of this particular planet."[22]

But experiences like these are not reserved for the users of drugs. The American philosopher Charles Sanders Peirce, who anticipated at the end of the nineteenth century many of the new ideas of the twentieth, talks about a direct perception of the world as *haecceity*—"thisness." The Danish Peirce expert, the physicist Peder Voetmann Christiansen, describes *haecceity* as follows: "It is a direct, shocking experience of an object which causes language to evaporate like a drop of water on a glowing sheet of metal. All we can do is point our index finger and say 'that.' "[23]

Voetmann Christiansen illustrates Peirce's point of view by referring to a passage from anthropologist Carlos Castaneda's celebrated series of books about the South American sorcerer Don Juan and his teachings. " 'Just think,' he said, 'the world does not give itself to us directly, the description of the world stands in between. So really we are always a step away, and our experience of the world is always a recall of the experience. We recall all the time the instant that has just been, has just passed. We recall, recall, recall everything.' "[24]

Twenty-five years ago, the American psychologist Roger Shepard dreamed up a famous experiment one morning just before he woke up.

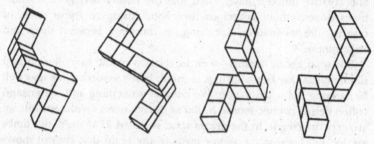

An object turned over. (After Shepard and Metzler)

Shepard saw some pictures in front of him, which he then re-created on his computer monitor. Simple pictures of little blocks put together in simple shapes like an unfinished Lego model.

In 1971, Shepard, with his colleague Jacqueline Metzler, published a study of pictures of such objects in *Science*. A series of subjects were asked to compare pictures of these constructions pair by pair. The two sets of blocks of which the subjects were shown pictures had been rotated so they were apparently not identical. The subjects were then asked whether the sets of blocks were identical or not.

What was interesting was how long it took people to answer. It turned out that the more the two sets of blocks had been rotated in relation to each other, the longer it took to figure out whether they were identical—or whether, for example, they were reflections of each other.

The conclusion was that humans actually carry out a rotation in their head when two objects are to be compared. Or they imagine a rotation. The image that is seen and experienced can be manipulated and handled in the head via a mental rotation.

People do not merely see. We simulate; make models so that we can compare.

"The idea for my original experiment with Jackie Metzler on mental rotation came to me ... in the form of a dynamic hypnopompic [waking-up] image of three-dimensional objects majestically turning in space," Roger Shepard writes in his book *Mind sights*. Shepard thinks it is no accident that it occurred just before waking up. "Many scientists and creative thinkers have noted that the mind's best work is sometimes done without conscious direction, during receptive states of reverie, idle meditation, dreaming, or transition between sleep and wakefulness."[25]

But what about dreams—seen in relation to the user illusion and simulations? One factor springs to mind: When we dream, we may well be carrying out a simulation: We visualize something and understand (often weird) connections in it. *But we do not use this simulation* while we are experiencing it. In the dream state, so-called REM sleep, our limbs are locked, because the motor areas of the brain that control movement are inhibited. Dream sleep is a state where there is no user but there are masses of illusion. In the light of how unexplained the function of dream sleep is, it is not unreasonable to suggest that dreams are a kind of simulation test bed.

The brain tests its simulation of reality by trying out new connections or by integrating new (or very old) memories and experiences. But the precondition for being able to test out crazy possibilities is precisely that they do not get used. So movement is specifically blocked during dream sleep while our other body functions run full steam ahead: Our pulse rises, our breathing increases, our eyes move, and oxygen metabolism in our brains is as it is when we are awake.[26]

If dreams are trial runs for peculiar new simulations, this is an example of a situation where *there is consciousness but the* I *is kept outside*. We cannot act with our bodies, nor can we influence our dreams with our *I*. But we are fully conscious when we dream. A user illusion without a user.

Conversely, we can describe a sleepwalker as a user devoid of illusion: As he sleepwalks he acts, but the actor has no awareness of doing so.

We can carry the poetic possibilities inherent in the term "user illusion" further: Hypnosis is an illusion with another user; meditation is a state with neither user nor illusion.

In December 1958, a fifty-two-year-old man received new corneas in a transplant operation at the Royal Birmingham Hospital in England. An eye infection had destroyed his own corneas when he was only ten months old. Since then, he had been completely blind.

The operation was seen as a great success and received considerable publicity in England; a series of articles in the *Daily Telegraph* reported on how the man's newly recovered sight started working only a few hours after the surgery.

Among the readers of the press coverage was a psychologist, Richard Gregory, who was interested in the psychology of knowledge (and whose work on visual illusions we met in Chapter Eight). With his colleague Jean Wallace, Gregory began studying what the world looked like to the patient, whom they dubbed S.B. in the scientific literature.

Prior to the operation, S.B. was an active, happy man, who had mastered many activities we do not normally associate with blind people: He could ride a bicycle (with a sighted assistant holding his shoulder) and use tools, and he'd walk without a white stick. S.B. felt his way around and enjoyed washing his brother-in-law's car while imagining its shape.

Gregory reports what happened after the operation: "When bandages were first removed from his eyes, so that he was no longer blind, he heard the voice of the surgeon. He turned to the voice, and saw nothing but a blur. He realised that this must be a face, because of the voice, but he could not see it. He did not suddenly see the world of objects as we do when we open our eyes."[27]

But when S.B. recovered his sight over the next few days, he had no trouble recognizing many objects once familiar to him only through touch: animals, cars, letters, clock hands. He quickly acquired the knack of drawing but made quaint mistakes: He gave a bus spoked wheels, even though buses did not have spokes at the beginning of the

1960s. He did so because as a child he had been allowed to feel a bus, which did have spoked wheels.

One of the only things that really astonished S.B. was the moon. He saw a quarter-moon in the sky and asked what it was. He puzzled over the answer, because he had always thought a quarter-moon looked like a quarter of a sponge cake.

S.B. drew on his recollections of touch to see with; and if there is anything we cannot touch, it is the moon.

One of the things S.B. had always dreamed of using was a lathe. Gregory and Wallace showed him a lathe in a glass case at the Science Museum in London, but S.B. said he could not see it. The case was opened, and he closed his eyes, ran his hands over the lathe for a minute, stepped back, opened his eyes, and said, "Now that I've felt it I can see."[28]

Initially S.B. could see only what he knew from his sense of touch.

S.B.'s story ends tragically. Only a year after his operation, he died, a victim of depression. Seeing the world had been a disappointment. S.B. often sat in the evening with all the lights off. The story of S.B. tells us how hard it is to see something we have not simulated beforehand. It is not true that seeing is believing. Believing is seeing.

In a normal person's perception of the world, sensations from different senses link up to form a single inner picture, which we then experience. We use one sense to support the other: It is easier to hear speech if we can see the speaker.

But it is not only when there is a paucity of sensory data from one sense that we use another. The entire project of our experience and thereby our consciousness is to combine the many different inputs into a single simulation of what we know.

Richard Gregory has posed the following question on the basis of S.B.'s story, among other things. "How much would we come to see if, as children, we had been brought up in a touchless mirror-like world of vision without hands-on experience of objects? The answer almost certainly is very little, for we would see patterns but not objects; as we would lack correlations to develop perceptual 'object hypotheses.' "[29]

Gregory's involvement in *exploratories,* science museums that emphasize touch and personal experience, is due to just such experiences of how important touch is to our sight.

The lesson Gregory says teachers can learn from this knowledge concerns the importance of touching things. He distinguishes between three kinds of learning:[30]

THREE KINDS OF LEARNING

Formal	(Handle-turning)
Intuitive	(Hand-waving)
Interactive	(Hands-on)

Formal learning is exemplified by mastering the formal mathematical apparatus so we can do our sums and manipulate numbers without necessarily knowing what is going on. The good old-fashioned way.

Intuitive learning consists of providing explanations based on common sense, which the recipient can understand. It is not the language or the symbols that convey the message (as is the case in formal learning); understanding is conveyed by an intuitive sense, which is put across by the teacher's use of gesture.

Interactive learning, where we touch objects, involves investigating them for ourselves, testing them in practice and getting our hands dirty.

The idea of the exploratories (but not of the many copies that have sprung up all over the world) is precisely this: to provide adults and children with a chance to play their way to knowledge through the physical manipulation of an experimental apparatus. The foundations of this strategy are not just that it is desperately boring to learn by the formal method (where one arrives at the correct result without knowing why). Nor that in the long run it is dissatisfying to learn through the intuitive method, where it is the understanding of the teacher that is put across through nonverbal signals in particular.

The *hands-on* strategy is important because it tells us that we do not learn only with our consciousness.

The first strategy, the *formal,* is pure consciousness, pure information: We learn codes, but not what they are codes for. There are nothing but explicit symbols.

The second strategy, the *intuitive,* is both consciousness and, particularly, nonconsciousness: both information and exformation. The learner acquires the teacher's simulation: re-creates it based on the arguments and states of mind conveyed by the teacher's words and gestures. Communication takes place at a higher bandwidth, because not only the verbal, symbolic bandwidth is used but also the visual bandwidth.

The third strategy, the *interactive*, implies a far higher bandwidth than purely formal learning. But there is no teacher: The learner has to take in the information and discard it by himself. However, the intelligently designed experimental apparatus enables the learner to alter his simulation, his perception of the aspect of reality the apparatus is about.

If we learned only with our consciousness, and it was thus the *I* that was responsible for all the knowledge we contain, however would we learn to ride a bike, dance, or think?

There are lots of skills we can use but not account for. In fact, more often than not, we cannot account for them.

What does Marilyn Monroe look like? Describe her! Blond, yes, smiling, yes, a beauty spot, yes. Can you say much more? Most people cannot, but a picture, even a part of a picture, and we recognize her face in an instant.

What does your family look like? Your boss? Your colleagues? The boy next door? You know, of course you do, but you cannot put it into words. It is impossible to describe a face in very many details, even though just one of these details is enough for you to recollect its owner.

The British philosopher Michael Polanyi described this phenomenon in the 1950s as *tacit knowledge*. Most of what we know cannot be stated. The example of the faces is Polyani's, whose view has been summarized by the Swedish philosopher Ingvar Johansson: "Polanyi says that when we direct our attention at *(attend to)* a face, for example, at the same time we direct our attention away from *(attend from)* the details of that face. What we attend from is what we have tacit knowledge of. It may be said that we are always attending to something or other when we possess knowledge, but if so, we must also be attending away from something. Tacit knowledge is essential if there is to be any knowledge at all."[31]

The vital aspect of the idea of tacit knowledge is that a skill—for example, that of a craftsman—contains more knowledge than can be described. "Green thumb" (having a way with plants) cannot be conveyed by a description: You can acquire green thumbs only by getting them dirty (and some of us never acquire them).

Everyday life contains countless examples like this, but they are just as common in science—the activity that perhaps more than any other is supposed to be based on stated, explicit knowledge. But in 1962, in the wake of Polanyi's insights, the American science historian Thomas Kuhn formulated his celebrated theory of the paradigms of science. A fundamental idea for Kuhn was precisely that a scientific field cannot account for its own values and norms; not even for its own theories. The way one becomes a scientist is by learning a few examples, which one repeats. One calculates one's way through Newtonian physics to learn tacit knowledge. One experiments one's way through Mendelian genetics by repeating a few examples. One learns things by doing them—i.e., one learns by repeated actions, not words (even though learning parrot fashion rewards just those people who are good at repeating words without investigating whether they can repeat what the words mean).

In modern scientific philosophy, the term "paradigm" means something other than it meant to Kuhn when he introduced it. Today a paradigm signifies something along the lines of "picture of the world," and many people are talking about a new paradigm, by which they mean a new picture of the world, whatever they mean by that.

When Kuhn was criticized for using the term "paradigm" (which is really the Greek for "the inflections of nouns, verbs, or other parts of speech") in twenty-two different ways,[32] he changed his language and talked of *exemplars:* "Concrete solutions to problems which students meet from the beginning of their scientific education, in the laboratory, at exams or at the ends of chapters in scientific textbooks," Kuhn writes.[33]

An *exemplar* contains all the tacit knowledge the formulae do not tell us about: what the symbols *mean.* It can be experienced only by trying out the symbols in practice; by using them to discard information with. We cannot learn anything by gazing at symbols. They reveal their power only when they are united with living human minds that can re-create some of the exformation that was present when the symbols were formulated.

Studies of *priming,* subliminal perception, which influences the conscious experience, are used nowadays to distinguish between what are known as *implicit* and *explicit* memory[34]—i.e., memory that works without or with the use of consciousness, respectively.

The performance of a task can be influenced by memories that are not consciously present during performance. What is remembered was conscious when it was remembered but is not so when it is used. John Kihlstrom writes of the phenomenon: "Implicit memory effects are conceptually similar to subliminal perception effects, in that both reveal the impact on experience, thought, and action of events that are not accessible to conscious awareness. However, the two effects should be distinguished. In contrast to subliminal perception, the events contributing to implicit memory effects were clearly detectable by the subject, attention was devoted to them, and they were represented in phenomenal awareness at the time they occurred."[35]

These phenomena can be seen most markedly in patients with severe memory loss, where a memory they can no longer recall consciously can still affect their ability to guess the rest of a word, for example, when only the beginning is presented to them. The patients cannot remember that they know it or where they know it from, but their behavior shows that they know it. It was actually the demonstration of severely amnesiac patients' ability to "guess" the whole word when they were presented with incomplete words that led to the entire modern interest in priming.[36]

But this is not only a phenomenon found in patients. Everyday life is presumably heavily marked by such implicit memory, where a memory affects behavior without our being consciously aware of it.

Recognition of faces is based on knowledge we cannot describe. This point of Michael Polanyi's has been drastically confirmed by studies of patients with severe memory loss as regards precisely their ability to recognize faces: prosopagnosia (the Greek *prosopon* means "face" and *agnosi* means "not knowing").

Two patients with prosopagnosia were shown fifty black-and-white photographs of faces. Forty-two of the people pictured were completely unknown to the patients, while the final eight were familiar, being either close relatives or in the public eye.

The patients were unable to recognize the faces they already knew, nor could they distinguish between the known and unknown faces. Not with their consciousness. But they could with their bodies!

Daniel Tranel and Antonio Damasio, from the University of Iowa, did not only ask whether the patients could recall the faces; they also measured the electrical conductivity of the skin to see if there was a reaction. This method is known as a lie detector, even though measuring the electrical properties of the skin is a far more valuable scientific method than the somewhat dubious praxis hinted at by the term.

Tranel and Damasio comment on their findings: "The dissociation between the absence of an experience of recognition and the positive electrodermal identification may mean that in these subjects an early step of the physiological process of recognition is still taking place, but that the results of its operation are not made available to consciousness."[37]

On the basis of an earlier study,[38] Tranel and Damasio proposed a model for the way we recognize faces: The immediate perception of the face is succeeded by recognition of memories, visually and through other senses, connected to the face. Only then does the conscious experience arise, according to Tranel and Damasio. In other words, a sequence similar to the *sense-simulate-experience* scheme.

The body remembers faces better than the consciousness does—in these patients. Do the rest of us have similar experiences? If so, and this knowledge becomes widespread, there may be reason to believe that one day it will be possible to say, "I can remember I have seen you before, but I cannot remember who you are," without necessarily insulting your interlocutor.

But of course, it is already an old trick among pickup artists. "Where have we met before?" is a line that can be employed even though the pickup artist probably experiences a characteristic change in the electrical conductivity of his skin rather than remembers the face he is looking at.

In the light of this knowledge, one may ask what significance, if any, the conscious *I* has for learning and skills. Does it play any role at all, when cycling, scientific experiments, and the completion of the washing up are based on routines that are not conscious?

The role of the *I* in learning is precisely to force the nonconscious, the *Me*, to practice, rehearse, or just attend. The *I* is a kind of boss who tells the *Me* what it must practice. The *I* is the *Me*'s secretary.

During an *I*-controlled learning session, performance is not very good: It is quite hard to learn to ride a bike or speak a new language. But it does not get any easier if you are aware of it while you are trying to learn it, not to mention if you are aware that other people are aware that you are trying to learn it; because then you have not just your own but also other people's eyes upon you.

Our consciousness is disturbing during both learning and exercising skills. That is precisely why overload and mantras, described in the previous chapter, can be useful.

But the consciousness and the *I* are useful because they can perceive a context and see a purpose in things one does not feel like doing—for example, practicing. The *I* can cause great pleasure in the *Me* when one is undertaking something one feels confident about. Because, of course, the confidence comes from achievement in situations where one had not been confident. The *I* affords discipline, even though it can hold very few bits per second.

But the real strength of the *I* appears only when it displays humility toward the *Me*, which is capable of so much more because the bandwidth is so much higher. The consciousness is a wonderful entity when it knows its own limitations.

As a rule it does so. We have already seen how AT&T engineer John Pierce was shocked in the early 1960s when he realized that the capacity of the human consciousness was as low as fifty bits a second at most. As he asked, why bother, then, to transmit TV at millions of bits a second?

The answer, of course, is that it is not only the consciousness that watches television. The conscious *I* does not perceive very much of what happens in a television program or a movie. Nor can it, for the bandwidth of the *I* is far too low. Far more information is transmitted (in principle) than we can grasp.

In practice, this phenomenon manifests itself in the fact that a film or a videotape editor, along with the person artistically responsible for a movie or TV program, spends hours editing every minute of the final sequence of moving images. Sometimes a whole day is spent on a single sequence lasting just a few seconds. There is loads of information to be decided on: the individual edits, the rhythm of the edits, text and graphics, the music and effects—often several layers at a time.

But before the film reaches the editing table, a vast number of decisions have already been made: How should the lighting be arranged during shooting? Sharp or soft, warm or cold? Is an actor or a scene to be shot close-up or in long shot? Up or down? Will the camera move? Will the focus change? What will the ratio of foreground to background noise be? And so forth.

One who works with moving images often spends days on details the audience will not be aware of. Indeed, the whole point is that they should not be aware of them. But they *know*.

A "ravishing" production is imbued with profound love of detail: Every single camera angle, every single edit, every single sound, is deliberate and slots harmoniously into the whole. From start to finish, the moving images are experienced as a smooth flow of narrative that expresses things at lots of different levels.

Quality in moving images is a matter of details the audience does not experience consciously but nevertheless notes nonconsciously.

You can tell by gut reaction if a program is good television. But only if you make the program yourself can you describe in words what makes it good. This applies in principle to every craft and skill: Only if you have tried it for yourself—i.e., only if you have spent many years of consciousness on it—can you put into words and be conscious of what quality is.

But it is very important to insist that the criterion for the experience of quality is not whether it is conscious! Most people think that Bach, the Beatles, and Bob Dylan are quality. But that does not mean they can give a lecture on the mathematical structure of Bach's works for organ (some of those who can do so have trouble actually experiencing the music). If art "works" in such a way that one is given a good, rousing experience that leads to good thoughts, feelings, or moods, why it works is not so important. Unless one wants to do it oneself.

Artists, craftsmen, scientists—indeed, everyone—display in their work an enormous tacit knowledge of what works on people and how. This tacit knowledge is necessary in order to communicate with quality, but it need not necessarily be experienced at the receiving end. Any shrewd songwriter knows precisely which chords to strike for a number to win the Eurovision Song Contest. The exploitation of a craftsman's tacit knowledge in order cynically to influence people, without any desire to give of himself, soon results in cliché art. But all human expression teeters between "surefire hits" and profound emotion.

The exformation in a piece of television or some other form of communication is far greater than the information there. Most consumers do not experience the exformation consciously. But it is there, and it works.

≈

"If you watch a film or a TV programme from so far away that you can neither hear the sound nor recognize the faces you will almost certainly be struck by a staccato interruptedness, something of which you are not aware if the same display is seen from close up."[39]

No; this is not from a television training manual. It is a quotation from a collection of lectures given in 1986 to the Royal Society. The theme of the lectures was "Images and Understanding"—and most of them dealt with what we know about sight and what sight sees, from a scientific point of view.

But one of the lecturers, Jonathan Miller, dedicated a lecture to moving images. "The problem is that the more successful an editor is, that is to say the more practised he becomes, the harder it is to recognize how much craft has gone into the achievement."[40]

The point may be said to be a kind of film editor's Zen: The more work you put into something, the less it is noticed. The whole idea is that the audience should not notice the circumstances but understand the message. Miller's point, though, is primarily that film editors know a great deal about how people see pictures that not many other people know. A series of more or less well-defined rules state how one can put pictures together so people will believe them: Two people edited into a news report must have their noses pointing at each other even though the two shots are from completely different situations; the bank manager and the staff association representative must look left and right respectively if viewers are not to be given a peculiar feeling that the two cannot talk to each other (and indeed, maybe they cannot).

Miller believes that we should be interested in what film editors know about the way people see. Not in order to make films, but to understand sight. For the reason the film editors' tricks work is that they work on people who do not know the principles involved. Film editors exploit tacit knowledge of how a scene can be portrayed that is inherent in everyone's way of seeing things (or consists of culturally acquired codes that most of us understand unconsciously even if we've never heard of them—that a scene shot in blue light will be seen as an evening or night scene, for example).

So scientists studying vision can learn a lot from film editors. As long as they do not think it is beneath them. The history of science shows that most great scientific theories were preceded by practical applications: Steam engines were in use long before thermodynamics put their behavior into words; people were being cured long before the doctors claimed they knew why; people talked on the phone long before Claude Shannon came up with his information theory.

In general, one may regard science as an articulation and explication of knowledge that is already being applied. Science lends words to an accumulation of skills, which it thereafter becomes much easier to develop to show new, astonishing aspects: terrain hitherto not on the map.

There is no disparagement of science in this view. On the contrary. Science tells us what we already know about the world but cannot tell one another.

Or as Jonathan Miller so beautifully puts it: "An important source of information is the intuitive folklore which is shared by movie editors, but up till now no one has bothered to make this practical wisdom explicit."[41]

Perhaps the science of consciousness and communication in centuries to come will learn just as much from actors, radio producers, and film editors as thermodynamics learned from boilermen, pyrotechnists, and charcoal burners in centuries past.

"The whole of science is nothing more than a refinement of everyday thinking,"[42] Albert Einstein wrote in 1936 in an article about physics and reality that had been provoked by arguments with Niels Bohr about modern quantum physics. Quantum mechanics had demonstrated that it is hard to describe the world without reference to the fact that one is describing it. Einstein did not like this image, which Bohr championed vigorously.

Einstein's point was that the physicist absolutely cannot think about his physics without "considering critically a much more difficult problem, the problem of analyzing the nature of everyday thinking."[43]

This was not just civility on the part of the world's most celebrated scientist; everyday life is much more complicated than the scientific world, for the trick science pulls is precisely to ignore everything it cannot get the better of.

But everyday life and its language make their mark on scientific thought nevertheless, even when far simpler problems than those of everyday life are involved. On the issue of the depth of the everyday world compared to the scientific one, Bohr and Einstein were completely in accord: "We are suspended in language in such a way that we cannot say what is up and what is down,"[44] Bohr said. His point was that in the final analysis, science is about what we say to each other in *an unambiguous way.* Actually, this fact constitutes what is characteristic of science: It is about everything we can say to each other in an unambiguous way.

That is not much, compared to everything we experience, sense, and think—not to mention what we feel. Science is a collective project aimed at knowing the world in a way we can tell each other about. Knowledge becomes scientific knowledge only after it is told in a way that allows other people to reproduce that knowledge. In an unambiguous way.

Other human cognitive activities have not submitted to this restriction. Art is also about what we can share, but not about whether we can share it in an unambiguous way. That is why these other cognitive activities have not been subjected to the massive demand for *expressibility,* the ability to be explicit, that is characteristic of science.

This demand makes it impossible for science to abandon the language of everyday life even when dealing with phenomena that are hard to express in everyday language, such as that electrons simultaneously have the properties of waves and of particles. Certainly, a great deal of science appears quite outlandish in its choice of language, but the premise is always that a new generation of scientists can learn these signs and symbols in an unambiguous way; that ten years at university will be enough to know what is being talked about. Therefore science cannot just abandon concepts and words from everyday life when atomic phenomena refuse to correspond to them. What is learned in science has to be explicable in the language of a young student.

A word to be learned is not necessarily learned by thinking long and deeply about it; rather, it is learned, perhaps, by *using* it. "After all, strictly speaking, conscious analysis of any idea excludes its immediate application," Bohr wrote.[45]

A scientific education consists, then, of working one's way through a vast number of experiments, calculations, and arguments so that the student knows what others mean by these activities. In an unambiguous but not necessarily conscious way, everyone who performs the same experiment achieves the same result, even if the details are not all, or cannot all be, completely identical.

The relationship between conscious learning and nonconscious skills is alike when one compares science and ballet. Both involve hard work in order to learn something that at bottom one cannot put into words but that one can share with a lot of other people nevertheless.

Precisely the fact that our everyday knowledge is not trivial but very deep means that we can never be rid of it but must trace all our cognitive activity back to it. This *backward tracing problem*[46] is the real problem of the philosophy of quantum physics: "we are hanging in language,"[47] but it cannot say what we want to say.

We cannot abandon language, because then we would not be able to talk to each other. Nor can we say what we would like to say, because we have only language with which to get our message across.

The problem of science, the problem of *backward tracing*, is due, then, to a more ordinary factor: The bandwidth of language is far lower than the bandwidth of sensation. Most of what we know about the world we can never tell each other.

The problem of quantum physics is just a particularly acute version of an ordinary factor: Our sociolinguistic fellowship with one another is based on exchanges at a bandwidth of sixteen bits a second. Our direct-natural fellowship with the world is based on exchanges via a band-width with a capacity of many millions of bits per second.

Therefore we can only talk about what matters when we do not talk but act. We can show things to one another, feel things together, learn from each other's green thumbs, take pleasure in one another's skills. But we cannot describe them in detail to one another.

The *I* may say, "I can ride a bike." But it cannot. It is the *Me* that can.

As Lao-tzu, the Chinese savant who founded Taoism, put it as he rode into the mountains to die, "Those who know do not talk. Those who talk do not know."[48]

CHAPTER 12

THE ORIGIN OF CONSCIOUSNESS

A hundred years ago, when the psychologists still took introspection seriously, William James wrote, "The universal conscious fact is not that 'feelings and thoughts exist,' but 'I think' and 'I feel.' "[1]

The conscious *I* is the most immediate thing we experience. It precedes all other experiences. It is the point from which each of us as a modern human being sees the world that created us.

But where does the *I* itself come from?

In 1976, Julian Jaynes, of Princeton University, proposed a shocking theory: Three thousand years ago, man had no consciousness, Jaynes asserted in *The Origin of Consciousness in the Breakdown of the Bicameral Mind.*

"If our reasonings have been correct, it is perfectly possible that there could have existed a race of men who spoke, judged, reasoned, solved problems, indeed did most of the things that we do, but who were not conscious at all."[2]

The great epics of ancient Greece, Homer's *Iliad* and *Odyssey*, are about people who do not possess consciousness but are as if automatons who act on the basis of the gods' speech through them. But the *Odyssey*, especially, was written during the period in which consciousness began to mark human life: The origin of consciousness is a historical process, which can be traced in the evidence surviving from the oldest civilizations, Jaynes claimed.

Consciousness, he explained, is not at all so essential to a human's functioning as is thought. Consciousness is a relatively new invention: a historical phenomenon. The notion of the *I* is part of the historical product that consciousness constitutes. Consciousness and the notion of the *I* were created historically and can therefore be changed historically.

Julian Jaynes's theory aroused attention—and opposition. Both because the theory changes our understanding of consciousness and because it changes our understanding of a whole range of events in historic time. Jaynes reinterprets the history of mankind, with the origin of consciousness as a central theme. ,

His idea is as follows: In the very old days, more than three thousand years ago, no consciousness existed, no notion of the *I*, no idea that people had a mental space inside them. This did not mean there were no social structures, experiences, or language. But it meant that the perception of man's actions was completely different: People acted at the gods' command, not because of their own urges. Emotions, desires, and decisions were the result of the gods' working through man: They were caused by divine intervention.

According to Jaynes, the human mind was bicameral—had two chambers, corresponding to the right and left hemispheres of the brain. All the nonlinguistic activity in the right brain half was passed on to the left brain half in the form of voices talking inside people's heads. Just as schizophrenics can hear voices when there are none, these ancients could hear the gods speaking inside them, telling them what to do. Through the bicameral mind, the social order could speak to the individual in the form of divine voices. Nowadays we call such voices hallucinations.

The central difference between this and our own view of man was that there was no independent reflective activity in people's heads: no consciousness and no decisions. The gods—called demons—looked after that kind of thing.

Men had no free will at all in those times; they did not even have will, in our sense. "Men and women were not conscious as are we, were not responsible for their actions, and therefore cannot be given the credit or blame for anything that was done over these vast millennia of time," Jaynes wrote.[3]

But how could this be possible? How could people have built cities, ships, and roads without consciousness? How was man able to function?

It is actually not that hard to imagine, even though the thought does seem strange. Think of a trip through town, using the form of transport to which you are most accustomed and a route you travel almost every day. Think about how the trip takes shape: You move along, you are not much aware of the traffic, but you may be thinking about what you will do when you arrive. Or about the weather this morning, or quite another matter. The actual transport more or less takes care of itself; you have lots of time to let your mind wander while your legs and arms manage the rest. Obviously you are not completely out of touch with the traffic en route, but your mind is on other things. A whole range of functions take place without your being aware of them. Your consciousness is elsewhere.

"Now simply subtract that consciousness and you have what a bicameral man would be like," Jaynes wrote.[4]

Precisely because as a rule we think about something other than what we are doing, our consciousness does not mean much for our normal functioning. After all, if it did, we would not be able to think about anything except what we were doing.

So a human being without consciousness is simply just like us but without an ongoing flow of thought that is about something else. The only difference arises when something unexpected or tricky occurs— e.g., a traffic jam. An individual is then forced to pay attention: be conscious about what is happening and what needs to be done. Conversely, a human being with a bicameral mind has to wait for instructions from the gods: an inner voice that tells him what to do. His experience of life will be expressed not in the form of conscious recollection and reflection but through the voices of the gods from his nonconscious.

One can certainly function without *I*-consciousness. In fact, most of us function most of the time without *I*-consciousness. We just do not know it, because we are not conscious of it while we do so. For if we were, we would not be without consciousness of it: We cannot be conscious of not being conscious. Only the conscious is conscious.

"The gods were at the same time a mere side effect of language evolution and the most remarkable feature of evolution of life since the development of Homo sapiens himself. I do not mean this simply as poetry," Jaynes wrote. "The gods were in no sense figments of the imagination of anyone. They were man's volition."[5]

But in the long run it did not work. In the end, the gods deserted man. "My God has forsaken me,"[6] runs one of the oldest surviving texts from Mesopotamia, "My goddess has failed me and keeps at a distance. The good angel who walked beside me has departed."

There were hard times in the penultimate millennium¯B.C. (2000–1000 B.C.). Natural disasters, wars, and mass migration led to upheaval and chaos throughout the civilizations of the Middle East. People became acquainted with other races, written language weakened the power of speech, the old wisdom that had been expressed in the speech of the gods had grown too old; the world was being transformed.

The bicameral mind collapsed, and an enormous cultural shift led to the origin of consciousness, according to Jaynes's theory.

The idea of reading the Greek epic poems as evidence of the development of the structure of the human mind is not in itself new; the psychoanalytical tradition has long mooted this view: in Freud, for example, through the myths about Oedipus (Oedipus murdered his father and married his mother) and Narcissus (who fell in love with his own reflection).

In 1949, an explicator of the psychoanalytical tradition founded by C. G. Jung, Erich Neumann, described the *Odyssey* as a key document in our understanding of the origin of consciousness. The *Odyssey* is the tale of King Odysseus from Ithaca, who had made his mark in the Trojan War, most notably by conceiving the hollow horse to smuggle troops into the besieged city. On his way home, he ran into countless difficulties because he had displeased Poseidon, the sea god. Many of these difficulties were in the form of temptations, which Odysseus overcame thanks to his willpower and cunning: siren songs, evil giants, and a seductress who turns suitors into swine.

In the American historian Morris Berman's summary of Neumann's interpretation, we can read, "Again and again, Odysseus experiences the enormous pull of that great unconscious, undifferentiated female power, the desire to melt or merge back into it, to go unconscious, as he once was as a very young infant or a fetus. But what makes him a hero is that he refuses that option. He is not interested in the dark energy of the unconscious, and his 'victory' over this is symbolized by the blinding of the Cyclops, whose eye is the 'third eye' of intuitive understanding."

Berman continues: "With the birth of the hero, which is really the birth of the ego, the world becomes ambivalent. It gets split into masculine and

feminine, black and white, left and right, God and the devil, ego and unconscious, and this becomes the great drama that all cultures (according
to Neumann) have to deal with."[7]

But the *Odyssey*, in this view, is still only the tale of the earliest origins
of consciousness and the temptations the unconscious subjects it to.

The most precise historical dating of the origin of consciousness is
traced by Jaynes to the Greek statesman and legislator Solon of Athens,
who lived from about 640 to 560 B.C. Solon introduced democracy to
Athens in the century when Greek philosophy was founded by figures
such as Thales, Anaximander, and Pythagoras.

It is known with certainty that Solon used the word *noos* as an expression for a subjective mind. One of the dogmas attributed to him but
also to many other contemporary Greek thinkers is the famous "Know
thyself"—an expression that makes sense only *if one has an idea of oneself
seen from without*. Seeing oneself from outside is an advanced mental
operation that presupposes an idea of who one is.

Jaynes finds signs of the origin of consciousness in many civilizations: the Greek, the Indian, the Chinese, and the Egyptian. Of all the
remarkable cultural breakthroughs that occurred on the planet at
once, in many different cultures, about half a millennium B.C., in
Jaynes's view it is the Old Testament that contains the best textual
description of the origin of consciousness. There the whole story is told
in one go, from the disappearance of the gods to the taking over of the
mind by consciousness.

Moreover, the religion of the Old Testament involves *monotheism*.
Religions with lots of gods correspond to the bicameral mind, while
those with a single God correspond to the conscious mind.

For the really huge difference between polytheism and monotheism
is not so much superstition, hallucinations, or rain dancing: The big
difference is the perception of who the real executor of human
action is.

Prior to the era of consciousness, in the period of the bicameral
mind, people did not have free will; they had no will at all, in fact. After
the advent of consciousness, man was given free will—to a certain
extent. The problem of ethics arose, and Moses descended from
Mount Sinai with the tablets containing God's Ten Commandments.

Suddenly there was something to think about: how one ought to act.
The hugeness of the contrast between "Know thyself" and moral direc-
tives on the one hand and the freedom from responsibility of the

bicameral mind on the other are apparent from this passage from Jaynes's book:

"An old Sumerian proverb has been translated as 'Act promptly, make your god happy.' If we forget for a moment that these rich English words are but a probing approximation of some more unknowable Sumerian thing, we may say that this curious exaction arches over into our subjective mentality as saying, 'Don't think: let there be no time space between hearing your bicameral voice and doing what it tells you.' "[8]

The idea that people are happiest when they feel free to act freely, without intervention from the consciousness, can be traced in this ancient quotation.

Translated into the language of this book, the Sumerian proverb would sound thus: "Avoid vetoes—make your *Me* happy." But this involves a dramatic shift in meaning, for nowadays we do not hear the gods (and we lock up anyone who does). So the focus is not on following an inner voice but on acting without too much consciousness and prior reflection.

But the assertion itself—act without conscious consideration—was probably no less absurd to the ancient Sumerians than it is today, if we isolate it from its context and adopt it as a rule of conduct.

During the transformation from the bicameral mind to the conscious mind, a long period of transition occurred, in which the voices of the gods may not have spoken through very many people but many listened to anyone who could still hear them.

"Greek oracles were the central method of making important decisions for over a thousand years after the breakdown of the bicameral mind,"[9] Jaynes writes. The oracle at Delphi, the most famous of them all, consisted of young women who through frenzied mouths and bodily contortions gave answers to the questions put to them. The questions were not trivial but concerned: colonies, war, legislation, hunger, music, and art. Just as remarkably, "The replies were given *at once*, without any reflection, and uninterruptedly," Jaynes writes, then asks, "How was it conceivable that simple rural girls could be trained to put themselves into a psychological state such that they could make decisions at once that ruled the world?"[10]

One may wonder how unschooled the priestesses at Delphi really were. It is said, for example, of Aristoxenus, who was a student of Aristotle and who wrote a biography of the mathematician and philosopher Pythagoras, that "Aristoxenus says that Pythagoras got most of his ethical doctrines from the Delphic priestess Themistocleia."[11] One may also question how categorical were the answers the young priestesses gave. Heraclitus writes, "The lord whose oracle is in Delphi neither speaks out nor conceals, but gives a sign."[12] So the young women may have given answers, but they had to be interpreted before they were of any use. But whatever the details, it is remarkable that Greece could be ruled through consultations at Delphi.

The explanation, Jaynes thinks, is a general pattern in which a common faith is expressed through specially chosen individuals, who can, through rituals and trances, establish contact with powers (in themselves) with which other people are no longer in contact. The whole range of sorcerers, medicine men, oracles, witches, fortune-tellers, and their modern successors express a longing for the contact the bicameral mind had with the gods. As history unfolds, mankind is losing his faith in the chosen few who can still sense the will of the gods. Or perhaps the message is now conveyed in another guise.

The epoch of the bicameral mind came to its conclusion: Man's image of himself had changed—and with it, his view of the divine. The panoply of Greek deities gave way to Christianity, which is the religion of consciousness. "A full discussion here would specify how the attempted reformation of Judaism by Jesus can be construed as a necessarily new religion for conscious men rather than bicameral men," writes Jaynes. "Behavior now must be changed from within the new consciousness rather than from Mosaic laws carving behavior from without. Sin and penance are now within conscious desire and conscious contrition, rather than in the external behaviors of the decalogue and the penances of temple sacrifice and community punishment."[13]

Jaynes does not pursue these considerations of religious history, but the fundamental point is the same as that which arose from a comparison of Judaism and Christianity based on Benjamin Libet's veto principle: Where Judaism affects man's mind from without, through social ceremonies and moral prohibitions, Christianity tries to change the mind from within, by demanding that people have a disposition that is itself capable of exercising the controls formerly located outside the mind, in the social fellowship. Christianity is the religion of consciousness because it makes consciousness—instead of something from outside—the regulator of human behavior.

This suggests a tripartite division of the historical process. First there is a *preconscious phase,* where people do not possess free will but act directly and without reflection upon the gods' commands. A *socially conscious phase* follows, in which free will is regulated via a social contract (the Ten Commandments) pronounced by a human being (Moses) with special abilities to hear God; focus is on the community and ceremonies. In the third phase, a *personally conscious phase,* the relationship between man and God is again internal (as in the preconscious phase) but now is conscious: Free will implies the possibility of sin in mind as well as deed.

Polytheistic religions all belong in the first phase, while Judaism and, in part, Roman Catholicism belong to the second; Protestantism is a pure cultivation of the third phase.

The question, though, is whether the attempts by the Christian tradition to render man totally conscious and transparent can succeed. If Benjamin Libet is right, and consciousness can veto nonconscious urges so they are not implemented in real life but it can never control the origin of urges, man is quite simply not so transparent as Western philosophy and religion since the Renaissance have made out. From the total absence of consciousness in times of yore, the modern era has been an attempt to insist on the absence of nonconsciousness.

Two very important concepts in Jaynes's analysis of the origin of consciousness are those of "I" and "me." An "I" arises at the same time as the idea of a world. When you have a picture of an outside world that you can think about, you can also think about yourself in that world: You can see yourself from without; you can think your way into situations and ask how you would react. The "I" concept is closely associated with seeing yourself from without: having a map of the world where you, too, are present. The "Me" concept, which Jaynes himself admits is unclear compared to the "I" concept,[14] also in Jaynes involves a self seen from without.

In the light of the *I/Me* distinction, we could put things another way: A preconscious person is only a *Me,* whereas a conscious person believes he is only an *I.* Man has moved from a period in which there was only a *Me* to a period where there is apparently only an *I*. In the *Me* period, behavior was controlled by voices, while in the *I* period, consciousness thinks it controls everything.

Once it has arisen, the *I* must necessarily insist that it has control of the person. That is the very idea of an *I*. The idea of an *I* with free will is irreconcilable with a bunch of gods operating through commanding voices. Because then it would not be the *I* doing the deciding.

But conversely, the *I* faces the problem that it cannot explain or necessarily accept all that happens in the person covered by the *I*. The *I* view, which would claim that the *I* supervises and sees through everything, runs into the problem that this is obviously just not the case. Neither the happiness and joy a person can feel nor the hatred and vileness he or she can contain are anything the *I* can explain.

The *I* must necessarily bow and kneel to something greater than itself. But it is a central characteristic of an *I* that this greater thing cannot be the person him- or herself, for that is controlled by the *I*.

The solution is monotheism: the idea that there is one, and only one, God.

The notion of God is the *I*'s salvation when it is confronted with characteristics of the *Me* that it cannot explain: a power that is far greater than the *I* and that operates through every thing and event in the world. Divine intervention can be used to explain everything the *I* cannot explain in the person that the *I* ostensibly sees through and controls.

We can go even further and make the following assertion: The concept of God covers everything about the *Me* that is not the *I*. Instead of acknowledging subliminal perception, nonconscious thinking, and a pile of other activities in a person that the *I* cannot explain, the *I* can say it is not the person that embodies this providence and these abilities: It is a divine principle.

The inability of the *I* to explain the *Me* is thus shielded by the notion of God, a notion that permits an irrationality that the *I* claims does not exist in the person.

Consciousness cannot accept that it does not have control of the person. On the other hand, consciousness has to admit that it does not quite have tabs on everything. Hence monotheism.

Almost every monotheistic religion contains more or less dominant traditions that "heaven is inside you"—that the divine principle is in every man: not just out there but also in here.

In his attempt to summarize millennia of religious thought in *The Perennial Philosophy*, Aldous Huxley emphasizes precisely this God within: "God within and God without—these are two abstract notions, which can be entertained by the understanding and expressed in words. But the facts to which these notions refer cannot be realized and experienced except in 'the deepest and most central part of the soul.' And this is true no less of God without than of God within."[15]

The religions have cultivated the fact that the *I* must necessarily realize there is something that is greater than itself. They have also cultivated a series of methods to help the *I* gain composure toward this something. The religions offer a fellowship to people who wish to cultivate these factors.

One may interpret prayer and meditation, ceremonies and blessings, as contact to this divinity within. But we can go a step further and assert that what the *I* tries to contact via prayer, chanting, and scriptures is the very *Me* that the *I* must consciously deny the existence of.

A very significant part of what Huxley refers to as the "God within" is the aspect of man that consciousness cannot explain. If we claim as much, we can say that the theme of the religions is really a reworking of the theme of consciousness and thus the theme of the *I*: equanimity toward the fact that we are more than we ourselves can know.

There are thus good reasons for taking the experiences of religion seriously; from an atheistic point of view, too, one must say that religions involve something real and genuine that is concerned not merely with a yearning for the simplicity and innocence of the bicameral mind but with a highly contemporary authentic drama: the relationship between consciousness and nonconsciousness in a person. Atheists also have to live with the conflict described by the religions. Religion is far too important for atheists to leave to the religious.

The American Julian Jaynes is far from the only person to have explored the origin of consciousness. German and French *mentalité* historians have studied the history of *I*-consciousness. Their conclusions do not always accord with Jaynes's.

The European studies indicate that establishing consciousness apparently did not go as smoothly as Jaynes claimed it did in his 1976 theory that consciousness first arose about 1000 B.C. Later on, *consciousness disappeared again!*

This occurred in about A.D. 500 and lasted for over five hundred years. Morris Berman writes of recent studies of this period: "Human self-awareness, for reasons not entirely clear, seemed to disappear during this time and then mysteriously reappeared in the eleventh century. Behavior during the period A.D. 500–1050 had a kind of 'mechanical' or robotic quality to it."[16] The view of crime also changed: "There was virtually no discussion of the issue of intentionality in a criminal act. It was only the *act* that counted, the overt physical behavior."[17]

The end of the Middle Ages is characterized by the reappearance of consciousness, the breakthrough of self-awareness. Berman describes the period around A.D. 1500 in the following remarkable terms: "We find a sharp, simultaneous increase in self-awareness and in the quantity and technical quality of mirror production."[18]

The use of mirrors became widespread during the Renaissance, the period imprinted with the rebirth of the individual—the beginning of the modern age. Looking at oneself in a mirror, seeing oneself from without, was a literal communication of self-awareness or *I*-awareness. Likewise, books of etiquette began to spread, instructing people in how to behave in the presence of others: how to eat, dress, converse, and in general be *cultured*.

It may seem completely absurd to interpret the proliferation of mirrors this way. But the mirror is precisely an instrument that allows you to see yourself the way you appear to others. The preconscious person only saw the world, and his own actions in the world, from within. The idea of comparing oneself to other people presupposes that one can see oneself the way others see one. Mirrors permit that.

(Or do they? In a mirror, we see ourselves *reflected* in two senses: not just optically, but also socially. We do not actually see what everyone else sees, because we see a person who sees no one but himself. It is a closed circuit; there is no sociality, as when we look at someone else.)

The French *Annales* school of historians, the German Norbert Elias, and many others have explored the peculiar historical detail that the mirror and consciousness go hand in hand. The important thing is of course not the mirror in itself; the important thing is the reflection. After all, we can look deeply into a smooth piece of water if we want to see ourselves. Mirror technology, like so much other technology, is merely a method of ensuring that we ourselves can determine when we want to achieve an effect—in this case, the effect of seeing ourselves from without—and not just when there is a calm sea.

The ancient Greek myth about Narcissus, who fell in love with his own reflection, can be read in many ways and has many levels. In the most widespread version today, the myth is about a human being who falls in love with his own reflection and is therefore not interested in the deeply interested and interesting woman, Echo. He thus incurs the wrath of the gods and gets turned into a flower.

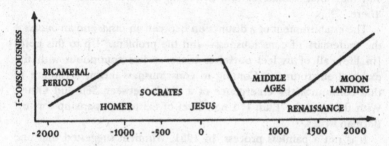

Major events in the history of consciousness

In this context we can interpret the myth as expressing the risk inherent in being too absorbed in oneself seen from without—the way others see one. One thereby loses the ability to sense one's needs immediately and directly. Narcissus' problem is not love of himself; it is love of himself in the eyes of others.

With self-consciousness and the mirror and good table manners, a problem arises: A person's sphere of action is no longer limited to what his desires urge and the law permits; suddenly the gaze of others becomes important. The *I* unavoidably gains control, for it is only the *I* that can imagine what other people might be thinking; the *Me* knows only its own impulses.

The British psychoanalyst Donald Winnicot has pointed out that the mother's face is the infant's first mirror. "In individual development, the precursor of the mirror is the mother's face,"[19] Winnicot wrote. Studies reveal that the infant's expression becomes hectic and disorganized unless the mother's face registers emotion when she looks at her baby.

But the infant has no sense of itself. "There is no such thing as an infant," Winnicot asserts in a famous remark. The infant exists only together with the mother or other people. The notion of an "I," an identity, does not appear until the third year of life. The original state of the infant is an experience of nonseparation, nonidentity.

Morris Berman labels this learning of the difference between oneself and other people as "the basic fault" in modern man's view of the world. "Exactly where one comes to consciousness is totally arbitrary; the thing that remains constant is the awareness that 'I' am 'here' and that 'that' (whatever one is looking at, or is outside of one) is 'there.' "[20]

The establishment of a distinction between an *inside* and an *outside* is the trademark of consciousness—and the problem. "Up to this point [in life], all of us feel ourselves more or less continuous with the external environment. Coming to consciousness means a rupture in that continuity, the emergence of a divide between Self and Other. With the thought 'I am I' a new level of existence opens up for us," Berman writes.[21]

It is not a painless process. In 1951, Winnicot suggested that one could interpret children's use of teddy bears as *transitional objects* between the inside and the outside. To smooth the passage between the self and the rest of the world, children use comforters and teddy bears. Later on, more advanced things take over: art, religion, alcohol, pills, and books. The fundamental angst arising from the idea that we are separated from the world is dulled by whatever means we can find.

In his remarkable book *Coming to Our Senses*, Morris Berman employs this childhood separation as the key to understanding why we deny our own body and the feelings we register in it. For when we distinguish between our self and the rest of the world, a conflict arises: How do they relate to each other? We may deny the existence of our consciousness (and experience an ecstatic sense of oneness with the world by forgetting ourselves), or we can deny the existence of the outside world and its *differentness*, allowing the consciousness and the *I* to rule without being contradicted.

Against the background of his knowledge of a wide range of psychoanalytical and philosophical traditions, including figures like Winnicot, Elias, the psychoanalyst Jacques Lacan, and the philosopher M. Merleau-Ponty, Berman claims it is the latter strategy that is dominant in our culture. The distinction between self and *differentness* becomes a recurrent theme in history: We learn to distinguish between friend and foe, tame and wild, worldly and heavenly. The more or less desperate attempt to keep alive the idea that we possess control over ourselves is manifested in national states and standing armies (which arose at the same time as the mirror and self-consciousness).

But the real drama is not these outer conflicts; to Berman, the real drama is the inner conflict: You are a person with a body, but you do not want to acknowledge that body, for it is uncontrollable, weird, and revolting. What really terrifies is everything you cannot control: spiders, sexuality, emotions, angst, and your body.

In other words, everything the *I* cannot control, however much it would like to. The result of this denial of what you cannot control is a feeling of intense emptiness, an inner disturbance that constantly needs compensating for with transitional objects. Like dictators who finally go mad because nobody dares contradict them, the *I* ends up in a lifelong despair: Everything uncontrollable is a threat to the *I*, and we seek to eradicate it through intensive use of pesticides, zoos, and television. We have got to get the *different* under control, for "The mere idea of an Outside is the real source of angst," as the German philosophers Max Horkheimer and Theodor Adorno wrote in 1944.[22]

"While in one sense the body is the most abiding and inescapable presence in our lives, it is also essentially characterized by absence," the American philosopher Drew Leder wrote in his book *The Absent Body* (1990). He asks "why the body, as a ground of experience, yet tends to recede from direct experience."[23]

Leder builds upon the so-called phenomenological school in twentieth-century philosophy, founded by the German philosopher Edmund Husserl, who tried to find the basis of all knowledge in science and everyday life. Husserl started by studying "the phenomena"—what we experience immediately. In about 1913, he began to describe all experiences from the basis of a "transcendental I." The word "transcendental" indicates that Husserl is talking about something that transcends the experience itself and precedes it. The transcendental I is not the same as the empirical I, a person, but rather—in the language of this book—the principles for the simulation behind the user illusion. But the vital thing was that Husserl showed that one could analyze the human experience—the phenomena we immediately perceive—and not just abstract concepts.

The Frenchman Maurice Merleau-Ponty emphasized that these

immediate experiences are anchored in the sensations of the body. We can sense things only because we have a body.

But Drew Leder goes further than Husserl and Merleau-Ponty. For their tradition mainly involves perception and "motility." "It is through these modalities that we directly experience and act upon the world," Leder writes. "Yet such functions arise within a series of impersonal horizons: the embryonic body prior to birth, the autonomous rhythms of breathing and circulation, the stilled body of sleep, the mystery of the corpse. It is precisely because such bodily states involve various forms of experiential-absence that they have tended to be neglected by philosophers of experience."[24]

To Leder, the fundamental problem in philosophy's view of the body is that the philosophers' distinction between body and mind means they have never understood the body's fundamental ties to the world. We eat, breathe, and experience; we move, dance, and wave. The body is connected to its surroundings in a way we do not experience, because we are not aware that we breathe, and officially do not want to be aware that we go to the lavatory.

"Almost all spiritual traditions use posture and gesture as a means whereby we enter into relation with the divine," Leder writes. "This body's roots reach down into the soil of an organismic vitality where the conscious mind cannot follow."[25]

The body knows a link to the world that the consciousness cannot sense. That is why almost all spiritual traditions involve body positions and many therapeutic traditions body attitudes. One might say that our bodily attitudes to the universe express far more than our consciousness knows: By crossing our arms we display closedness toward our fellow human beings; by stretching we experience well-being and show trust, because one is vulnerable when one stretches.

In 1981, the Danish psychologist Olav Storm Jensen formulated a theory of "the two bodies," which expresses many of the same points as Leder. Storm Jensen distinguishes between a body that is controlled by consciousness ("the cognitive-voluntary body" or "the ego-body") and one that cannot be consciously controlled ("the emotional-vegetative body").[26]

The consciously controlled body deals with everything to do with willpower and thinking: everything "one can do" with one's body if one wants. The other body does everything "one" cannot control: It deals with the circulation, the reflexes, digestion, sexuality, and emotional reactions.

The most important bridge between the two bodies is respiration. Normally, this is controlled totally by the nonconscious body. We do not think about the fact that we are breathing; we do not even think about the fact that we sometimes hold our breath in excitement or surprise (indeed, we do not even think about the fact that breathing is a very important part of a telephone conversation). But we can control our breathing consciously. Many mental and spiritual techniques are based on just this: developing our breathing.

Another important bridge is sexuality, which cannot be controlled by the conscious body alone but has a tendency to go off on its own (frigidity, impotence, neurotic fear of the body, and other dysfunctions).

But characteristically, the conscious body cannot prevent the nonconscious body from carrying out its functions: We cannot hold our breath for more than a minute or so; we cannot hold water for more than a few hours; we cannot halt the sexual functions, whether we want to or not.

We can express this fact in another, rather macabre way: It is very difficult to commit suicide. In the final analysis, the part of the body not regulated by the consciousness does not allow us to hold our breath long enough to kill ourselves. Similarly, it is hard to refrain from bodily contact and sexuality, eating and drinking, going to the toilet, and sleeping.

Consciousness, then, has only limited control of the person. "The other body" lives its own life, which consciousness cannot control. The *I* cannot get the *Me* to do whatever it wants it to do. A vast number of processes take place that handle a vast amount of information the consciousness never hears about.

To some extent we can control whether the consciousness is to know what is going on. We can—if we direct our attention there—feel that we have clothes on our bodies or that we are sitting in a chair. But we cannot feel the way our immune defenses are routing an ordinary virus this very minute (we feel it only when there are such major problems that steps are taken to reinforce the immune defenses, such as by raising our body temperature). Nor do we feel the way the blood moves through our left thigh.

Some people, who have worked on it for a very long time, using

Eastern concentration techniques, for example, can bring vital body functions—blood pressure, body temperature, etc.—under the control of the consciousness to a certain extent. Western techniques such as visualization and biofeedback have been introduced to the treatment of disease in recent years and have yielded promising results. Directing his attention to parts of the body that are seats of disease or unbalance, the sufferer imagines the healing function of the body and so is aware of the abilities of the body to heal itself. In recent years, the study of the link between the psyche and the immune defenses has become an important area of medical research: psychoneuroimmunology.

But fundamentally, the nonconscious body is not under the control of consciousness. Whether we want it that way or not. The body is part of a biological metabolism with the living system on the planet—and this participation is not subject to the power of the consciousness. We do not have access, via the body's own means, to changing the role each of us plays on earth. We are part of a living system to which we are so adapted that there is no freedom to get off.

As the Chinese savant Lin Yutang put it, "Even the most spiritually dedicated man cannot help thinking about food for more than four or five hours."[27]

The body is in a state of interaction with the world: We eat, drink, and dispatch matter back into the cycle of nature. In no more than five years, practically every atom in the organism gets replaced. The vast majority of atoms are replaced far more often. Identity, body structure, appearance, and consciousness are preserved—but the atoms have gone.[28]

The feeling of individual continuity is real enough, but it has no material foundation. Material continuity is to be found only in a greater cycle.

In 1955, the American physicist Richard Feynman put it thus: "The atoms that are in the brain are being replaced; the ones that were there before have gone away. So what is this mind of ours: what are these atoms with consciousness? Last week's potatoes! They now can remember what was going on in my mind a year ago."[29]

The memory, the *I*, the personality and individuality, are a dance, a pattern, a whirl in the world: a pattern in a stream of matter.

"All bodies are in a state of perpetual flux like rivers, and the parts are continually entering in and passing out," wrote the visionary German philosopher Gottfried Wilhelm Leibniz in 1714.[30]

At the end of the seventeenth century, Leibniz formulated a number of contributions to mathematics, physics, and philosophy. A recurrent theme was his study of the significance of tiny differences, stemming from his view that every change in nature takes place smoothly and not in abrupt movements. The study of the human mind also concerned Leibniz. As the Danish philosopher Harald Høffding relates:

"Leibniz was the first to draw attention to the importance of infinitesimal elements in psychology (as he did in mathematics and physics).... Using the unconscious elements (which he calls 'petites perceptions'), he explains the individual's connection with the whole universe, to which the individual is far more profoundly related than he is conscious of."[31]

Subliminal perception and nonconscious mental activity mean that man's link to the world is far stronger than consciousness suspects. Leibniz knew this, and psychology knew it at the end of the nineteenth century. But the twentieth century has been a story of forgetting this link; of regarding consciousness as the whole story of man's connection with the world.

Now the wind is changing, and people are again realizing that they are far more than they themselves can know.

The beauty of science has often filled scientists with wonder. But the scientific tradition was founded in the attempt to understand the divine principles behind the world. As Julian Jaynes sees it, the origin of science lies in the study of omens, which started in Assyria during the breakdown of the bicameral mind. In ancient Greece, Pythagoras studied mathematics because he wanted to find the divine principle expressed in the world of numbers. The great figures of modern science were often deeply motivated religiously: Kepler, Newton, Einstein. As Jaynes put it, "Galileo calls mathematics the speech of God."[32]

Thought is not conscious; scientific thought is not conscious either, but our concept of consciousness encompasses everything we human beings are proud of in ourselves, which means, not least, science.

But perhaps it is not so strange that beauty can play such an enormous role in scientific work. For it is not the conscious *I* that thinks at all, but the nonconscious *Me*. Everything the *I* cannot explain.

So we can continue the exchange at the end of Chapter Ten:

Boltzmann: "Was it a god that wrote these signs?"

Maxwell: "No, it was me!"

God: "Yes, it was me."

PART IV

≈

COMPOSURE

CHAPTER 13

INSIDE NOTHING

"Once a photograph of the Earth taken from the outside is available . . .
a new idea as powerful as any other in history will be let loose,"[1] wrote
the British astronomer Fred Hoyle. That was in 1948.

Just two decades later, the whole world was given the opportunity to
see such a photograph, when the U.S. spaceship Apollo 8 orbited the
moon at Christmas 1968 with three men on board and sent the captivating photograph of the earth above the lunar horizon back to . . . the
earth.

We saw ourselves from without, even though we were not in the photograph, because we are so small. For the first time ever, the planet saw
itself in the mirror.

It revolutionized our image of ourselves. Previously we had viewed
the stars and the other planets from without, as they appeared in the
heavens. We already knew our own planet, but only from its own surface. We distinguished between heaven and earth. What we knew of the
skies we knew only from here. What we knew of the earth we knew only
from here.

But suddenly the earth had become a heavenly body.

The space program was based on the defense and industry interests of a
superpower rather than on those of science, let alone the earth's environment. But its consequence was the peculiar fact that only after we
had set out did we discover the place from which we had set out. We

peered over our shoulders—and saw an abyss of beauty. An indescribably beautiful azure-blue planet suspended in the middle of infinity: an orgy of color, a place unlike any other celestial body man had ever seen.

The surface of the moon is a desert of craters, a dead sphere of random, untidy remnants of collisions between a dead lump of rock and loose-flying fragments of stone in the solar system. The space program also showed that our closest neighbors in space, the planets Venus and Mars, are similarly barren, crater-pocked deserts.

When it became possible to compare heaven and earth, it became obvious that we know of no other place in outer space even remotely resembling the earth: Our planet is quite unique.

When scientists began pondering why this was so, it became clear that there was a reason for the fact that we know of nowhere else in space even remotely like the earth: We know of no other place in space that hosts life.

It is life on earth that makes it completely different from anything we know in space. Not that there cannot be other places in space where there is life; we just have not found them yet.

In the wake of this shocking sight of the planet from without followed a consciousness raising no less powerful than that which happened to mankind when we started looking at ourselves in the mirror. Environmental awareness and knowledge of the planet as our dwelling place spread at a dramatic pace across the globe, and by the end of the 1980s it was common property.

In the industrialized countries, the rich and technically habituated populations slowly began to realize that the preindustrial civilizations contain a wealth of experience about the living environment on the planet from which the scientific civilizations can learn plenty. In the United States, on television news programs on annual Earth Days, prominent cultural figures could be heard proclaiming that it was fortunate that we could still learn from the culture of the Indians before it disappeared for good. In the U.S.S.R., there was a slowly growing realization that the suppressed Buddhist and shamanic cultures of Siberia might possess valuable knowledge from which centrally planned industrialism could learn a great deal about nature.

The cultures that manifested a culture of consciousness and science began to see that man had in fact been capable of other—and perhaps more important—things in the days before he started looking at himself in the mirror.

All because our own planet, thanks to the people who had seen themselves in the mirror, was for the first time given the chance to see itself from without.

The space flights provided us with a perspective of the earth as a planet. In the 1960s, NASA set a task for a number of scientists, including the British atmospheric chemist James Lovelock. The task was this: How would we find out whether there was life on Mars once we had landed a space probe there?

Lovelock's response was simple, even though it took him some years to arrive at the result: We do not need to go to Mars to see if there is life there. We can see from the earth that there is no life on Mars. A rather inconvenient answer for an organization that was working on sending a spaceship there and was using the question of life or no life as a major argument in its efforts to procure funds. But also a very important answer. Because one can turn the argument around: From Mars, one can see that there is life on earth.

From without, the earth offers very clear evidence of life. The atmosphere has quite a different composition than it would have if there were no life. For example, there would not be any free oxygen in the earth's atmosphere if it wasn't for living creatures. In turn, free oxygen means that the atmosphere is very clean and transparent, so we can see the surface from far away, in the form of oceans, which are blue. The blue sea reflects the color of the atmosphere as it looks from within, in the form of our blue sky. If there were no life on earth, the sky would not be blue but would more likely be yellowish or pink.[2]

A large number of factors on the earth's surface are coregulated by living creatures: the composition of the atmosphere, temperature, the salinity of the seas, the erosion of rock from the continents, cloud formation, the ability of the surface to reflect sunlight, etc., etc. Along with the American biologist Lynn Margulis, James Lovelock therefore formulated the Gaia theory: The earth *is* a living organism. Gaia is the name the ancient Greeks gave the earth goddess.

Lovelock and Margulis are among the cheekier scientists and have no qualms about getting into a scientific clinch with colleagues who regard the idea of the earth as a single living organism as going a bit too far. As the two scientists ask, why not accept the fact that every aspect of the environment in which we live is regulated by life—why not say that the whole place is one big living organism?

Everything we eat was once alive (or still is). Even table salt is the result of the way living processes regulate the salinity of the sea. All the air we breathe is the result of living processes: The vital oxygen is a product of photosynthesis in plants, which in turn obtain energy from the rays of the sun.

A human being combines chemical compounds obtained from plants (or other animals that eat plants) with oxygen, which also comes from the activities of the plants. Through this combination of plant matter and plant waste (oxygen), energy is released, which allows people to grow or gather even more plants.

The combination of plant matter and oxygen results in a release of carbon dioxide, which is the gas the plants inhale, obtaining their nourishment; the air is the plants' food.

Animals and plants form part of a cycle where one living thing's doo-doo is another thing's food: Animals eat plants and expel plant food in

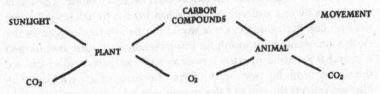

Flora and fauna: A chain of exchanges converts solar energy into movement and keeps a cycle of complexity going.

the form of exhaled air and plant manure in the form of excretion. Animals can do this because they use the plants' waste products in the form of oxygen.

Together, the two life forms constitute an effective alliance for the exploitation of the sun's energy: The plants stand still and grow with the help of the sunlight; the animals rush around collecting the plant matter—an endless breathing in and out, alternating between plants and animals, between spreading out and gathering in.

Humans and other animals have a clear, important role in this cycle: a role we can fulfill precisely because we breathe. Every single second, by breathing, we reinforce the fact that we are part of an enormous living organism that needs a circulation of matter on a planet shone upon by the radiation from a star.

Seen from the Gaia system's point of view, the important thing about humans is that we breathe—and demonstrate a corresponding if slightly slower alternation between gathering in and spreading out solid matter. Breathing is the bridge to Gaia—confirmation that we are part of a living system.

As organisms, as *Me*'s, we are rooted in this cycle. The parts of our body that consciousness cannot control are just the ones most important to Gaia: breathing, digestion, sexuality, survival. The parts we control consciously are the execution of activities that support the functions most important to Gaia: gathering food, choosing reproduction partners, disposal of waste.

Consciousness and human societies are organizations and effectuations of these activities, but always on the premise that they have to operate in the cycle comprising living organisms on earth. In recent centuries, conscious civilization has permitted an evolution of these activities to a degree that has created problems for the cycle of the living planet. Pollution, resource depletion, and the selection of species to be promoted or not have altered important flows of matter and energy on the planet.

The emergence of human consciousness has changed the development of the planet decisively because the extent and character of the nonconscious functions has changed. But also because these activities have allowed Gaia to see herself from without, through man's photographs of her from the moon. (One might object that of course it is not the whole of Gaia who sees herself just because people look at a picture of the earth from without. No, but neither do your ears see themselves in the mirror.)

But no matter how big the changes are that have occurred, it is still a fact that the *Me* is part of a greater living organism: The person is rooted in the planet. The relationship between the *I* and the *Me* is also the relationship between the conscious person and the planet: However vast the quantity of information we receive through the outer surface of the body and its senses, it is as nothing compared to the enormous flow of information constantly being exchanged across the inner surface: the lungs and the gastrointestinal system. We breathe and eat and thus exchange enormous quantities of matter, energy, and information with the earth as a living system. Gaia passes right through us from front to back. A human being is a kind of chocolate whirl surrounding a flood of matter from Gaia: a whirl on a whirl in Gaia.

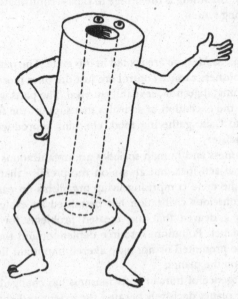

The inner surface. A stream of matter flows through man from lips to the other end. A very big amount of information is exchanged across this inner surface to Gaia.

The *I* is rooted in the *Me*. The *Me* is rooted in Gaia. I am in Me. Me is in Gaia.

Modern biology is founded upon Charles Darwin's theory of evolution, formulated in the nineteenth century. Its concept is simple: Living organisms, once they have come into being, will develop, because natural selection occurs. The individuals who do well will have lots of offspring, so there will be more of them. There is therefore a process of selection constantly taking place, bringing evolution in its train.

It has always been difficult to understand intuitively how something as wonderful as a human being could emerge after a few billion years of evolution. It is hard to conceive of such a marvelous design as the human eye as the result of blind evolution.

Lynn Margulis, along with James Lovelock the chief spokespersons for the Gaia theory, has argued for years in favor of a variant of Darwin's theory, a variation dubbed *endosymbiosis*. The idea is that living organisms such as humans are themselves the result of a collaboration, involving many different living organisms that have gotten together and formed the cells we are made of.

Originally, the evolution of life led to the formation of microorganisms such as bacteria, which developed properties that ensured their survival. At first the bacteria tried to eat or infect each other. But instead of one bacteria emerging victorious, they ended up cooperating.

Together, two such organisms influenced each other so much that they developed a *symbiotic* relationship and could not survive without each other. Symbiotic relationships are common in nature, but what made Margulis's idea special was that they could exist within the cells— i.e., inside the living organisms themselves. An organism could thus consist of an internal cooperation: an endosymbiosis, with *endo* meaning "inside."

The elegance of the theory is that it explains how evolution can happen in great leaps: Suddenly two properties that gain great benefits from each other are combined—the ability to move and the ability to burn oxygen, for example. This causes a dramatic improvement, which in turn changes the living environment of other organisms, which are then forced to alter, perhaps through cooperation.

Margulis's theory was highly controversial when she proposed it in the 1960s, but since then it has made considerable headway, because scientists have now proved that some of the most important parts of animal cells were once independent living creatures: bacteria that survived by becoming part of something greater.

This goes for such vital components of animal cells as the mitochondria, responsible for oxygen metabolism, and such vital components of plant cells as the plastids, responsible for photosynthesis.

This means that precisely those parts of animal and plant cells that promote the great cycle were originally independent microorganisms, which then opted for teamwork.

We may therefore regard a plant as a platform for bacteria, which are raised into the light by being plastids in the leaves of the plant. We may regard an animal as a heat tank that carries bacteria around to places with plant food, which can be combined with the oxygen of the air.

Lynn Margulis is fond of provoking people by emphasizing that human beings are walking ecosystems of microorganisms—and by emphasizing that the very purpose of human beings from the Gaia point of view is to act as heat tanks for a few kilograms of microorganisms that will produce carbon dioxide for the plants.[3]

If we combine the Gaia and the endosymbiosis points of view, we get a series of Russian dolls: Inside every single cell in the human body, originally independent microorganisms are working together. This teamwork itself constitutes a walking ecosystem that is part of a much bigger ecosystem, which eventually embraces the entire planet. There is teamwork within teamwork, and the only question is where we should draw the line. What is an individual?

If there is teamwork inside *Me*, and *Me* is part of another team effort, where all the other team-working animal and plant species are made up of the same microbiological building blocks that work together inside *Me*, what is the sense of insisting that *Me* is so distinct and special?

Further, if all our atoms are replaced within five years and the body is merely a pattern in a greater flow, what is the sense of distinguishing so sharply between oneself and the rest of this living organism? Would there not be more sense in seeing the whole as an intricate system of endosymbioses within endosymbioses within endosymbioses? This does not exclude the sense of drawing a line between two organisms, even though they consist of atoms that are constantly being replaced. But it does underline that the individual and the organism compose merely one way of regarding the living cycle.

One may point out the analogy with the human mind, which apparently consists of many different layers and elements of personality quite happy to argue about which is to answer the experimenter's questions. One might formulate a theory of the *endosymbiotic I*: Consciousness, the user illusion, is merely one *mental symbiont*, one point of view, which has taken control of a piece of teamwork and refuses to acknowledge that others are involved in the team as well.

Without coworkers, this endosymbiotic *I* would be utterly incapable of survival. It may even be a good thing that the symbiont that has "won" the struggle for consciousness refuses to listen to the others: If all the bacteria inside us had to vote on where we were to go when we were hungry, we might never make a move at all.

But in the final analysis, the living system on the earth is a giant organism, in turn consisting of an enormous system of Russian dolls, one inside another. Where the line is drawn is not so important, even though our normal perspective on ourselves may be said to be a trifle narrow.

We may regard ourselves as symbionts within an organism whose outer membrane is the blue sky stretched out above us.

It may seem absurd to describe the earth as a living organism: After all, most of our planet consists of dead rock deep beneath the surface. James Lovelock's answer to this objection is the analogy that a big tree is alive only on the surface.

But one could conceive another answer, based on the image of the earth's ties with the rest of the solar system that has emerged in recent years.

Earth as a planet consists of two different layers, formed at two different times. One of them, which makes up the bulk of the planet, was formed when the solar system was formed 4.6 billion years ago, when a huge cloud of matter between the stars of the Milky Way contracted and formed a star surrounded by a disk of matter that later became the planets.

The earth's outer layer, especially the oceans, came later. The reason is that the solar system was split into two layers. In the inner solar system, where the earth is located, the heavy elements dominated, because more volatile matter evaporated in the heat of the newborn sun. In the outer layer of the solar system, the more volatile matter was able to congregate into big planets like Jupiter and Saturn, and even farther out the comets could hold sway: mighty snowballs of light, volatile matter that froze to ice far from the mother star.

But the comets are the vagabonds of the solar system. They exist in enormous numbers, and some of them move into the inner solar system, where they strike the tiny conglomerations of heavy matter that make up the planets.

There is much that indicates that it was such comet strikes that formed the outer, lighter layers of the earth, especially the oceans. This occurred during a dramatic bombardment when the solar system was much younger, between 3.5 and 4.5 billion years ago.[4] The most important organic substances, which later formed the basis of living creatures, presumably originated from these comet strikes too.[5]

This picture[6] indicates that life on earth, which inhabits the outer layers of the planet, has a deep cosmic origin. The history of the solar system is a process where at first heavy planets were formed in the inner regions, where the volatile matter could not condense. Later, lumps of frozen volatile matter fell upon the heavier planets, where they melted but were held in place by the gravity of the rocky planets. A delicate balance between evaporation and new precipitation has developed on one planet, earth, while the others proved unable to "hold water." A decisive reason why the earth was able to hold on to these volatile layers of melted comets was the emergence of living organisms, which regulated crucial climatic conditions and kept them constant.

A planet like the earth is thus a place where comets are boiled into living organisms. Against this background, it is not so senseless to say that the earth is alive. Perhaps it is not the whole earth but only the younger, outer layers that are alive. But these outer layers constitute all our living conditions, everything we are familiar with from our everyday lives: earth, air, fire, and water.

Everything we are familiar with from everyday life consists of cooked comets. We ourselves are cooked comets.

The original earth, composed of heavy matter, captured comets from the distant reaches of the solar system. They formed a layer of water, soil, and air, which caught life. In this version of the Gaia theory, we may say that what happened is that *the earth caught life.*

Life is characterized by order. Amidst a colossal flow of atoms and energy, a shape arises, its identity maintained even though all the atoms are constantly being replaced. Stable shapes emerge in a fluid flow. As time passes, these shapes grow and grow, until they die and disappear because their atoms go their own ways and are not replaced by new ones.

How can this be possible when the world is subject to the second law, which says, after all, that it is disorder that grows, not order? What makes it possible is that *the universe is expanding.* Yet, strangely, at the same time this expansion is the explanation of why the disorder is growing.

Living creatures are open systems: They exchange energy and matter with their surroundings. So, strictly speaking, the disorder need not necessarily grow inside a living system. Thermodynamics requires only that the overall disorder grow in the living creature and its surroundings.

When a baby eats bananas and turns them into poop, there is more disorder in the diaper than in the spoon. A net production of disorder occurs around the living being. The being creates disorder around it, partly in the shape of excrement, partly as heat. It constantly needs feeding, so order can be created in the living creature while disorder is being created in its surroundings.

But other living creatures have to live in the same environment as the baby. How can this be possible when these other creatures also have to import more order than they export? Or we could ask it another way: How can the whole earth, regarded as a planet that has caught life, abide by this rule when enormous numbers of living creatures are creeping and crawling around on the planet—all eating, defecating, and breathing?

The earth must export more disorder than it imports. Otherwise there could not be life on it. And this is just what the earth does.

Sunlight consists of highly organized radiation, which strikes the earth and is useful for building structure in living creatures. These living creatures then eat each other in a closed circuit of matter that ends up producing body heat, which is transmitted into the environment. This heat eventually results in radiation from the earth in the form of microwaves.

If we look at the energy received and given off by the earth, there is no difference. The earth does not get warmer all the time. There is just as much energy in the microwaves transmitted from the earth in the form of heat radiation as in the sunlight the earth receives. The earth's energy budget balances. The books are straight; the earth does not receive energy from its surroundings at all—or more correctly, all the energy is retransmitted into space.

But there is one vital difference: sunlight has a shorter wavelength than the microwaves transmitted by the earth. The wavelength states the distance between the peaks of the electromagnetic radiation. Light is short-wave, while microwaves are long-wave.

The earth receives a certain amount of energy in the form of short-wave light but returns the same amount of energy in the form of long-wave microwaves.

The difference is dramatic, because there is a great difference in the same quantity of energy when it is in the form of light and when it is in the form of microwaves. Quantum mechanics has shown that all radia-

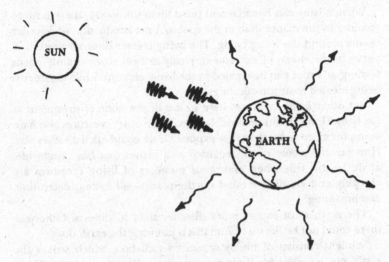

The earth's entropy balance. Highly organized sunlight is received, and lowly organized heat radiation is returned. The energy in the two forms of radiation is the same, but there is more entropy in the heat radiation.

tion energy appears in the form of quanta, tiny packages that constitute a kind of lowest unit of currency for radiation at a given wavelength. But there is a difference. Light appears in quanta that each contain more energy than the quanta microwaves appear in. So the same amount of energy must appear in the form of far more quanta when it exists as microwaves than when it exists as light.

The earth thus gives off more quanta than it receives from the sun. For the same amount of energy is received in the form of "big packets" but is shipped out again in the form of "small packets."

If more quanta are radiated from the earth, it means more disorder.

It is harder to describe the same amount of energy in the form of microwaves than in the form of light, because there are more quanta to keep track of, more degrees of freedom, more possible ways of doing it.[7]

So the earth is a net exporter of disorder, entropy. More disorder is transmitted from the earth than the earth receives.

If the earth were not alive, the temperature would be several hundred degrees hotter than it is today, the Gaia theory explains.[8] If that were the case, the radiation that reexported the energy from the sun to space would come from a slightly hotter body and would therefore be more like the light from the sun than it is today, when there is life. The radiation from the earth would have a slightly shorter wavelength. This in turn would mean that fewer quanta were shipped off from the earth—i.e., a little less disorder.

As life has regulated the temperature on the earth to be a bit lower than it would have been on a dead earth, this means that a little more disorder is exported than there otherwise would have been. This difference means that order can be created on the earth.

It is harder to describe energy radiation from the earth than to describe the energy that strikes the earth. There are more quanta to keep track of. More disorder means that more information can be transferred.

The earth discards a vast amount of information, then. It receives order, which is converted to heat and beamed out again in the form of discarded information. Thanks to this discarding, complexity can also arise on the earth in the form of life.

The same thing goes for the earth as for babies: It is easier to describe what goes in than what comes out.

But how can space contain all this information, all the mess shipped out from the earth? The answer is that the universe is expanding. It is constantly growing. More and more space is appearing, and therefore everything is constantly being cooled down.

Two kinds of processes take place in the universe: expansion and contraction. The universe as a whole is expanding dramatically and has been doing so throughout its fifteen billion years of existence. This expansion means that there is ever more space between things. The gaps between the galaxies are growing.

Meanwhile, locally in the universe, stars are formed by the contraction of vast quantities of matter, caused by their gravity. Thus squeezed, the matter heats up, begins to glow, and transmits energy into space.

The expansion means that the universe in general is dark and cold—and is getting ever darker and colder. The stars transmit light into the darkness, where it disappears.

But on its way, it may strike a little planet that has captured a few comets, which melt and make the planet catch life. Precisely because the universe is expanding, the planet's life can get rid of the increase in disorder: the information that life discards.

If we look at the night sky above the earth, we see a huge amount of darkness speckled with a few shining stars. If we look at the day sky, we see a single star, so close that it outshines all the other stars.

The earth receives light from one place, the sun, but sends its own microwaves off in all directions. A highly ordered signal from the sun is dispersed into a disordered noise beaming off in every direction.

The expansion of the universe means that entropy is growing: Everything is, generally, getting constantly farther apart; distances are growing; more space is appearing without there being more matter. Everything is being diluted with nothing; more and more degrees of freedom are appearing: Things are becoming more difficult to describe.

But the expansion also means that local accumulations of order are possible: Stars can appear that shine without problems in disposing of their light. There is lots of space for them to shine into. That is why planets can appear that are warmer than their surroundings and can ship their energy onward.

The expansion ensures in one go that entropy can grow globally and yet fall locally—into the living world.

There is somewhere into which all that information can be pitched.

"On the overall it's nothing. Locally it's very active,"[9] said the American cosmologist James Peebles in 1979 when he was asked to describe the results of his investigations into the large-scale structure of the universe. *On the overall*, the matter and radiation of the universe are equally distributed, with no structure or direction. But locally there are piles of Milky Ways populated with stars orbited by planets which in turn—in one case, at any rate—are populated by wonderful little creatures who bustle around in the starlight.

On the overall, the universe is just a smooth soup of matter that is constantly expanding; everything is alike, but there is constantly more nothing; everything is distributed evenly and is forever being diluted with nothing. But locally there is structure; locally there are differences—and these differences do not disappear. They merely get diluted. And while they are being diluted, complexity can arise.

The complexity can arise because the dilution permits information to be discarded, disorder exported, from the local units limited by cell walls, skin surfaces, and blue skies.

In behind these limits, in behind the membranes encompassing living beings, the order arises that does not contain masses of information but is the result of colossal amounts of information that have passed through the area defined by the membranes—the cell walls, skin surfaces, and blue skies.

Because the universe is expanding, complexity can grow on the other side of the membranes. Because the universe is expanding, differences can flood out through the membranes that differentiate it from the surroundings and can create order inside it. This local order apparently contradicts the expansion's creation of even more disorder, ever more degrees of freedom in the universe as a whole.

But there is no conflict: *On the overall,* disorder is growing, and for precisely that reason, order can arise locally through the export of disorder. The expansion of the universe means that there is space for such exportation.

Because the universe *on the overall* is nothing, locally there may be activity that leads to everything we are familiar with as living organisms; and because such living organisms constantly export disorder—information—inside them, locally, a consciousness can arise that is itself the result of an enormous discarding of information, a dramatic export of disorder.

Because everything is constantly being diluted by nothing, we can experience it as everything.

The expansion started fifteen billion years ago with the big bang, observable today in the way the galaxies fly apart in the sky. Distant accumulations of ancient stars are receding from us faster than close accumulations of younger stars. The farther away something is, the faster it is receding.

This is known as the Hubble expansion, discovered at the end of the 1920s by the American astronomer Edwin Hubble. It does not imply that it is from *us* everything is receding; it implies that from any viewpoint in the universe you would see every other viewpoint receding from you. Rather like the way ants would see each other along the surface of a balloon that is being inflated: Every ant will feel that every other ant is on its way away from it. Perhaps none of the ants will figure out that things look like this because the balloon is expanding.

Today the big bang theory is the dominant view in cosmology, the science of the universe as a whole. If we calculate backward from the expansion Hubble discovered, we can conclude that the expansion started somewhere between ten and twenty billion years ago. As the oldest clusters of stars in the universe are about twelve billion years old, the expansion must be at least as old. So fifteen billion years is a very good figure to use.

The picture astronomers and cosmologists have of what has happened during this fifteen-billion-year period is becoming clearer and clearer (even though there *are* difficulties in completing the jigsaw puzzle[10]). From an evenly distributed state, of which we still find remnants in the radiation that permeates the universe, whole clusters of galaxies crystallized out, which led to star formation and solar systems. We do not know how the smooth distribution of matter led to the coarseness we see in matter today; thus we do not understand why there are stars in a dark sky, rather than just a thin cloud of matter.

But perhaps that is not the most important question anyway.

The most pressing question is how everything began when the expansion began. The expansion consists of everything being diluted by nothing. If we go back in time, everything is still there, but there is less nothing. Distances shrink, the world gets smaller back in time. The matter exists, but space is smaller.

If we go all the way back, fifteen billion years, there is almost nothing of space but lots of matter and radiation. The density grows massively back toward time zero. The cosmologists have provided a very good description of the universe back to the very first seconds of its existence. Indeed, we have an idea of the very first fractions of a second in the history of the universe; in fact, right back to a time known as the Planck time, after the German physicist Max Planck, who discovered the quantum in 1900 and sparked the whole branch of physics that became known as quantum mechanics, which describes atoms and other particles.

The Planck time covers the first 0.000000000000000000000000000000-000000000000001 (10^{-43} second after the beginning of everything. At that time, the whole of the visible universe we can observe today was not diluted by much nothing. Everything was very dense; in fact, one may say that everything was one. But it did take up a bit of room, even though the bit of room corresponding to our universe today was less than one hundredth of a centimeter in diameter.

All our normal concepts break down when we try to describe a universe back at the Planck time: time, space, and matter cannot be told apart. Everything is marked by quantum fluctuations, disturbances associated with the fundamental character of uncertainty that quantum mechanics tells us the world is marked by. Time and space keep changing place; we cannot distinguish between them the way we can in the universe today.

Actually, the laws of physics do not operate in such a world. We cannot apply the natural laws we know from today. So many astronomers are happy just to trace the history of the universe back to the Planck time. "These physical conditions are so extreme that it seems entirely appropriate to regard the Planck time as the moment of creation of the universe,"[11] writes the American astronomer Joseph Silk in a standard textbook on cosmology.

But not all cosmologists are satisfied, because the real question, of course, is what happened at the creation, not what happened just afterward. It is a bit much to undertake a mental voyage fifteen billion years back in time to find the beginning of everything, only to give up a fraction of a second before it all began!

"We discussed it during the drive from Albuquerque," John Wheeler explained, "but the only answer we could find was the black holes." It was Monday, 16 April 1990, in the lecture room at the Santa Fe Institute's charming little building at 1120 Canyon Road. The seminar on complexity, entropy, and information physics had just started, and the great names were busy suggesting questions for discussion that week.

Wheeler had driven from the airport in Albuquerque, the first city of New Mexico, up to the beautiful mountain town of Santa Fe, which smart alecks call Fanta Se because the residents of the town are almost all involved in art galléries, crystal healing, and the manufacture of atom bombs. As a tourist destination built in the Indian style, Santa Fe is a center for art and spirituality surrounded by an incomparable mountainscape of tableland. It possesses just that element of grandiose beauty which made J. Robert Oppenheimer settle on a nearby nowhere called Los Alamos as the voluntary prison where hundreds of the world's leading physicists, in deepest secrecy, were to produce the atom bomb during the Second World War. Ever since, Los Alamos has been a leading site for nuclear weapons research—and science in general—in the United States.

The Santa Fe Institute is one of the world's centers for interdisciplinary studies of complexity. During the drive with some of his former students, who now work in Albuquerque, Wheeler had put a very simple question to which he knew only one answer: black holes.

Wheeler's question went: "If we can make a thermometer that measures heat, why can't we make an entropy meter that measures disorder?"

Why can we not design a piece of apparatus capable of telling us unambiguously how much entropy there is in a physical system?

The initial answer is that entropy is a quantity that always requires you to define your microstates and macrostates. You have to refer to an observer before you can speak of entropy. For only when you know the observer's abilities can you say how much of the energy present in the system cannot be used for anything. Only when you know how coarse the observer's description—and thereby his skills—are can you say what he can get out of the system. Entropy, just like information, is therefore defined only when you specify how coarse your analysis is—when you announce the size of the holes in the net you want to go fishing with.

So you cannot make an entropy meter that measures the quantity of disorder or entropy in a system.

Except for black holes.

Black holes are a fascinating consequence of the theory of gravity, the theories of relativity, in which Einstein's student John Wheeler is a leading expert. In fact, it was Wheeler who dubbed these peculiar phenomena "black holes," in 1968. A black hole is a volume of space where gravity is so powerful that nothing can escape from it. All matter is held in place by the powerful gravitational field; all light likewise. To escape from a black hole, you would have to be traveling faster than the speed of light—and nothing can do that. So a black hole is surrounded by a membrane that permits passage only one way: into the hole.

Such black holes can arise as the final phase in the life of a star, when there is no more radiation energy to keep the star going and it simply collapses under the enormous force exerted by its gravity. Black holes can also be created in the center of young galaxies, where a number of stars have come together.

In the 1960s, black holes were explored along theoretical lines, and during the 1970s it became clear that they do exist in the universe. Today we may assume that they play a very big role in many of the phenomena of the cosmos.

But in a sense it does not matter in the slightest what a black hole is made of. It is just black. All we can say about a black hole is how much mass there is inside it. Everything else is utterly inaccessible to outsiders. All that is left is the field of gravity. The rest has gone. To oblivion. Away.

What is inside a black hole is in a sense outside our universe: inaccessible to the rest of us.

The black hole membrane has a surface that defines a limit, a point from which there is no return. Once you are in, you do not come out again. So the surface area of a black hole can only grow: It can suck in new matter, never release anything. The greater the mass, the greater the surface of the membrane; and the mass is always growing.

So the surface area of a black hole is always growing too. It cannot decrease. If two holes combine and absorb each other, we get a surface area that is at least twice that of the two original holes together. This law was discovered by Roger Penrose (along with R. M. Floyd, Stephen Hawking, and others).

In 1970, one of Wheeler's students at Princeton, Jacob Bekenstein, made a remarkable observation: The ever-increasing surface of a black hole resembles another quantity, from quite a different end of physics, which also only grows and can never decrease—entropy.

Bekenstein decided to explore the analogy between black holes and thermodynamics, and he arrived at an epochmaking conclusion: Black holes have entropy.[12] Their entropy is simply expressed by the surface of the one-way membrane surrounding the hole. The bigger the hole, the greater the entropy. And it can only grow.

The explanation is precisely that we cannot know what the hole is made of. A vast amount of matter has collapsed so we cannot see it but can see only its field of gravity. We have lost the knowledge of what made the hole. No matter what is inside it, we can never know more about it than the fact that it is there—and producing a field of gravity. From without, what is within does not matter. The world without has simply lost the information.

No matter what microstate led to the hole, the whole thing is expressed by the same macrostate, in the form of a field of gravity. A black hole represents a load of information that is not accessible to the outside world. Hidden history.

"We have come to realize in this century that entropy represents unavailable information,"[13] John Wheeler writes in a poetic overview of modern knowledge of gravity and space-time. A realization physicists have attained not least through theoretical studies of black holes on the basis of Bekenstein's idea.

The *entropy* of a black hole is expressed through its size. But size is a purely geometric property, which involves the structure of space. Astonishingly, something involving space has a property obtained from thermodynamics that is about the rules for building steam engines.

Even more interestingly, black holes possess *unequivocally* defined entropy: We do not need to ask who is asking about their entropy in order to define it. There is no need to ask about the observer's coarse graining, for the simple reason that all observers outside the hole are in utterly the same position. *Nobody* can know what is inside a black hole without being there himself. So a black hole has a well-defined entropy to anyone who observes it from without. The amount of missing knowledge is equally great no matter how one investigates the hole.

Historically, Bekenstein's idea led to the important result that black holes also possess temperature, which means that through quantum mechanical processes they can in fact radiate into their surroundings. But this radiation, which was discovered by Stephen Hawking, is not related in any way to what created the hole. It depends only on the surface of the hole. The history is still forgotten, the information still lost.

≈

The most important thing about Bekenstein's idea was that it led to the first entropy meter: the first system for which we can unequivocally define the entropy and ask, "How much information has gotten lost here?"

For example, we can take a black hole with the mass of the visible universe at the beginning, at the Planck time, and ask, "How much entropy did the universe have then? How much information is there in such a universe?"

This question is the same as asking the number of ways this young universe could have been composed. How many microstates correspond to the macrostate described as a newborn universe?

Today the visible universe has a very large information content: a very large entropy. We calculate the entropy of the universe as the entropy in the background radiation that fills the universe—a smoothly distributed echo of the big bang.

The amount of entropy is very great in the universe today: It takes colossal amounts of information to describe the universe in every detail. After all, the second law of thermodynamics has applied for fifteen million years, so an enormous amount of mess has been created to keep track of.

The integer that describes the entropy of the visible universe, the number of bits in the universe, is written as a 1 followed by 88 zeros (10^{88}). If we compressed the entire universe into a black hole, the entropy would be somewhat greater: The number of bits would be represented by a 1 followed by 120 zeros (10^{120}). But how big was the entropy at the Planck time?

The question was posed at the end of the 1980s.[14] The answer was shocking, even when one remembers that the second law of thermodynamics at the Planck time had only *just* started making entropy, the description of which requires information. If we regard this completely newborn universe as a black hole, its entropy—i.e., its hidden information content—is equal to one bit.

The world began as something that can be described using just one single bit. That is the only hidden information it contains. The rest of the disorder came later.

In principle, the astronomers manage to describe the universe back to the very first bit but no further. Then the laws break down.

One bit is enough information to answer yes or no to a question. But not to ask it.

What was the question?

≈

In 1973, the American physicist Edward Tryon launched a peculiar idea: Such a tiny early universe as the one existing at the Planck time could perhaps have arisen from nothing, *ex nihilo*. The explanation would be that the uncertainty principle of the laws of quantum mechanics actually allows something tiny to arise from nothing, as long as it lasts only an instant. The smaller it is, the longer it can last.

Tryon pointed out that if everything in the universe was added together—matter, energy, gravity, rate of expansion, and all the intermediate calculations—the sum would actually be zero. There are equal amounts of positive and negative energy in the universe: just as much energy bound in matter and in the moving of the matter caused by the expansion. In strictly technical terms, the sum of everything is nothing.[15] This presupposes certain theoretical assumptions, but since 1973 they have become increasingly well founded.

But if everything adds up to a big round 0, an interesting consequence of the laws of quantum mechanics emerges. For they state that nothing—empty space—sometimes divides, and for a split second becomes something. The smaller this something is, the longer it is allowed to exist. A zero can be allowed to exist as long as it likes. So if the universe is a zero, it can exist forever.

Tryon's idea was that nothing sometimes suffers a disturbance that turns it into a complete universe. A very small one, true, but expanding rapidly. Technically speaking, this universe constitutes one big 0, but does that matter, as long as it lasts forever?

Since then, the cosmologist Alexander Vilenkin has refined Tryon's theory, which is nowadays taken perfectly seriously: The universe arose *ex nihilo*. Studies in the last few years as to how we can derive a theory of gravity from quantum mechanics have also focused on ideas about everything being one big zero.[16]

So there are grounds for taking Tryon's idea seriously: Everything emerged from nothing thanks to a chance disturbance that has since inflated into a universe that may be a zero but, conversely, can last forever. Nothing is quaking in an eternity.

In the nineteenth century, the German philosopher G. W. F. Hegel proposed ideas on being and nothing (which are also found in numerous Eastern philosophies and in early Greek philosophers such as Heraclitus). Hegel wrote, "Formation is the vanishing of being into nothing and the vanishing of nothing into being."[17]

This made Søren Kierkegaard, who was highly critical of Hegel's concept-juggling style of philosophy, describe the idea of everything beginning in nothing as "spice-seller's explanations": "The idea of 'Beginning with Nothing' is no more and no less than a new rewriting of the very Dialectics of the Beginning," he wrote. " 'The Beginning begins with Nothing.' This is merely a new statement, not a single step further. . . . 'The Beginning is Not' and 'the Beginning begins with Nothing' are utterly identical statements, and take me not one step further." Kierkegaard immediately moots his own proposal: "What if, instead of talking or dreaming of an absolute Beginning, we talked of a Leap?"[18]

A leap! In his *Concluding Unscientific Postscript* (1846), Kierkegaard anticipates—at any rate, viewed with the benefit of hindsight—Tryon and Vilenkin's theory that the universe began as a quantum fluctuation, a disturbance of Nothing, a *quantum leap*.

In 1983, the physicist Peder Voetmann Christiansen showed how Niels Bohr's formulation of the quantum leap smacked of inspiration from Kierkegaard.[19] But the cosmologists can hardly have read Kierkegaard. Nor was it a physical leap the philosopher was hinting at, but an act of will, an existential choice. His point is one of conceptual analysis, and he emphasizes that saying "everything began with nothing" tells us nothing. For what else could it have done? And what would we have thereby said at all, apart from nothing?

But Kierkegaard's point is nevertheless interesting in relation to the idea of a creation *ex nihilo:* What do we really achieve by saying that everything started with nothing? As a disturbance in nothing; a leap?

Perhaps it would be better to say that it was precisely that: a disturbance *in* nothing, *in nihilo,*[20] rather than *ex nihilo.* The universe did not arise out of nothing: the universe arose inside nothing. Everything is nothing, seen from the inside. *The world without is really nothing seen from within.* We are inside nothing.

Seen from without, there is zilch, nothing. Seen from within, there is everything we know. The whole universe.

But we might ask how we can know that it is possible to get inside nothing?

Technically, the answer is very simple: As everything we see around us adds up to one big round zero, the world *is* nothing. The question as to whether we can get inside it is not very meaningful, for as soon as we ask it, we already know the answer.

"There is no *out there* out there," was John Wheeler's summary of what mankind knows in the light of what quantum mechanics has told us. He likes to illustrate his idea with a sketch[21] which describes the fact

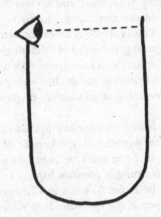

Wheeler's U

that we are participators in a universe rather than mere observers; we are participant-observers, as Wheeler calls it. Our observations help to create the universe we are observing. The sketch consists of a large U, where one ascender bears an eye that is observing the other ascender. We can express Wheeler's idea another way:

The universe began when nothing saw itself in the mirror.

As the physicist Fred Alan Wolf put it in his book on quantum mechanics, adapting Shakespeare's famous lines from *Hamlet*:

"To be or not to be is not the question; it is the answer."[22]

But then what *was* the question?

CHAPTER 14

ON THE EDGE OF CHAOS

"More Is Different" was the title of a 1972 article in *Science*[1] in which the American solid-phase physicist and Nobel laureate P. W. Anderson punctured what, in the 1980s, was to become the controversy of holism versus reductionism in the scientific worldview.

Holism is the view that the world consists of wholes that cannot be described solely in terms of their component parts, while reductionism, the dominant view among the practitioners of the natural sciences, holds that the many-sided phenomena of the universe can best be described by reducing them to a small number of component parts, which one may then study separately. Through the 1980s, the view spread that reductionism was bankrupt, because its focus on individual components and separated aspects of reality had driven the world into the environmental crisis that has increasingly become the dominant problem for modern civilization.

Holism was even promoted as a *new paradigm* in science: a new scientific view of the world that emphasized wholes and connections, as opposed to the obsession of established science with component parts.[2]

This criticism of reductionism had much justification, for the practitioners of the natural sciences had become arrogant toward their own understanding of the world: After all, reductionism says precisely that we reduce, simplify, abbreviate, and discard information when we draw up an abstract description of the world. But many natural scientists, and perhaps engineers in particular, acted in the technologically optimistic 1960s and 1970s as if the natural science view of the world was synonymous with the world itself. Since then, a great deal of experience in technologies such as nuclear power has made natural scientists and laymen rather wiser.

The natural science view of the world is no more and no less than a map of the terrain: a description that discards much of the information one may experience when observing the world, maintaining certain simple basic features, which can then be talked about unambiguously. Holism, on the other hand, emphasizes hunches and associations, which are hard to talk about: the interplay with the universe when it is so rich in information that it cannot be made an object of conversation over the low bandwidth of language.

For decades, reductionism represented an unintelligent belief that if only we understood the parts, we would grasp the whole: an arrogant blindness toward the lack of knowledge inherent in believing that the study of the parts is enough to understand the whole. As research ideology—forget the wider contexts—reductionism has been reactionary and uncurious. But that does not alter the fact that the holism-contra-reductionism controversy today is a debate that may be said to be passé: false opposites.

Actually, none of the parties to this debate had grasped the real point, which P. W. Anderson had already formulated in his slogan "More Is Different," which originates from a lecture he gave in 1967: "The ability to reduce everything to simple fundamental laws does not imply the ability to start from those laws and reconstruct the universe."[3]

Anderson, then employed at the Bell Telephone Laboratories, confessed to reductionism from the very start of his lecture: Everything is composed of the same fundamental elements, each of which can be studied separately. But he added a criticism of another viewpoint often reckoned to be part of reductionism: *constructionism.* This is the notion that knowledge of the fundamental particles and fundamental laws means that we can work out how the world is arranged.

But we cannot do so, because we run into two decisive problems: scale and complexity. Everything may indeed consist of atoms, but that does not mean that knowledge of their construction and behavior enables us to work out how an elephant drinks water. When we put lots of atoms together, phenomena arise that do not exist when there are only a few atoms present. And most of the phenomena that interest us in our everyday lives contain considerably more atoms than any nuclear physicist has ever studied in his laboratory.

Anderson's point, therefore, is that reductionism does not necessarily conflict with the view that complexity exists and new natural phenomena arise every time we step up the scale and study new layers of the universe.

Just because we know the fundamental laws and particles of nature does not mean that we necessarily know very much about the world. For many atoms may behave quite differently from few atoms: More Is Different.

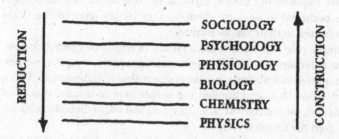

The levels of science. At each level a new complexity arises. Even though the higher levels consist of elements from the lower ones, you cannot construct the higher levels just because you know the lower ones.

The use of computers has dramatically demonstrated Anderson's point. For centuries, physicists had believed they knew a vast amount about the world because they knew Newton's laws of gravity and motion. Children at school and students in university learned that they had a grip on the universe because they knew Newton's equations.

So they did, too; after all, they could do all the sums in the textbooks and see that indeed they could work out how a system functioned if they knew the right equations.

However, it turned out that the physicists had never done their sums. Most of what we learned at school is simply not correct. The textbook examples were no more than that: cunning special cases, designed to allow us to ignore friction and other confusions that occur in the real world. The real phenomena are so complicated that they cannot be solved at all, so they were ignored, to allow us to concentrate on a few textbook examples so simple they could be worked out and put in examination papers.

Not until we had computers to do all the laborious calculations for us did we realize that we did not know Newton's laws after all; we had no idea of the confusion, untidiness, disorder, and incalculability they contained.

Through the 1980s, terms like "complexity," "chaos," and "fractals" became key words in our dawning understanding of the fact that just because we know the laws of the world does not mean we know the world. We may well know the formulae; perhaps we have even learned them by heart. But it makes no difference, for very extensive computations are required in order to arrive at the real world. Scientists could not be bothered to perform them, so they simply ignored the world and delighted in their simple formulae.

A simple rule can easily make a system of highly complex behavior. All that is required is that we do our sums properly—i.e., that we perform a mass of calculations, a massive discarding of information. When we have done that, and applied the simple rule to discard masses of information, we can harvest rich, complex, and unpredictable behavior out of even the simplest recipes.

This is the lesson to be learned from the theory of chaos, which is in turn the lesson from the computer; for computers were built by the very people who thought they could so easily work out the world.

It's a very important lesson, not only because it set classroom boredom in its proper perspective (and proves that pupils display no lack of intelligence if they are bored by having to learn formulae from a teacher who refuses to tell them how these formulae relate to reality). It is also important because it set consciousness in its proper perspective, because it gives cause for consciousness to keep its composure.

However good, however relevant the simple rules laid down in a map of the terrain, we should never believe that we can guess what the terrain is like on the basis of the map. We may be able to find our way through it, but we cannot experience the terrain from the map.

The contemporary philosophical controversy on holism contra reductionism reflects a controversy between two fundamental views, which can be expressed in the spirit of P. W. Anderson. The first of them is the belief that there are wholes that can be apprehended and permit us to understand everything in simple but holistic terms—in fact, the belief that consciousness can comprehend the world because the world consists of wholes and guiding principles that can be comprehended.

The second is the belief that the world consists of lots of individual components that can be described separately but, collectively, display a behavior that is quite different from when we study them on their own—in fact, the belief that consciousness will never be able to comprehend the world, because the world consists of a mass of tiny elements, which behave quite capriciously and differently when there are enough of them.

Holism is an attempt to say that there is a whole we can apprehend. Nonconstructionist reductionism is an attempt to appreciate that we can never describe the world exhaustively, either in its parts or as a whole. At each new layer of description, new forms of behavior will emerge with the addition of nothing but a few of the particles from the level below—but now enough to form a flock.

The dominant theme of our times, in the terms used in this book, is consciousness regaining composure through the recognition of the nonconscious; computer formalism regaining composure through the recognition of unpredictability; descriptions regaining composure through the recognition of what is being described; the low bandwidth regaining composure through the recognition of the high bandwidths. The point being that we can never understand the world exhaustively without understanding the whole world exhaustively—that is, every single element of the world. Everything is connected, so we cannot comprehend anything exhaustively at all unless we comprehend everything exhaustively. But this raises the problem that such a totally exhaustive description necessarily contains just as much information as what it describes; a complete description of the world takes up just as much room as the world itself. So it is not accessible to a subject: a consciousness that is describing the environment. The only map that displays every detail of the terrain is the terrain itself. But then, that is not a map.

Holism insists that we can understand the world as a whole. So as a worldview, holism is profoundly reactionary.[4]

A more composed view is that we cannot understand the world at all. But we can describe it; and every description will have to accept that it is a description—i.e., something is missing, information has been discarded; it is not the terrain, it is a map.

The reactionary aspect of holism is its belief that one can describe the world meaningfully by understanding a few general principles. The dramatic breakthrough in the wake of computers and chaos theory is that even the simple fundamental laws of nature we have learned over the last few centuries are infinitely inscrutable when they are allowed to exert themselves in practice. They are computationally irreducible, to use Stephen Wolfram's expression, mentioned in Chapter Four.

"We are entering the gray zone," the physicist Chris Langton responded cautiously to the question as to how far we have already crossed the line. "It will happen anyway," he added. "We might as well study it, in order to influence the way it develops."[5]

The scene possessed almost overwhelming symbolic force. The young, long-haired American was standing in the parking lot outside the modest barracks housing CNLS—the Center for Nonlinear Studies—at Los Alamos National Laboratory in New Mexico. Langton was on his way to his office at the Theory Division, Department 13, in another building on the lot.

Between the two buildings is the museum, where one can inspect relics, photographs, and flickering displays explaining why Los Alamos was home to the development of the atom bombs dropped on Hiroshima and Nagasaki in August 1945, putting an end to the war in the Pacific.

The subject of Langton's remarks was *artificial life*—a new field of research that had been born at a workshop in Los Alamos in September 1987, chaired by Chris Langton. What he meant was that a development had been set in motion, whether we liked it or not: the development of artificial life forms on earth—life forms that live in the technology that man has created but can no longer control. When we had discussed the topic in Langton's office the same morning, he replied as scientists so often do: "It will happen anyway." But for once it was not just an excuse to develop a technology containing great risks, but a corresponding fascination. It was a simple, factual observation that computer networks on earth have now become such extensive interconnected circuits of flowing information that we no longer have a free choice: We have created the seedbed for artificial life, and a handful of teenagers have sparked it off. Evolution possesses its own remorseless logic: When the conditions are present, living creatures arise to exploit them. Whether these conditions are created by incognizant biological processes or incognizant technological processes, life exploits them.

Chris Langton has a profound sense of responsibility. He convened a workshop on artificial life for precisely that reason: An evolution is beginning to take place; there are ethical and moral issues that need debating. "Such issues must be discussed before we go much further down the road to creating life artificially," he wrote in his preface to the proceedings from the first conference on artificial life.[6] "It is, perhaps, not coincidental that the first workshop on Artificial Life was held at Los Alamos, site of the mastery of atomic fission and fusion."

It began as a pest: quietly, persistently, irritatingly, but just as a pest. Computer viruses, fragments of programs capable of moving into computer memory, where they immediately order the computer to make copies of themselves. They were originally created by mischievous programmers who wanted to tease one another, then their employers, and finally vast networks of communicating computers. Then teenagers, so-called hackers, started playing hide-and-seek with technological and defense colossi by infecting their computer networks with pranks. The idea is that a short length of program code inserted in a computer propagates as a "virus," infecting the host computer and any other computer the infected host is in contact with.

On the face of it, an apparently innocent, harmless game, which merely goes to show that there is not much security surrounding computers: that computers all over the world chattering away together make it possible to spread messages never meant to be spread.

The problem is just that we have not yet succeeded in eradicating such viruses. Computers can be sanitized individually. But that does not mean a virus has disappeared. According to many of the criteria we could list, a computer virus is alive—and cannot be killed. Or at least, it's as alive as the viruses we know from biological organisms.

"Artificial life is the greatest challenge facing mankind,"[7] wrote the American physicist Doyne Farmer when he was head of the complex systems study group from the Theory Division at Los Alamos. In a treatise, Farmer and Aletta d'A. Belin propose a number of criteria of being alive. Life is a pattern in space and time rather than a material object (after all, atoms keep getting replaced); life can replicate; life contains information about itself in its genes; life metabolizes; life inter-relates with its surroundings; life can mutate, etc.

Look for these properties in computer viruses, and it is hard to see why they should not be alive. True, they are just short fragments of computer code, and just as dependent on the existence of the computer as many parasites are on the existence of their hosts or as man is on Gaia's. Such viruses can spread only because the computer is powered up, but similarly, no living creature could survive on earth if the sun was switched off. Computer viruses can replicate and leap from host to host. They can change their host's metabolism of electrical signals; they contain information about themselves; they interrelate to their surroundings, and they mutate.

Computer viruses are just as alive as biology's viruses, which similarly exist on the edge between the living and the dead.

"The analogy is a strong one," writes the robot scientist Hans Moravec, "because today's million-bit computer programs have about the same information content as the genetic codes of bacteria, and the few thousand bits of a typical computer virus is a good match for the small genetic code of a biological virus."

Moravec has no doubt that computer viruses will gain in strength: "Today's computer systems are like bodies with skin, but without immune defenses."[8]

Doyne Farmer writes, "It seems that whenever there is a medium capable of supporting large amounts of specific information, organizational patterns emerge that propagate themselves by taking over the resources of this medium."[9]

Man has created a vast flow of information in the global computer networks. They are about to catch life. Started as japes and pranks, they are now impossible to eradicate. An autonomous organization is proliferating, with its own logic beyond our intentions. As soon as there are sufficient resources, something or someone will exploit them.

Our bodies have developed immune defenses and self-recognition in order to keep viruses and bacteria out. But computers do not yet have an image of themselves as different from other things, which would allow them to remain clean as regards infections from outside. We have constructed machines but not equipped them with the ability to distinguish themselves from the world. So new life forms are spreading inside them uninhibitedly.

"We shall not try to judge whether the cooperative structures we have evolved in the core are alive or not," write four Danish physicists in a paper[10] on *Coreworld*, a kind of Battleships game for the computer, which they have developed to a degree of complexity that means they can no longer ascertain whether the system they are studying is alive. Their statement is a touch coquettish, because the system is clearly not alive, but it is nevertheless peculiar that such simple systems display characteristics such as cooperation and evolution to a degree reminiscent of living beings.

Research into artificial life has explored numerous examples of the way simple recipes can lead to complicated behavior as long as there is enough time. Computation time.

Chris Langton has created artificial ants on a computer monitor, tiny creatures that follow simple patterns but together display a general behavior as complicated as that of the anthill. The moral is not that real ants are as simple as Langton's artificial ones; the moral is that simple rules can lead to complicated behavior as long as there is enough computation time; as long as loads of information is discarded in the process.

It does not take especially complicated or advanced systems to create complicated and advanced behavior: It takes time. Time to discard information.

So various new fields of research are on their way with automated processes that display nonautomatic behavior.

The recipe for something complicated does not itself have to be complicated. Simple laws can lead to complex behavior and complex systems. The key is to allow simple mechanisms to work over time.

The consequence of this knowledge is that it is extremely difficult to have an overview of what one is doing. If one makes a simple recipe, like the one found in a computer virus, it may lead to incalculable consequences, because it thrives in a system where reiterations, copies, and computations are performed over and over again.

The discarding of information can lead to structures that are far richer and more varied than the rules governing the discard of information. The value lies not in knowing the rules but in knowing their evolution.

Since the 1950s, scientists working on artificial intelligence have been trying to build machines that could display intelligence. But with no success whatsoever. The scientists tried to understand humans as rule-based creatures that followed simple, clear patterns in their mental lives: general rules that were easy to understand and easy to associate with the task they wanted to solve; rules that were explicit and clear.

Precisely for that reason, research into AI is now becalmed, while research into computer systems that involve not rules but the learning of examples has made more progress. So-called neural networks are an example of computer systems that do not try to find the rules for a complex task, such as image analysis, but instead are trained through a large number of examples that finally result in behavior similar to the behavior desired—e.g., human behavior. The idea is not to make the rules explicit and clear, but to make the wealth of experience big and wide. What matters is being conscious not of how the machine does it but of what it does and what it has experienced.

It is like the learning of human skills: The road to complexity is simple but long. It involves repeating simple operations over and over again, building up a great wealth of experience. It does not involve stitching together a clutch of simple, robust recipes that can be followed everywhere. It does not involve knowing everything before you start. It involves undergoing experiences. More Is Different.

The code word is *emergence*. When simple rules are allowed to beaver away long enough in time or in a sufficient number of component parts, completely new properties appear; they emerge, break out, pop up, come into view.

These emergent properties cannot be found by studying a small collection of component parts. They can be seen only when there are so many parts that collective influences, group properties, can occur. Temperature, for example, is a property that yields no meaning if we observe very few molecules. A large number is required before temperature is present. We cannot see from the individual molecule what temperature it is part of, for temperature is a collective property manifested as a statistical relation: A temperature describes the distribution of velocities among lots of molecules.

At a higher level, molecules of a certain temperature can form part of a larger organization such as a living organism, even though by looking at the individual molecule you cannot see that it is part of a living organism. Life is an emergent property of matter, not a property of matter's component parts.

The notion of emergence is traditionally based in the school of biology which insists that the animate is more than physics and chemistry; that there is more to living organisms than can ever be described by the laws of physics and chemistry. This is the antireductionist view: You cannot reduce biology to physics.

But in recent decades, emergent properties and collective influences have begun to appear again and again in the descriptions physicists try to provide of the most simple structures, such as nuclei and simple molecular systems. In the past, scientists could not be bothered to compute whether simple systems could display emergence, but the computer has made it clear that it does not take particularly complicated conditions for such properties to appear.

The point is thus not that emergence does not appear in biology; the point is that before the computer age, biological systems were the only examples of simple systems that were allowed to work long enough in time for emergence to appear. So it seemed as if living beings were completely different from inanimate nature. Living beings had the property of emergence, which we did not think existed in inanimate nature. But with the computer, it has become clear that emergence is a common characteristic of everything, of both animate and inanimate nature.

The German chemist Bernd-Olaf Küppers thus writes, "The phenomenon of emergence . . . is a phenomenon of our real world, which we encounter at all levels of scientific description, and not a special characteristic of living systems that prevents biology from being placed on physical foundations."[11]

In fact, emergence is the result of Gödel's theorem for the basis of mathematical description: A formal system, that cannot contain very much information, cannot "predict" what will happen to it when it is allowed to run. Precisely because mathematics is brimming with indeterminable problems, we can never know where a formal description will end if we pursue it long enough. Gregory Chaitin's development of Gödel's theorem into algorithmic information theory (discussed in Chapter Three) has proved that emergence is a perfectly ordinary property in any closed system. We cannot work out in advance or tell by looking at the component parts what they will become.

"In addition, the algorithmic approach also allows a formal treatment of the problem of emergence," Küppers writes. "That 'the whole is more than the sum of its parts' is true for every structured system S, independently of whether the system is living or inanimate."[12]

There is, then, no difference between animate and inanimate systems. It is generally the case that More Is Different.

Consciousness is a phenomenon imbued with the same factor: Characteristics arise that we cannot deduce or understand by looking at individual rules or component parts in isolation. Douglas Hofstadter writes in *Gödel, Escher, Bach*: "Gödel's proof offers the notion that a high-level view of a system may contain explanatory power which simply is absent on the lower levels." He continues: "Gödel's proof suggests—though by no means does it prove!—that there could be some high-level way of viewing the mind/brain, involving concepts which do not appear on lower levels, and that this level might have explanatory power that does not exist—not even in principle—on lower levels."[13]

Hofstadter tries to solve the problem of determinism and free will along this path. He describes human beings as if they were calculators running a program. "It is irrelevant whether the system is running deterministically; what makes us call it a 'choice maker' is whether we can identify with a high-level description of the process which takes place when the program runs. On a low (machine language) level the program looks like any other program: on a high (chunked) level, qualities such as 'will,' 'intuition,' 'creativity,' and 'consciousness' can emerge."[14]

Hofstadter's point is that even a fully defined and determined system of simple rules can display such complex behavior that it is meaningful to describe it in terms of decisions and will, quite irrespective of the fact that the laws affecting the simple level govern completely.

A completely implemented version of a set of simple rules can display properties we cannot find in the rules themselves; the reason we cannot find the properties in the rules is a general condition of the world that is described in Gödel's theorem and Chaitin's extension of it. Precisely because we can never decide whether a computation will halt or not, as Turing proved, we can never know in advance what laws will lead to.

In a sense, it is quite irrelevant whether man possesses free will or not: There may well be simple laws that, in the final analysis, determine what we do—laws we can know and the initial conditions of which we can know, enabling us in principle to compute what a human being will do in a given situation. But these laws will most probably be *computationally irreducible*, so that we can compute these consequences only by having all the information these laws handle. In other words, we have to know everything a person has learned, and undergo all the experiences a person has undergone, before we have enough information to compute what that person will do. Everywhere that person has been, we must have been; everywhere that person has acted, we must have acted. But in that case we must necessarily be that person ourselves.

You can never predict what a person will do, because it would require all the information that person has and has had; but the person does not even have that himself, for most of a human's experiences and operations are nonconscious.

Neither the individual nor anybody outside him can know what that individual is destined to do, even though it may be fully determined by laws and initial conditions.

Chaos theory has demonstrated a perfectly analogous situation for even the simplest physical systems. According to the theory of *deterministic chaos,* even fully determined systems are unpredictable. The point is that even if the laws for a system are simple and known, the system is very sensitive to its initial conditions. If we want to know exactly how the weather is going to develop just a few weeks into the future, we must know the current weather situation on earth in every detail.

The reason for this is that most physical systems (apart from textbook cases!) have the characteristic that they display chaos. This means that even the teeniest mistake in our knowledge of the initial conditions for the system will grow explosively, indeed, exponentially, in time. In practice, this means that it is quite impossible to know how the phase of the atmosphere will develop a mere few weeks into the future, unless we know the position and speed of every single molecule in the atmosphere with perfect precision. And we shall never know, for practical reasons.

The world is unpredictable, not because it does not have laws or that they are not known, but because the world is not known with complete accuracy. And we shall never know it, precisely because we are subjects in this world of ours: We are cognizers without full knowledge.

If we want complete knowledge of what is happening to a system, we must be the system itself and undergo its evolution in its own time. We cannot take any shortcuts or compress matters into approximate, manageable models. Only the world knows what it will do—and we are not the world.

Thermodynamics describes the world's fundamental character of irreversibility, irrevocability, and inconvertibility in time. For more than a hundred years, physicists have wondered how Newton's laws, which are so beautiful and reversible in time, can live side by side with the picture presented by thermodynamics of a messier world imbued with irreversibility and statistics. Dissatisfaction with this discord in physics' world picture has led many physicists to object to either thermodynamics or Newtonian laws.

The most famous modern representative of the view that there is something wrong with Newton's world picture because it fails to include irreversibility is the Belgian physicist and Nobel laureate Ilya Prigogine. As one of the gurus of the holistic movement, Prigogine is well known for his poetic, captivating philosophy of the necessity of time and irreversibility in the modern cosmography. Prigogine has made huge contributions to the development of thermodynamics, but his philosophy is more respected among laymen than among his colleagues. The reason for this is that he refuses to respect the law that More Is Different. Prigogine wants irreversibility built in at the microscopic level.

"Irreversibility is either true on all levels or on none,"[15] Prigogine writes in his extensive work *Order Out of Chaos*, in which he and Isabelle Stengers try to formulate a theory that irreversibility is not an effect of our level of description but is true at the microscopic level too. To him, irreversibility is a deficiency in Newton's laws rather than an emergent property that appears when the simple, time-reversible laws work for long enough on sufficiently large systems.

Prigogine's view is criticized by both friends[16] and adversaries[17] among physicists. There is no particular basis in physical theories for the view that Prigogine succeeded in formulating a theory of microscopic irreversibility.

The question is also whether such a theory is required. Perhaps it is precisely the fact that there are different levels at which we can describe the world that is interesting: We lose knowledge of the world when we approach it from one level rather than from another. It is precisely the fact that we want to describe not everything at once, but only whatever it is about the world that interests us, that gives rise to irreversibility.

The physicist Rolf Landauer, who is highly critical of Prigogine, has tried to formulate a solution to the problem of irreversibility by insisting that there will always be physical limits to our capacities to carry out calculations: No matter how big a computer we may build, it will always be smaller than the universe. So we will never—even in principle—be able to follow any process randomly far into the future, because the process displays chaotic behavior. In the final analysis, this chaotic quality the world possesses means that we cannot pursue all molecules randomly far into the future. Even if we had control of the world, we would not continue to have it. Things escape our grasp and do so in an irreversible way.

"While chaos, by itself, is not a source of unpredictability or irreversibility, it obviously does cause the need for computation to grow very rapidly with elapsed time,"[18] Landauer writes.

Even in the case of deterministic chaos, where all laws and effects are fully determined in practice, we can never quite get things under control in a finite area of the universe because we have to face the fact that our computer power is limited. For any limited observer, the world must, then, be imbued with irreversibility, even if the laws for that world are not.

Landauer describes his solution as speculative, but his point is clear enough: It is only because we have gotten used to believing that in principle we have infinite computing power available that we believe that deterministic laws must lead to behavior we can understand in practice as reversible. But we do not have all the computer power in the universe at our disposal, and even if we did, we would not be able to compute the future of the world faster than the world itself does. "In contrast to this physical situation, mathematics has taught us to think in terms of an unlimited sequence of operations," Landauer writes in an article entitled "Information Is Physical,"[19] and that is an unrealistic situation. Computations are physical processes that take place in a physical universe, where our resources are limited.

We cannot grasp the world because More Is Different, and even more is even more different. In the final analysis, our difficulties in describing the world derive from our trying to compress an infinite universe into a finite description.

That cannot be done. Not even if we did as mathematics and the natural sciences do, and claimed that in principle our description is infinite. The only way forward is to face the fact that we cannot describe everything as long as we want to be us.

Rolf Landauer sees irreversibility as a measure of the fact that we can never keep hold of all the details of the systems we try to describe, and so we must accept that the world is constantly slipping away from us as time passes, getting harder and harder to describe. He concludes his discussion of irreversibility by quoting James Clerk Maxwell: "Dissipated energy is energy which we cannot lay hold of and direct at pleasure, such as the energy of the confused agitation of molecules which we call heat. Now, confusion, like the correlative term order, is not a property of material things in themselves, but only in relation to the mind which perceives them."

Landauer does not like the reference to the mind in this passage, which also appeared in the very first chapter of this book. For what matters is not the subjective experience in the mind but the coarse graining that we approach the world with: At our level of description, on the scale at which we describe the world, there is lots of energy present that we cannot exploit. Maxwell's demon taught us that we cannot exploit the enormous kinetic energy to be found in molecular motion in hot matter. This is not a subjective condition in any sense other than the fact that it reveals something about the level at which we describe the world. With our coarse graining, with the size of the holes in our physical fishing net, the energy irrevocably becomes increasingly more difficult to gain access to. Irreversibility is an effect of our possibilities for interaction with the world. Even if the rules for this interaction are themselves reversible laws.

≈

If we put an ice cube in our drink, it can remember its correct temperature: 0 degrees centrigrade. A mixture of ice and water will keep itself at freezing point until there is no more ice, because the hot afternoon keeps trying to create equilibrium by making the drink as warm as the air.

But as long as there is an ice cube in the glass, the drink remains at

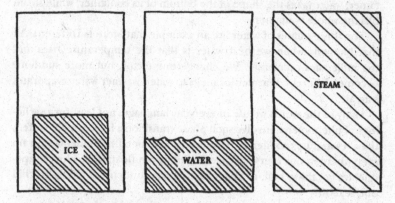

Ice, water, and steam. Three states with different properties, even though all that has changed is the temperature.

a constant temperature. It does not merely react passively to the temperature of the surroundings; it maintains its own. The reason why the drink can remember its temperature is that it contains a mixture of two *phases* of water: its solid phase, ice, and its liquid phase, water. The transition between the two phases is known as melting (or freezing, if the transition is in the other direction). These are phase transitions. The other important phase transition for water is evaporation/boiling or condensation/dew.

Phase transitions are very important phenomena in the physical world. A system that contains two phases can maintain such a mixed phase even when it is far from an equilibrium in which it has the same temperature as its surroundings.

The difference between the liquid and the solid phases of water can be explained by the molecular theory of matter: Ice consists of water molecules that maintain their relative positions, while water consists of molecules that can circulate freely among one another, rather like marbles in a bag. The gaseous phase of water, steam, consists of molecules that can circulate among one another with complete freedom. The molecular situation corresponds completely to the way the three phases behave on our level: Ice keeps its shape, irrespective of its container; water takes the shape of the bottom of its container; while steam fills the whole container.

The three phases of water are an example that More Is Different. All that happens when we heat water is that the temperature rises and the molecules accelerate. We change one factor, but more suddenly becomes different: Warmer ice melts to water, warmer water evaporates into air.

Many of the words we use in everyday language, not least for psychological phenomena, involve such phase transitions: freeze, melt, stiffen, thaw, evaporate, condense. The two fundamental movements pop up everywhere in our everyday speech: things can float, drift, blow, evaporate, let go, thaw, boil, or coagulate, freeze, condense, hold tight, chill out, seal off.

Of course, it is not so strange, because the three phases of water—solid, liquid, and gaseous—are among the most important experiences we have of the world.

And the phenomenon has in recent years proved far more universal than one might think.

"We propose that the solid and fluid phases of matter, with which we are so familiar from everyday experience, are much more fundamental aspects of nature than we have supposed them to be. Rather than merely being possible phases of matter, they constitute two fundamental universality classes of dynamical behavior," Chris Langton writes from Los Alamos in an article on computation at the edge of chaos, an article that encompasses some of the most auspicious research of recent years.[20]

The idea is as simple as it is refreshing. Langton not only conducts research into artificial life but explores the more general theoretical problem of how information-handling systems such as living organisms occur spontaneously in nature at all. How can physical systems assume the ability to handle information? How can the ability to compute arise as an emergent property in inanimate systems? In other words, issues that actually form a general version of the question: What is the origin of life?

Formulated in relation to how physical systems can acquire the ability to compute—i.e., handle information—this is a very difficult problem. So Langton has translated it into the question: When will simple computer versions of physical systems themselves develop the ability to compute? Specifically, the problem is expressed in a mathematical language known as *cellular automata*.

It uses very simple models in which lots of local units each follow very elementary rules. Picture a chessboard system: The local rule might be that all squares surrounded by three black neighboring squares must be white, while all the other squares must remain black. Such simple recipes can lead to astonishingly rich and varied behavior. More than anything else, it was the young physicist Stephen Wolfram's studies of the unpredictable behavior of such cellular automata that made it clear that many of reality's systems are computationally irreducible: Even a very simple recipe for cellular automata can lead to behavior that is quite impossible to predict.

By translating his problem into the language of cellular automata, Langton was able to attack it on the computer: What is necessary for cellular automata to develop the ability to handle information and create complexity?

Some cellular automata perish very rapidly. Their recipe does not lead to interesting behavior. Others live for a long time and could perhaps continue to infinity.

This corresponds exactly to the situation with ordinary calculations on computers: Some arrive quickly at an answer ($2 + 2 = 4$), others go on forever ($10/3 = 3.33333333\ldots$), while still others can be harder to guess at. Turing's halting problem tells us that in general we can never know whether a computation will halt until it halts.

Langton's cellular automata display the same three possible outcomes: (1) they perish, (2) they continue infinitely, (3) they are on the borderline, and it is hard to tell what will happen.

Computations that perish correspond to ice. You get your answer, and that's that. There is total order. The situation is frozen solid, and in the long term it is not especially interesting.

Computations that go on forever are like water: Everything is kept fluid. There is chaos, lack of clarity. It can be interesting for a while, but in the long term it's rather trivial, because nothing ever comes of it.

The really interesting computations are balanced between the frozen and the ever-liquid: We do not know if they will ever come to an end. Such computations often take place on the brink of the solid and the liquid—close to the transition between ice and water. It is therefore in such borderline situations that interesting things happen.

An interesting computational process capable of handling information has to be able to do two things: store information and erase information. Unless one can store, one cannot accumulate information. Unless one can erase, one cannot perform computations by composing the information in new ways. A system capable of doing anything interesting must therefore be capable of storing and erasing; remembering and moving; keeping and letting go; freezing and flowing. The system must also permit these processes to occur near each other.

Langton's idea was that there were only these two basic forms, freezing and liquid, in any dynamical system that could be emulated by cellular automata. In practice, this means that any physical system will be characterized by one of the two basic forms: solid or liquid.

Ultimately, there are only these two basic states or basic phases, and everything of interest takes place on the boundary between them: on the boundary between chaos and order, on the boundary between water and ice, on the boundary between the finite and the infinite computation process.

Right where we cannot know whether it all ends or not.

"Computation may emerge spontaneously and come to dominate the dynamics of physical systems when those systems are at or near a transition between their solid and fluid phases," writes Langton, adding, "Perhaps the most exciting implication is the possibility that life had its origin in the vicinity of a phase transition."[21]

Other researchers, especially James Crutchfield, from Berkeley, California, though critical of Langton's speculation, have come to the same conclusion,[22] using similar methods: It is on the boundary between order and chaos that the really interesting things happen. Here, on the edge of chaos, we can carry out computations where new structures can arise.

What is interesting is not having juice or other treats in the fridge and ice cubes in the freezer. The interesting thing is mixing them into a drink.

≈

In 1988, the German physicist and chaos scientist Peter Richter proposed an early version of these ideas in his phrase "the beauty of boundaries."[23] By observing computer images of phenomena from chaos theory and fractals, Richter had come to an analysis of where human beings settle on the earth: coasts, rivers, mountain chains, mountain passes. Near boundaries. Near the transition from one element to another.

The beauty of boundaries comes about because the boundary between sea and land is where something complicated and interesting takes place. Sea is trivial in the long term, just as land easily becomes so. But when the two principles meet at a coast or the mouth of a river, astonishing things may happen, just as most of life on earth is to be found at the boundary between sea and air or the boundary between land and air.

The same goes for our lives: If we are only in one domain, our lives are not as interesting as they would be if we lived on the boundary between different domains, where more factors tug at us and the result is therefore uncertain.

The natural sciences tend to be interested either in order or in chaos; either Newtonian reversibility or thermodynamic irreversibility; either simplicity or confusion.

The study of complexity really took shape when Bernardo Huberman and Tad Hogg pointed out in 1986 that the complex is precisely to be found midway between chaos and order. A few years later, Chris Langton, James Crutchfield, and others were able to show that the interesting things happen when and where order meets chaos.

Complexity grows on the edge of chaos.

In the final analysis, this is why knowing the simple equations and a series of textbook cases is not enough. Even if we know the formulae for the world, from the formulae we cannot guess what the world is like. Even if we could reduce a variegated world to a brief description, we would never be able to reconstruct the world from the description.

More Is Different, P. W. Anderson said—and added, as we have seen, "The ability to reduce everything to simple fundamental laws does not imply the ability to start from those laws and reconstruct the universe."

But that is what we are consciously trying to do with the artificial lives we live in our technological civilization.

CHAPTER 15

THE NONLINEAR LINE

In 1877, when the planet Mars was unusually close to earth, only sixty million kilometers away, the Italian astronomer Giovanni Schiaparelli announced that he had discovered canals—*canali*—on the surface of earth's neighbor. These canals constituted a colossal system of linked structures covering the whole surface of Mars. They were very difficult to see, because disturbance in the earth's atmosphere makes the study of planet surfaces very difficult. Photography was impossible: The atmospheric disturbance meant that the image of Mars was hazy in the eyepiece of the telescope and blurred completely in the course of the exposure time of the film. But Schiaparelli then spent many years charting the extensive system of linked lines on the surface of Mars.

In 1892, when Schiaparelli announced that his fading sight was forcing him to give up his studies, the enormously wealthy American diplomat Percival Lowell decided to build an observatory in an area with unusually little atmospheric disturbance—Flagstaff, Arizona—so that study of the canals could continue.

Percival Lowell's studies of the planets proved very important, not least because he launched a search for the ninth and remotest of the planets in the solar system. His search was crowned with success in 1930, when Lowell's successor at the observatory, Clyde Tombaugh, discovered the planet, which was dubbed Pluto, not only because it is the name of the god of death's dark realm, but also because it started with Lowell's initials.

But it was the study of the Martian canals that most occupied Lowell, until his death in 1916. Lowell thought he could see extensive systems of straight canals connecting dark patches spread around the surface of the planet. This intricate system of straight lines was thought to constitute a planetary irrigation system, which collected water from the Martian ice caps and carried it to the dry areas closer to the equator. Mars is clearly a dry planet, so life quite simply had to obtain water from the poles, which, like those on earth, are covered by eternal snow.

Many years later, the American astronomer and science writer Carl Sagan put it this way: "The turning point of the argument was the straightness of the canals, some of them following great circles for thousands of miles. Such geometrical configurations, Lowell thought, could not be produced by geological processes. The lines were too straight. They could only have been produced by intelligence."[1]

Lowell's conclusion was therefore the controversial one that Mars was not only the home of living creatures but also a completely civilized planet, shaped and regulated so the meager fluid could be spread across the whole globe.

The Martian canals continued to be discussed for decades, and only visits by space program probes made it completely clear that there are no such straight canals on Mars. There are, however, dried-up riverbeds from an epoch in which Mars did have running water, but they are not at all straight; they are crooked and irregular, like rivers here on earth, the result of geological activity that can be explained without invoking intelligent intervention. What is more, they are too small for Lowell to have seen through his telescope.

What Lowell saw was an illusion. There were no canals, no straight lines; but the eye is trained to see patterns and wants to see patterns even where there are none. All kinds of irregular blotches and patches on the surface of Mars that could just be glimpsed through the atmospheric haze were interpreted as straight lines, even when there were no straight lines.

Lowell saw something that was not there: a pattern where in actual fact there were only random, dispersed patches.

As Carl Sagan remarked, "Lowell always said that the regularity of the canals was an unmistakable sign that they were of intelligent origin. This is certainly true. The only unresolved question was which side of the telescope the intelligence was on."[2]

There are practically no straight lines in nature. While civilization created by man is imbued with straight lines, right angles, and round shapes everywhere, the straight line is absent from the collection of shapes in natural nature.

There are lots of natural shapes that we may perceive as straight with a little goodwill, but only if we do not look too hard. Trees grow upright, but we have to be quite a long way off for them to look perfectly smooth and straight (even if we ignore the branches): They are gnarled and knotty, their bark is rough, and their trunks narrow as they ascend. Similarly, no blade of grass is quite straight and no animal back perfectly erect. Frost and crystals can present straight lines, but their straightness covers only short distances. Rivers and coastlines are irregular, mountain chains are saw-toothed, and clouds are irregular in the extreme.

The horizon looks straight, yes, but that is only because we see it on a very specific scale. If we saw a little more of the horizon (from a spaceship, for example), we would discover that the earth is not flat at all, but round; if we went closer (using a telescope), we would discover that the straight horizon is composed of innumerable tiny wave crests that the eye smooths out into a straight line.

Rays of light travel along straight lines, but we cannot see them. If we look directly into a ray of light, we see only a point. If we view it from the side, we can see it only because the light is being scattered by dust or smoke particles in the air. If we examined these illuminated particles in more detail, we would discover that they make up not straight lines but series of separate dots.

All the shapes we learn about in our geometry lessons are absent in nature: the straight line, the right angle, the right-angled triangle. We do not find them even though at first sight we may think we see them. Apart from the rectilinearity of crystals, the circle is the only simple geometric shape we can find in nature in its pure form: We see it in the sky in the form of the sun and the full moon, far, far away.

Nature uses a very different language of shapes than does school geometry, which is a way of describing shapes that we owe the ancient Greeks.

A raindrop on its way down a mountain will not follow a straight line. Of course, from an abstract point of view it will, because gravity will tug at it; but there is more in the world than the earth's gravity. There is also the earth's surface—and that is irregular. So a raindrop on its way down a mountain will not fall in a straight line. For at every single point along the way it must determine which direction is down, and down is not always straight ahead. There may be a pebble or a prominence that will make the raindrop's route irregular, a touch zigzag. The raindrop's path reflects the local conditions at every single point on the way down. Raindrops do not consider where to go, work out a route, and follow it. At every single point, raindrops move in a downward direction. Rain-

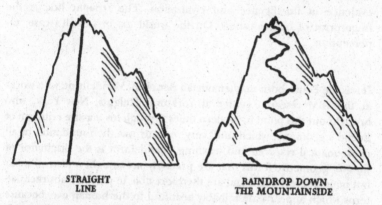

STRAIGHT
LINE

RAINDROP DOWN
THE MOUNTAINSIDE

Raindrops do not follow a straight line as they run off a mountain. It is more difficult to describe their route than to describe a straight line.

drops navigate by the local situation, not the global one. They decide step by step.

That is why raindrops do not follow a straight line. When it is raining they may, unless it is windy. But on their way down a mountain they do not.

That is why rivers and streams are not straight either. They follow winding, agitated courses that do not merely go by the general slope of the terrain but go also by local differences in the softness of the soil. A big rock may make the streambed zig, while a deposit of gravel causes it to zag. If we observe a river from an airplane or a space probe, we see large bends in its course; if we stroll along its bank, we notice lots of much smaller bends within the big bends we see from the air.

But if we go to Holland, we see almost nothing but straight waterways. The reason is that Holland is, generally speaking, an unnatural landscape, which lies below sea level, protected by dikes. So all the water in the country is thoroughly regulated, as regards water height and flow, by dikes and controls; these are easiest to keep track of if the water runs in straight lines along man-made canals.

Holland's waterways are like something out of a geometry book: The rushing spring streams that carry meltwater from the mountain peaks look like anything but what science taught us.

The straight line is, as Percival Lowell quite correctly realized, evidence of intelligence and civilization. The straight line is the fingerprint of consciousness. On the world or, in Lowell's case, on perception.

It was the Polish-born mathematician Benoit B. Mandelbrot, who works at the IBM research center at Yorktown Heights, New York, who brought out this point in modern times through his massive criticism of Euclid's geometry, which until very recently was the foundation of all mathematical research and teaching. Mandelbrot is the originator of *fractals*, geometric forms that are precisely *not* straight and rectilinear but bend at every point and are therefore able to produce abstract patterns which appear indescribably beautiful to the human eye, because they seem to possess the same complexity as the geometry of nature proper: forms of great depth and complexity, forms that get richer the more closely one studies them.

In a book on the fractal geometry of nature, published in 1983, Mandelbrot wrote, "Why is geometry often described as 'cold' and 'dry'? One reason lies in its inability to describe the shape of a cloud, a mountain, a coastline, or a tree. Clouds are not spheres, mountains are not cones, coastlines are not circles, and bark is not smooth, nor does lightning travel in a straight line. More generally, I claim that many patterns of Nature are so irregular and fragmented that, compared with Euclid, Nature exhibits not simply a higher degree but an altogether different level of complexity."[3]

One may ask why a scientist working for a computer corporation would write a book with a point like this. The reason is, in fact, the computer.

Most of the mathematics we learned at school is about forms and functions that are continuous and differentiable. In practice, this means that they are composed of smooth, regular shapes and mathematical functions. A small change does not mean much. A big change means more.

In about 1700, Isaac Newton and Gottfried Leibniz created differential and integral calculus, on which almost all natural science is based. Wonderful mathematical aids for analyzing forms and functions that are smooth. Newton and Leibniz invented devious maneuvers that permit us to summarize a study in a few simple formulae that are easy to manipulate on a piece of rough paper. One can calculate all the way through the problems by hand, because they have been simplified by the mathematical tricks the two great scientists came up with.

Any problems that we cannot solve via this kind of mathematics have to be solved numerically—i.e., we have to calculate them out number by number, digit by digit. Nobody can be bothered to do that. So nobody was interested in nondifferentiable forms and functions—all the irregular stuff—until the computer arrived.

With the computer, it suddenly became possible to calculate all the way through all kinds of problems that could be described by other forms of mathematics than well-behaved differential and integral calculus: that is to say, all the forms that cannot be described through simple geometric figures and all the functions that cannot be described by methods that are easy to calculate to the end.

Benoit Mandelbrot explored such complicated forms and called them fractals; but Mandelbrot did not actually discover them. They were discovered around the time of the First World War by the French mathematicians Gaston Julia and Pierre Fatou, but they could not be explored because they were so complicated. So they were just called monsters and shelved (alongside even older approaches to fractal mathematics). By the 1990s, any child was familiar with their beauty— thanks to the computer, which does not mind calculating its way through the innumerable tiny decisions that have to be made when one builds up a fractal image.

The fractals are not based on really complicated mathematics, even though they form highly complex patterns. Many fractals can be defined by extremely simple formulae, repeated again and again in a process known as *iteration:* One takes a formula and calculates a number by using the formula. Then one takes the result and puts it into the formula again, yielding a new result, which in turn gets put into the formula.

The result is an iteration, an endless repetition that leads to highly complex patterns from very simple rules. The secret is the repetition.

They are the kinds of repetitions human beings cannot be bothered to perform. But computers do not mind—and nature is also happy to perform them.

Many of the recipes in the genes of living creatures, Mandelbrot points out, possess precisely the character of recipes for a process that has to be repeated again and again, so that, for example, one slowly builds up a tree by repeating the same form again and again, inside itself. Take a cauliflower; separate it into florets; they can be divided again into even smaller florets; in the end, they are far smaller than the nail on your little finger. The same basic form, repeated again and again inside itself.

Access to computers convinced scientists that *linear mathematics* could describe only a special case from the world. A very tiny corner. Most of the world has to be described through *nonlinear mathematics*— i.e., formulae and forms that are not regular and smooth but marked by the fact that the tiniest change can lead to a huge difference, because things bend and break everywhere. The phenomenon of chaos is a nonlinear effect, just as fractals are. In the 1980s, the computer led to the nonlinear revolution in the natural sciences: a revolution that seriously opened our eyes to the fact that our civilization is completely different from nature.

When, in 1986, the two German fractal scientists Heinz-Otto Peitgen and Peter Richter wrote the foreword to their beautiful and now world-famous landmark book, *The Beauty of Fractals*, they quoted the Austrian artist Friedensreich Hundertwasser:

"In 1953 I realized that the straight line leads to the downfall of mankind. But the straight line has become an absolute tyranny. The straight line is something cowardly drawn with a ruler, without thought or feeling; it is the line which does not exist in nature. And that line is the rotten foundation of our doomed civilization. Even if there are places where it is recognized that this line is rapidly leading to perdition, its course continues to be plotted. . . . Any design undertaken with the straight line will be stillborn. Today we are witnessing the triumph of rationalist know-how and yet, at the same time, we find ourselves confronted with emptiness. An esthetic void, a desert of uniformity, criminal sterility, loss of creative power. Even creativity is prefabricated. We have become impotent. We are no longer able to create. That is our real illiteracy."[4]

But what is the problem of living in a civilization based on the straight line? That it contains very little information. There is almost nothing to sense.

A raindrop's path down a mountain is very difficult to describe. There are all kinds of detours that require detailed explanations. A length of string stretched between the starting point and the destination of the raindrop is in principle far easier to describe. It is enough to specify the two points at which the string is attached—and that it is taut; then you have said all there is to say about that line.

A straight line does not require much information before it is settled. However, a nonlinear line that bends and turns requires a great deal of information before it is described.

It is very easy to describe a modern concrete apartment tower, compared to an old-fashioned house where artisans laid the bricks one by one, not to mention a completely old-fashioned thatched cottage.

Linear civilization is easy to describe and thus easy to predict. There is far less information in a beautifully smooth highway than in a cobbled alley. When we asphalt a town square, we discard the information from the terrain that used to be there, and make it easier to describe that particular area of the earth's surface than it was before we flattened it.

Civilization is about attaining predictability; and predictability is the opposite of information, because information is a measure of the surprise value of a message: the astoundment it unleashes.

"There's a hole in the road," we say—and this is useful information to the traveler. There is information in the statement, precisely because it is a road and not just a potholed strip of land.

Civilization keeps information out of our lives: information about the terrain we are passing through; information about precipitation while we sleep; information about air temperature fluctuations throughout the day; information about the bacteria content of the water before treatment; information about the form of the wood our floor is covered in; information about what we spilled on the floor before we did the cleaning.

We straighten and clean in order to avoid knowing what the world is like. A good thing too. If we want to ride our bikes, it is a good thing the road is smooth; if we want to sleep, it is a good thing we can keep the rain out; if we want to avoid diarrhea, it is a good thing the water has been treated; if we want to dance, it is a good thing the floor is level; if we want to get on with life, it is a good thing to tidy up.

Yet there is a limit. Linear civilization is very boring to look at. Its cities easily become sterile, empty settings, which do not supply the eye with any experiences or the mind with any relief. So we go on holiday, to places overgrown by nature, and enjoy chopping firewood and wielding the sickle. We love spending a whole day simply ensuring the sustenance of life and the refreshment of the body. We enjoy being forced to receive information about just how many biting insects nature actually has to offer. But meanwhile we cannot *work*. At any rate, not in the contemporary sense of the word.

Civilization is about removing information about our surroundings; discarding information about nature so our senses are not burdened with all that information and our consciousness can concentrate on other matters. We cut away loads of information from our surroundings in order to devote ourselves to the inner lives inside our heads and in society. The relationship between human beings and their inner lives becomes more important and takes up more room in our awareness, precisely because we do not have to spend all our time thinking about the weather. Instead we can think about one another.

Technology is about making things predictable and repeatable so we do not need to devote so much time and attention to them. Oil furnaces are fueled with something that requires much less attention than if we all had to go out and chop firewood. The fridge has turned obtaining and storing food into a chore that requires much less attention. The road network and our bicycles make reaching a distant point much more predictable and much quicker. Technology aims to make perception and attention superfluous, allowing us to perceive and attend to something other than the things we use technology to help us with.

But technology is therefore dull too. In itself, it aims to remove us from the process we are carrying out: to make our attention superfluous by removing the need to crunch a quantity of information.

A typewriter or a typesetting machine removes information from the process of writing: There is far more information in handwriting's agitated characters that reveal the writer's state of mind than in the predefined characters of a computer. A telephone conversation contains far less information than a conversation face-to-face, but more than a letter. A handwritten letter contains more information than the same letter produced on a typewriter or word processor.

Civilization removes "naturally grown" information from our lives to leave room for other information: work, private lives, culture, television, entertainment. We do not constantly need to use our entire sensory apparatus on rain and snakes; instead we can talk to each other. Our surroundings become so little of a burden to us that we can certainly allow ourselves to relocate consciousness half a second behind reality so we can talk about it.

When we are bored by technology, in a sense we are bored by our own perception of the world. Technology can be defined as *objectified simulations*. Our experience of the world is based on the *sense-simulate-experience* sequence, as discussed earlier. We form a hypothesis about what we are sensing; we simulate the surroundings that are filling us with sensory data. Only then do we experience this simulation. We do not see the spectrum of electromagnetic waves: We see a red fire engine. Our brain apprehends something that resembles what it has already experienced.

This simulation is normally not at all conscious, but science is about making the rules for this simulation explicit and conscious. Science summarizes the part of our simulation of the world that we can talk to each other about because we can express it unambiguously.

When we know the way we simulate something, we can reconstruct it. We can build another one, because we know the principles behind it. We can simulate it in our minds and convert this simulation into an object the principles of which we understand. We can objectify our simulation.

We know the principles of flight, so we can build a flying machine. Actually, in practice it is more the other way around: We start building a flying machine, but cannot. Then we look at the birds and everything we know about the air, and a few hundred years later we build a flying machine.

The problem is then that we simulate the world as if it consisted of straight lines and other tidy shapes. All our terms for describing the world are linear and tidy, so all we can build are things that are linear and tidy. This perception is ingrained right down into our nervous system: The straight line is built into the functions of our nerve cells.

We therefore build a linear world when we objectify our understanding of the world in the form of technology.

Our concepts are linear, and often in ways we do not even realize.

≈

"How long is the coast of Britain?" Benoit Mandelbrot asked in the first article in which he mentioned fractals, a revolutionary treatise in *Science* in 1967.[5] The point was the simple one that the length of a coastline is not a well-defined term, even though we all learned at school how long various coastlines and rivers are.

The Danish coastline, for example, is said to be 7,474 kilometers long.[6] But strictly speaking, this is nonsense. Because it all depends on how many of the little curves in the coastline you include. If you take an aerial photograph of Denmark, you can see a certain degree of detail and measure how long the coast is. But if you walk along the coastline, you will see more small curves inside the bigger curves, and this means that the coastline gets longer the more details you include.

So when we say that the coastline is 7,474 kilometers long, we do so because we have tacitly defined a particular yardstick, a particular degree of coarseness that we use to see how long various coastlines are. But strictly speaking, every coastline is infinitely long: The more details we include, the longer the coastline, until we could start going around every single grain of sand. Similarly, rivers are infinitely long if we count all the tiny bends. But of course the Nile is still longer than the Gudenå at any given scale.

We can pose the problem in another way: If we have a stretch of coastline between two piers 167 meters apart, how long is that stretch?

In principle, there is an endless piece of coastline between the two piers. But if we skip all the tiny curves along the coast, it assumes a well-defined length. If we just draw the line of sight between the two piers, skipping all the irregular details, the coastline becomes just 167 meters long. But if we include a few twists, the coastline gets longer.

We can ask another way: If we walk 167 meters along the coast from pier A to pier B, how far do we walk?

That depends on the length of our stride!

The concept of *length*, which is one of the most common in everyday life, is not defined until we define an observer: somebody who experiences that length.

Distance is a well-defined term, but a highly abstract one: It involves the line of sight or beeline between two points in a terrain. Length follows a naturally defined boundary such as a coastline, a river, or a surface in a terrain, and thus becomes defined only when we define a scale, a coarseness—in other words, an observer. Lengths do not exist in reality, not until we define who experiences that reality.

Mind you, a length is perfectly well defined if we mean the road from Copenhagen to Roskilde. That is because the road was laid by human beings, who had already objectified a certain scale, a coarse-

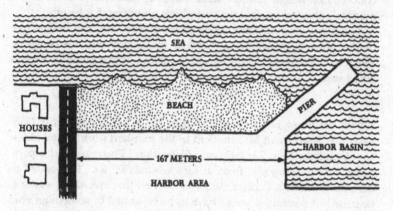

An infinite coastline

ness, to show which yardstick was the right one. The road is precisely linear and flat on one specific scale. On that scale, the length of the road is unequivocally defined. On a microscopic scale, it may be rough and fuzzy on the surface, and therefore longer than the highway authorities want it to be. But any traveler knows which scale is intended when people talk about the length of a road.

The concept of length is not well defined in nature until human beings arrive. The concept is well defined in any civilized context, but of course human beings have already gotten there.

In everyday language, however, we take it for granted that concepts like length are always well defined. This is quite sensible, because everyday language is based on the common sense that will always admit that it is pigheaded nonsense to want to talk about a length without acknowledging that there is somebody talking about it; and as somebody is talking about a length, the scale is already defined, for the conversation reveals—perhaps implicitly—which context this length is part of. There is always a reference to a praxis, and this praxis (motoring, house building, painting) makes the presupposed scale perfectly clear. The praxis may even aim at objectifying the desired scale by planing, sanding, or asphalting, with a view to linearity on a particular scale.

The problem arises when consciousness begins to want to define a concept like length without acknowledging that such a definition is possible only after one has defined who is observing that length.

This is the kind of thing philosophers wrestle with, and indeed one of the greatest problems of Western philosophy and mathematics, which is more than 2,500 years old, involves just this question: Zeno's paradoxes.

"Of all the Presocratics, Zeno has most life in him today," write G. S. Kirk, J. E. Raven, and M. Schofield in the standard work on the oldest Greek philosophers, *The Presocratic Philosophers*.[7] The reason is his paradoxes, which Zeno, who lived in Elea around 500 B.C., formulated to defend his teacher, Parmenides, who asserted that everything was one, because if it was not, it would have to be separated by something else, which must therefore also exist and thus be part of the everything that was one.

One of Zeno's paradoxes concerns movement: If you want to move from one place to another, you must first traverse half the distance, and before that, half of the half of the half. You must thus traverse an infinite number of halves before you reach your destination; and as you cannot do that in finite time, you never get anywhere.

Another of the paradoxes concerns an arrow: If at any given time the arrow is in a given place, where is it when it is moving? If it is not in a given place at any given time, where is it at any given time? Is it moving where it is or where it is not?

Since Zeno's day, philosophers and mathematicians have wrestled with these paradoxes, which clearly originate from the idea of the infinite divisibility of space and time: what is technically known as the hypothesis of a *continuum*.

But the idea that space and time are infinitely divisible and continuous has come under violent attack from many physicists in recent years. Rolf Landauer has criticized the idea of a continuum because in the final analysis it implies that the universe contains an infinite amount of information (there is no end to the yes/no questions you

can ask of something that can go on being divided to infinity).[8] John
Wheeler has criticized the idea of a continuum because it fundamentally conflicts with quantum mechanics.[9]

As soon as we leave the idea of a continuum, the problems of having
to traverse half of half of half before we even get moving disappear.

Zeno's paradoxes derive from the desire to talk of a length as being
infinitely divisible. But that is precisely what a length is not. Certainly, a
coastline is infinitely long, but as soon as we say that it is of a certain
length, we introduce a coarse graining, a mesh size for our net, which
allows us to talk about a length in the first place.

Implicit in the everyday concept of length, then, is the precondition
that there is no such thing as a continuum but an infinity depicted as if
it were of finite length. When an infinite quantity is described as finite,
this implies an observer who defines a scale, a minimum measuring
rod, below which we leave out the details.

The problems arise because the concept of length is an abstract one,
which can be used only if we have defined a scale: a coarse graining. We
do not normally consider this but imagine that we can divide a length
infinitely.

The same goes for time: Zeno indicates that it is impossible to determine whether something is moving where it is. Because if it is, it is not
there, and if it is not, where is the movement?

The problem resembles one we encounter when we take moving pictures: We cannot take a picture of a movement. We can only take lots of
pictures, which freeze a whole series of frozen fragments of a sequence
of movement and then show them rapidly one after the other, giving
the spectator an illusion of movement. But the movement itself cannot
be photographed (except as a blurred image).

There is a relatively sharp limit to the number of pictures we need to
see if we are not to see a series of individual images but a continuous
movement: about eighteen frames per second. The same goes for our
sense of hearing, where at least sixteen pulses a second are required if
we are to hear not a series of pulses but a continuous tone.

Movements and tones are "illusions" that arise when we integrate
sensory data we cannot separate because they take place within the
same subjective time quantum, or *SZQ (subjektives Zeitquant)*, to put it in
the language of the German cybernetics tradition (introduced in
Chapter Six). Our concepts reflect the fact that the bandwidth of consciousness is about sixteen bits per second.[10]

The concept of movement and the concept of continuous tones, like the concept of length, therefore imply a certain coarse graining, a certain scale, an observer who quantizes the experience. When everyday language talks of length, movement, and continuous tones, it is presupposed that there is somebody who experiences the length, movement, or tone. Otherwise the concepts would be meaningless.

Zeno's paradoxes indicate, then, that language allows itself to talk of these concepts as if no coarse graining were required for them to be defined. But if we abstract away the observer's coarse graining, we also abstract away the concepts that presuppose that observer's coarse graining.

What Zeno points out is that even if the terrain is infinitely divisible, the map can never be so, for it was drawn by a consciousness of limited bandwidth.

Civilization objectifies our simulation of the world: We imagine how we can build houses, roads, and cities—and we build them according to blueprints full of straight lines. Civilization thus introduces the straight line, so the quantity of information diminishes and everyday terms take on immediate meaning. Where there was infinity, finity arises.

The fractal geometry Mandelbrot launched and many mathematicians have continued to develop operates with a beautiful concept that reveals something about how much space there is "between" our everyday notions: the concept of *fractal dimension*. We are used to regarding space as three-dimensional (and roll our eyes when Einstein talks about a fourth dimension derived from time). The three dimensions are easy to visualize: up and down, left and right, forward and back.

We are also used to the fact that something can be three-dimensional—namely, space; two-dimensional—namely, a plane; or one-dimensional—namely, a line.

But Mandelbrot proposed that something could have a dimension that lay between 1 and 2 or 2 and 3! For example, a coastline might have a dimension of 1.23. This means that though it may be a line of infinite length, it twists so much that it fills some of the plane. A line with a fractal dimension of 1.98 is so twisted that it fills almost the entire plane; while a line with a dimension of 1.02 is very close to being a straight line.

Likewise a surface can have a dimension of 2.78 because it is so dented that it almost fills the space above and below. It is characteristic that natural forms most frequently have dimensions that are not whole numbers. Coastlines practically never have a dimension of 1.0, even though they are precisely lines. They may have 1.09 if they are very straight, or be higher if there are lots of fjords.

While civilization almost always creates objects with dimensions in whole numbers, nature almost always creates objects of nonwhole number dimensions. That is the same as saying that the straight line almost never exists in nature, while civilization makes almost nothing but straight lines.

BROWNIAN MOTION

STRAIGHT LINE

Random movement (Brownian motion) contains lots of information, because at every single point it is random events that determine its course. A straight line contains very little information, because it is described merely by stating two points.

That qualifying "almost" is necessary. For nature also makes objects with dimensions in whole numbers.

The contrast to the straight line is the pure randomness known as the *random walk*: a totally random movement that arises if at every single point one tosses a coin to determine the direction to proceed in.

An example from physics is the Brownian motion of particles in a liquid: The particles are constantly being struck by the molecules of the liquid and thus pushed in random directions. Brownian motion contains an unfathomable amount of information because it is very difficult to describe.[11] But the fractal dimension of this line of random coincidences is precisely 2.0; in the long run, it fills up the plane.

Pure randomness ends up creating objects of whole-number dimensions. Pure order and planning ends up creating objects of whole-number dimensions. The interesting stuff lies between the completely random and the completely planned.

The ideal is not lines with as much information as possible; but it is certainly not lines with as little information as possible—i.e., straight lines.

The most interesting milieus are imbued with complexity, nontriviality: somewhere between total order and total chaos, total linearity and total nonlinearity, total civilization and total decay.

Nature occupies such a place: Nature is never quite linear, but neither is she totally disordered. Nature, including inanimate nature, is imbued with organization and complexity; with information, but only in limited quantities; with information that is present, but even more information that used to be.

Observing nature therefore gives us endless joy.

A quay is a coast
in one dimension.
1.0

A tile is a mainland
in two dimensions.
2.0

A room is outer space
in three dimensions.
3.0

A vault is a quake
in nothing.
0.0

The answer to linear civilization is not to ban objects of whole-number dimensions—i.e., the linear objects of civilization. It is nice when the table is flat and the creativity of the artist is what imparts information to the sketch, not the roughness of the table.

But the city dweller, perhaps, experiences a surfeit of objects of whole-number dimensions, and the ecosystems have trouble surviving when far too many river deltas are straightened out into canal systems, because it then becomes too difficult to deposit pollution along meandering riverbeds.

The balance between the linear and the nonlinear is a major challenge for civilization. In the final analysis, it is closely related to the challenge of finding the balance between the conscious and the nonconscious. After all, the difference between consciousness and nonconsciousness is precisely that there is very little information in consciousness. It can therefore apprehend only straight lines, having trouble with crooked ones, which contain far too much information.

The tendency of civilization toward linearity is therefore precisely the power of consciousness over nonconsciousness; the power of projection over spontaneity; the power of the gutter over the raindrop. The straight line is the medium of planning, will, and decision. The crooked line is the medium of sensory perception, improvisation, and abandon.

The *I* is linear; the *Me* is nonlinear. The social domain, the conversational domain, tends to be linear, unalloyed chatter. The personal domain, the domain of sensory perception, is more able to preserve the nonlinear.

Art seeks out the nonlinear; science the linear. The computer demolishes the difference, because it gives consciousness the ability to convert large quantities of information by machine.

If we want to see linear civilization on the really grand scale, we must go to places where great power is concentrated. Not just Manhattan, but perhaps Moscow in particular.

The now collapsed communism of the planned economy created a civilization with an utterly inconceivable number of straight lines in the form of vast boulevards and apartment blocks, which look like an architect's dream from the air but are devoid of habitability.

The absurd illusions of grandeur in Stalinist architecture are a measure of consciousness's unopposed imposition of drawing-board designs. Ultimately, an absurdity inherent in the very notion of the planned economy is that a central consciousness can know how many shoes are required on the other side of a continent.

The problem of communism is that where the decisions are made, there is not enough information about the situation in society. The same problem arises in the very large capitalist monopolies, where market domination is so great that no real feedback comes from consumers, because the price mechanism has been disabled.

The market mechanism is the only known mechanism for creating feedback from consumer to producer in industrialized society. In preindustrial economies, social units were so small and production so simple that individuals could agree on how production should be arranged (even though as a rule it ended with a king or a great landowner deciding everything).

During industrialism, communities have become so integrated that it is no longer possible for a single subject to monitor all of society's needs. But through supply and demand, the market mechanism ensures a flow of information from society about the needs out there, so that the people in charge of the means of production know something about the market.

The individual consumer in the marketplace makes a yes/no decision: Do I want that ware at that price or not? The consumer does not decide what she would like; there is not full awareness of a need. There is only a decision in relation to a particular product at a particular price.

The planned economy presupposes that in principle people can formulate their needs consciously: I want this and that, and I am prepared to pay so much for it. So I will vote for this person or that person, who will then ensure that the decision to produce what I want is made. Communism with a planned economy presupposes that society can formulate its needs. The market economy presupposes only that consumers can choose among various options with which they are presented.

For a planned economy to work, people must be transparently conscious and know what they want. This is not realistic. For a market economy to function as a need fulfiller, man would have to be autonomously self-managing and able to say no to anything he did not want. This is not realistic either. But it is less unrealistic than the idea that people can actively formulate and table their needs and thus facilitate central planning.

The collapse of communism is a manifestation of the low bandwidth of the social domain, the low capacity of language compared to the actual wealth of information in our needs. Feedback from society to the planners cannot take place efficiently enough over the conscious linguistic bandwidth. Supply and demand are better at returning this information.

This is ironic, for the whole idea of socialism is that barter and the market economy discard too much information.

Karl Marx's criticism of capitalist exchange of commodities involved precisely that: discarded information. Instead of looking at the use value of a good—i.e., its actual quality and material ability to meet a need—the market concentrates on the exchange value of the good— i.e., the price—which, in Marx's eyes, is a measure of the work that went into it.

Karl Marx pointed out again and again that exchange value is an abstraction, a looking-away-from, the result of a discarding of information. The entire social domain had become regulated through this abstraction, which said nothing about genuine needs and genuine use values but spoke only about a reduced judgment: Do I want that commodity at that price?

His point was therefore that people cheated themselves by believing that it was gold that possessed a magic power—a power that really had nothing to do with the gold but was all about its exchange value. Instead of pleasing one another by carrying out a piece of real work, which led to a real product, which they knew would meet a real need, people submitted to an abstraction, exchange value, measured through the price. In honor of this abstraction, people go to work and manufacture things they do not know if anybody needs—and manufacture them in a way they do not know is apt or not.

Marx's criticism also demonstrated how industrialization robs the artisan of his knowledge and turns it into a template for building machines that pump out identical products on a production line.

Marx proposed that conscious, socially regulated production would be far more capable of meeting social wants and create much more job satisfaction. The idea was of "socialized man, the associated producers, rationally regulating their interchange with Nature rationally, bringing it under their common control, instead of being ruled by it as by the blind forces of Nature."[12]

The collapse of communism has demonstrated that there is no alternative to the market mechanism when it comes to the feedback of information from society to the powers that control the means of production. The market alone has proved effective at communicating whether a product meets a need. The conscious conversation cannot communicate sufficient information in a reliable fashion.

It is ironic, because Marx's criticism was precisely that too much information about needs was discarded when goods were produced for a market.

It is no coincidence that Karl Marx's criticism of the capitalist economy was rooted in a suggestion that too much information was being discarded. Marx's entire work is based on Hegel's philosophy, which is concerned, by and large, precisely with the discarding of information. Hegel stressed the importance of dialectic in contrast to classical logic. Dialectic is a method of logical discourse which emphasizes that entities are defined through a conflict of opposites, and one must think in opposites in order to understand things. Where classical Aristotelian logic is based on black and white opposites, dialectic stresses that one always loses knowledge when one thinks in abstract concepts. One must necessarily discard information when one creates a concept.

If we say that a person is a bank clerk, there is a great deal that we do not say but which would be just as true of that person: gender, religion, hobbies, marital status, political observance, cosmic interests, upbringing, etc. So dialectics stresses the conflict of opposites: If we bring out one aspect, the other will appear, in the form of secret associations and inner contradictions. The Danish Hegel expert, philosopher Jørgen K. Bukdahl, defines dialectic thus: "Generally, dialectic is an account of the loss of knowledge in abstract analysis. Every time we abstract elements from their undetermined context, there are—perhaps—associations and links and conditions which we overlook."[13]

Marx's criticism of capitalism was precisely an attempt to point out that the market mechanism overlooked too much—e.g., the natural conditions for production. What Marx overlooked was that the conscious social domain has the same tendency to discard too much information and ignore the needs of man and nature.

It is important to maintain that Marx's criticism may be correct, even though the attempts to replace the market mechanism with party discipline only made things worse.

The ever-increasing amount of state regulation in capitalist economies shows that there *is* a problem with the way the market mechanism discards information: In the completely free market economy, there are natural and human needs that must be taken care of but are not. But these problems are as nothing compared to the problems that have arisen in economies without market mechanisms.

Communism's weird obsession with the unwavering line in the political management of society shows that completely new concepts of politics are required before it is possible to formulate an alternative to the market mechanism.

Today there is no alternative, but in the longer term one may imagine that people will think it is unsatisfactory that industrialism forces them to work for abstractions rather than specific needs. So one may envisage that an alternative to the market mechanism will one day appear on the agenda again.

But the most fundamental problem is perhaps that people are not transparent to themselves and are therefore unable to formulate their needs through the low bandwidth of language.

Information society is at the door and promises to alleviate many of the pains capitalism has inflicted on man: unhealthy work processes, repetitive-strain injuries, and environmental destruction.

But information society presents another danger: *a lack of information*. For just as there is far too little information in a linear city, there is far too little information in information society—a society where most people's jobs are performed body, mind, and soul via the low bandwidth of language.

Granted, many people are already complaining that information society means far too much information. But the opposite is true: Where man is equipped to manage millions of bits per second in a meaningful way, he now processes only a few bits a second from the computer monitor. The sensuality of material processing has been stripped from the work process, and consciousness must make do with very few bits per second for nourishment. It is like fast food: There is almost nothing to digest, no bones and fiber to discard during and afterward.

Where artisans in the past used to possess vast tacit knowledge of materials and processes and crops, they now have to relate to consciously designed technical solutions presented via computer monitor.

The computer has an enormous ability to handle information, which has enabled scientists to study complexity. But it also has the ability to present its user with very little information: In its user interface, it makes use mainly of the bandwidth of language.

Information society can seem stressful because it contains not too much information but too little.

So in information society, people have to excite colossal amounts of exformation in order to do their jobs: Meaning has to be read into a few numbers on a computer monitor. There is no longer an abundance of detail and sensuality in the work process but a dry, cool minimal diet of information, which has to be "dressed" with exformation before it is meaningful.

Sensory poverty is on its way to becoming a major problem in society, provoking a cry for meaning amidst the flow of information. Man has moved down to a lower bandwidth, and he is getting bored.

In the long run, the problem is that nobody will traverse the material terrain anymore; people will merely sit plotting routes on a map. The linear civilization threatens to replace the terrain with a map, so that it will be only in his time off that man knows he possesses materiality; that the *I* is rooted in a *Me;* that his head is planted on a body.

Consciousness is taking man over: The straight line is vanquishing the crooked one, and the amount of information in life is getting too small.

The simulation of the world is replacing the world. Information is being discarded, and life is becoming a laborious attempt to climb higher up the tree on the basis of a smidgen of information from a TV screen.

To an increasing degree, politics will be about demands for *something to sense*. The demand will no longer be for clothes, food, and housing. We also want bits! The uprisings of the future will be under slogans such as *Senses Make Sense! Make Sense of the World! Common Sense Belongs to Everybody!*

Out of the boredom of artificial civilized life, new technologies are being introduced under the banner of *virtual reality*. One simply replaces the experience of eleven million bits a second from a beautiful forest with a corresponding eleven million bits a second from the same forest—or from the inside of a lobster pot, so we can feel what it is like to be a lobster. A TV over our eyes, headphones on our ears, and sensory gloves on our hands (and in the long run our whole bodies): We are in virtual reality, getting the bits we lack from the real, artificially created reality.

We are even being offered virtual sex—guaranteed free of HIV and any other differentness.

The author of *Alice in Wonderland*, the mathematician Lewis Carroll, predicted this development a hundred years ago when he wrote the story of "Sylvie and Bruno Concluded." At one point, the narrator meets a figure by the name of Mein Herr, with whom he exchanges the following remarks:

"Mein Herr looked so thoroughly bewildered that I thought it best to change the subject. 'What a useful thing a pocket-map is!' I remarked.

" 'That's another thing we've learned from *your* Nation,' said Mein Herr, 'map-making. But we've carried it much further than *you*. What do you consider the *largest* map that would be really useful?'

" 'About six inches to the mile.'

" 'Only *six inches!*' exclaimed Mein Herr. 'We very soon got to six yards to the mile. Then we tried a *hundred* yards to the mile. And then came the grandest idea of all! We actually made a map of the country, on the scale of a *mile* to the *mile!*'

" 'Have you used it much?' I enquired.

" 'It has never been spread out, yet,' said Mein Herr: 'the farmers objected: they said it would cover the whole country, and shut out the sunlight! So we now use the country itself, as its own map, and I assure you it does nearly as well.' "[14]

CHAPTER 16

THE SUBLIME

An almost inconceivable beauty rests over the Jemez Mountains at Rio Grande in northern New Mexico. Plateaus have been scarred by river courses and erosion, so precipitous walls rear up toward isolated islands of horizontality called *mesas,* after the Spanish word for "table." An orgy of soil colors adorns the steep walls of the tableland, which was created by volcanic activity still traceable in the hot springs that have given the mountains their name. *Jemez* is Indian for "place of the boiling springs."

The mountainous horizon around the plateaus endows the place with a unique alliance of open sky and closed land: one of the world's greatest enclosures, with a spaciousness that can contain even the grandest feelings of inspiration.

At the end of the 1930s, a physicist with a penchant for poetry crossed the mesas on horseback. A few years later, the U.S. government asked him to recommend a hideaway where a couple of dozen scientists could work in secret on a new weapon that there was reason to fear Hitler was developing too—a weapon that would do away with all the usual notions of warfare.

The young man, J. Robert Oppenheimer, recommended Los Alamos, a tiny community with a boy's school, set on a mesa northwest of Santa Fe. A few years later, when the Second World War had concluded with the detonation of the bombs over Hiroshima and Nagasaki, the scientific leader of the project declared that the physicists had sinned forever.

They had created the bomb in an incomprehensible fury of activity from March 1943, when they moved into Los Alamos, until August

1945, when Japan capitulated. It had been their belief that the bomb would be used only for demonstration purposes over desert areas; never against civilians. They had imagined that such a weapon would put an end to any ideas of war.

They were right, but there was a forty-five-year delay.

As recently as in the mid 1980s, the world was living beneath the shadow of the absurd possibility of the holocaust of nuclear war. The two superpowers, the U.S.A. and the U.S.S.R. had each built up an insane stock of weapons, more than fifty thousand bombs, sufficient to put an end to the life of every mammal on earth and knock out most other life on the planet. There was no lack of warnings, even before the first atom bomb was detonated.

During the war, Niels Bohr had warned the Western heads of state, and in 1950, in an open letter, the United Nations (and thus the general public), that the secrecy surrounding atom bombs would lead to "a fateful competition about the formidable weapon."[1]

But at the same time, Bohr argued for something else. Nuclear weapons held a hitherto unknown opportunity, a promise and "the means for making all mankind a co-operating unit": an open world.

Bohr's idea was so simple that it appeared to his contemporaries to be deeply naive: Nuclear weapons are so dangerous that they force nations to talk to each other about how to get them under control; with nuclear weapons, man has reached a technological stage where coexistence and conversation have become a necessity of life, whether one likes it or not.

"Closedness," fortifications, and isolation are no longer sustainable options. Nuclear weapons force people to open up to each other in dialogue.

The first decades after Bohr's open letter did not point in the direction he had foreseen. The 1960s saw a dramatic rearmament with nuclear weapons, where the U.S.S.R. began to achieve parity with the U.S.A. in terms of destructive power. Both parties acquired more and more weapons and more and more methods of delivering them to each other's territories: rockets, planes, submarines, intercontinental ballistic missiles. Throughout the 1960s, many Western critics of rearmament protested violently and aroused considerable public discussion. But it died slowly and until the end of the 1970s remained merely a rumble of angst that underlay society's activities.

But from the end of the 1970s, violent criticism grew across the globe and among military leaders in the two superpowers. The criticism focused on *the obvious insanity of the idea of nuclear war as defense:* Every military analyst knew that any use of nuclear weapons at all would lead to a complete exchange of the arsenals. The consequence of the use of nuclear weapons was mutual collective suicide.

The situation had in fact become critical. In the 1960s, the U.S.A. had far more arms than the U.S.S.R., which provided a certain stability. At the beginning of the 1970s, the two countries had approximately the same number of warheads, also a form of balance. But a technological transformation suddenly rendered the situation completely unstable: MIRV—a system for placing more than one warhead on a single missile, each aimed at a different target.

Before MIRV, a nuclear war would have been conducted like the phase of a chess game where the players swap pawns. Each party would launch its missiles against the enemy's missiles to destroy them. Each missile would use its payload to destroy one of the enemy's missiles and its payload. The atom bomb would be used to destroy the opposition's atom bombs on a one-to-one basis. This kind of pawn exchange meant that there was no real advantage in using one's nuclear weapons before the opposition did so. The situation, however absurd it may seem, was fundamentally stable: A first strike did not pay.

But MIRV changed the picture. With MIRV (Multiple Individually-targeted Reentry Vehicles), once the missile approached the enemy it dispatched each warhead to its own target. This changed the game completely: If each missile carried ten warheads, each capable of hitting one of the enemy's missiles, there was a major advantage in striking first. One missile takes out ten enemy missiles, each carrying ten warheads; just one of your missiles can destroy a hundred of the enemy's warheads. As soon as you had a well-founded suspicion that the enemy was going to use his weapons, you had better launch your own missiles to prevent him from launching his arsenal. For once he did so, you would not have many missiles of your own left.

MIRV rendered the nuclear balance of power unstable. Even military leaders of the highest rank began to be really afraid—on both sides.

Dramatic popular and political attention flared up through the first half of the 1980s, and after the middle of the decade, the situation suddenly changed drastically. Both superpowers showed an interest not only in stopping the arms race but also in genuine disarmament. The security of a superpower was suddenly inversely proportional to the number of nuclear weapons on the ground. For they were merely inducements to an enemy first strike.

In 1985, when the University of Copenhagen invited a large number of the world's worried nuclear weapons experts to a conference in connection with the hundredth anniversary of the birth of Niels Bohr, there was very great concern among the scientists.[2] Just four years later, when the same university invited the same participants to continue the debate, the mood had been transformed fundamentally: Optimism and relief ran through the otherwise professionally concerned scientists.[3]

This total change of mood occurred not just because the superpowers had begun to talk seriously about disarmament; primarily, the world realized that nuclear war was not a sensible military option. It had become clear that nuclear weapons simply cannot be used for defense.

The peculiar thing about this development is how people reacted to it. In the early 1980s, the threat of nuclear war was in the foreground of most people's consciousness. Almost everyone expressed views on the problem, through discussions or activities. Some thought that nuclear weapons were necessary to defend the West/the East; others believed they were absurd and a problem in themselves. But nobody was neutral or untouched.

Today it is as if the problem has disappeared. The weapons are mostly all still there, but there is practically nobody who imagines they will ever be employed in full-scale nuclear war, though there is fear of their use in local conflicts in the Third World. The situation is *radically different* from a decade ago.

What has happened? Few people have learned all the details of MIRV; there are actually very few treaties and pieces of legislation resulting in the scrapping of weapons; few weapons have actually been physically scrapped.

But the mood is totally transformed. So transformed that it no longer appears on the political agenda, nor does it dominate discussion in the social sciences. Considering that nuclear weapons were—with good reason—regarded a decade ago as humanity's greatest problem but are forgotten today, one must ask why nobody discusses just why they have been forgotten.

Of course, one can claim that it is simply because the enemy has disappeared; the collapse of world communism and the upheavals in Eastern Europe have led to the end of the Cold War. Capitalism has won, as they say. But as yet no situation has become established that is markedly stable. The army of the former U.S.S.R. is strongly opposed to what is happening in the now dissolved superpower, and it still has inconceivable stocks of nuclear weapons at its disposal.

In fact, the breakup of the Eastern bloc is more the result of the reduced tension in the nuclear arms field than a contributing factor to it. The end of the mutual paranoia preceded the thaw. The security advantages of scrapping one's arsenal were emphasized by the late peace specialist Anders Boserup, for example, before Gorbachev arrived and unleashed the dissolution of the Eastern bloc.[4]

What has happened is perhaps precisely what Niels Bohr dreamed about: The nuclear menace became so imminent and ominous that it forced the two superpowers to talk to each other; and when they began to do so, their leaders and their peoples (who became acquainted in various ways) realized that the others were not so hostile after all. People began to understand each other's concerns and troubles, and realized the rather comical situation they were both in. Just like two people who, having gotten off on the wrong foot, feel hatred or fear for each other: When they meet and have a good talk, all their paranoia and all the ghosts vanish like dew before the sun.

Nuclear weapons were created to defend the national state and defend the borders between peoples; but precisely because these weapons are so destructive, they are breaking down the closedness and national states they were created to defend.

Nuclear weapons were made to defend closedness but have led to openness. Nuclear weapons have utterly transcended the horizon within which they were created: the horizon of the national state. They have shown the world that national states are meaningless when weapons of ultimate destruction are available.

Nuclear weapons are an example of the way science and technology can *transcend their own horizon of origin* and lead to precisely the opposite of what they were intended for when they were created.

Other technologies, too, have transcended their horizon of origin—

for example, the technology for conquering space led to the understanding of the life on our planet; and the technology for carrying out computations led to the knowledge that we cannot compute everything.

The history of nuclear weapons is an example of what one might call *emergent politics:* A transformation has taken place without anybody really noticing or any legislation passing through a parliament. In the early 1980s, everyone was concerned by the problem of nuclear weapons, and practically everybody did something about it. Not many of us felt we were doing enough, but almost all of us did something: warned the children, went to meetings, supported movements, discussed it during the lunch hour, read a book about it, or asked about it at the sports club. Everybody did something that appeared completely insubstantial, indifferent, and insignificant, and was certainly not the reason why the problem suddenly began to thaw out and give way to our efforts.

But perhaps that *was* the reason: Perhaps it was precisely because an incredible number of people took up the issue at once, and all in their own way tried to do something, that an enormous phase transition suddenly took place and everybody suddenly saw that nuclear weapons are pretty odd things, which make no military sense.

Perhaps it was simply because enough individuals did what they could to improve the situation that the situation became improved. Even though we cannot trace the causal chain and identify the links, perhaps it was the sum of incomprehensibly many tiny actions that made the difference.

Many tiny activities in the right direction led to an enormous emergent transformation. Suddenly we all dared to believe that nuclear war was unthinkable. And it became so.

The above is naive. Very naive. But not necessarily wrong.

There is a very long tradition in the social sciences of understanding changes and structures in society through concepts of collective behavior: laws and developments that gain sway behind the individual's back, circumventing or even spiting our conscious perception of what we are up to. Especially, but not exclusively, the Marxist tradition has

emphasized that man's consciousness of what he does as part of society
is not reliable. The effect of our actions can be quite different from
what we believe. We can have a "false consciousness" about what we do;
the individual conscious experience is not necessarily the valid one.

This means that it is not necessarily acts of parliament or ballots that
determine the path of developments. Rather, they seem like tardy rationalizations of what has already taken place.

The most important changes in society occur as emergent effects of
actions the original intentions of which were not their final results.
Society can change overnight, not due to violent revolutions but due to
the effect of accumulated trifles. By and large, people cannot supervise
what they do.

What is the consequence of this naive view? That we should leave well
enough alone and forget all the conscious attempts to influence the
development of society? Lean back and wail like babies in the expectation that some kind of emergent effect will surely occur to solve the problem in ways we cannot foresee? Definitely not, not at all, precisely not.

Even if we assume that just as, in the "naive" analysis above, the
nuclear weapon problem disappeared due to a sudden emergent transformation, this does not mean it could have happened without an
abundance of tiny events. Niels Bohr's point was not that we should sit
with our hands in our laps; his point was that the talks between nations
forced on them by nuclear weapons would themselves pave the way for
an open world.

The disappearance of the nuclear weapon problem does not make
single one of those pamphlets, mass meetings, discussions at work,
and dialogues between peace activists and military leaders redundant.
On the contrary, the emergent change was precisely the result of
a whole army of parents discussing the problem at nursery school, of
politicians changing their minds, of proponents of nuclear weapons
entering into dialogue, of the horrors of nuclear war being depicted in
works of art, and of scientists computing the impossibility of treating
the casualties.

Emergent politics does not consist of leaving well enough alone; it
consists of acting according to one's convictions even when doing so
seems completely useless. Emergent politics consists of doing something one is completely convinced is good for oneself and the people
one knows, even if it seems naive. Emergent politics is an acceptance of
naïveté, not an acceptance of passiveness.

Emergent politics consists of doing what one feels is right, right there on the spot—and of changing if necessary. It is an acceptance that the most important thing one can do is to do something: to act and change in a way that is good as far as one can tell.

It is an acceptance, too, of the fact that because people know far more about each other than their consciousness knows, and because people do far more to each other than their consciousness knows about, it is not enough to decide on the right point of view and then convey it via the low bandwidth of language: One must simply do something that one believes is right to the depths of one's organism. Because the effects are greater than we are conscious of.

Consciousness must not direct our actions in the sense that we should do only what we realize consciously and on reflection is the most appropriate thing. We should do what our gut feeling tells us. We must take our own lives seriously, and thereby everybody else's. We must have the courage to believe that life is greater than we know.

As Niels Bohr did, we must have the courage to say naive things; do naive things, persistently and amicably over the decades, simply because we believe they are right and feel they are right and are conscious that they are right.

Then we are entitled to believe that we are doing our best. After all, we can do no more than that.

The touching naïveté of these views can be defended in only one way, by the question: How else can we explain that the nuclear weapons problem disappeared; that a whole world became aware of environmental problems at the end of the 1980s; that the populations of the wealthy nations are slowly realizing the necessity of solidarity with the poor ones?

How else can we explain that we are still here?

The American historian Morris Berman raises the problem of man's instinct for collective suicide. In his book *Coming to Our Senses*, published in 1989, Berman explains the instinct as a societal version of the individual's panicky fear of otherness. In industrialized cultures, everyone undergoes the traumatic separation between what is one-self and what is not (Self/Other); between what one is conscious of as oneself and what one is conscious of as different. The *I*-consciousness that originates in our first years of infancy causes a radical self-alienation, from which emerges the inextinguishable question of how to relate to otherness: the bestial, slimy, and spiderlike; the uncontrollable and corporeal and wild and primitive.

Berman interprets a great deal of modern history as civilization's attempt at solving the problem of otherness through zoos, pesticides, visual pornography, alcohol, and religions, all of which can control the wild stuff. The fundamental separation between a self and the world creates dread, disquiet, and loneliness. Culture puts taboos on blood, semen, spit, sweat, and other bodily fluids because they arouse this fundamental problem: the difference between my surroundings and myself. To modern man, the body is an unpleasant, frightening reminder that we ourselves are like the world: that in the final analysis we are nature, slimy inside.

"Nuclear holocaust is really a scientific vision of utopia, in which the world is finally expunged of the messy, organic, and unpredictable—by being wiped out—'purified.' Suicide, whether on the political, environmental, or personal level, is the ultimate (and most effective) solution to the problem of Otherness," Berman writes. Examples include not only nuclear war but extermination of the Jews, homosexuals, and other minorities by the Nazis, the way modern households exterminate spiders and tame wild animals as pets. Berman continues: "We shall solve it all, destroy any vestige of wild, disorganized Other entirely, so that Self now reigns supreme in a pure, dead and totally predictable world."[5]

Morris Berman's words seem strangely obsolescent, even though they are only a decade old. Oddly enough, the panicky dread and the feeling of imminent doom have vanished. Since nuclear war according to Berman is an attempt to solve the fundamental impotence of consciousness vis-à-vis both the world without and that within oneself, we may ask what it *means* that the danger of nuclear war has passed and the environmental crisis is something people are beginning to dare to face up to. Does it mean that our relationship to ourselves has in fact fundamentally changed? That a fundamental shift has occurred in man's balance between conscious and nonconscious in recent years?

My thoughts turned to the hot springs of the Jemez Mountains when the Siberian fisherman refused to sail out into the fog on open Lake Baikal. We changed course and camped for the night on a tiny beach beside the mighty Central

Siberian lake, which is the size of an ocean and contains 23 percent of all the planet's fresh water. Local biologists and environmentalists had invited Western theater people, musicians, and researchers to an environmental and cultural festival to draw attention to the pollution problems afflicting Lake Baikal. The area near the city of Ulan-Ude, where we were based, had until the year before the festival, in 1990, been closed territory, not just to foreigners but also to people from the other ends of the U.S.S.R. This area of wondrous beauty, home to spiritual powers and to the region's Tibetan Buddhists, is riddled with nuclear missile silos.

The opening up of Soviet society meant that we could visit this unique lake, which both geologically and biologically contains unique examples of the life of the planet. We were on our way to inspect an island on which a large flock of the unique Baikal seal resides, but in the fog we had to seek shelter for the night. This gave us time to bathe in the hot springs in the area.

In the dark Siberian summer nights we could hear the locals singing their mournful songs about Baikal, beautiful brooding plaints. The wonderful desolate countryside around Baikal has always been used for prison camps for enemies of the czar, Stalin, and others in power. Almost all the songs about Baikal tell of prisoners who try to flee across the mighty lake and make their way back to society from captivity, where they have been locked out amidst the beauty.

The thought that this magnificent natural area and its proud, thrifty fishermen should be the enemy of another superpower appeared so shudderingly insane that the only possible explanation for the hostility, which had now begun to thaw, was simple ignorance and paranoia, derived from closedness. These people might be different and their lives poorer than where we came from, but to bomb this lake and its fishermen back to the ice age seemed incomprehensible and inconceivable.

It was just as beautiful here as in the Jemez Mountains of New Mexico. In one place, the atom bomb had been invented. In the other, people had been ordered to shut the rest of the world out because the bomb was present here. The spiritual and temporal leader of the Buddhists, the Dalai Lama, has declared both landscapes sacred.

In neither place did it seem that the beauty was quite bearable. In both places, 1990 was the year in which the industrial culture began to invite the people's culture to participate in a dialogue about how we manage nature. In New Mexico, it was the Indians; in Siberia, the Mongolian tribesfolk, who were invited down from the mountains to sing and dance and talk of a cleaner lake.

When the turn came for us Western Europeans to explain why we had come all this way to attend a festival for a lake, no lengthy speech proved necessary.

The interpreter listened to my draft for the address and said, "Dostoyevsky says the same thing: 'Beauty will save the world.' "⁶

Information is a measure of unpredictability, disorder, mess, chaos, amazement, indescribability, surprise, otherness. Order is a measure of the opposite.

Consciousness does not consist of very much information and regards itself as order. It is proud that by discarding information it can reduce all the disorder and confusion around it to simple, predictable laws for the origin of phenomena.

Civilization consists of social and technological organization that rids our lives of information. As civilization has progressed, it has enabled the withdrawal of consciousness from the world.

It has enabled a worldview in which the acknowledged picture of the world is identified with the world; where the map is identified with the terrain; where the *I* denies the existence of the *Me;* where all otherness is disclaimed, except in the form of a divine principle; where man can live only if he believes that the *otherness* is also *good.*

But consciousness has also reached the age of composure. Through conscious studies of man and his consciousness, it has become clear that man is much more than his consciousness. It has become clear that people perceive far more than consciousness knows; that people do far more than their consciousness knows. The simulation of the world about us, which we experience and believe is the world itself, is made possible only through systematic illusions and reductions that result from discarding most of the unpredictable otherness that imbues the world outside us.

The conscious *I* must realize that it cannot account for the world out there. The formal and unequivocal description we can give of the world will never ever be able to predict or even describe that world exhaustively. The richness of a simplified formal description that can be contained in a consciousness with a bandwidth as low as ours will never be sufficient to describe the richness of what is different and outside us.

Inside us, in the person who carries consciousness around, cognitive and mental processes take place that are far richer than consciousness can know or describe. Our bodies contain a fellowship with a surrounding world that passes right through us, in through our mouths and out the other end, but is hidden from our consciousness. The body is part of a mighty living system, which totally forms and manages a planet that has caught life.

The conscious *I* can account for neither the World Without nor the World Within—and not, therefore, for the link between the World Without and the World Within.

The religious philosopher Martin Buber belongs to the Hasidic movement that arose among Polish Jews in the 1700s. Its point is that union with the divinity is attained not by turning one's back on the world but by going out into the world with one's whole being, right in the middle of things. What is sacred is the enjoyment of life here and now. In his famous book *Ich und Du* ("I and Thou"), from 1923, Buber writes of God as "the wholly Other" but also as "the wholly Same, the wholly Present." God changes and transforms, but is also "the mystery of the self-evident, nearer to me than my I."[7]

Both the World Without and the World Within are closer to my *Me* than to my *I*. The World Without and the World Within are more closely related to each other than to my *I*.

In 1930, Kurt Gödel described how a limited formal system could never be complete and free of contradiction at once. How a finite description would never be able to describe an infinite world.

Consciousness will never be able to describe the world, neither within nor without itself. Both the person who is within and the world that is without are richer than consciousness can know. They each constitute a depth that can be charted and described, but not exhaustively known. They have links that consciousness cannot know about. Together, these depths, the inner and the outer, could be called "Gödel's Deep," and we could say that consciousness floats in Gödel's Deep: The *I* floats in Gödel's Deep.

Gödel's theorem is based on a modern version of the liar paradox, which was discovered in ancient Greece when consciousness made its breakthrough. "I am a liar," the simplest version runs; "All Cretans lie" is a version from antiquity formulated by Epimenides of Crete.

Consciousness gave man the faculty of lying; of making assertions that are not true; of maintaining a gap between what is said and what is meant.

The content of the modern version, Gödel's theorem, has been formulated by the Polish philosopher Alfred Tarski as the knowledge that it is impossible for a statement to prove about itself whether it is true or false.

What is characteristic of the statement "I am a liar" is therefore not the word "liar," even though it gave the paradox its name. What is characteristic is the word "I"—a speaker speaking about his own speech.

It is self-reference that is the problem. The body cannot lie. Its bandwidth is too high for that. But the *I* can. In fact, the *I* can do nothing else. The *I* refers to itself as if it were the *Me*. But it is not. The *I* simulates being the *Me*, having control of the *Me*. But the *I* is just a map of the *Me*. A map can lie. A terrain cannot.

"I am a liar" is not a liar paradox. It is the truth about consciousness.

Consciousness is a wonderful creation, brought about by biological evolution on earth. An eternal awareness, a bold interpretation, a life-giving measure.

But consciousness is about to retain composure by appreciating that it does not master the world; that an understanding of simple rules and principles of predictability in the world does not provide the possibility of guessing what the world is like.

Consciousness is not very old, but it has changed our world in the course of the few thousand years it has dominated human life. It has brought about so much change that it is falling victim to the mechanisms that created it. Consciousness pretends that the simulation of the world it experiences is the actual sensation of the world; that what people consciously experience *is* what they sense; and that what they sense *is* the world itself.

A consciousness that is not conscious that it is just consciousness, and not the world as it really is, has therefore become a danger to itself. Man can perceive and become aware of rapid changes in his surroundings. Consciousness has developed in order for us to be aware of certain forms of change in our surroundings. It seeks out rapid shifts, flashing lights, and known dangers.

But the civilization that consciousness has created is now creating a completely new form of change: slow change, insidious change, global change—the extinction of species and the erosion of the terrestrial environment.

The environmental crisis is exposing mankind to dangers and challenges toward which our attention is not automatically directed. As a species, we have learned to be aware of factors in our surroundings that no longer represent the true dangers.

"The world that made us is now gone, and the world we made is a new world, one that we have developed little capacity to comprehend," write cognitive scientist Robert Ornstein and biologist Paul Ehrlich in their book *New World, New Mind.*[8]

The two scientists argue that we human beings will have to change our way of perceiving the world. "Civilization is threatened by changes taking place over years and decades, but changes over a few years or decades are too *slow* for us to perceive readily."[9]

We must therefore, they argue, create "a new evolutionary process, a process of conscious evolution. . . . We need to replace our old minds with new ones."[10] A new form of education and training must help new generations to learn to apprehend the world in a way that is relevant to the problems the world is facing. Schools and universities will have to tell students about visual illusions, unconscious experiences, and how to "adapt to change," for *"the only thing constant in life is change itself."*[11]

Ornstein and Ehrlich, then, suggest a consciously trained change in consciousness as the answer to the problems consciousness has created. We must learn to know what we do not know: learn to be aware of the fact that we are not aware of everything; learn to be conscious that consciousness is limited.

A genuine, necessary strategy, certainly, which corresponds completely to the fact that the scientific-technological tradition is an absolute necessity if we are to solve the pollution problems created by the scientific-technological tradition. But the question is whether more is required than a change in the way we teach future generations; more than a change *in* our consciousness.

The question is whether there must be a change in the way we live; in the values we set for what it means to be human and to live a good life; a reassessment of the role of consciousness in our existence.

There is one value that almost everybody seeks out and sets store by: a value that concerns the utmost and most wonderful thing about being human. A word we use for describing actions and thoughts, landscapes and scenes, experiences and intercourse, exertions and achievements when they are most entrancing: the *sublime*.

When a ballet dancer, a singer, or an instrumentalist pull our attention toward them and make us quiver with presence; when a sudden remark refines weeks of argument to a simple idea that suddenly grasps everything that is positive about a situation; when a piece of carpentry executed with incomparable beauty testifies to total artisanal devotion; when a session with friends is imbued with total openness and ebullient feelings of togetherness—we talk of the sublime.

The word possesses the dull ring of intellectual snobbery and sophistication, yet still it is susceptible to the idiom "from the sublime to the ridiculous there is only one step."[12]

The word "sublime" comes from Latin and means elevated, raised above the ordinary and humdrum. More precisely, "sublime" derives from two words: *sub*, "under," and *limen*, "roof, threshold, or lintel." The sublime is something that rises toward an upper limit; actually, "what rises up in an oblique line."[13] The word shares the same root as "subliminal," described in Chapter Seven, which in psychology refers to perception beneath the threshold that applies to conscious awareness.

Not only are the words related; the phenomena are also. In a sublime artistic performance, the artist draws on far more information than consciousness can administer. The great artist dares let herself give far more than she consciously controls.

In a sublime performance, the *Me* is given permission by the *I:* There is such trust present that art comes to life.

Similarly, it is characteristic of the great feat of athletics, the great thought process, the great piece of craftsmanship, that an enormous amount of information and experience is processed; far more than consciousness can control.

In social contexts, too, we seek situations where we dare to let our hair down and be there for and with each other without worrying about how we appear to the others; thus, in conversation, in bed, or in the kitchen, we can give our all. The untranslatable Danish word *hygge*[14] covers situations in which we do not veto ourselves constantly but simply live, confident in each other's company. In moments of *hygge*, we may experience a sublime togetherness.

The sublime comprises situations and feats where consciousness trusts the person sufficiently to let life flow freely.

Seeking the sublime is not the same as seeking the absence of consciousness. It is seeking such well-prepared, familiar confidence in tasks and surroundings that one may give one's all. The way to this confidence and *hygge* does in fact pass through the *I*, for it is the discipline in life and its social relationships, and the discipline in acquiring a skill that is the domain of the *I*, which provide access to the confidence and familiarity that allow the *Me* to be given a chance of practicing the skill to the full.

There is no real conflict between consciousness and the sublime, for consciousness is the way to the sublime; discipline is the way to improvisation; stability is the way to surprise; cohesion is the way to openness.

But consciousness is only the servant of the sublime: the method by which we may attain the feeling of familiarity, confidence, and closeness that means we dare to give. Consciousness is not a goal in itself; it is a means to being here now. Without consciousness.

Experience can be more than subliminal: It can also be sublime. The sublime experience is the one where we draw on our entire apparatus for experiencing and dare to mark the world as it really is: chaotic and contradictory, dread-provoking and menacing, painful and merry.

Experiencing the state of the planet can generate angst and disquiet, because there are problems on the globe. But perhaps precisely this is the way to getting something done about the problems: Trust that we dare take our own experience seriously is the way to daring to experience what is, even if it is unpleasant.

Theodore Roszak claimed in 1979 that there was a close relationship between the *needs of a planet* and the *needs of a person*. That the environmental crisis manifests itself in our minds as a personal problem. That we can understand the state of the globe from our own bodies and from our own dread. The road to a more sustainable civilization is therefore through our willingness to dare to take note of ourselves. Only when we dare to do so can we take care of our own world: the planet we are so related to. We must learn to dare to be persons, Roszak wrote in his book *Person/Planet.*[15]

The sublime as a value is the emphasis on the value of consciousness when it is in equilibrium with the nonconscious interaction with the world, which is so much richer in information, otherness, surprises, slime, spiders, and snubs than our consciousness can ever be.

It is the emphasis on the fact that we can never guess what the world is like even if we know its laws; that we can never lend words to or make rules for everything we can do; that most skills must necessarily remain languageless and can be demonstrated only as an ability, such as riding a bike or having a green thumb.

Søren Kierkegaard's doctorate was titled *On the Concept of Irony with Reference to Socrates.* At the final assumption of power by consciousness in ancient Greece, that greatest of all the philosophical personalities in history continued to recognize the wisdom of unschooled man. Through his technique of asking questions, Socrates led a peasant slave to derive Pythagoras' theorem (of right-angled triangles), even though the man was ignorant of geometry. The moral was that we do know everything already but we cannot always put it into words.

Kierkegaard writes, "Socrates' purpose was *not* to make *the abstract concrete,* but through the immediately concrete to allow *the abstract* to *appear.*"[16]

We can derive knowledge from the world; but we cannot derive the world from knowledge.

The culture and civilization of consciousness has celebrated huge triumphs, but it also creates huge problems. The more power consciousness has over existence, the greater the problem of its paucity of information becomes. Civilization fills people with a lack of otherness and contradiction, which leads to the same kind of insanity we find in dictators surrounded by yes-men.

It is important to dare to be pleased that we are not in full control, are not conscious all the time; to enjoy the liveliness of nonconsciousness and combine it with the discipline and reliability of consciousness. Life is really more fun when you are not conscious of it.

Consciousness does not contain much information, for information is otherness and unpredictability. Consciousness will find composure by acknowledging that people need more information than consciousness can supply. Man also needs the information contained in consciousness, just as we need a map to find our way around the terrain. But what really counts is not knowing the map—it is knowing the terrain.

The world is far richer than we know from looking at a map of it. We ourselves are far richer than we know from looking at the map of ourselves.

Joy, physical pleasure and love, the sacred and the sublime, are not so far away as consciousness thinks. Human consciousness, floating freely in Gödel's Deep, is not in as much trouble as it thinks in its dread of otherness: only half a second ago, I was *Me*.

Heaven is only half a second away—in the other direction.

"What is done by what is called myself is, I feel, done by something greater than myself in me," said James Clerk Maxwell.

He did not suffer from the user illusion.

NOTES

Chapter 1: Maxwell's Demon

1. Ludwig Boltzmann, in Theodor Des Coudres, "Ludwig Boltzmann, Nekrolog," *Berichte über die Verhandlungen der königlich sächsischen Gesellschaft der Wissenschaften zu Leipzig, Mathamatisch-Physische Klasse* 58 (1906), 615–627; here p. 622. The Goethe quote is from *Faust*, which Boltzmann regarded as "perhaps the greatest of all works of art": see Engelbert Broda, *Ludwig Boltzmann, Man—Physicist—Philosopher* (Woodbridge, Conn.: Ox Bow Press, 1983), pp. 21, 33.

2. James Clerk Maxwell, "On Faraday's Lines of Force" (1855–56), *The Scientific Papers of James Clerk Maxwell* (Cambridge University Press, 1890), vol. 1, p. 155.

3. Heinrich Herz, in Morris Kline, *Mathematics and the Search for Knowledge* (New York: Oxford University Press, 1985), p. 144.

4. Letter dated 4 February 1882 from Professor F. J. A. Hort to Professor L. Campbell, in Lewis Campbell and William Garnett, *The Life of James Clerk Maxwell*, rev. ed. (London: Macmillan, 1884), pp. 322–26, here p. 326. The letter refers to two conversations during "Maxwell's last illness." Ivan Tolstoy, *James Clerk Maxwell: A Biography* (Edinburgh: Canongate, 1981), p. 85, and Martin Goldman, *The Demon in the Aether: The Story of James Clerk Maxwell* (Edinburgh: Paul Harris, 1983), p. 69, both mention that the conversation with Hort took place "on his deathbed." The context in which Campbell and Garnett quote Hort's letter also indicates the justification of mentioning the statement to Hort as a deathbed statement: death came (pp. 316–26) just afterward, according to accounts by the priest who administered the last rites, the doctor who attended Maxwell at the end, and a close relative who was present.

5. James Clerk Maxwell, "Recollections of Dreamland," in Campbell and Garnett (note 4), pp. 391–93, here p. 393. See also Tolstoy (note 4), pp. 84–5.

6. W. Zurek, ed., *Complexity, Entropy and the Physics of Information*, Santa Fe Institute Studies in the Sciences of Complexity, vol. 8 (Redwood City, Cal.: Addison-Wesley, 1990), p. vii.

7. John Wheeler at Santa Fe Institute workshop on "Complexity, Entropy and the Physics of Information," April 16–21, 1990. I am grateful to the chairman of

the workshop, Wojcieh Zurek, Los Alamos National Laboratory, for allowing me to attend the meeting and to Danish physicist Steen Rasmussen, Los Alamos, for establishing contact.

8. Ludwig Boltzmann, in Martin J. Klein, *Paul Ehrenfest*, vol. 1: *The Making of a Theoretical Physicist*, 3d ed. (Amsterdam: North-Holland, 1985), p. 77.

9. Ibid., p. 76.

10. On the link between the scientific argument and Boltzmann's suicide, see, e.g., Broda (note 1), pp. 29–33, and Klein (note 8), pp. 75–7.

11. Harvey P. Leff and Andrew F. Rex, *Maxwell's Demon: Entropy, Information, Computing* (Princeton University Press, 1990), p. 2.

12. Letter to Peter Guthrie Tait, in Martin Goldman (note 4), p. 123.

13. Letter to Tait, in Leff and Rex (note 11), p. 5.

14. Ibid., p. 290.

15. Letter to J. W. Strutt (Lord Rayleigh), in ibid., p. 290.

16. William Thomson, "Kinetic Theory of the Dissipation of Energy," *Nature* 9 (1874), 441–44, in Leff and Rex (note 11), pp. 34–6, here p. 34.

17. James Clerk Maxwell, "Diffusion," *The Scientific Papers of James Clerk Maxwell*, vol. 2, pp. 625–46, here pp. 645–46. According to Daub in Leff and Rex (note 11), p. 41, the article is said to be from the *Encyclopaedia Britannica*, 9th ed., 1878.

Chapter 2: Throwing Away Information

1. Leo Szilard, "Über die Entropieverminderung in einem thermodynamischen System bei Eingriffen intelligenter Wesen," *Zeitschrift für Physik* 53 (1929), 840–56, quoted from the translation printed in Leff and Rex, *Maxwell's Demon*, pp. 124–33, here p. 127.

2. Edward E. Daub, "Maxwell's Demon," *Stud. Hist. Phil. Sci.* 1 (1970), 189–211, in Leff and Rex (note 1), pp. 37–51, here p. 48.

3. Ibid., p. 49.

4. Ibid., pp. 48–49.

5. Rolf Landauer, "Computation, Measurement, Communication and Energy Dissipation," in P. Haykin, ed., *Selected Topics in Signal Processing* (Englewood Cliffs, N.J.: Prentice-Hall, 1989), p. 18.

6. Leff and Rex (note 1), p. 16. See also p. 20 on the criticism of Szilard's successor, Brillouin. Rudolf Carnap's criticism anticipates later arguments by physicists.

7. L. Brillouin, "Maxwell's Demon Cannot Operate: Information and Entropy. I," *J. Appl. Phys.* 22 (1951), 334–37, in Leff and Rex (note 1), pp. 134–37.

8. Leon Brillouin, *Science and Information Theory* (New York: Academic Press, 1956). The book was vastly influential. L. Brillouin, "Life, Thermodynamics, and Cybernetics," *Am. Sci.* 37 (1949), 554–68, in Leff and Rex (note 1), pp. 89–103.

9. Brillouin (note 7), p. 134.

10. Ibid.

11. Ibid., p. 136.

12. Brillouin (note 8), p. 168.

13. Charles Bennett, "Demons, Engines and the Second Law," *Scientific American* 257:5 (1987), 88–96, here p. 96.

14. Seth Lloyd, "Use of Mutual Information to Decrease Entropy: Implications for the Second Law of Thermodynamics," *Physical Review A* 39 (1989), 5378–86, here p. 5384, col. 1.

15. There are 6×10^{23} molecules in a mole of air (22 liters). The total bandwidth of the brain is 10^{12} bits per second and life lasts approximately 2×10^9 seconds.

16. Bennett (note 13), p. 96.

17. Martin J. Klein, "Maxwell, His Demon, and the Second Law of Thermodynamics," *Am. Sci.* 58 (1970), 84–97, in Leff and Rex (note 1), pp. 75–88, here p. 84.

18. This example is thanks to David Layzer, *Cosmogenesis* (New York: Oxford University Press, 1990), pp. 25–7.

19. Edwin Jaynes, in Leff and Rex (note 1), p. 17.

20. Paul Feyerabend quoted in Engelbert Broda, *Ludwig Boltzmann*, (Woodbridge, Conn.: Ox Bow Press, 1983) p. *v.*

21. K. G. Denbigh and J. S. Denbigh, *Entropy in Relation to Incomplete Knowledge* (Cambridge University Press, 1985), p. 104.

22. Søren Brunak and Benny Lautrup, *Neurale netværk* (Neural Networks) (Copenhagen: Munksgaard, 1988), p. 44. Karl Steinbuch, *Automat und Mensch* (Berlin: Springer-Verlag, 1965), p. 263.

23. John R. Pierce and Michael Noll, *Signals* (New York: W. H. Freeman, 1990), p. 50.

24. Norbert Wiener, *Cybernetics or Control and Communication in the Animal and the Machine* (Cambridge, Mass.: The MIT Press, 1961 [orig. 1948]), p. 10.

25. Ibid., p. 11.

26. Brillouin (note 7), pp. 134–35, and *Science and Information Theory* (note 8), p. 161, where Brillouin claims that it was Shannon who used the term. See also Leff and Rex (note 1), pp. 6–7, 18–21, 28–9.

27. As told to the author; printed in a slightly different version in Peder Voetmann Christiansen, "Informationens elendighed," in Thomas Söderqvist, *Informationssamfundet*, (Copenhagen: Forlaget Philosophia, 1985), pp. 61–72, here p. 63.

28. Richard P. Feynman, R. B. Leighton, and M. Sands, *The Feynman Lectures on Physics* (Reading, Mass.: Addison-Wesley, 1977 [orig. 1963]), vol. I, pp. 46–7.

CHAPTER 3: INFINITE ALGORITHMS

1. David Hilbert, in Constance Reid, *Hilbert* (New York: Springer-Verlag, 1970), reprinted in Reid, *Hilbert-Courant* (Springer-Verlag, 1986), p. 196.

2. Hilbert, in Morris Kline, *Mathematics: The Loss of Certainty* (New York: Oxford University Press, 1980), p. 259.

3. Reid (note 1), p. 195.

4. Ibid., p. 196.

5. Ibid.

6. See John W. Dawson, Jr., "The Reception of Gödel's Incompleteness Theorems," *Philosophy of Science Association* 2 (1984), printed in P. G. Shanker, ed., *Gödel's Theorem in Focus* (London: Routledge, 1988), pp. 74–95, here pp. 76–8; and Hao Wang, *Reflections on Kurt Gödel* (Cambridge, Mass.: The MIT Press, 1987), p. 85. Historians and biographers imply that Gödel's announcement came at

the same meeting as Hilbert's address—e.g., Andrew Hodges writes in Alan Turing, *The Enigma of Intelligence* (London: Unwin Paperbacks, 1985 [orig. 1983]), p. 92, that it occurred "at the very same meeting." But according to Wang, Hilbert's address was given "presumably on 9 September," while many sources place Gödel's announcement on 7 September. However, there is no doubt that the two events took place within a couple of days and in the same town.

7. See Dawson (note 6), p. 78, and Wang (note 6), p. 87.
8. Paul Bernays, in Reid (note 1), p. 198.
9. Reid (note 1), p. 220.
10. Bertrand Russell, in Dawson (note 6), p. 90.
11. Kurt Gödel, "Über formal unentscheidbare Sätze der Principia mathematica und verwandter Systeme I," in Kurt Gödel, *Collected Works*, vol. I (S. Feferman et al., eds.), (New York: Oxford University Press, 1986), pp. 144–94, here p. 148.
12. Stephen C. Kleene, "The Work of Kurt Gödel," *The Journal of Symbolic Logic* 41: 4 (1976), printed in Shanker (note 6), pp. 48–71, here p. 54.
13. Hodges (note 6), p. 92.
14. Roger Penrose, *The Emperor's New Mind* (London: Vintage, 1990 [orig. 1988]), p. 141.
15. Johannes Witt-Hansen, *Videnskabernes historie i det 20. århundrede: Filosofi* (Copenhagen: Gyldendal, 1985), e.g., pp. 196, 206.
16. Solomon Feferman, "Kurt Gödel: Conviction and Caution" (1983), in Shanker (note 6), pp. 96–114, here p. 113, footnote 18, where the dating of Gödel's publication is compared to the year of Hilbert's death.
17. Ibid., p. 96.
18. Ibid., p. 111.
19. Wang (note 6), pp. 133–34. See also John W. Dawson, "Kurt Gödel in Sharper Focus," *The Mathematical Intelligencer* 6: 4 (1984), in Shanker (note 6), pp. 1–16, here pp. 7, 12. Also Shanker, p. 84 (Dawson) and pp. 96, 111 (Feferman).
20. Wang (note 6), p. 46. The quote is from "Some Facts About Kurt Gödel," based on conversations between Wang and Gödel in 1975–76. Gödel suggested the title himself and gave Wang permission to publish an article after his death. Its tone is thus appropriate, although there are factual errors (see Dawson, note 19), p. 14, ref. 1.
21. Hodges (note 6), p. 109.
22. Kline (note 2), Preface.
23. Rudy Rucker, *Mind Tools. The Five Levels of Mathematical Reality* (London: Penguin Books, 1988 [orig. 1987]), p. 226.
24. For more on the philosophers, see Witt-Hansen (note 15), p. 207. It is worth noting that according to Witt-Hansen, Tarski presented his analysis as early as 21 March 1931.
25. Douglas Hofstadter, *Gödel, Escher, Bach—An Eternal Golden Braid* (Harmondsworth: Penguin Books, 1980 [orig. 1979]).
26. Ian Stewart, "The Ultimate in Undecidability," *Nature* 332 (1988), 115–16, here p. 116.
27. Gregory J. Chaitin, "Gödel's Theorem and Information," *International Journal of Theoretical Physics* 22 (1982), 941–54; reprinted in Chaitin, *Information, Ran-*

domness and Incompleteness (Singapore: World Scientific, 1987), pp. 55–65, here p. 55.

28. Stewart (note 26), p. 116.

29. Gregory J. Chaitin, "Randomness in Arithmetic," *Scientific American* 259:1 (July 1988), 52–7, here pp. 56–7.

30. Ibid., p. 57.

31. W. H. Zurek, "Algorithmic Information Content, the Church-Turing Thesis, Physical Entropy, and Maxwell's Demon," in Zurek, ed., *Complexity, Entropy and the Physics of Information,* pp. 73–89.

32. Ibid., p. 85.

33. Proceedings from 1990 meeting not available at time of writing. But the content of the discussions is touched upon by Zurek (note 31), Carlton Caves, "Entropy and Information: How Much Information Is Needed to Assign a Probability?" in Zurek (note 31), pp. 91–113, particularly pp. 112–13, and Caves, "Quantitative Limits on the Ability of a Maxwell Demon to Extract Work from Heat," *Physical Review Letters* 64 (1990), 2111–14. Bill Unruh is thanked p. 2114, sp. 2, for a good question (here put to Caves). The formulation in the Watergate question is also present in this paper (p. 2112), which was accepted in 1989—i.e., before Zurek's address in April 1990. Caves is very explicit in crediting Zurek for the central results of the discussion. But I cannot be sure that at the meeting in 1990 I was adequately aware of Zurek's verbal thanks to Caves.

34. Caves, in Zurek (note 33), p. 113.

35. W. H. Zurek, "Thermodynamic Cost of Computation, Algorithmic Complexity and the Information Metric," *Nature* 341 (1989), 119–24.

36. Bernd-Olaf Küppers, *Information and the Origin of Life* (Cambridge, Mass.: The MIT Press, 1990 [German ed. 1986]), p. 106.

CHAPTER 4: THE DEPTH OF COMPLEXITY

1. Heinz Pagels, *The Dreams of Reason: The Computer and the Rise of the Sciences of Complexity* (New York: Bantam Books, 1989 [1st ed. 1988]), p. 66.

2. Feynman, Leighton, and Sands, *The Feynman Lectures on Physics,* Chapter 46, p. 5.

3. Stephen Wolfram, "Undecidability and Intractability in Theoretical Physics," *Physical Review Letters* 54 (1985), 735–38.

4. Stephen Wolfram, "Computer Software in Science and Mathematics," *Scientific American* 251:3 (1984), 140–51, here p. 151.

5. Stephen Wolfram, "Cellular Automata as Models of Complexity," *Nature* 311 (1984), 419–24, here p. 419.

6. Peter Grassberger, "How to Measure Self-Generated Complexity," *Physica* 140A (1986), 319–25, here p. 321. This volume of *Physica A* contains Invited Lectures from the 16th International Conference on Thermodynamics and Statistical Mechanics, Boston University, August 11–15, 1986.

7. Peter Grassberger, "Toward a Quantitative Theory of Self-Generated Complexity," *International Journal of Theoretical Physics* 25 (1986), 907–44, here p. 908. This article is based on a lecture at a seminar on cellular automata in Lisbon.

8. B. A. Huberman and T. Hogg, "Complexity and Adaptation," *Physica* 22D (1986), 376–84. A preprint of the article was circulated in 1985.

9. Herbert A. Simon, "The Architecture of Complexity," *Proceedings of the American Philosophical Society* 106 (1962), 467–82. Grassberger credits Simon in footnote 8 in P. Grassberger, "Problems in Quantifying Self-Generated Complexity," MS.

10. Grassberger (note 6), p. 325, and Grassberger (note 7), p. 938; see also footnote 2, orig. p. 908.

11. Charles Bennett, "Logical Depth and Physical Complexity," in Rolf Herken, *The Universal Turing Machine. A Half-Century Survey*, Oxford University Press, 1988, pp. 227–57, here p. 230. An almost identical passage is to be found in Bennett, "Dissipation, Information, and the Definition of Organization," in David Pines, ed., *Emerging Synthesis in Science* (Reading, Mass.: Addison-Wesley, 1987), pp. 297–313; see Pagels (note 1), p. 66. The idea of logical depth is first mentioned with Bennett as the source in Gregory Chaitin, "Algorithmic Information Theory," *IBM J. Rep. Develop.* 21 (1977), 350–59, reprinted in Chaitin, *Information, Randomness and Incompleteness*, pp. 38–52, here p. 48.

12. Charles H. Bennett, "On the Nature and Origin of Complexity in Discrete, Homogenous, Locally-Interacting Systems," *Foundations of Physics* 16 (1986), 585–92, here p. 585.

13. Charles Bennett, "How to Define Complexity in Physics, and Why," in Zurek, *Complexity, Entropy and the Physics of Information*, pp. 137–48.

14. Seth Lloyd, "The Calculus of Intricacy," *The Sciences* 30:5 (1990), 38–44. See also Grassberger (note 9).

15. Hans Kuhn, "Origin of Life and Physics: Diversified Microstructure-Inducement to Form Information-Carrying and Knowledge-Accumulating Systems," *IBM J. Rep. Develop.* 32:1 (1988), 37–46.

16. Seth Lloyd and Heinz Pagels, "Complexity as Thermodynamic Depth," *Annals of Physics* 188 (1988), 186–213, here p. 187.

17. Seth Lloyd, interview, Pasadena, Cal., 29 March 1991.

18. Rolf Landauer, "A Simple Measure of Complexity," *Nature* 336 (1988), 306–7, here p. 307.

19. W. H. Zurek, "Thermodynamic Cost of Computation, Algorithmic Complexity and the Information Metric," *Nature* 341 (1989), 119–24, here p. 124.

20. Landauer (note 19), p. 306.

21. Ibid., p. 306.

22. Among the other suggestions for measures of complexity that express ideas closely related to the notions of depth, the following deserves special emphasis: James P. Crutchfield and Karl Young, "Inferring Statistical Complexity," *Physical Review Letters* 63 (1989), 105–8.

CHAPTER 5: THE TREE OF TALKING

1. *The Guinness Book of Records 1996*, Facts on File, Inc., 1995, Arts and Entertainment section, Literature subsection, Diaries and Letters sub-subsection, page 141.

2. Sybille Kramer-Friedrich, "Information Measurement and Information Tech-

nology: A Myth of the Twentieth Century," *Boston Studies in the Philosophy of Science* 90 (1986), pp. 17–28.

3. Theodore Roszak, *The Cult of Information* (New York: Pantheon, 1986), pp. 15–16.

4. Pedro II, in John R. Pierce and A. Michael Noll, *Signals: The Science of Telecommunications* (New York: Scientific American Library, 1990), p. 17.

5. Claude Shannon, "The Mathematical Theory of Communication," in Claude E. Shannon and Warren Weaver, *The Mathematical Theory of Communication* (Urbana: The University of Illinois Press, 1963 [originally 1949]), pp. 3–91, here p. 3.

6. Warren Weaver, "Recent Contributions to the Mathematical Theory of Communication," in Shannon and Weaver (note 5), pp. 94–117, here p. 99.

7. Ibid., p. 99.

8. Ibid., p. 100 (Weaver's italics).

9. Kenneth M. Sayre, "Intentionality and Information Processing: An Alternative Model for Cognitive Science," *The Behavioral and Brain Sciences* 9 (1986), 121–66, here p. 125.

10. Donald M. MacKay, "The Nomenclature of Information Theory with Postscript on Structural Information-Content and Optical Resolution" (orig. 1950), in Donald M. MacKay, *Information, Mechanism and Meaning* (Cambridge, Mass.: The MIT Press, 1969), pp. 156–77, here p. 171.

11. Wendell R. Garner, *Uncertainty and Structure as Psychological Concepts* (New York: John Wiley, 1962), p. 15.

12. Fred I. Dretske, "Précis of Knowledge and the Flow of Information," *The Behavioral and Brain Sciences* 6 (1983), pp. 55–90.

13. Sayre (note 9), p. 131. The reference from p. 131, col. 1, chap. 9.1, to Kenneth M. Sayre, *Cybernetics and the Philosophy of Mind* (London: Routledge & Kegan Paul, 1976), contains only the information in the reference, cf. p. 160 of the book, ref. 6.

14. Weaver (note 6), p. 116.

15. Rolf Landauer, "Dissipation and Noise Immunity in Computation and Communication," *Nature* 335 (1988), 779–784. Results first published in 1987 (ref. 36 in the above article).

16. Landauer cited in John Horgan, "Profile: Claude E. Shannon," *Scientific American* 262:1 (1990), 16–19.

17. Ben Schumacher, "How Much Does Information Weigh?" Paper at "Complexity, Entropy and Physics of Information" workshop, Santa Fe Institute, 20 April 1990.

18. The idea that meaning is constituted not through the act of communication but in the subject was launched by the German philosopher Edmund Husserl in his *Studies in Logic* (1900–1901); I am grateful to Ole Fogh Kirkeby for putting me onto this. In a piece on Husserl, Kirkeby writes, "To Husserl, communication cannot thereby constitute the concept of meaning. The primary meaning-giving activity takes place in the subject, in the speaker, and there is no criterion indicating that conversation establishes an actual transfer of meaning from the sender to the receiver of verbal signals." Ole Fogh Kirkeby, "Event and Corporal Thought," MS, 1991, p. 142. Kirkeby refers to Edmund

Husserl, *Logische Untersuchungen, Zweiter Band, II Teil* (Tübingen: Max Neimeyer Verlag, 1980), chap. 1. This particular point of Husserl's is the object of criticism from pupils such as Merleau-Ponty. The notion of exformation, which is new, is thus closely related to Husserl's thinking.

The notion of exformation also has a kind of precursor in the concept of "non-knowledge" (Danish: *ikke-viden*), which I used in my thesis in 1992 (later published as Tor Nørretranders, *Naturvidenskab og ikke-viden* (Science and Non-Knowledge) (Århus: Kimære, 1987). Jesper Hoffmeyer also used the concept of non-knowledge in his *Naturen i Hovedet* (Nature in the Head) (Copenhagen: Rosinante, 1984) and in a periodical, *OMverden, Munksgaard*. The term itself is old, appearing in Jens Himmelstrup, *Terminologisk Ordbog in Søren Kierkegaard: Samlede Værker* (Collected Works) (Copenhagen: Gyldendal, 1964 [orig. 1936]), vol. 20, p. 102; Georges Bataille also gave three lectures on non-knowledge in 1952. But the term "exformation" is far more closely related to Husserl's thinking than to the concept of non-knowledge. The concept of exformation is defined within the framework of understanding that is defined by Shannon's notion of information and is reminiscent of the notion of depth from the theory of complexity, but it is not clear how the notion of non-knowledge is rooted theoretically. Moreover, the two concepts emphasize different factors: exformation emphasizes the buildup of complexity through the discarding of information, while non-knowledge emphasizes the reductive loss of cognition in abstract cognition. The kinship between the two concepts is thus likely to provoke the wrong associations altogether.

19. Peter Bastian, *Ind i musikken* (Into the Music) (Copenhagen: Gyldendal, 1987), p. 37.

20. John Davies, "The Musical Mind," *New Scientist*, 19 January 1991, 38–41, here p. 40.

21. Niels A. Lassen, David H. Ingvar, and Erik Skinhøj, "Brain Function and Blood Flow," *Scientific American* 239 (1977), 62–71.

22. P. E. Roland and L. Friberg, "Localization of Cortical Areas Activated by Thinking," *Journal of Neurophysiology* 53 (1985), 1219–43. Lars Friberg and Per E. Roland, "Functional Activation and Inhibition of Regional Cerebral Blood Flow and Metabolism," in J. Olesen and L. Edvinsson, eds., *Basic Mechanisms of Headache* (Amsterdam: Elsevier, 1988), pp. 89–98.

23. Per E. Roland et al., "Does Mental Activity Change the Oxidative Metabolism of the Brain?" *The Journal of Neuroscience* 7 (1987), 2373–89.

24. Lars Friberg, "Auditory and Language Processing," in D. H. Ingvar et al., ed., *Brain Work II, Abstracts*, Alfred Benzon Symposium 31, p. 44.

25. Louis Sokoloff, "Local Cerebral Energy Metabolism Associated with Local Functional Activity: Where and Why?" in Ingvar (note 24), p. 10.

26. The word appears in an 1826 letter in which a Swede, Jöns Jacob Berzelius, complains to Friedrich Wöhler, a German, about the tradition of naming newly discovered minerals after people. Berzelius writes that one could aptly name one after his good friend Miguel Erecacoexecohonerena. My source, E. Rancke-Madsen, *Grundstoffernes Opdagelseshistorie* (The History of the Discovery of the Elements) (Copenhagen: G. E. C. Gad, 1987), p. 99, fails to mention wherefrom Miguel acquired his surname.

CHAPTER 6: THE BANDWIDTH OF CONSCIOUSNESS

1. M. Zimmermann, "The Nervous System in the Context of Information Theory," in R. F. Schmidt and G. Thews, eds., *Human Physiology*, 2d ed. (Berlin: Springer-Verlag, 1989) (transl. of *Physiologie des Menschen*, 23d ed.), pp. 166–73, here p. 172.

2. M. Zimmermann, "Neurophysiology of Sensory Systems," in Robert F. Schmidt, ed., *Fundamentals of Sensory Physiology* (Berlin: Springer-Verlag, 1986), pp. 68–116, here p. 116.

3. Dietrich Trincker, "Aufnahme, Speicherung und Verarbeitung von Information durch den Menschen," *Veröffentlichungen der Schleswig-Holsteinischen Universitätsgesellschaft, Neue Folge*, nr. 44 (Kiel: Verlag Ferdinand Hirt, 1966), p. 11.

4. This is an indirect quote by Edwin G. Boring: "To be aware of a conscious datum is to be sure that it has passed." E. G. Boring, *The Physical Dimensions of Consciousness* (New York: Dover, 1963 [orig. 1933]), p. 228.

5. The three exercises have been invented for this occasion but are hardly original. No. 3 was derived from talking to recording engineers during TV recording (as inspired by Bastian, *Ind i musikken*, pp. 143–53). Numerous similar exercises have been reported in spiritual and psychological literature.

6. W. R. Garner and Harold W. Hake, "The Amount of Information in Absolute Judgements," *Psychological Review* 58 (1951), 446–59.

7. Hamilton in G. A. Miller, "Information Theory," *Scientific American* 195:2 (August 1956), 42–46, here p. 43.

8. G. A. Miller, "The Magical Number Seven, Plus or Minus Two," *Psychological Review* 63 (1956), 81–87, p. 81; see also Howard Gardner, *The Mind's New Science* (New York: Basic Books, 1987 [orig. 1985]), p. 89.

9. Miller (note 8), p. 86.

10. Miller (note 7), p. 46.

11. The table is constructed by merging data reviewed in Fred Attneave, *Applications of Information Theory to Psychology* (New York: Holt, 1959), pp. 67–75, and E. R. F. W. Crossman, "Information Theory in Psychological Measurement," in A. R. Mettham and R. A. Hudson, eds., *Encyclopedia of Linguistics, Information and Control* (Oxford: Oxford University Press, 1969), pp. 232–38, here p. 233.

12. Karl Steinbuch, *Automat und Mensch* (Berlin: Springer-Verlag, 1965), p. 263. The exact figures in Steinbuch are given for German, and are here rounded to match Danish conditions. Steinbuch gives 1 bit/letter in words and 4.1 bits/letter in the alphabet—i.e., 24.6 bits for 6 letters.

13. W. E. Hick, "On the Rate of Gain of Information," *Quarterly Journal of Experimental Psychology* 4 (1952), pp. 11–26.

14. Richard Gregory, "Bit," in Richard L. Gregory, *The Oxford Companion to the Mind* (Oxford: Oxford University Press, 1987), pp. 93–4, here p. 94.

15. Henry Quastler, "Studies of Human Channel Capacity," in Colin Cherry, ed., *Information Theory, Proceedings of the Third London Symposium* (London: Butterworths, 1956), pp. 361–71. Tennis quote pp. 367–68; Mandelbrot quote and reply p. 371.

16. J. R. Pierce, *Symbols, Signals and Noise* (New York: Harper, 1961), p. 229.

17. Ibid., p. 236.

18. Ibid., pp. 248–49.

19. Karl Küpfmüller, "Grundlagen der Informationstheorie und Kybernetik," in O. H. Grauer, K. Kramer, and R. Jung, *Physiologie des Menschen*, Band 10: *Allgemeine Neurophysiologie* (München: Urban & Schwarzenberg, 1971), pp. 195–231, here p. 203. The same figures were published by Küpfmüller in 1959.

20. K. Küpfmüller, "Nachrichtenverarbeitung im Menschen," in K. Steinbuch, ed., *Taschenbuch der Nachrichtenverarbeitung* (Berlin: Springer, 1962), pp. 1481–1501, here p. 1500.

21. Helmuth Frank, *Kybernetischen Grundlagen der Pädagogik*, Zweiter Band (Baden-Baden: Agis-Agis Verlag, 1962 [2. Auflage 1969]), p. 69.

22. Ibid., p. 71.

23. Ibid., p. 82.

24. H. J. Eysenck, "The Theory of Intelligence and the Psychophysiology of Cognition," in Robert J. Sternberg, *Advances in the Psychology of Human Intelligence*, vol. 3 (Hillsdale, N.J.: Lawrence Erlbaum, 1986), pp. 1–34, here p. 8 et seq.

25. S. Lehrl and B. Fischer, "Der maximale zentrale Informationsfluss bei Küpfmüller und Frank: beträgt er 50 bit/s oder 16 bit/s? Zum Nutzen und Schaden von Küpfmüllers Angaben für die Verbreitung der Informationspsykologie," *Grundlagenstudien aus Kybernetik und Geistenswissenschaft/Humankybernetik* 26 (1985), 147–54, here p. 154.

26. Crossman (note 11), p. 236.

27. Elizabeth Spelke, William Hirst, and Ulric Neisser, "Skills of Divided Attention," *Cognition* 4 (1976), 215–30, here p. 226.

28. Ibid., p. 229.

29. Richard Jung, "Perception, Consciousness and Visual Attention," in P. A. Buser and A. Rougeul-Buser, *Cerebral Correlates of Conscious Experience, INSERM Symposium No. 6* (Amsterdam: Elsevier/North-Holland, 1978), pp. 15–36, here p. 18.

30. Zimmermann (note 1), p. 172.

31. After Küpfmüller (note 19), p. 220.

32. Eigil Nyborg, *Den indre linie i H. C. Andersens eventyr: En psykologisk studie* (The Inner Lines in the Fairy Tales of Hans Christian Andersen: A Psychological Study) (Copenhagen: Gyldendal, 1983 [orig. 1962]), p. 195.

33. Gregory Bateson, "Problems in Cetacean and Other Mammalian Communications," in Gregory Bateson, *Steps to an Ecology of Mind* (New York: Ballantine, 1972), pp. 364–78, here p. 370. Bateson describes the limited channel capacity of consciousness in qualitative terms in "Style, Grace, and Information in Primitive Art" (1967), ibid., pp. 128–76, see esp. pp. 136, 142–43.

34. Bent Ølgaard, *Kommunikation og Økomentale Systemer* (Communication and Ecomental Systems) (Åbyhøj: Ask, 1986), p. 78.

35. Edward T. Hall, *The Silent Language* (New York: Doubleday, 1981 [orig. 1959]), pp. 61–2. See also Edward T. Hall, *The Hidden Dimension* (New York: Doubleday, 1982 [orig. 1966]).

36. K. S. Lashley, in Warren Weaver, "Recent Contributions to the Mathematical Theory of Communication," in Shannon and Weaver, *The Mathematical Theory of Communication*, pp. 94–117, here p. 96, footnote 1.

37. Umberto Eco, *The Name of the Rose*, trans. William Weaver (London, Mandarin: 1994 [orig. 1983]), pp. 477, 491.

38. Steinbuch (note 12), p. 264.

39. It is also said to be very difficult to lie in the sign language used by the deaf. Thanks to Kijo Sofeza for pointing this out.

40. Stephen Toulmin, "The Charm of the Scout" (1980), in Stephen Toulmin, *The Return to Cosmology* (Berkeley: University of California Press, 1982), pp. 201–13, here p. 212.

CHAPTER 7: THE BOMB OF PSYCHOLOGY

1. Harald Høffding, *Psykologi*, 6th ed. (Copenhagen: Gyldendal, 1911), p. 102.

2. Norman Dixon, "Subliminal Perception," in Gregory, *The Oxford Companion to the Mind*, pp. 752–55, here p. 752.

3. Norman Dixon, *Subliminal Perception: The Nature of a Controversy* (London: McGraw-Hill, 1971), p. 5.

4. J. V. McConnell, R. L. Cutler, and E. B. McNeil, "Subliminal Stimulation: An Overview," *Amer. Psychol.* 13 (1958), 229–42, here p. 238, quoted in Dixon (note 3), p. 224.

5. Norman Dixon, *Preconscious Processing* (Chichester: John Wiley, 1981), p. 183. This book is a much-edited revision of Dixon's 1971 book (note 3).

6. Vance Packard, *The People Shapers* (London: MacDonald and Jane's, 1978), p. 136.

7. Hermann von Helmholtz, in Richard L. Gregory, *Mind in Science* (Harmondsworth: Penguin, 1984 [orig. 1981]), p. 363.

8. P. N. Johnson-Laird, *The Computer and the Mind* (London: Fontana, 1988), p. 18.

9. Daniel C. Dennett, "Consciousness," in Gregory (note 2), pp. 160–64, here p. 162.

10. C. G. Jung, *Jeg'et og det ubevidste* (The Ego and the Unconscious) (Copenhagen: Gyldendal, 1987 [orig. 1933]), pp. 13–14.

11. Joseph Weiss, "Unconscious Mental Functioning," *Scientific American* 262:3 (1990), 75–81, here p. 75.

12. Ibid., p. 81.

13. See, e.g., Dixon (note 3), pp. 103–52; Dixon (note 5), pp. 91–112; and Kihlstrom (note 17), p. 1448.

14. C. S. Peirce and J. Jastrow, "On Small Differences of Sensation," [*Memoirs of the*] *National Academy of Sciences*, vol. 3, Fifth Memoir (1884), 73–83. See October 17, 1884.

15. Peder Voetmann Christiansen, *Charles P. Peirce: Bricks and Mortar to a Metaphysics*, IMFUFA, Text no. 169 (Roskilde: Roskilde Universitetscenter, 1988), p. 49. (In Danish)

16. L. Weiskrantz, *Blindsight: A Case Study and Implications*, Oxford Psychology Series no. 12 (Oxford: Clarendon Press, 1986), p. 24.

17. John F. Kihlstrom, "The Cognitive Unconscious," *Science* 237 (1987), 1445–52, here p. 1448.

18. Ibid., p. 1447.

19. Endel Tulving and Daniel L. Schacter, "Priming and Human Memory Systems," *Science* 247 (1990), 301–6.

20. Kihlstrom (note 17), p. 1450.

21. Daniel Holender, "Semantic Activation Without Conscious Identification in Dichotic Listening, Parafoveal Vision, and Visual Masking: A Survey and Appraisal," *The Behavioral and Brain Sciences* 9 (1986), 1–66.

22. Julian Jaynes, *The Origin of Consciousness in the Breakdown of the Bicameral Mind* (Boston: Houghton Mifflin, 1982 [orig. 1976]), p. 23.

23. Ibid., p. 24.

24. Richard Latto and John Campion, "Approaches to Consciousness: Psychophysics or Philosophy?" *The Behavioral and Brain Sciences* 9:1 (1986), 36–7, here p. 37.

25. Jacques Hadamard, *An Essay on the Psychology of Invention in the Mathematical Field* (Princeton: Princeton University Press, 1949 [orig. 1945]), p. 75.

26. Albert Einstein, in Hadamard (note 25), p. 142.

27. Jaynes (note 22), p. 41.

28. Henri Poincaré, in Hadamard (note 25), p. 40.

29. William James, *The Principles of Psychology* (London: Macmillan, 1891 [orig. 1890]), p. 284.

30. Ibid., pp. 288–89. The sculptor metaphor reappears in modern accounts of irreversible information processing in computation and consciousness; e.g., Søren Brunak and Benny Lautrup, *Neural Networks* (Singapore: World Scientific, 1990), p. 71.

31. H. H. Kornhuber, "The Human Brain: From Dream and Cognition to Fantasy, Will, Conscience, and Freedom," in Hans J. Markowitsch, ed., *Information Processing by the Brain* (Toronto: Hans Huber Publishers, 1988), pp. 241–58, here p. 246.

CHAPTER 8: THE VIEW FROM WITHIN

1. Francis Crick, Preface, in Horace Barlow, Colin Blakemore, and Miranda Weston Smith, *Images and Understanding* (Cambridge University Press, 1990), pp. ix–x, here p. ix.

2. David Marr, *Vision. A Computational Investigation into the Human Representation and Processing of Visual Information* (New York: W. H. Freeman, 1982), p. 16.

3. T. Poggio, "Vision: The 'Other' Face of AI," in K. A. Mohyeldin Said et al., eds., *Modelling the Mind* (Oxford: Clarendon Press, 1990), pp. 139–54, here p. 139.

4. Jaynes, *The Origin of Consciousness in the Breakdown of the Bicameral Mind*, p. 25.

5. Gregory, *The Oxford Companion to the Mind*, p. 508.

6. Gaetano Kanizsa, "Subjective Contours," *Scientific American*, April 1976, reprinted in Irvin Rock, ed., *The Perceptual World* (New York: W. H. Freeman, 1990), pp. 155–63.

7. Barbara Gillam, "Geometrical Illusions," *Scientific American*, January 1980, in Rock (note 6), pp. 164–76.

8. Vilyanur Ramachandran, "Perceiving Shape from Shading," *Scientific American*, August 1988, in Rock (note 6), pp. 127–51. David Brewster's observations are mentioned in Richard L. Gregory (note 11), p. 193.

9. Zeke Berman, "Vases or Faces?" Postcard, Exploratorium, San Francisco's Museum of Science and Human Perception, 1978.

10. K. C. Cole, *Vision: In the Eye of the Beholder* (San Francisco: Exploratorium, 1978), p. 48.

11. Richard L. Gregory, *Eye and Brain: The Psychology of Seeing*, 4th ed. (Princeton University Press, 1990 [orig. 1966]), here pp. 21–2.

12. Ibid., p. 20.

13. Ludwig Wittgenstein, *Tractatus Logico-Philosophicus* (Copenhagen: Gyldendal, 1963 [orig. 1921]), p. 106. Norwood Russell Hanson, *Patterns of Discovery* (Cambridge University Press, 1965 [orig. 1958]), pp. 8–24. Thomas S. Kuhn, *Videnskabens revolutioner* (Copenhagen: Fremad, 1973 [orig. 1962]), pp. 130–49. For an overview, see Richard L. Gregory, *Mind in Science* (Harmondsworth: Penguin, 1984 [orig. 1981]), pp. 383–414.

14. Irvin Rock and Stephen Palmer, "The Legacy of Gestalt Psychology," *Scientific American* 263:6 (1990), pp. 48–61.

15. J. B. Deregowski, "Real Space and Represented Space: Cross-Cultural Perspectives," *The Behavioral and Brain Sciences* 12 (1989), 51–119, here p. 57.

16. Colin Turnbull, in Robert Ornstein and Paul Ehrlich, *New World, New Mind* (London: Paladin, 1991 [orig. 1989]), p. 87.

17. Pablo Picasso and fellow passenger, in Heinz R. Pagels, *The Dreams of Reason* (New York: Bantam, 1988), p. 163.

18. Philippe Brou, Thomas Sciascia, Lynette Linden, and Jerome Y. Lettvin, "The Colors of Things," *Scientific American* 254:9 (1986), pp. 84–91. See also Gregory (note 11), pp. 127–39; John Mollon, "The Tricks of Colour" in Barlow et al. (note 1); Edwin Land, "The Retinex Theory of Color Vision," in Rock (note 6), pp. 39–62.

19. Richard Gregory, interview, Bristol, Eng., October 1989.

20. J. Y. Lettvin, H. R. Maturana, W. S. McCulloch, and W. H. Pitts, "What the Frog's Eye Tells the Frog's Brain," *Proceedings of the IRE* 47 (1940–51), p. 1959.

21. Ibid., p. 1951, col. 2: "The character of these contexts, genetically built in, is the physiological synthetic a priori."

22. Ibid., col. 1.

23. H. B. Barlow, "Single Units and Sensation: A Neuron Doctrine for Perceptual Psychology?" *Perception* 1 (1972), 371–94, here p. 373, from Marr (note 2), p. 12.

24. Barlow (note 23), p. 380, from Marr (note 2), p. 13.

25. David Marr (note 2), pp. 11–19, provides an overview of this development.

26. Horace Barlow, "What Does the Brain See? How Does It Understand?" in Barlow et al. (note 1), pp. 5–25, here p. 20.

27. Thomas Nagel, *What Does It All Mean? A Very Short Introduction to Philosophy* (New York: Oxford University Press, 1987), pp. 20, 22, 23.

28. Ibid., p. 11.

29. Peter Zinkernagel, *Omverdensproblemet* [Eng.: *Conditions for Description* (London: Routledge & Kegan Paul, 1962)] (Copenhagen: G. E. C. Gad, 1957); *Virkelighed* (Reality) (Copenhagen: Munksgaard, 1988); and Tor Nørretranders, *Det udelelige* (The Indivisible) (Copenhagen: Gyldendal, 1985).

30. C. Crone et al., ed., *Fysiologi* (Copenhagen: Foreningen af Danske Lægestuderendes Forlag, 1990), pp. 99–100. The author of this chapter, Arne Mosfeldt Laursen, does allow in his *Hjernevindinger* (Copenhagen: Munksgaard, 1990),

p. 2, that the thalamus perhaps acts as a filter that prevents "the cortex from being flooded by trivial information."

31. F. Crick and C. Asanuma, "Certain Aspects of the Anatomy and Physiology of the Cerebral Cortex," in J. L. McClelland and D. E. Rumelhart, *Parallel Distributed Processing* (Cambridge, Mass.: The MIT Press, 1986), vol. 2, pp. 333–71, here pp. 346–49.

32. A. R. Luria, *Hjernen: En introduktion til neuropsykologien* (The Brain: An Introduction to Neuropsychology), Danish trans. (Copenhagen: Nyt Nordisk, 1989 [orig. 1973]), p. 40.

33. Francis Crick, "Function of the Thalamic Reticular Complex: The Searchlight Hypothesis," *Proceedings of the National Academy of Sciences, USA*, 81 (1984), pp. 4586–90.

34. Francisco Varela, "Laying Down a Path in Walking," in William Irwin Thompson, *Gaia: A Way of Knowing* (Great Barrington, Mass.: Lindisfarne Press, 1987), pp. 48–64, here pp. 59–60.

35. Humberto R. Maturana, "What Is It to See?" *Arch. Biol. Med. Exp.* 16 (1983), 255–69.

36. Humberto Maturana and Francisco Varela, *Kundskabens træ* (The Tree of Knowledge), Danish trans. (Århus: 1987 [orig. 1986]), p. 160.

37. Humberto Maturana, interview, 14 April 1991, Espergærde, Denmark. I'm grateful to the DISPUK-center for arranging this interview.

38. Maturana and Varela (note 36), p. 135.

39. Niels Bohr from Aage Petersen, "The Philosophy of Niels Bohr," *Bulletin of the Atomic Scientist* 19 (1963), 8–14, p. 12.

40. Nørretranders (note 29).

41. This problem has also been described as the "cocktail-party effect" (how one hears what one's wife is talking about at the other end of the room, if she is talking to another man), equated with *das Figur-Hintergrund-Problem*, see W. Schneider (1986) in Ch. von der Malsburg and W. Schneider, "A Neural Cocktail-Party Processor," *Biological Cybernetics* 54 (1986), 29–40.

42. Charles M. Gray, Peter König, Andreas K. Engel, and Wolf Singer, "Oscillatory Responses in Cat Visual Cortex Exhibit Inter-Columnar Synchronization Which Reflects Global Stimulus Properties," *Nature* 338 (1989), 334–37.

43. Marck Baringa, "The Mind Revealed?" *Science* 249 (1990), 856–58.

44. Francis Crick and Christof Koch, "Towards a Neurobiological Theory of Consciousness," *Seminars in the Neurosciences* 2 (1990), 263–75.

45. Malsburg and Schneider (note 41).

46. Report of lack of confirmation from simian experiments is thanks to Christof Koch, interview at the California Institute of Technology, 28 March 1991.

47. Crick and Koch (note 44), here p. 274.

48. Francis Crick and Christof Koch, "Some Reflections on Visual Awareness," *Symposia on Quantitative Biology*, vol. 55 (Cold Spring Harbor Press, 1990), MS, p. 10.

49. Ibid., p. 16.

50. Crick and Koch (note 44), p. 263.

CHAPTER 9: THE HALF-SECOND DELAY

1. Hans H. Kornhuber and Lüder Deecke, "Hirnpotentialänderungen bei Willkürbewegungen und passiven Bewegungen des Menschen: Bereitschaftspotential und reafferente Potentiale," *Pflügers Archiv fir dir gesamte Physiologie des Menschen und Tieren* 284 (1965), 1–17.

2. Lüder Deecke, Berta Grözinger, and H. H. Kornhuber, "Voluntary Finger Movement in Man: Cerebral Potentials and Theory," *Biological Cybernetics* 23 (1976), 99–119.

3. Benjamin Libet, interview, 26 and 27 March 1991, San Francisco. Unless otherwise indicated, the Libet quotations in this chapter are from this interview. A number of the statements in the interview originate from the manuscript of Libet's article "The Neural Time-Factor and the Concepts of Perception, Volition and Free Will," *Revue de Metaphysique et de Morale*, Paris, 1991.

4. Benjamin Libet, "Unconscious Cerebral Initiative and the Role of Conscious Will in Voluntary Action," *The Behavioral and Brain Sciences* 8 (1985), 529–66, here p. 529.

5. Ibid.

6. Johannes Mørk Pedersen, *Psykologiens Historie, Psykologisk Laboratorium* (Copenhagen University, 1990), p. 21.

7. Benjamin Libet, Curtis A. Gleason, Elwood W. Wright, and Dennis K. Pearl, "Time of Conscious Intention to Act in Relation to Onset of Cerebral Activity (Readiness-potential)," *Brain* 106 (1983), 623–42, here pp. 625, 627.

8. Ibid., p. 640.

9. Libet (note 4), p. 536.

10. John Eccles, "Mental Summation: Time Timing of Voluntary Intentions by Cortical Activity," in Libet (note 4), pp. 542–43, here p. 543.

11. Some of the counterarguments are repeated in Libet's words (note 4): Argument No. 2 is by Gary Rollman (pp. 551–52); Argument No. 5 by Geoffrey Underwood and Pekka Niemi (pp. 554–55) and Charles C. Wood (pp. 557–58). Argument No. 6 derives from Eccles (pp. 542–43).

12. Lüder Deecke, "The Natural Explanation for the Two Components of the Readiness Potential," *The Behavioral and Brain Sciences* 10 (1987), 781–82, here p. 782.

13. Lüder Deecke, interview, Copenhagen, 15 August 1990.

14. R. Näätänen, "Brain Physiology and the Unconscious Initiation of Movement," in Libet (note 4), p. 549.

15. The reference to Jensen's work can be found in B. Libet, "The Experimental Evidence for a Subjective Referral of a Sensory Experience Backwards in Time," *Philosophy of Science* 48 (1981), 182–97, here pp. 185–86.

16. I. Keller and H. Heckhausen, "Readiness Potentials Preceding Spontaneous Motor Acts: Voluntary vs. Involuntary Control," *Electroencephalography and Clinical Neurophysiology* 76 (1990), 351–61.

17. B. Libet, W. W. Alberts, E. W. Wright, Jr., L. D. Delatytre, G. Levin, and B. Feinstein, "Production of Threshold Levels of Conscious Sensation by Electrical Stimulation of Human Somatosensory Cortex," *J. Neurophysiol.* 27 (1964), 546–78, here p. 549.

18. Benjamin Libet, "Cortical Activation in Conscious and Unconscious Experience," *Perspectives in Biology and Medicine* 9 (1965), 77–86.

19. See, e.g., Bryan Kolb and Ian Q. Whishaw, *Fundamentals of Human Neuropsychology*, 3d ed. (New York: W. H. Freeman, 1990), pp. 335–36.

20. Bruce Bridgeman, *The Biology of Behavior and Mind* (New York: Wiley, 1988), p. 429. The bibliography indicates, p. 513, that Bridgeman here does not use Libet's work from 1979.

21. Benjamin Libet, Elwood W. Wright, Jr., Bertram Feinstein, and Dennis Pearl, "Subjective Referral of the Timing for a Conscious Sensory Experience," *Brain* 102 (1979), 193–224.

22. B. Libet, W. W. Alberts, E. W. Wright, Jr., & B. Feinstein, "Responses of Human Somatosensory Cortex to Stimuli Below Threshold for Conscious Sensation," *Science* 158 (1967), 1597–1600, here p. 1600.

23. Libet et al. (note 21), pp. 194–95.

24. B. Libet, W. W. Alberts, E. W. Wright, Jr., and B. Feinstein, "Cortical and Thalamic Activation in Conscious Sensory Experience," in G. G. Somjen, ed., *Neurophysiology Studied in Man* (Amsterdam: Excerpts Medica, 1972), pp. 157–68.

25. See, e.g., R. F. Schmidt, ed., *Fundamentals of Sensory Physiology* (Berlin: Springer-Verlag, 1986), pp. 78–81.

26. In the actual experiment, the necessary duration of the stimulus for the area of the thalamus, medial lemniscus, ventrobasal thalamus, is only 200 milliseconds, but in this account we call it 500 ms so as to avoid unnecessary confusion; see Libet et al. (note 8), p. 202. In practice, the minimal duration depends on the strength of the stimulus compared to the conscious threshold. For very powerful stimuli, 100 ms can suffice.

27. Karl R. Popper and John C. Eccles, *The Self and Its Brain* (Berlin: Springer International, 1985 [orig. 1977, rev. 1981]), p. 364.

28. Patricia Smith Churchland, *Neurophilosophy: Towards a Unified Science of the Mind-Brain* (Cambridge, Mass.: The MIT Press, 1986), p. 486, note 8.2. See also P. S. Churchland, "On the Alleged Backwards Referral of Experiences and Its Relevance to the Mind-Body Problem," *Philosophy of Science* 48 (1981), 165–81; Benjamin Libet, "The Experimental Evidence for Subjective Referral of a Sensory Experience Backwards in Time: Reply to P. S. Churchland," *Philosophy of Science* 48 (1981), 182–97; P. S. Churchland, "The Timing of Sensations: Reply to Libet," *Philosophy of Science* 48 (1981), 492–97.

29. Ted Honderich, "The Time of a Conscious Sensory Experience and Mind-Brain Theories," *Journal of Theoretical Biology* 110 (1984), 115–29; Benjamin Libet, "Subjective Antedating of a Sensory Experience and Mind-Brain Theories: Reply to Honderich (1984)," *Journal of Theoretical Biology* 114 (1985), 563–70.

30. Ian M. Glynn, "Consciousness and Time," *Nature* 348 (1990), 477–79; Benjamin Libet, "Conscious vs. Neural Time," *Nature* 352 (1991), 27.

31. Rodney Cotterill, *No Ghost in the Machine* (London: Heinemann, 1989), pp. 267–71.

32. Roger Penrose, *The Emperor's New Mind* (New York: Vintage, 1990), p. 574. Penrose in fact misinterprets Libet and obtains a delay from the results that is actually too long (pp. 572–74) because he adds the Kornhuber-Deecke delay to

Libet's, resulting in several seconds between consciousness and "reality"; see also Benjamin Libet, "Time-Delays in Conscious Processes," *The Behavioral and Brain Sciences* 13 (1990), 672. But this factor is not critical to Penrose's view.

33. Daniel Dennett and Marcel Kinsbourne, "Time and the Observer: The Where and When of Consciousness in the Brain," *The Behavioral and Brain Sciences* 15 (1992), 213–75. I am grateful to Daniel Dennett for making parts of the manuscript available.

34. Daniel Dennett, *Consciousness Explained* (London: Allan Lane, 1992), chaps. 5, 6.

35. Benjamin Libet, "Models of Conscious Timing and the Experimental Evidence," *The Behavioral and Brain Sciences* 15 (1992), 213–75.

36. Benjamin Libet, Dennis K. Pearl, David Morledge, Curtis A. Gleason, Yoshio Morledge, and Nicholas M. Barbaro, "Control of the Transition from Sensory Detection to Sensory Awareness in Man by the Duration of a Thalamic Stimulus," *Brain* 114 (1991), 1731–57.

37. Terrence J. Sejnowski, Christof Koch, and Patricia A. Churchland, "Computational Neuroscience," *Science* 241 (1988), 1299–1306.

38. Libet (note 4), p. 538.

39. Ibid., p. 539.

40. Walter Kaufmann, *The Faith of a Heretic* (New York: Doubleday, 1961), p. 225.

41. Adin Steinsaltz, *The Essential Talmud* (London: Weidenfeld and Nicolson, 1976), p. 26. Steinsaltz's work, written in Hebrew, was translated into English by Chaya Galai. Compare Galai's "Do not unto others that which you would not have them do unto you" with Kaufmann's "What you don't like, don't do to others" (note 40, p. 225).

42. Matthew 5:21–22, 27–28; 7:12. Holy Bible, King James Version.

43. Kaufmann (note 40), p. 250.

44. Benjamin Libet acknowledges this point. In a letter to the author dated 18 September 1991 he writes, "I think you are correct in thinking that even when an urge is vetoed, and not acted out, that there could be other clues about one's urges that could affect another person."

45. Benjamin Libet, letter to the author, 1 July 1991.

46. Harald Høffding, *Psykologi,* p. 429.

Chapter 10: Maxwell's Me

1. Michael Laudrup, interview, Vedbæk, Denmark, 21 October 1989.

2. Michael Laudrup to the author in a TV program (*Den intuitive elektronhjerne*), DR-TV, 24 October 1989.

3. Janet L. Taylor and D. I. McCloskey, "Triggering of Preprogrammed Movements as Reactions to Masked Stimuli," *Journal of Neurophysiology* 63 (1990), 439–46, here p. 445.

4. Ibid.

5. George Gamow, *Tredive År der rystede Fysikken* (Thirty Years That Shook Physics) (Copenhagen: Gyldendal, 1968 [orig. 1966]), p. 59.

6. This interpretation can be seen in, e.g., Rodney Cotterill, *No Ghost in the Machine* (London: Heinemann, 1989), p. 268 et seq.

7. The distinction between *I* and *Me* as used here is philosophically naïve; especially in the phenomenological-existential tradition, this distinction has been drawn up in a more technical form which does not coincide with the one used here. See, e.g., the *I* and the *Me* chapter in Jean-Paul Sartre, *The Transcendence of the Ego* (New York: Noonday Press, 1957), pp. 31–60, originally published in French in *Recherches Philosophiques* VI (1936–37). In the distinction used in this book, we are simply talking about the conscious *I* versus the rest of the person. A closer reflection of the distinction in relation to the concept of the transcendental *I* in Kant and Husserl is not attempted here but would certainly have been rewarding.

8. Thomas Nagel, "Is that you, James?" *London Review of Books* 9:17 (1 October 1987), 3–6, here p. 5, col. 2. Nagel has decisively affected the modern cognitive philosophy formulation of the within/without distinction, which is also vital to Libet. See Thomas Nagel, *The View from Nowhere* (New York: Oxford University Press, 1986).

9. Ibid., p. 5, col. 2.

10. Andrew Hodges, *Alan Turing: The Enigma of Intelligence*, p. 488.

11. Ibid., p. 489.

12. Wilhelm Furtwängler, in Bastian, *Ind i musikken*, p. 129.

13. Glenn Gould, *Afskaf bifald!* (Copenhagen: Gyldendal, 1988), pp. 70–6.

14. Bastian, in Tor Nørretranders, "En rejse ind i Peter Bastians lyd" (A Journey into the Sounds of Peter Bastian), *Levende Billeder*, April 1987, pp. 12–15, here p. 15.

15. Bastian, *Ind i musikken*, p. 160.

16. John C. Lilly, *Communication Between Man and Dolphin* (New York: Crown, 1978).

17. John C. Lilly, *The Centre of the Cyclone: An Autobiography of Inner Space* (London: Paladin, 1973 [orig. 1972]), p. 173.

18. Abraham Maslow, *The Psychology of Science* (New York: Harper, 1966), pp. 95–101.

19. Barry Green and W. Timothy Gallwey, *The Inner Game of Music* (London: Pan, 1987 [orig. 1986]), p. 117.

20. Ibid.

21. Keith Johnstone, *Impro: Improvisation and the Theatre* (New York: Theatre Arts Books, 1985 [orig. 1979]), pp. 111, 91.

22. Bernard Dixon, *Beyond the Magic Bullet* (London: Allen & Unwin, 1978).

23. Adrian Furnham, "Hooked on Horoscopes," *New Scientist* 26 (January 1991), pp. 33–6, here p. 33.

24. Søren Kierkegaard, *Begrebet Angst* (The Concept of Anxiety), *Samlede Værker* (Collected Works) (Copenhagen: Gyldendal, 1963), vol. 6, p. 136. Kierkegaard's concept *Angst* has been translated variously as anxiety, fear, and dread.

25. Søren Kierkegaard, *Sygdommen til Døden* (The Sickness unto Death), *Samlede Værker* (Collected Works), vol. 15, p. 73.

CHAPTER 11: THE USER ILLUSION

1. Michael S. Gazzaniga, *The Social Brain* (New York: Basic Books, 1985), p. 81.
2. "Dichotomania" is an expression for an exaggerated urge to split the functions of the two hemispheres of the brain. See Sally P. Springer and Georg Deutsch, *Left Brain, Right Brain*, 3d ed. (New York: W. H. Freeman, 1989), p. 287. "Right brain" and "Left brain" are Gazzaniga's terms.
3. Gazzaniga (note 1), p. 72.
4. Ibid.
5. Joseph E. LeDoux, "Brain, Mind and Language," in David A. Oakley, ed., *Brain and Mind* (London: Methuen, 1985), pp. 197–216, here p. 206.
6. Ibid., p. 207.
7. Gazzaniga (note 1), p. 72.
8. LeDoux (note 5), p. 209.
9. Ibid., p. 210.
10. David A. Oakley and Lesley C. Eames, "The Plurality of Consciousness," in David A. Oakley, ed., *Brain and Mind* (London: Methuen, 1985), pp. 215–51, here p. 247.
11. Ibid., p. 248.
12. Helen Crawford, Hugh Macdonald, and Ernest R. Hilgard, "Hypnotic Deafness: A Psychophysical Study of Responses to Tone Intensity as Modified by Hypnosis," *American Journal of Psychology* 92 (1979), 193–214, here pp. 198–99.
13. See also Oakley and Eames (note 10), here p. 238.
14. John F. Kihlstrom, "The Cognitive Unconscious," *Science* 237 (1987), 1445–52, here p. 1450.
15. John Kulli and Christof Koch, "Does Anesthesia Cause Loss of Consciousness?" *TINS* 14:1 (1991), 6–10, here p. 6.
16. Ibid. Patient quoted.
17. Benjamin Libet, interview, 26–27 March 1991, San Francisco.
18. Alan Kay, "Computer Software," *Scientific American* 251:3 (1984), 41–7, here p. 42.
19. The immediate objection to this metaphor is that once again we are equating man's mental functions with the latest technological invention: First the human brain was part of a steam engine, then a telephone switchboard, and now it is the computer. But the point is that new technology always expresses and objectifies whatever it is about man and the world that people have just understood.
20. Richard Dawkins, *The Selfish Gene* (Oxford University Press, 1976), excerpted in Douglas R. Hofstadter and Daniel C. Dennett, *The Mind's I* (Harmondsworth: Penguin, 1982), pp. 124–44, here p. 141.
21. Aldous Huxley, *The Doors of Perception*, in *The Doors of Perception and Heaven and Hell* (London: Chatto & Windus, 1968 [orig. 1960]), pp. 11–12.
22. Ibid., p. 16.
23. Peder Voetmann Christiansen, *Charles Sanders Peirce: Mursten og mørtel til en metafysik* (Bricks and Mortar for a Metaphysics) (Roskilde: RUC/IMFUFA Text no. 169, 1988), p. 35.
24. Carlos Castaneda, in Christiansen (note 23), p. 36.
25. Roger N. Shepard, *Mind sights* (New York: W. H. Freeman, 1990), pp. 37–8.

26. J. Allan Hobson, *The Dreaming Brain* (London: Penguin, 1990 [orig. 1988]); and Jonathan Winson, "The Meaning of Dreams," *Scientific American* 263:5 (1990), 42–8. I am grateful to Peter Lund Madsen, Clinical Physiology Dept., Bispebjerg Hospital, for the information about oxygen metabolism.

27. Gregory, *Eye and Brain*, p. 202. For the background to the story, see also Richard M. Restak, *The Brain* (New York: Warner Books, 1979), pp. 96–103.

28. S.B., in Gregory (note 27), p. 206.

29. Richard Gregory, "Turning Minds on to Science by Hands-on Exploration: The Nature and Potential of the Hands-on Medium," in *Sharing Science* (London: The Nuffield Foundation, 1989), pp. 1–9, here p. 4.

30. Ibid., p. 5.

31. Ingvar Johansson, "Angelsaksisk videnskabsteori" ("Anglo-Saxon Scientific Theory") in I. Johansson, R. Kalleberg, and S.-E. Liedman, *Positivisme, marxisme, kritisk teori* (Copenhagen: Gyldendal, 1974), pp. 11–78, here p. 73. Michael Polanyi, *Personal Knowledge* (London: Routledge & Kegan Paul, 1958).

32. Margaret Masterman, "The Nature of a Paradigm," in Imre Latakos and Alan Musgrave, eds., *Criticism and the Growth of Knowledge* (Cambridge University Press, 1974 [orig. 1970]), pp. 59–89, here p. 61.

33. Thomas P. Kuhn, "Efterskrift" ("Postscript") [orig. 1969], in Thomas P. Kuhn, *Videnskabens revolutioner* (Copenhagen: Fremad, 1973 [orig. 1962]), pp. 182–212, here p. 192.

34. Daniel L. Schacter and Peter L. Graf, "Effects of Elaborative Processing on Implicit and Explicit Memory for New Associations," *Journal of Experimental Psychology: Learning, Memory and Cognition* 12 (1986), 432–44.

35. John F. Kihlstrom, "The Cognitive Unconscious," *Science* 237 (1987), 1445–52, here p. 1449.

36. Elizabeth K. Warrington and L. Weiskrantz, "New Method of Testing Long-term Retention with Special Reference to Amnesic Patients," *Nature* 217 (1968), 972–74. E. K. Warrington and L. Weiskrantz, "Amnesic Syndrome: Consolidation or Retrieval?" *Nature* 228 (1970), 628–30. The dating of interest in priming as deriving from these studies is to be found in Endel Tulving and Daniel L. Schacter, "Priming and Human Memory Systems," *Science* 247 (1990), 301–6, here p. 301.

37. Daniel Tranel and Antonio R. Damasio, "Knowledge Without Awareness: An Autonomic Index of Facial Recognition by Prosopagnosics," *Science* 228 (1985), 1453–54, here p. 1453.

38. Antonio R. Damasio, Hanna Damasio, and Gary W. Van Hoesen, "Prosopagnosia: Anatomic Basis and Behavioral Mechanisms," *Neurology (Ny)* 32 (1982), 331–41.

39. Jonathan Miller, "Moving pictures," in Horace Barlow, Colin Blakemore, and Miranda Weston-Smith, *Images and Understanding* (Cambridge University Press, 1990), pp. 180–94, here p. 190.

40. Ibid., p. 191.

41. Ibid.

42. Albert Einstein, "Physik und Realität," *The Journal of The Franklin Institute* 221 (1936), 313–47 (Eng. trans. pp. 349–82), here p. 313 (349).

43. Ibid., p. 314 (349).

44. Bohr in Aage Petersen, *Quantum Physics and the Philosophical Tradition* (New York: Yeshiva University, 1968), p. 188.

45. Niels Bohr, "Virkningskvantet og naturbeskrivelsen" (Quantum Effect and Describing Nature), in Niels Bohr, *Atomteori og Naturbeskrivelse* (Copenhagen: Bianco Lunos Bogtrykkeri, 1929), pp. 69–76, here p. 72.

46. Tor Nørretranders, "Videnskab and hverdagssprog," *Bogens Verden* 68 (1986), 395–98, here p. 397.

47. Bohr, in Petersen (note 44), p. 188.

48. Lao-tzu, *Tao Te Ching* (New York: Vintage, 1972), text 56.

CHAPTER 12: THE ORIGIN OF CONSCIOUSNESS

1. William James, *The Principles of Psychology* (London: Macmillan, 1891 [orig. 1890]), p. 226.

2. Jaynes, *The Origin of Consciousness in the Breakdown of the Bicameral Mind*, p. 47.

3. Ibid., p. 201.

4. Ibid., p. 85.

5. Ibid., p. 202.

6. Ibid., p. 225.

7. Morris Berman, *Coming to Our Senses* (New York: Bantam New Age Books, 1990 [orig. 1989]), p. 329.

8. Jaynes (note 2), p. 204.

9. Ibid., p. 321.

10. Ibid., p. 322.

11. In G. S. Kirk, J. E. Raven, and M. Schofield, *The Presocratic Philosophers* (Cambridge University Press, 1983), p. 233, note 1.

12. Ibid., p. 209, text 244.

13. Jaynes (note 2), p. 318.

14. Ibid., p. 63, point 4.

15. Aldous Huxley, *The Perennial Philosophy* (New York: Harper & Row, 1970 [orig. 1944]), p. 2.

16. Berman (note 7), p. 47.

17. Ibid., p. 180.

18. Ibid., p. 48.

19. Winnicot quoted ibid., p. 28.

20. Ibid., p. 25.

21. Ibid.

22. Max Horkheimer and Th. W. Adorno, *Oplysningens dialektik* (Copenhagen: Gyldendal, 1972 [orig. *Dialektik der Aufklärung*, 1944]), p. 29.

23. Drew Leder, *The Absent Body* (University of Chicago Press, 1990), p. 1.

24. Ibid., p. 2.

25. Ibid., p. 173.

26. Olav Storm Jensen, "Kropspsykologi og orgasme," in Tor Nørretranders, ed., *Hengivelse—en debatbog om mænds orgasmer* (Copenhagen: Information Forlag, 1981), pp. 144–61, here p. 151.

27. Lin Yutang, *Jordisk Lykke* (Worldly Happiness) (Copennagen: Gyldendal, 1968 [orig. 1937]), p. 57.

28. Larry Dossey, *Lægevidenskabens krise* (Space, Time and Medicine [Boulder, Colo.: Shambala Publications, 1982]) (Copenhagen: Borgen, 1984), p. 100. The significance of breathing was particularly emphasized by David Abram, "The Perceptual Implications of Gaia," *The Ecologist* 15:3 (1985), 96–103.

29. Richard P. Feynman, "The Value of Science" (1955), in Richard P. Feynman, *What Do You Care What Other People Think?* (New York: W. W. Norton, 1988), pp. 240–48, here p. 244.

30. Leibniz's Monadologi in Leder (note 23), p. 30.

31. Harald Høffding, *Psykologi*, pp. 106–7.

32. Jaynes (note 2), p. 434.

CHAPTER 13: INSIDE NOTHING

1. Hoyle, in Norman Myers, ed., *The Gaia Atlas of Planet Management* (London: Pan Books, 1985), p. 21.

2. James Lovelock, *The Ages of Gaia* (Oxford: Oxford University Press, 1988), p. 85. Lovelock's argument about the blue sky as a result of life on earth was presented for the first time in Tor Nørretranders, *Den blå himmel* (The Blue Sky) (Copenhagen: Munksgaard, 1987), pp. 55–7.

3. Lynn Margulis and Dorion Sagan, *Mikrokosmos* (Copenhagen: Munksgaard, 1990). See also Arthur Fisher, "The Wheels Within Wheels in the Super-kingdom Eucaryotae," *Mosaic* 20:3 (1989), 2–13; Charles Mann, "Lynn Margulis: Science's Unruly Earth Mother," *Science* 252 (1991), 378–81.

4. Christopher F. Chyba, "Impact Delivery and Erosion of Planetary Oceans in the Inner Early Solar System," *Nature* 343 (1990), 129–33.

5. Christopher F. Chyba, Paul J. Thomas, Leigh Brookshaw, and Carl Sagan, "Cometary Delivery of Organic Molecules to the Early Earth," *Science* 249 (1990), 366–73.

6. An early formulation can be found in Takafumi Matsui and Yutaka Abe, "Evolution of an Impact-Induced Atmosphere and Magma Ocean on the Accreting Earth," *Nature* 319 (1986), 303–5.

7. Roger Penrose, *The Emperor's New Mind* (London: Vintage, 1990 [orig. 1989]), pp. 413–15. See also Werner Ebeling and Michail V. Volkenstein, "Entropy and the Evolution of Biological Information," *Physica A* 163 (1990), 398–402.

8. Lovelock (note 2), p. 9.

9. James Peebles, interview, Copenhagen, 29 June 1979.

10. John Peacock, "More Hubble Trouble?" *Nature* 352 (1991), 378–79.

11. Joseph Silk, *The Big Bang* (New York: W. H. Freeman, 1989), p. 113.

12. Jacob D. Bekenstein, "Black Holes and Entropy," *Physical Review D* 7 (1973), 2333–46.

13. John A. Wheeler, *A Journey into Gravity and Spacetime* (New York: Scientific American Library, 1990), p. 221.

14. P. C. W. Davies, "Why Is the Physical World So Comprehensible?" in W. Zurek, ed., *Complexity, Entropy and the Physics of Information*, pp. 61–70, here p. 67. John Wheeler, "Information, Physics, Quantum: The Search for Links," in Zurek, pp. 3–28.

15. Edward P. Tryon, "What Made the World?" *New Scientist*, March 8, 1984,

pp. 14–16. Edward P. Tryon, "Is the Universe a Vacuum Fluctuation?" *Nature* 246 (1973), 396–97.

16. Jan Ambjørn, interview, Copenhagen, 28 February 1991.

17. Hegel, in Justus Hartnack, *Hegels Logik* (Copenhagen: C. A. Reitzels Forlag, 1990), p. 19, note 13.

18. Søren Kierkegaard, *Samlede Værker*, vol. 9, p. 98.

19. Peder Voetmann Christiansen, "Retur til virkeligheden" (Back to Reality), *Gamma* 52 (1983), pp. 12–30, reprinted in Christiansen, *Tegn og Kvanter* (Signs and Quanta) (IMFUFA/RUC, Text no. 202, 1990), pp. 53–78.

20. I am grateful to Anette Krumhardt and Villy Sørensen for their comments on the correctness of the expression *in nihilo*.

21. The sketch and a number of Wheeler's most remarkable formulations can be found reprinted in the article "John Archibald Wheeler: A Few Highlights of His Contributions to Physics," compiled and edited by Kip S. Thorne and Wojcieh H. Zurek, in W. H. Zurek, A. van der Merwe, and W. A. Miller, *Between Quantum and Cosmos* (Princeton University Press, 1988), pp. 2–13, here p. 2.

22. Fred Alan Wolf, *Taking the Quantum Leap* (San Francisco: Harper & Row, 1981), p. 176.

CHAPTER 14: ON THE EDGE OF CHAOS

1. P. W. Anderson, "More Is Different," *Science* 177 (1972), 393–96. The article is an expanded version of a Regents' Lecture at the University of California, La Jolla, 1967.

2. Fritjof Capra, *Vendepunktet* (Copenhagen: Borgen, 1986 [orig. 1982]), is a characteristic example.

3. Anderson (note 1), p. 393, col. 2.

4. Many readers over the years have identified my views with holism and will therefore be surprised to see holism described here as reactionary. But even though I have criticized reductionism even more often, for many years I have been a critic of holism. See, e.g., my criticism in *Det udelelige* (The Indivisible) (Copenhagen: Gyldendal, 1985), chap. 18; in *Naturvidenskab og ikke-viden* (Natural Science and Non-Knowledge) (Århus: Kimære, 1987 [orig. 1982]); in my article "Helhedstænkningen er en jernkakkelovn" (Thinking in Wholes Is a Catachresis), *Fredag* 16:3 (1988), 15–20. The view is not that reductionism is better than holism; not at all. The view is that this is a false antithesis. One may also note that the Gaia theory, which many people regard as holistic, is precisely not so: See Lovelock, *The Ages of Gaia*, p. 13. Thinking in wholes is not necessarily reactionary, but neither is it the same as holism.

5. Chris Langton, interview, 23 April 1990, Los Alamos, New Mexico.

6. Christopher G. Langton, *Artificial Life: Proceedings of an Interdisciplinary Workshop on the Synthesis and Simulation of Living Systems*, Santa Fe Institute Studies in the Sciences of Complexity, vol. 6 (Redwood City, Cal.: Addison-Wesley, 1989), p. xxiii.

7. J. Doyne Farmer and Aletta d'A. Belin, "Artificial Life: The Coming Evolution," in *Proceedings in Celebration of Murray Gell-Man's 60th Birthday* (Cambridge University Press); preprint LA-UR-90-378, p. 2.

8. Hans Moravec, *Mind Children: The Future of Robot and Human Intelligence* (Cambridge, Mass.: Harvard University Press, 1988), pp. 128, 129.

9. Farmer and Belin (note 7), p. 16.

10. Steen Rasmussen, Carsten Knudsen, Rasmus Feldberg, and Morten Hindsholm, "The Coreworld: Emergence and Evolution of Cooperative Structures in a Computational Chemistry," *Physica D* 42 (1990), 111–34.

11. Küppers, *Information and the Origin of Life*, p. 122.

12. Ibid., p. 153.

13. Hofstadter, *Gödel, Escher, Bach*, pp. 707–8. The idea is closely related to Gödel's basic argument that problems which arise in simple systems can be solved in more complicated systems. See Hao Wang, *Reflections on Kurt Gödel* (Cambridge, Mass.: The MIT Press, 1987), p. 170.

14. Hofstadter (note 13), pp. 713–14. The idea that computational irreducibility can describe free will has been formulated in recent times against the background of the chaos theories of Doyne Farmer: See James Gleick, *Kaos* (Copenhagen: Munksgaard, 1989 [orig. 1987]). The same idea can be found in Brunak and Lautrup, *Neurale netværk*, pp. 139–41 (*Neural Networks*, pp. 152–55).

15. Ilya Prigogine and Isabelle Stengers, *Order Out of Chaos* (New York: Bantam Books, 1984), p. 285.

16. Peter V. Coveney, "The Second Law of Thermodynamics: Entropy, Irreversibility and Dynamics," *Nature* 333 (1988), 409–15.

17. Rolf Landauer, "Nonlinearity, Multistability, and Fluctuations: Reviewing the Reviewers," *Am. J. Physiol.* 241 (1981), R107–13.

18. Rolf Landauer, "Computation, Measurement, Communication and Energy Dissipation," in S. Haykin, ed., *Selected Topics in Signal Processing* (Englewood Cliffs, N.J.: Prentice-Hall, 1989), p. 40.

19. Rolf Landauer, "Information Is Physical," *Physics Today*, May 1991, pp. 23–29, here p. 28.

20. Chris Langton, "Computation at the Edge of Chaos: Phase Transitions and Emergent Computation," *Physica D* 42 (1990), 12–37 (preprint LA-UR-90-379, p. 30).

21. Ibid., p. 3.

22. James P. Crutchfield and Karl Young, "Computation at the Onset of Chaos," in Zurek, *Complexity, Entropy and the Physics of Information*, pp. 223–69.

23. Peter Richter in the Danish TV series "Hvælv": *Det kosmiske kaos*, DR-TV, 16 May 1988.

CHAPTER 15: THE NONLINEAR LINE

1. Carl Sagan, *The Cosmic Connection* (New York: Anchor, 1973), p. 130.

2. Carl Sagan, *Cosmos* (New York: Random House, 1980), p. 110.

3. Benoit B. Mandelbrot, *The Fractal Geometry of Nature* (New York: W. H. Freeman, 1983 [orig. 1977]), p. 1.

4. Friedensreich Hundertwasser, in H.-O. Peitgen and P. H. Richter, *The Beauty of Fractals* (Berlin: Springer-Verlag, 1986), p. v.

5. Benoit B. Mandelbrot, "How Long Is the Coast of Britain? Statistical Self-Similarity and Fractional Dimension," *Science* 156 (1967), 636–38.

6. *Gyldendals Tibinds Leksikon* (Copenhagen: Gyldendal, 1983), vol. 2, p. 308.
7. Kirk, Raven, and Schofield, *The Presocratic Philosophers*, p. 279.
8. Landauer, "Information Is Physical," pp. 28–9. The argument of the infinite information content of the universe was proposed at the workshop on "Complexity, Entropy and the Physics of Information."
9. John Wheeler, "Information, Physics, Quantum: The Search for Links," in Zurek, *Complexity, Entropy and the Physics of Information*, pp. 9–10.
10. Helmar G. Frank, *Kybernetischen Grundlagen der Pädagogik* (Baden-Baden: Agis-Verlag, 1969 [orig. 1962]), p. 69.
11. Bernard H. Lavenda, "Brownian Motion," *Scientific American* 252:2 (1985), 56–67.
12. Karl Marx, *Capital* (London: Lawrence & Wishart, 1954), vol. 3, part 7 ("Revenues and Their Sources"), p. 820.
13. Jørgen K. Bukdahl, "Naturdialektik som bidrag til en ædruelig kritik af den instrumentelle fornuft" (Natural dialectic as a contribution to sober criticism of instrumental common sense), *Teori og Praksis* 4 (1975), 7–17, here p. 8.
14. Lewis Carroll, "Sylvie and Bruno Concluded," *The Complete Works of Lewis Carroll* (New York: The Modern Library, date unknown), pp. 616–17. The preface to the story is dated Christmas 1893.

CHAPTER 16: THE SUBLIME

1. Niels Bohr, *Open Letter to the United Nations, June 9th, 1950* (Copenhagen: J. H. Schultz Forlag), p. 6.
2. A. Boserup, L. Christensen, and O. Nathan, eds., *The Challenge of Nuclear Armaments* (Copenhagen: Rhodos, 1986).
3. N. Barfoed, T. Bredsdorff, L. Christensen, and O. Nathan, eds., *The Challenge of an Open World* (Copenhagen: Munksgaard, 1989). "Hvælv," *Rundbohr*, DR-TV, 29 May 1989.
4. Anders Boserup, Ove Nathan, and Tor Nørretranders, "McNamara's Plan," *Nature* 307 (1984), 680. Anders Boserup, in Tor Nørretranders, *Det udelelige* (Copenhagen: Gyldendal, 1985), pp. 358–73.
5. Morris Berman, *Coming to Our Senses* (London: Unwin, 1990 [orig. 1989]), p. 98.
6. *Baikal Cultural Express*, Ulan-Ude, Buryat, July 1990. I am grateful to Elena Yudenova for the quotation.
7. Martin Buber, *I and Thou* (Edinburgh: T. & T. Clark, 1987 [orig. German ed. 1923; Eng. trans. 1937]), p. 104.
8. Robert Ornstein and Paul Ehrlich, *New World, New Mind: Changing the Way We Think to Save Our Future* (London: Paladin, 1991 [orig. 1989]), p. 7.
9. Ibid., p. 10.
10. Ibid., p. 12.
11. Ibid., p. 217.
12. A. P. Cowie, R. Mackin, and I. R. McCaig, *Oxford Dictionary of English Idioms*, 1993, p. 210 (orig. published as *Oxford Dictionary of Current Idiomatic English*, vol. 2, 1983). Also ascribed to Napoleon Bonaparte after the retreat from Moscow, 1812: "From the sublime to the ridiculous there is only one step," *Pen-*

guin Dictionary of Quotations (London: Book Club Associates, 1977 [orig. 1960]), p. 268. *Ordbog over Det Danske Sprog* (Copenhagen: Gyldendal, 1931), vol. 12, sp. 444. See also *Shorter Oxford English Dictionary* (1975), vol. 2, p. 2168.

13. *Ordbog over Det Danske Sprog* (note 12), vol. 22, sp. 444.

14. The closest one can get is "a feeling of comfort and bonhomie." "It is what the Danes pursue rather than happiness" (translator's note). "Everybody pursues it, but only Danes get there!" (author's reply).

15. Theodore Roszak, *Person/Planet* (London: Gollancz, 1979 [orig. 1977]).

16. Søren Kierkegaard, *Om Begrebet Ironi med stadigt Hensyn til Socrates, Samlede Værker* (Collected Works) (Copenhagen: Gyldendal, 1962), vol. 1, p. 281.

BIBLIOGRAPHY

This list includes only works quoted or mentioned in the body of the book and its notes. Works reprinted in anthologies included elsewhere in the list are not indicated under separate headings (as they are in the notes).

Abram, David. "The Perceptual Implications of Gaia." *The Ecologist* 15:3 (1985), 96–103.

Anderson, P. W. "More Is Different." *Science* 177 (1972), 393–96.

Attneave, Fred. *Applications of Information Theory to Psychology.* New York: Holt & Co., 1959.

Barfoed, N., T. Bredsdorff, L. Christensen, and O. Nathan, eds. *The Challenge of an Open World.* Copenhagen: Munksgaard, 1989.

Baringa, Marck. "The Mind Revealed?" *Science* 249 (1990), 856–58.

Barlow, Horace, Colin Blakemore, and Miranda Weston-Smith. *Images and Understanding.* Cambridge, Eng.: Cambridge University Press, 1990.

Bastian, Peter. *Ind i musikken.* Copenhagen: Gyldendal, 1987.

Bataille, Georges. *Den indre erfaring.* Copenhagen: Rhodos, 1972.

Bateson, Gregory. *Steps to an Ecology of Mind.* New York: Ballantine Books, 1972.

Bekenstein, Jacob D. "Black Holes and Entropy." *Physical Review D* 7 (1973), 2333–46.

Bennett, Charles H. "On the Nature and Origin of Complexity in Discrete, Homogenous, Locally-Interacting Systems." *Foundations of Physics* 16 (1986), 585–92.

———. "Demons, Engines and the Second Law." *Scientific American* 257:5 (1988), 88–96.

———. "Logical Depth and Physical Complexity." In *The Universal Turing Machine. A Half-Century Survey,* by Rolf Herken. Oxford: Oxford University Press, 1988.

Berman, Morris. *Coming to Our Senses.* London: Unwin Paperbacks, 1990.

Bohr, Niels. "Virkningskvantet og naturbeskrivelsen." In *Atomteori og Naturbeskrivelsen.* Copenhagen: Bianco Lunos Bogtrykkeri, 1929.

————. *Open Letter to the United Nations, June 9th, 1950.* Copenhagen: J. H. Schultz Forlag, Denmark.

Boring, E. G. *The Physical Dimensions of Consciousness.* New York: Dover, 1963.

Boserup, Anders, Ove Nathan, and Tor Nørretranders. "McNamara's Plan." *Nature* 307 (1984), 680.

Boserup, A., L. Christensen, and O. Nathan, eds. *The Challenge of Nuclear Armaments.* Copenhagen: Rhodos, 1986.

Bridgeman, Bruce. *The Biology of Behavior and Mind.* New York: Wiley, 1988.

Brillouin, Leon. *Science and Information Theory.* New York: Academic Press, 1956.

Broda, Engelbert. *Ludwig Boltzmann: Man—Physicist—Philosopher.* Woodbridge, Conn.: Ox Bow Press, 1983.

Brou, Philippe, Thomas Sciascia, Lynette Linden, and Jerome Y. Lettvin. "The Colors of Things." *Scientific American* 254:9 (1986), 84–91.

Brunak, Søren, and Benny Lautrup. *Neurale netværk.* Copenhagen: Munksgaard, 1988.

Buber, Martin. *I and Thou.* Edinburgh: T. & T. Clark, 1987.

Bukdahl, Jørgen K. "Naturdialektik som bidrag til en ædruelig kritik af den instrumentelle fornuft." *Teori og Praksis* 4 (1975), 7–17.

Campbell, Lewis, and William Garnett. *The Life of James Clerk Maxwell,* Rev. ed. London: Macmillan, 1884.

Capra, Fritjof. *Vendepunktet.* Copenhagen: Borgen, 1986.

Carroll, Lewis. "Sylvie and Bruno Concluded." In *The Complete Works of Lewis Carroll.* New York: The Modern Library, n.d.

Caves, Carlton. "Quantitative Limits on the Ability of a Maxwell Demon to Extract Work from Heat." *Physical Review Letters* 64 (1990), 2111–14.

Chaitin, Gregory J. *Information, Randomness & Incompleteness.* Singapore: World Scientific, 1987.

————. "Randomness in Arithmetic." *Scientific American* 259:1 (1988), 52–7.

Christiansen, Peder Voetmann. "Informationens elendighed." In *Informationssamfundet,* by Thomas Söderqvist. Copenhagen: Forlaget Philosophia, 1985.

————. *Charles S. Peirce: Mursten og Mørtel til en Metafysik.* IMFUFA, Text no. 169. Roskilde: Roskilde Universitetscenter, 1988.

————. *Tegn og Kvanter.* IMFUFA/RUC, Text no. 202. Roskilde: Roskilde Universitetscenter, 1990.

Churchland, P. S. "On the Alleged Backwards Referral of Experiences and Its Relevance to the Mind-Body Problem." *Philosophy of Science* 48 (1981), 165–81.

————. "The Timing of Sensations: Reply to Libet." *Philosophy of Science* 48 (1981), 492–97.

————. *Neurophilosophy: Towards a Unified Science of the Mind-Brain.* Cambridge, Mass.: The MIT Press, 1986.

Chyba, Christopher F. "Impact Delivery and Erosion of Planetary Oceans in the Inner Early Solar System." *Nature* 343 (1990), 129–33.

Chyba, Christopher F., Paul J. Thomas, Leigh Brookshaw, and Carl Sagan. "Cometary Delivery of Organic Molecules to the Early Earth." *Science* 249 (1990), 366–73.

Cole, K. C. *Vision: In the Eye of the Beholder.* San Francisco: Exploratorium, 1978.

Cotterill, Rodney. *No Ghost in the Machine.* London: Heinemann, 1989.

Coveney, Peter V. "The Second Law of Thermodynamics: Entropy, Irreversibility and Dynamics." *Nature* 333 (1988), 409–15.

Crawford, Helen, Hugh Macdonald, and Ernest R. Hilgard. "Hypnotic Deafness: A Psychophysical Study of Responses to Tone Intensity as Modified by Hypnosis." *American Journal of Psychology* 92 (1979), 193–214.

Crick, Francis. "Function of the Thalamic Reticular Complex: The Searchlight Hypothesis." *Proceedings of the National Academy of Sciences, USA,* 81 (1984), 4586–90.

Crick, F., and C. Asanuma. "Certain Aspects of the Anatomy and Physiology of the Cerebral Cortex." In *Parallel Distributed Processing,* edited by J. L. McClelland and D. E. Rumelhart. Vol. 2. Cambridge, Mass.: The MIT Press, 1986.

Crick, Francis, and Christof Koch. "Towards a Neurobiological Theory of Consciousness." *Seminars in the Neurosciences* 2 (1990), 263–75.

———. "Some Reflections on Visual Awareness." *Symposia on Quantitative Biology.* Vol. 55. Cold Spring Harbor, N.Y.: Cold Spring Harbor Press, 1990.

Crone, C., et al., eds. *Fysiologi.* Copenhagen: Foreningen af Danske Lægestuderendes Forlag, 1990.

Crossman, E. R. F. W. "Information Theory in Psychological Measurement." In *Encyclopedia of Linguistics,* edited by A. R. Mettham and R. A. Hudson. Oxford: Information and Control, 1969.

Crutchfield, James P., and Karl Young. "Inferring Statistical Complexity." *Physical Review Letters* 63 (1989), 105–8.

Damasio, Antonio R., Hanna Damasio, and Gary W. Van Hoesen. "Prosopagnosia: Anatomic Basis and Behavioral Mechanisms." *Neurology (Ny)* 32 (1982), 331–41.

Davies, John. "The Musical Mind." *New Scientist,* 19 January 1991, 38–41.

Deecke, Lüder. "The Natural Explanation for the Two Components of the Readiness Potential." *The Behavioral and Brain Sciences* 10 (1987), 781–82.

Deecke, Lüder, Berta Grözinger, and H. H. Kornhuber. "Voluntary Finger Movement in Man: Cerebral Potentials and Theory." *Biological Cybernetics* 23 (1976), 99–119.

Denbigh, K. G., and J. S. Denbigh. *Entropy in Relation to Incomplete Knowledge.* Cambridge: Cambridge University Press, 1985.

Dennett, Daniel, and Marcel Kinsbourne. "Time and the Observer: The Where and When of Consciousness in the Brain." *The Behavioral and Brain Sciences,* in press.

Deregowski, J. B. "Real Space and Represented Space: Cross-Cultural Perspectives." *The Behavioral and Brain Sciences* 12 (1989), 51–119.

Des Coudres, Theodor. "Ludwig Boltzmann. Nekrolog." *Berichte über die Verhandlungen der könglich sächsischen Gesellschaft der Wissenschaften zu Leipzig, Mathamatisch-Physische Klasse,* 58 (1906), 615–27.

Dixon, Bernard. *Beyond the Magic Bullet.* London: Allen & Unwin, 1978.

Dixon, Norman. *Subliminal Perception: The Nature of a Controversy.* London: McGraw-Hill, 1971.

———. *Preconscious Processing.* Chichester: John Wiley, 1981.

Dossey, Larry. *Space, Time and Medicine.* Boulder, Colo.: Shambhala Publications, 1982.

Dretske, Fred I. "Précis of Knowledge and the Flow of Information." *The Behavioral and Brain Sciences* 6 (1983), 55–90.

Ebeling, Werner, and Michail V. Volkenstein. "Entropy and the Evolution of Biological Information." *Physica A* 163 (1990), 398–402.

Eco, Umberto. *The Name of the Rose.* Translated by William Weaver, 1983. Reprint,
Mandarin, 1994.

Einstein, Albert. "Physik und Realität." *The Journal of The Franklin Institute* 221
(1936), 313–47.

Eysenck, H. J. "The Theory of Intelligence and the Psychophysiology of Cognition."
In *Advances in the Psychology of Human Intelligence,* by Robert J. Sternberg. Vol. 3.
Hillsdale, N.J.: Lawrence Erlbaum, 1986.

Farmer, J. Doyne, and Aletta d'A. Belin. "Artificial Life: The Coming Evolution."
Preprint LA-UR-90-378.

Feynman, Richard P. *What Do You Care What Other People Think?* New York: W. W.
Norton, 1988.

Feynman, Richard P., R. B. Leighton, and M. Sands. *The Feynman Lectures on Physics.*
Reading, Mass.: Addison-Wesley, 1977.

Fisher, Arthur. "The Wheels Within Wheels in the Superkingdom Eucaryotae."
Mosaic 20:3 (1989), 2–13.

Frank, Helmuth G. *Kybernetischen Grundlagen der Pädagogik.* Vol. 2. Baden-Baden:
Agis-Agis Verlag, 1962.

Friberg, Lars, and Per E. Roland. "Functional Activation and Inhibition of Regional
Cerebral Blood Flow and Metabolism." In *Basic Mechanisms of Headache,* edited by
J. Olesen and L. Edvinsson. Amsterdam: Elsevier, 1988.

Furnham, Adrian. "Hooked on Horoscopes." *New Scientist,* 26 January 1991, 33–6.

Gamow, George. *Tredive År der rystede Fysikken.* Copenhagen: Gyldendal, 1968.

Gardner, Howard. *The Mind's New Science.* New York: Basic Books, 1987.

Garner, Wendell R. *Uncertainty and Structure as Psychological Concepts.* New York:
John Wiley, 1962.

Garner, W. R., and Harold W. Hake. "The Amount of Information in Absolute
Judgements." *Psychological Review* 58 (1951), 446–59.

Gazzaniga, Michael S. *The Social Brain.* New York: Basic Books, 1985.

Gleick, James. *Kaos.* Copenhagen: Munksgaard, 1989.

Glynn, Ian M. "Consciousness and Time." *Nature* 348 (1990), 477–79.

Gödel, Kurt. *Collected Works.* Vol. I, edited by S. Feferman et al. New York: Oxford
University Press, 1986.

Goldman, Martin. *The Demon in the Aether: The Story of James Clerk Maxwell.* Edinburgh: Paul Harris, 1983.

Gould, Glenn. *Afskaf bifald!* Copenhagen: Gyldendal, 1988.

Grassberger, Peter. "How to Measure Self-Generated Complexity." *Physica* 140A
(1986), 319–25.

———. "Toward a Quantitative Theory of Self-Generated Complexity." *International Journal of Theoretical Physics* 25 (1986), 907–44.

Gray, Charles M., Peter König, Andreas K. Engel, and Wolf Singer. "Oscillatory
Responses in Cat Visual Cortex Exhibit Inter-Columnar Synchronization Which
Reflects Global Stimulus Properties." *Nature* 338 (1989), 334–37.

Green, Barry, and W. Timothy Gallwey. *The Inner Game of Music.* London: Pan,
1987.

Gregory, Richard L. *Mind in Science.* Harmondsworth: Penguin, 1984.

———. *The Oxford Companion to the Mind.* Oxford: Oxford University Press, 1987.

———. "Turning Minds on to Science by Hands-on Exploration: The Nature and Potential of the Hands-on Medium." In *Sharing Science.* (London: The Nuffield Foundation, 1989).

———. *Eye and Brain: The Psychology of Seeing.* 4th ed. Princeton, N.J.: Princeton University Press, 1990.

Guinness Book of Records 1996. In Arts and Entertainment section, Literature subsection, Diaries and Letters sub-subsection. Facts on File, Inc., 1995.

Hadamard, Jacques. *An Essay on the Psychology of Invention in the Mathematical Field.* Princeton, N.J.: Princeton University Press, 1949.

Hall, Edward T. *The Silent Language.* New York: Doubleday, 1981.

———. *The Hidden Dimension.* New York: Doubleday, 1982.

Hanson, Norwood Russell. *Patterns of Discovery.* Cambridge: Cambridge University Press, 1965.

Hartnack, Justus. *Hegels Logik.* Copenhagen: C. A. Reitzels Forlag, 1990.

Hick, W. E. "On the Rate of Gain of Information." *Quarterly Journal of Experimental Psychology* 4 (1952), 11–26.

Hobson, J. Allan. *The Dreaming Brain.* London: Penguin, 1990.

Hodges, Andrew. *Alan Turing: The Enigma of Intelligence.* London: Unwin Paperbacks, 1985.

Høffding, Harald. *Psykologi.* 6th ed. Copenhagen: Gyldendal, 1911.

Hoffmeyer, Jesper. *Evolution, Økologi, Historie.* Copenhagen: politisk revy, 1980.

———. *Naturen i hovedet.* Copenhagen: Rosinante, 1984.

Hofstadter, Douglas. *Gödel, Escher, Bach—An Eternal Golden Braid.* Harmondsworth: Penguin Books, 1980.

Hofstadter, Douglas R., and Daniel C. Dennett. *The Mind's I.* Harmondsworth: Penguin, 1982.

Holender, Daniel. "Semantic Activation Without Conscious Identification in Dichotic Listening, Parafoveal Vision, and Visual Masking: A Survey and Appraisal." *The Behavioral and Brain Sciences* 9 (1986), 1–66.

Honderich, Ted. "The Time of a Conscious Sensory Experience and Mind-Brain Theories." *Journal of Theoretical Biology* 110 (1984), 115–29.

Horgan, John. "Profile: Claude E. Shannon." *Scientific American* 262:1 (1990), 16–19.

Horkheimer, Max, and Th. W. Adorno. *Oplysningens Dialektik.* Copenhagen: Gyldendal, 1972.

Huberman, B. A., and T. Hogg. "Complexity and Adaptation." *Physica* 22D (1986), 376–84.

Huxley, Aldous, *The Perennial Philosophy.* New York: Harper & Row, 1970.

———. *The Doors of Perception.* In *The Doors of Perception and Heaven & Hell.* London: Chatto & Windus, 1968.

"Hvælv." *Det kosmiske kaos.* DR-TV, 16 May 1988.

"Hvælv." *Rundbohr.* DR-TV, 29 May 1989.

"Hvælv." *Den intuitive elektronhjerne.* DR-TV, 24 October 1989.

Ingvar, D. H., et al., eds. *Brain Work II, Abstracts.* Copenhagen: Alfred Benzon Symposium 31, 1990.

Jahnsen, Henrik, and Arne Mosfeldt Laursen. *Hjernevindinger*. Copenhagen: Munksgaard, 1990.

James, William. *The Principles of Psychology*. London: Macmillan, 1891.

Jaynes, Julian. *The Origin of Consciousness in the Breakdown of the Bicameral Mind*. Boston: Houghton Mifflin, 1982.

Jensen, Olav Storm. "Kropspsykologi og orgasme." In *Hengivelse—en debatbog om mænds orgasmer*, edited by Tor Nørretranders. Copenhagen: Informations Forlag, 1981.

Johansson, I., R. Kalleberg, and S.-E. Liedman. *Positivisme, marxisme, kritisk teori*. Copenhagen: Gyldendal, 1974.

Johnson-Laird, P. N. *The Computer and the Mind*. London: Fontana, 1988.

Johnstone, Keith. *Impro: Improvisation and the Theatre*. 4th ptg. New York: Theatre Arts Books, 1985.

Jung, C. G. *Jeg'et og det ubevidste*. Copenhagen: Gyldendal, 1987.

Jung, Richard. "Perception, Consciousness and Visual Attention." In *Cerebral Correlates of Conscious Experience*, by P. A. Buser and A. Rougeul-Buser. INSERM Symposium no. 6. Amsterdam: Elsevier/North-Holland, 1978.

Kaufmann, Walter. *The Faith of a Heretic*. New York: Doubleday, 1961.

Kay, Alan. "Computer Software." *Scientific American* 251:3 (1984), 41–7.

Keller, I., and H. Heckhausen. "Readiness Potentials Preceding Spontaneous Motor Acts: Voluntary vs. Involuntary Control." *Electroencephalography and Clinical Neurophysiology* 76 (1990), 351–61.

Kihlstrom, John F. "The Cognitive Unconscious." *Science* 237 (1987), 1445–52.

Kirk, G. S., J. E. Raven, and M. Schofield. *The Presocratic Philosophers*. Cambridge, Eng.: Cambridge University Press, 1983.

Kirkeby, Ole Fogh. *Begivenhed og kropstanke*. Unpublished Ms. 1991.

Kierkegaard, Søren. *Samlede Værker*. Copenhagen: Gyldendal, 1964.

Klein, Martin J. *Paul Ehrenfest*. Vol. 1: *The Making of a Theoretical Physicist*. 3d ed. Amsterdam: North-Holland, 1985.

Kline, Morris. *Mathematics: The Loss of Certainty*. New York: Oxford University Press, 1980.

———. *Mathematics and the Search for Knowledge*. New York: Oxford University Press, 1985.

Kolb, Bryan, and Ian Q. Whishaw. *Fundamentals of Human Neuropsychology*. 3d ed. New York: W. H. Freeman, 1990.

Kornhuber, H. H. "The Human Brain: From Dream and Cognition to Fantasy, Will, Conscience, and Freedom." In *Information Processing by the Brain*, edited by Hans J. Markowitsch. Toronto: Hans Huber Publishers, 1988.

Kornhuber, Hans H., and Lüder Deecke. "Hirnpotentialänderungen bei Willkürbewegungen und passiven Bewegungen des Menschen: Bereitschaftspotential und reafferente Potentiale." *Pflügers Archiv fir dir gesamte Physiologie des Menschen und Tieren* 284 (1965), 1–17.

Kramer-Friedrich, Sibylle. "Information Measurement and Information Technology: A Myth of the Twentieth Century." *Boston Studies in the Philosophy of Science* 90 (1986), 17–28.

Kuhn, Hans. "Origin of Life and Physics: Diversified Microstructure-Inducement to

Form Information-Carrying and Knowledge Accumulating Systems." *IBM J. Res. Develop.* 32:1 (1988), 37–46.

Kuhn, Thomas S. *Videnskabens revolutioner.* Copenhagen: Fremad, 1973.

Kulli, John, and Christof Koch. "Does Anesthesia Cause Loss of Consciousness?" *TINS* 14:1 (1991), 6–10.

Küpfmüller, K. "Nachrichtenverarbeitung im Menschen." In *Taschenbuch der Nachrichtenverarbeitung,* edited by K. Steinbuch. Berlin: Springer, 1962.

———. "Grundlagen der Informationstheorie und Kybernetik." In *Physiologie des Menschen,* edited by O. H. Grauer, K. Kramer, and R. Jung. Vol. 10. Munich: Urban & Schwarzenberg, 1971.

Küppers, Bernd-Olaf. *Information and the Origin of Life.* Cambridge, Mass.: The MIT Press, 1990.

Landauer, Rolf. "Nonlinearity, Multistability, and Fluctuations: Reviewing the Reviewers." *Am. J. Physiol.* 241 (1981), R107–13.

———. "Dissipation and Noise Immunity in Computation and Communication." *Nature* 335 (1988), 779–84.

———. "A Simple Measure of Complexity." *Nature* 336 (1988), 306–7.

———. "Computation, Measurement, Communication and Energy Dissipation." In *Selected Topics in Signal Processing,* edited by S. Haykin. Englewood Cliffs, N.J.: Prentice-Hall, 1989.

———. "Information Is Physical." *Physics Today,* May 1991, 23–9.

Langton, Christopher G. *Artificial Life: Proceedings of an Interdisciplinary Workshop on the Synthesis and Simulation of Living Systems.* Santa Fe Institute Studies in the Sciences of Complexity VI. Redwood City, Cal.: Addison-Wesley, 1989.

———. "Computation at the Edge of Chaos: Phase Transitions and Emergent Computation." *Physica D* 42 (1990), 12–37.

Lao-tzu. *Tao te ching.* New York: Vintage Books, 1972.

Lassen, Niels A., David H. Ingvar, and Erik Skinhøj. "Brain Function and Blood Flow." *Scientific American* 239 (1977), 62–71.

Latto, Richard, and John Campion. "Approaches to Consciousness: Psychophysics or Philosophy?" *The Behavioral and Brain Sciences* 9:1 (1986), 36–7.

Lavenda, Bernard H. "Brownian Motion." *Scientific American* 252:2 (1985), 56–67.

Layzer, David. *Cosmogenesis.* New York: Oxford University Press, 1990.

Leder, Drew. *The Absent Body.* Chicago: The University of Chicago Press, 1990.

Leff, Harvey S., and Andrew F. Rex. *Maxwell's Demon: Entropy, Information, Computing.* Princeton, N.J.: Princeton University Press, 1990.

Lehrl, S., and B. Fischer. "Der maximale zentrale Informationsfluss bei Küpfmüller und Frank: beträgt er 50 bit/s oder 16 bit/s?" *Grundlagenstudien aus Kybernetik und Geistenswissenschaft / Humankybernetik* 26 (1985), 147–54.

Lettvin, J. Y., H. R. Maturana, W. S. McCulloch, and W. H. Pitts. "What the Frog's Eye Tells the Frog's Brain." *Proceedings of the IRE* 47 (1940–51), 1959.

Libet, Benjamin. "Cortical Activation in Conscious and Unconscious Experience." *Perspectives in Biology and Medicine* 9 (1965), 77–86.

———. "The Experimental Evidence for Subjective Referral of a Sensory Experience Backwards in Time: Reply to P. S. Churchland." *Philosophy of Science* 48 (1981), 182–97.

————. "Subjective Antedating of a Sensory Experience and Mind-Brain Theories: Reply to Honderich (1984)." *Journal of Theoretical Biology* 114 (1985), 563–70.

————. "Unconscious Cerebral Initiative and the Role of Conscious Will in Voluntary Action." *The Behavioral and Brain Sciences* 8 (1985), 529–66.

————. "Conscious Subjective Experience vs. Unconscious Mental Functions: A Theory of the Cerebral Processes Involved." In *Models of Brain Function*, edited by R. M. J. Cotterill. Cambridge, Eng.: Cambridge University Press, 1989.

————. "Time-Delays in Conscious Processes." *The Behavioral and Brain Sciences* 13 (1990), 672.

————. "Conscious vs. Neural Time." *Nature* 352 (1991), 27.

————. "Models of Conscious Timing and the Experimental Evidence." *The Behavioral and Brain Sciences* 15, (1992), 213–75.

Libet, B., W. W. Alberts, E. W. Wright, Jr., and B. Feinstein. "Responses of Human Somatosensory Cortex to Stimuli Below Threshold for Conscious Sensation." *Science* 158 (1967), 1597–1600.

————. "Cortical and Thalamic Activation in Conscious Sensory Experience." In *Neurophysiology Studied in Man*, edited by G. G. Somjen. Amsterdam: Excerpta Medica, 1972.

————, L. D. Delatytre, and G. Levin. "Production of Threshold Levels of Conscious Sensation by Electrical Stimulation of Human Somatosensory Cortex." *J. Neurophysiol.* 27 (1964), 546–78.

Libet, Benjamin, Elwood W. Wright, Jr., Bertram Feinstein, and Dennis Pearl. "Subjective Referral of the Timing for a Conscious Sensory Experience." *Brain* 102 (1979), 193–224.

Libet, Benjamin, Curtis A. Gleason, Elwood W. Wright, and Dennis K. Pearl. "Time of Conscious Intention to Act in Relation to Onset of Cerebral Activity (Readiness-potential)." *Brain* 106 (1983), 623–42.

Libet, Benjamin, Dennis K. Pearl, David Morledge, Curtis A. Gleason, Yoshio Morledge, and Nicholas M. Barbaro. "Control of the Transition from Sensory Detection to Sensory Awareness in Man by the Duration of a Thalamic Stimulus." *Brain* 14, (1991), 1731–57.

Lilly, John C. *The Centre of the Cyclone. An Autobiography of Inner Space.* London: Paladin, 1973.

————. *Communication Between Man & Dolphin.* New York: Crown, 1978.

Lloyd, Seth. "Use of Mutual Information to Decrease Entropy: Implications for the Second Law of Thermodynamics." *Physical Review A* 39 (1989), 5378–86.

————. "The Calculus of Intricacy." *The Sciences* 30:5 (1990), 38–44.

————. and Heinz Pagels. "Complexity as Thermodynamic Depth." *Annals of Physics* 188 (1988), 186–213.

Lovelock, James. *The Ages of Gaia.* Oxford, Eng.: Oxford University Press, 1988.

Luria, A. R. *Hjernen: En introduktion til neuropsykologien.* Copenhagen: Nyt Nordisk, 1989.

MacKay, Donald M. *Information, Mechanism and Meaning.* Cambridge, Mass.: The MIT Press, 1969.

Mandelbrot, Benoit B. "How Long Is the Coast of Britain? Statistical Self-Similarity and Fractional Dimension." *Science* 156 (1967), 636–38.

————. *The Fractal Geometry of Nature.* New York: W. H. Freeman, 1983.

Mann, Charles. "Lynn Margulis: Science's Unruly Earth Mother." *Science* 252 (1991), 378–81.

Margulis, Lynn, and Dorion Sagan. *Mikrokosmos.* Copenhagen: Munksgaard, 1990.

Marr, David. *Vision: A Computational Investigation into the Human Representation and Processing of Visual Information.* New York: W. H. Freeman, 1982.

Marx, Karl. *Capital.* London: Lawrence & Wishart, 1954.

Maslow, Abraham. *The Psychology of Science.* New York: Harper, 1966.

Masterman, Margaret. "The Nature of a Paradigm." In *Criticism and the Growth of Knowledge,* edited by Imre Latakos and Alan Musgrave. London: Cambridge University Press, 1974.

Matsui, Takafumi, and Yutaka Abe. "Evolution of an Impact-Induced Atmosphere and Magma Ocean on the Accreting Earth." *Nature* 319 (1986), 303–5.

Maturana, Humberto R. "What Is It to See?" *Arch. Biol. Med. Exp.* 16 (1983), 255–69.

Maturana, Humberto, and Francisco Varela. *Kundskabens træ.* Århus: Ask, 1987.

Maxwell, James Clerk. *The Scientific Papers of James Clerk Maxwell.* Cambridge, Eng.: Cambridge University Press, 1890.

Miller, G. A. "Information Theory." *Scientific American* 195:2 (1956), 42–6.

————. "The Magical Number Seven, Plus or Minus Two." *Psychological Review* 63 (1956), 81–7.

Moravec, Hans. *Mind Children: The Future of Robot and Human Intelligence.* Cambridge, Mass.: Harvard University Press, 1988.

Mountcastle, Vernon B. "The View from Within: Pathways to the Study of Perception." *The Johns Hopkins Medical Journal* 136 (1975), 109–31.

Myers, Norman, ed. *The Gaia Atlas of Planet Management.* London: Pan Books, 1985.

Nagel, Thomas. *What Does It All Mean? A Very Short Introduction to Philosophy.* New York: Oxford University Press, 1987.

————. "Is That You, James?" *London Review of Books* 9:17 (1 October 1987), 3–6.

Nørretranders, Tor. *Det udelelige.* Copenhagen: Gyldendal, 1985.

————. "Videnskab og hverdagssprog." *bogens verden* 68 (1986), 395–98.

————. *Naturvidenskab og ikke-viden.* Århus: Kimære, 1987.

————. *Videnskabsvurdering.* Copenhagen: Gyldendal, 1987.

————. "En rejse ind i Peter Bastians lyd." *Levende Billeder,* April 1987, 12–15.

————. *Den blå himmel.* Copenhagen: Munksgaard, 1987.

Nyborg, Eigil. *Den indre linie i H. C. Andersens eventyr: En psykologisk studie.* Copenhagen: Gyldendal, 1983.

Oakley, David A., ed. *Brain and Mind.* London: Methuen, 1985.

Ølgaard, Bent. *Kommunikation og Økomentale Systemer.* Åbyhøj: Ask, 1986.

Ordbog over det danske Sprog. Copenhagen: Gyldendal, 1977.

Ornstein, Robert, and Paul Ehrlich. *New World, New Mind.* London: Paladin, 1991.

Packard, Vance. *The People Shapers.* London: Macdonald and Jane's, 1978.

Pagels, Heinz. *The Dreams of Reason. The Computer and the Rise of the Sciences of Complexity.* New York: Bantam Books, 1989.

Peacock, John. "More Hubble Trouble?" *Nature* 352 (1991), 378–79.

Pedersen, Johannes Mørk. *Psykologiens Historie, Psykologisk Laboratorium.* Copenhagen: Copenhagen University, 1990.

Peirce, C. S., and J. Jastrow. "On Small Differences of Sensation." *National Academy of Sciences*, vol. 3, Fifth Memoir (1884), 73–83.

Peitgen, H.-O., and P. H. Richter. *The Beauty of Fractals.* Berlin: Springer-Verlag, 1986.

Penrose, Roger. *The Emperor's New Mind.* London: Vintage, 1990.

Petersen, Aage. "The Philosophy of Niels Bohr." *Bulletin of the Atomic Scientist* 19 (1963), 8–14.

———. *Quantum Physics and the Philosophical Tradition.* New York: Yeshiva University, 1968.

Pierce, J. R. *Symbols, Signals and Noise.* New York: Harper & Brothers, 1961.

Pierce, John R., and A. Michael Noll. *Signals: The Science of Telecommunications.* New York: Scientific American Library, 1990.

Poggio, T. "Vision: The 'Other' Face of AI." In *Modelling the Mind,* edited by K. A. Mohyeldin Said, et al. Oxford: Clarendon Press, 1990.

Polanyi, Michael. *Personal Knowledge.* London: Routledge & Kegan Paul, 1958.

Popper, Karl R., and John C. Eccles. *The Self and Its Brain.* Berlin: Springer International, 1985.

Prigogine, Ilya, and Isabelle Stengers. *Order Out of Chaos.* New York: Bantam Books, 1984.

Quastler, Henry. "Studies of Human Channel Capacity." In *Information Theory, Proceedings of the Third London Symposium,* edited by Colin Cherry. London: Butterworths, 1956.

Rancke-Madsen, E. *Grundstoffernes Opdagelseshistorie.* Copenhagen: G. E. C. Gad, 1987.

Rasmussen, Steen, Carsten Knudsen, Rasmus Feldberg, and Morten Hindsholm. "The Coreworld: Emergence and Evolution of Cooperative Structures in a Computational Chemistry." *Physica D* 42 (1990), 111–34.

Reid, Constance. *Hilbert-Courant.* New York: Springer-Verlag, 1986.

Restak, Richard M. *The Brain.* New York: Warner Books, 1979.

Rock, Irvin, ed. *The Perceptual World.* New York: W. H. Freeman, 1990.

Rock, Irvin, and Stephen Palmer. "The Legacy of Gestalt Psychology." *Scientific American* 263:6 (1990), 48–61.

Roland, P. E., and L. Friberg. "Localization of Cortical Areas Activated by Thinking." *Journal of Neurophysiology* 53 (1985), 1219–43.

Roland, Per E., et al. "Does Mental Activity Change the Oxidative Metabolism of the Brain?" *The Journal of Neuroscience* 7 (1987), 2373–89.

Roszak, Theodore. *Person/Planet.* London: Gollancz, 1979.

———. *The Cult of Information.* New York: Pantheon Books, 1986.

Rucker, Rudy. *Mind Tools: The Five Levels of Mathematical Reality.* London: Penguin Books, 1988.

Russell, Bertrand. *Den vestlige verdens filosofi.* Copenhagen: Spektrum, n.d.

Sagan, Carl. *The Cosmic Connection.* New York: Anchor Press, 1973.

———. *Cosmos.* New York: Random House, 1980.

Sartre, Jean-Paul. *The Transcendence of the Ego.* New York: Noonday Press, 1957.

Sayre, Kenneth M. *Cybernetics and the Philosophy of Mind.* London: Routledge & Kegan Paul, 1976.

——. "Intentionality and Information Processing: An Alternative Model for Cognitive Science." *The Behavioral and Brain Sciences* 9 (1986), 121–66.

Schacter, Daniel L., and Peter L. Graf. "Effects of Elaborative Processing on Implicit and Explicit Memory for New Associations." *Journal of Experimental Psychology: Learning, Memory and Cognition* 12 (1986), 432–44.

Sejnowski, Terrence J., Christof Koch, and Patricia A. Churchland. "Computational Neuroscience." *Science* 241 (1988), 1299–1306.

Shanker, S. G., ed. *Gödel's Theorem in Focus.* London: Routledge, 1988.

Shannon, Claude E., and Warren Weaver. *The Mathematical Theory of Communication.* Urbana: The University of Illinois Press, 1963.

Shepard, Roger N. *Mind sights.* New York: W. H. Freeman, 1990.

Silk, Joseph. *The Big Bang.* New York: W. H. Freeman, 1989.

Simon, Herbert A. "The Architecture of Complexity." *Proceedings of the American Philosophical Society* 106 (1962), 467–82.

Spelke, Elizabeth, William Hirst, and Ulric Neisser. "Skills of Divided Attention." *Cognition* 4 (1976), 215–30.

Springer, Sally P., and Georg Deutsch. *Left Brain, Right Brain.* 3d ed. New York: W. H. Freeman, 1989.

Steinbuch, Karl. *Automat und Mensch.* Berlin: Springer-Verlag, 1965.

Steinsaltz, Adin. *The Essential Talmud.* London: Weidenfeld and Nicolson, 1976.

Stewart, Ian. "The Ultimate in Undecidability." *Nature* 332 (1988), 115–16.

Taylor, Janet L., and D. I. McCloskey. "Triggering of Preprogrammed Movements as Reactions to Masked Stimuli." *Journal of Neurophysiology* 63 (1990), 439–46.

Tolstoy, Ivan. *James Clerk Maxwell: A Biography.* Edinburgh: Canongate, 1981.

Toulmin, Stephen. *The Return to Cosmology.* Berkeley: University of California Press, 1982.

Tranel, Daniel, and Antonio R. Damasio. "Knowledge Without Awareness: An Autonomic Index of Facial Recognition by Prosopagnosics." *Science* 228 (1985), 1453–54.

Trincker, Dietrich. "Aufnahme, Speicherung und Verarbeitung von Information durch den Menschen." *Veröffentlichungen der Schleswig-Holsteinischen Universitätsgesellschaft, Neue Folge,* no. 44. Kiel: Verlag Ferdinand Hirt, 1966.

Tryon, Edward P. "What Made the World?" *New Scientist,* March 8, 1984, 14–16.

Tulving, Endel, and Daniel L. Schacter. "Priming and Human Memory Systems." *Science* 247 (1990), 301–6.

Varela, Francisco. "Laying Down a Path in Walking." In *Gaia: A Way of Knowing,* by William Irwin Thompson. Great Barrington, Mass.: Lindisfarne Press, 1987.

Von der Malsburg, Ch., and W. Schneider. "A Neural Cocktail-Party Processor." *Biological Cybernetics* 54 (1986), 29–40.

Wang, Hao. *Reflections on Kurt Gödel.* Cambridge, Mass.: The MIT Press, 1987.

Warrington, Elizabeth K., and L. Weiskrantz. "New Method of Testing Long-term Retention with Special Reference to Amnesic Patients." *Nature* 217 (1968), 972–74.

——. "Amnesic Syndrome: Consolidation or Retrieval?" *Nature* 228 (1970), 628–30.

Weiskrantz, L. *Blindsight: A Case Study and Implications.* Oxford Psychology Series no. 12. Oxford: Clarendon Press, 1986.

Weiss, Joseph. "Unconscious Mental Functioning." *Scientific American* 262:3 (1990), 75–81.

Wheeler, John A. *A Journey into Gravity and Spacetime.* New York: Scientific American Library, 1990.

Wiener, Norbert. *Cybernetics, or Control and Communication in the Animal and the Machine.* Cambridge, Mass.: The MIT Press, 1961.

Winson, Jonathan. "The Meaning of Dreams." *Scientific American* 263:5 (1990), 42–8.

Wittgenstein, Ludwig. *Tractatus Logico-Philosophicus.* Copenhagen: Gyldendal, 1963.

Witt-Hansen, Johannes. *Videnskabernes historie i det 20. århundrede: Filosofi.* Copenhagen: Gyldendal, 1985.

Wolf, Fred Alan. *Taking the Quantum Leap.* San Francisco: Harper & Row, 1981.

Wolfram, Stephen. "Cellular Automata as Models of Complexity." *Nature* 311 (1984), 419–24.

———. "Computer Software in Science and Mathematics." *Scientific American* 251:3 (1984), 140–51.

———. "Undecidability and Intractability in Theoretical Physics." *Physical Review Letters* 54 (1985), 735–38.

Yutang, Lin. *Jordisk Lykke.* Copenhagen: Gyldendal, 1968.

Zimmermann, M. "Neurophysiology of Sensory Systems." In *Fundamentals of Sensory Physiology,* edited by Robert F. Schmidt. Berlin: Springer-Verlag, 1986.

———. "The Nervous System in the Context of Information Theory." In *Human Physiology,* edited by R. F. Schmidt and G. Thews. 2d ed. Berlin: Springer-Verlag, 1989.

Peter Zinkernagel. *Omverdensproblemet.* Copenhagen: G. E. C. Gad, 1957.

———. *Virkelighed.* Copenhagen: Munksgaard, 1988.

———, A. van der Merwe, and W. A. Miller. *Between Quantum and Cosmos.* Princeton: Princeton University Press, 1988.

Zurek, W. H. "Thermodynamic Cost of Computation, Algorithmic Complexity and the Information Metric." *Nature* 341 (1989), 119–24.

———, ed. *Complexity, Entropy and the Physics of Information.* Santa Fe Institute Studies in the Sciences of Complexity, vol. 8. Redwood City, Cal.: Addison-Wesley, 1990.

INDEX

Page numbers in *italicized* type refer to illustrations.

FOR THE BEST IN PAPERBACKS, LOOK FOR THE

In every corner of the world, on every subject under the sun, Penguin represents quality and variety—the very best in publishing today.

For complete information about books available from Penguin—including Penguin Classics, Penguin Compass, and Puffins—and how to order them, write to us at the appropriate address below. Please note that for copyright reasons the selection of books varies from country to country.

In the United States: Please write to *Penguin Group (USA), P.O. Box 12289 Dept. B, Newark, New Jersey 07101-5289* or call 1-800-788-6262.

In the United Kingdom: Please write to *Dept. EP, Penguin Books Ltd, Bath Road, Harmondsworth, West Drayton, Middlesex UB7 0DA.*

In Canada: Please write to *Penguin Books Canada Ltd, 10 Alcorn Avenue, Suite 300, Toronto, Ontario M4V 3B2.*

In Australia: Please write to *Penguin Books Australia Ltd, P.O. Box 257, Ringwood, Victoria 3134.*

In New Zealand: Please write to *Penguin Books (NZ) Ltd, Private Bag 102902, North Shore Mail Centre, Auckland 10.*

In India: Please write to *Penguin Books India Pvt Ltd, 11 Panchsheel Shopping Centre, Panchsheel Park, New Delhi 110 017.*

In the Netherlands: Please write to *Penguin Books Netherlands bv, Postbus 3507, NL-1001 AH Amsterdam.*

In Germany: Please write to *Penguin Books Deutschland GmbH, Metzlerstrasse 26, 60594 Frankfurt am Main.*

In Spain: Please write to *Penguin Books S. A., Bravo Murillo 19, 1° B, 28015 Madrid.*

In Italy: Please write to *Penguin Italia s.r.l., Via Benedetto Croce 2, 20094 Corsico, Milano.*

In France: Please write to *Penguin France, Le Carré Wilson, 62 rue Benjamin Baillaud, 31500 Toulouse.*

In Japan: Please write to *Penguin Books Japan Ltd, Kaneko Building, 2-3-25 Koraku, Bunkyo-Ku, Tokyo 112.*

In South Africa: Please write to *Penguin Books South Africa (Pty) Ltd, Private Bag X14, Parkview, 2122 Johannesburg.*